Realizing the
Full Potential of
Social Safety
Nets in Africa

Realizing the Full Potential of Social Safety Nets in Africa

Kathleen Beegle, Aline Coudouel, and Emma Monsalve, Editors

A copublication of the Agence Française de Développement and the World Bank

Africa Development Forum Series

The Africa Development Forum Series was created in 2009 to focus on issues of significant relevance to Sub-Saharan Africa's social and economic development. Its aim is both to record the state of the art on a specific topic and to contribute to ongoing local, regional, and global policy debates. It is designed specifically to provide practitioners, scholars, and students with the most up-to-date research results while highlighting the promise, challenges, and opportunities that exist on the continent.

The series is sponsored by the Agence Française de Développement and the World Bank. The manuscripts chosen for publication represent the highest quality in each institution and have been selected for their relevance to the development agenda. Working together with a shared sense of mission and interdisciplinary purpose, the two institutions are committed to a common search for new insights and new ways of analyzing the development realities of the Sub-Saharan Africa region.

Advisory Committee Members

Agence Française de Développement
Gaël Giraud, Executive Director, Research and Knowledge
Mihoub Mezouaghi, Deputy Director, Research and Knowledge
Pierre Icard, Director, Head of Knowledge Department on Sustainable Development
Sophie Chauvin, Head, Edition and Publication Division
Hélène Djoufelkit, Deputy Head, Research Department

World Bank
Albert G. Zeufack, Chief Economist, Africa Region
Markus P. Goldstein, Lead Economist, Africa Region

Sub-Saharan Africa

Titles in the Africa Development Forum Series

Tourism in Africa: Harnessing Tourism for Growth and Improved Livelihoods (2014) by Iain Christie, Eneida Fernandes, Hannah Messerli, and Louise Twining-Ward

* *Safety Nets in Africa: Effective Mechanisms to Reach the Poor and Most Vulnerable*, «Les fi lets sociaux en Afrique : Méthodes effi caces pour cibler les populations pauvres et vulnérables en Afrique» (2015) edited by Carlo del Ninno and Bradford Mills

* *Land Delivery Systems in West African Cities: The Example of Bamako, Mali*, «Le système d'approvisionnement en terres dans les villes d'Afrique de l'Ouest: L'exemple de Bamako» (2015) by Alain Durand-Lasserve, Maÿlis Durand-Lasserve, and Harris Selod

Enhancing the Climate Resilience of Africa's Infrastructure: The Power and Water Sectors (2015) edited by Raffaello Cervigni, Rikard Liden, James E. Neumann, and Kenneth M. Strzepek

* *Africa's Demographic Transition: Dividend or Disaster?* «La transition demographique de lAfrique» (2015) edited by David Canning, Sangeeta Raja, and Abdo S. Yazbeck

The Challenge of Fragility and Security in West Africa (2015) by Alexandre Marc, Neelam Verjee, and Stephen Mogaka

Highways to Success or Byways to Waste: Estimating the Economic Benefits of Roads in Africa (2015) by Ali A. Rubaba, Federico Barra, Claudia Berg, Richard Damania, John Nash, and Jason Russ

Confronting Drought in Africa's Drylands: Opportunities for Enhancing Resilience (2016) edited by Raffaello Cervigni and Michael Morris

* *Reaping Richer Returns: Public Spending Priorities for African Agriculture Productivity Growth* (2017) by Aparajita Goyal and John Nash

Mining in Africa: Are Local Communities Better Off? (2017) by Punam Chuhan-Pole, Andrew L. Dabalen, and Bryan Christopher Land

Realizing the Full Potential of Social Safety Nets in Africa (2018) edited by Kathleen Beegle, Aline Coudouel, and Emma Monsalve

* Available in French

All books in the Africa Development Forum series are available for free at
https://openknowledge.worldbank.org/handle/10986/2150

Contents

Figures

Tables

Foreword

In less than a decade, social safety nets in Sub-Saharan Africa have become a core part of development strategies to address extreme poverty and protect households exposed to increasing shocks from disasters such as droughts, floods, epidemics and illnesses, international price shocks, and conflict. Consider this: every country in the region now has at least one social safety net program, and African countries now spend on average 1.2 percent of gross domestic product (GDP) on social safety nets—a rate slightly lower than the global average of 1.6 percent. Throughout the continent, cash transfer, public works, and school feeding programs have changed the lives of millions of vulnerable people for the better.

In Ethiopia, a productive social safety nets program is increasing food security while lowering the national poverty rate. Cash-for-work projects in Sierra Leone have increased savings of poor households and provided an incentive for income diversification. In Zambia, providing grants to households with children resulted in increased yields and higher sales of farm output, while increasing the bargaining power of women.

Since the introduction of cash transfer programs, both conditional and unconditional, a major concern has been that beneficiaries will misuse the cash and spend it on "temptation goods" such as alcohol or tobacco. Contrary to popular belief, a wealth of evidence shows that instead households use the support "productively": by increasing food security, sending children to school, or expanding income activities. When times get tough, such programs protect households, helping to avoid selling critical assets or taking children out of school. Among Africa's poor, a small positive shock to incomes can lift many out of poverty. However, though the number of social safety net programs has risen, coverage remains limited in Sub-Saharan Africa, with many of the poorest of the poor not covered. There is untapped potential for social safety nets to effectively address equity, raise resilience, and expand opportunities for poor and vulnerable.

What would it take? Bringing social safety nets to scale requires strong political will, technical expertise, and reliable and efficient spending, as this report highlights.

First, it is critical to understand the role of *politics* in shaping safety net programs. Such programs are appearing on political platforms and may help establish a relationship between vulnerable people and their government. The political appetite for such programs can be shaped by evidence on their effectiveness.

Second, programs need to be anchored in effective *institutions* with strong capacity and aligned incentives.

Third, scale-up will require innovative strategies to ensure *financial sustainability*. This includes a focus on ways to increase efficiency and volumes and to secure new sources of financing, with an emphasis on disaster risk management.

Paying greater attention to political economy, institutional capacity, and fiscal sustainability is a key factor for bringing social safety nets to scale in Africa. This report offers a strategic vision for supporting the scale-up of social safety nets to alleviate poverty and reduce vulnerability in Africa.

Makhtar Diop
Vice-President, Africa Region
World Bank Group

Foreword

Social safety nets have arrived in Africa. The number of programs is growing. And in several countries the coverage is expanding at a rapid pace. Long gone are the days when doubters dismissed safety nets as irrelevant development policy that was good only for rich or middle-income countries. There is now a strong body of evidence from Africa and other regions which establishes that households use cash and in-kind transfers in ways that benefit children, empower women, and enable poor and vulnerable households to live better lives. Safety nets enable households to work more and more productively. These programs tackle poverty and social exclusion for the most disenfranchised people. They help connect them with basic social services. And they help households better deal with shocks, without selling their assets or jeopardizing the health, nutrition, or education of their children. The case for safety nets has been made.

Africa has become a great innovator in social safety nets, pushing the frontiers in many areas. Other regions are learning from the creative use of technology in some programs (such as targeting in Sierra Leone), or from the way programs are designed with a scalable element to better respond to shock (in Kenya for example), or from the way productive inclusion is weaved into programs. As a partner with government, the World Bank team is at the forefront of the effort to innovate and build systems.

This report emphasizes various challenges countries face when bringing their social safety nets to scale, and ensuring their sustainability. In addition to important questions related to the technical design of social safety nets and of systemic instruments, this report points to three critical areas that are essential to successful scaling up: politics, institutions, and financing. First, understanding the politics of social safety nets is critical to shift the social contract progressively and achieve strong political support for such programs. Second, strong institutions are critical to implementing programs at large scale in a transparent and professional manner, and to ensuring coordination and efficiency in their delivery. Finally, bringing safety nets to scale, and reliably keeping them at such scale over time, requires innovative strategies to increase resources and to ensure their timely availability, including in the context of shocks and emergencies.

This broader focus on issues that go beyond technical considerations is relevant more generally—for regions beyond Africa and for other elements of social protection beyond social safety nets more broadly.

Michal Rutkowski
Senior Director and Head of Global Practice
Social Protection and Jobs
World Bank Group

Acknowledgments

This report has been prepared by a team led by Aline Coudouel and Kathleen Beegle. The core team is comprised of Colin Andrews, Thomas Bossuroy, Lucilla Maria Bruni, Sarah Coll-Black, Melis Guven, Maddalena Honorati, Allan Hsiao, Victoria Monchuk, Emma Monsalve, Laura Ralston, and Judith Sandford.

The team is grateful to Stefano Paternostro and Dena Ringold for their overall guidance throughout the process. The team has also benefited greatly from extensive consultations, discussions, and suggestions involving many colleagues throughout the preparation of the report. This includes the inputs and guidance of Elena Bardasi, Carlo del Ninno, Eric Zapatero, Dimitris Mavridis, John Van Dyck, and Andrea Vermehren (chapter 1); Ruth Hill, Laura Rawlings, and Jamele Rigolini (chapter 2); Badru Bukenya, Mathison Clore, Sam Hickey, Tom Lavers, Abla Safir, and Jennifer Turner (chapter 3); Susana Gamez, Mary Green, Sara Giannozzi, Jeffrey Maganya, and Yasuhiko Matsuda (chapter 4); and Francesca Bastagli, Julie Dana, Mareile Beate Stephanie Drechsler, Tina George, Bhavya Jha, Patrick Kabuya, Barry Patrick Maher, Solène Rougeaux, Jennifer Turner, and Sara Troiano (chapter 5). The team likewise received cross-cutting advice and inputs from Eva Kloeve, Lynne Sherburne-Benz, Thibault Van Langenhove, Ruslan Yemtsov, and Albert Zeufack.

The thoughtful comments of the peer reviewers—Markus P. Goldstein, Margaret E. Grosh, William Wiseman, and an anonymous reviewer—are greatly appreciated. The team appreciates the hard work of the ASPIRE group, particularly Maddalena Honorati, Oleksiy Ivaschenko, Marina Novikova, Claudia P. Rodriguez, and Linghui Zhu.

Special thanks to country teams that collected and validated detailed data on social safety net programs in Africa, including Mahamane Maliki Amadou, Philippe Auffret, Gbetoho Joachim Boko, Bénédicte de La Brière, Christabel E. Dadzie, Carlo del Ninno, Ivan Drabek, Heba Elgazzar, Randa G. El-Rashidi, Hadyiat El-Tayeb Alyn, Jordi Jose Gallego-Ayala, Rebekka E. Grun, Camilla

Holmemo, Alex Kamurase, Lisette Khonde, Toni Koleva, Matthieu Lefebvre, Phillippe George Leite, Dimitris Mavridis, Emma S. Mistiaen, Muderis Abdulahi Mohammed, Michael Mutemi Munavu, Suleiman Namara, Maniza B. Naqvi, Ana Ocampo, Foluso Okunmadewa, Serene Praveena Philip, Laura Ralston, Laura B. Rawlings, Nina Rosas Raffo, Solène Rougeaux, Manuel Salazar, Nadia Selim, Endashaw Tadesse Gossa, Cornelia M. Tesliuc, Maurizia Tovo, Fanta Toure, John Van Dyck, Andrea Vermehren, Emily Weedon, Penelope Williams, Briana Wilson, Sulaiman Adesina Yusuf, Giuseppe Zampaglione, and Eric Zapatero Larrio.

This task received financial support from the Office of the Chief Economist of the World Bank Group's Africa Region and the Nordic Trust Fund, which promotes knowledge and learning for human rights and development.

Robert Zimmermann provided assistance in the editing of the report. Lydie Billey supplied support in the management of this task and formatting the report. Gerry Quinn helped with graphic design.

The findings, interpretations, and conclusions are those of the authors and do not necessarily reflect the views of management, the reviewers, and other colleagues consulted or engaged in the preparation of the report.

About the Authors and Contributors

Colin Andrews is a Senior Economist in the Social Protection and Jobs Global Practice at the World Bank. He has over 10 years of experience working in social protection across Africa and South Asia and at the global policy level. Colin has been working on issues related to social safety net design, service delivery, and sector-related links with agriculture, education, and health. He has most recently been involved in issues in social protection financing, donor harmonization, and impact evaluation. He has published widely and has managed several lending operations in the Africa Region. Prior to joining the World Bank, he worked at the Food and Agriculture Organization of the United Nations, at the European Commission, and within international nongovernmental organizations. He received his master's degree in Economics from Trinity College, Dublin.

Kathleen Beegle is a Lead Economist in the World Bank's Africa Region. Based in Accra, she coordinates country programs in Ghana, Liberia, and Sierra Leone in education, health, poverty, social protection, gender, and jobs. She coauthored the 2016 World Bank regional study *Poverty in a Rising Africa*. She was Deputy Director of *World Development Report 2013*, on jobs. She was in the World Bank Research Group for over a decade, where her research focused on poverty, labor, and economic shocks. She was also a lead member of the World Bank Living Standards Measurement Study team; she led in the design and implementation of national household surveys for poverty and policy analysis, as well as methodological studies on survey design. Before joining the World Bank Research Group, she worked at RAND Corporation. Kathleen holds a PhD in Economics from Michigan State University.

Thomas Bossuroy is an Economist at the World Bank, where he works primarily on social safety nets and employment programs among the poor in West Africa. In addition to managing operations in Sahel countries, Benin, Nigeria, and Togo, he leads a range of analytical activities and experiments on employment and in livelihoods programs. In particular, he is managing several impact evaluations of skills development programs, productive inclusion strategies, and school feeding programs. His research also focuses on innovative service delivery strategies in health care, with a focus on combating tuberculosis in India. Prior to joining the World Bank, Thomas was a research fellow at the University of Cape Town, South Africa, where he evaluated national business development programs for the poor and vulnerable. He started his career as Executive Director of J-PAL South Asia, based in Chennai, India, where he oversaw randomized controlled trials and managed a growing organization with presence across India. After dedicating his doctoral research to the dynamics of social and political structures in Africa, Thomas received a PhD in Economics from the Paris School of Economics.

Lucilla Maria Bruni is an Economist in the World Bank's Social Protection Global Practice. Lucilla focuses on southern Africa, for which she leads a portfolio of operational and analytical activities related to social assistance, demographics, and labor markets. She also leads a series of training exercises on impact evaluation for government officers in Poland. In her previous assignments at the World Bank, Lucilla worked on social protection projects in East Asia and the Pacific and was on a field assignment in Cambodia. Prior to her work at the World Bank, Lucilla did research on poverty and inequality in Guatemala and was an economics consultant in London. Lucilla holds a Master of Public Administration in International Development from Harvard University and an M.Sc. and B.Sc. from the London School of Economics.

Sarah Coll-Black is a Senior Social Protection Specialist in the Social Protection and Jobs Global Practice at the World Bank. She has over 10 years of experience working on social protection in Africa, managing the design and delivery of safety nets, including links to disaster risk management and humanitarian response, risk financing, and youth employment. She coauthored the World Bank's Social Protection Strategy for Africa (2012–22) and led the World Bank's support to the Productive Safety Net Program in Ethiopia; she is currently focusing on West Africa. Prior to joining the World Bank, she worked in the Philippines with international organizations to extend basic services to the poorest people in Asia and the Pacific. She holds an MPhil from the Institute of Development Studies, University of Sussex, and an Economics degree from Dalhousie University.

Aline Coudouel is a Lead Economist with the World Bank, where she currently focuses on social assistance, social insurance, and labor markets in West Africa (especially Cabo Verde, Mauritania, and Senegal) after spending a few years working in Latin America and the Caribbean (Colombia, the Dominican Republic, Mexico, Nicaragua, and Panama). Previously, she was part of the poverty team at the World Bank, working on debt relief and poverty reduction strategies and as a member of the team that defined and promoted the poverty and social impact analysis of policies. She was a coauthor of the flagship *World Development Report 2012*, on gender equality and development, which sought to explain the driving forces behind gender equality and its effect on economic growth and helped to enhance the understanding of the role of public action in promoting this important issue. Prior to joining the Bank, she worked as a researcher for the United Nations Children's Fund, where she focused on the welfare of children and women in Europe and Central Asia. Aline holds a PhD in Economics from the European University Institute in San Domenico di Fiesole, Italy.

Melis Guven is a Senior Social Protection Economist in the World Bank's Africa Region. Melis focuses on safety nets and pensions and is the focal point and technical lead on pensions in the region. She is currently responsible for the social protection and labor programs of the World Bank in Botswana, Mauritius, and Seychelles. Prior to joining the Africa Region, she worked on a broad range of pension and safety net issues in Albania, Poland, Romania, and Turkey. Previously, Melis worked for the Turkish government (the Turkish Treasury) and was a core member of the health and pension reform team in Turkey. As a result, she has in-depth understanding of decision making and prioritization in governments.

Maddalena Honorati is a Senior Economist who joined the team in the Europe and Central Asia Region after working in the unit for strategy and operations and with teams in Africa within the Social Protection and Jobs Global Practice. Her areas of experience include social safety nets, labor market programs, skills, social protection systems, and methodological studies on household survey and administrative data collection for social protection. Before joining the Social Protection team in 2009, she worked for the Development Research Group at the World Bank on firm productivity, determinants of informality, and the impact of investment climate regulations on firm performance. Recently, her research interest has focused on the design and evaluation of social safety nets and active labor market programs as well as the measurement of social protection system performance. Maddalena holds a PhD in Economics from Bocconi University in Milan, Italy, and an MSc from Pompeu Fabra University in Barcelona, Spain. She has supported the operational implementation of programs in Albania, Armenia, Ecuador, Ghana, Kenya, and the Philippines.

Allan Hsiao is a PhD candidate in Economics at the Massachusetts Institute of Technology, where his research focuses on health care systems in Asia. His current research has involved studies on the rapid expansion of health care infrastructure in Indonesia, where residents benefit from a multilayered system of hospitals, clinics, and smaller facilities that has greatly enhanced access to health care over the last few decades. Allan's work applies frontier methods from industrial organization and development economics to draw policy prescriptions relevant to developing countries confronting rising health care needs under significant resource constraints. Other projects have focused on the impacts of large-scale school construction on local labor markets in Indonesia and rural-to-urban migration in China. He has contributed to the medical literature on cardiovascular outcomes and the global burden of disease. Prior to attending the Massachusetts Institute of Technology, he received an MPhil in Economics from the University of Oxford and a bachelor's degree in Economics from Harvard College.

Victoria Monchuk is a Senior Economist at the World Bank, where her fields of interest include social protection and cross-sectoral human development issues. Her work in the Social Protection and Jobs Global Practice has included supporting governments in Central and West Africa in building safety net systems and cash transfer programs. She is currently managing a decentralized service delivery program that seeks to expand equitable access to quality basic services in Ethiopia. She has also been involved in a number of assessments and evaluations of cash transfer, public works, and skills development programs. Previously, she was employed in the Fiscal Affairs Department of the International Monetary Fund, where she was engaged in analytical work on the efficiency of public expenditure on public health and education. Her research has focused on the impact of child labor and school achievement in Latin America.

Emma Monsalve is a Consultant in the World Bank's Social Protection and Jobs Global Practice in Africa. She joined the Bank in 2014 and worked with the Social Protection and Jobs Global Practice and the Poverty and Equity Global Practice in the Latin America and Caribbean Region. Before joining the Bank, she worked with the Inter-American Development Bank and the Central Bank of Colombia. She has developed technical and analytical expertise on a wide array of topics, including social protection and labor, poverty, education, health, and fiscal policy. In her most recent work at the World Bank, she has focused on assessing the efficiency and redistributional incidence of social spending in several countries in the Africa Region and the Latin America and the Caribbean Region and in designing and implementing poverty diagnostics. She has made numerous contributions to analytical work, systematic country diagnostics, country dialogue, lending operations, and the ASPIRE and Latin America and Caribbean Region Equity Lab databases. She holds a master's in Applied Economics from Johns Hopkins University and a bachelor's in Economics from the University of Antioquia in Colombia.

Laura Ralston is an Economist in the Social Protection and Jobs Global Practice at the World Bank, where she works on social insurance, human development, and labor markets. She has an interest in development in fragile and conflict-affected environments and works on Social Protection and Jobs projects in several fragile countries in Africa. She has contributed to the work of the World Bank's Fragility, Conflict, and Violence Group by tracking the progress and identifying challenges in projects and programs in these environments. She is seeking to develop cooperative approaches within the World Bank and with external partners, with a focus on innovation and the sharing of ideas. Toward these goals, she has coordinated impact evaluations across sectors in Africa, East Asia, Latin America and the Caribbean, and South Asia and has performed conflict and fragility analysis and monitoring in Africa and the Middle East. Laura received her PhD in Empirical Applied Microeconomics from the Massachusetts Institute of Technology. Her work there involved research on the determinants of conflict and violence using a wide range of methodologies, including quasi-experimental regression analysis, laboratory experiments, geospatial data science, and statistical learning.

Judith Sandford is a Social Protection and Food Security Specialist with 20 years of experience, currently working as an independent consultant. She has supported the design and implementation of government-led interventions and programs of nongovernmental organizations in Sub-Saharan Africa. Her experience includes long-term support for the Productive Safety Net Program in Ethiopia (PSNP) and the National Safety Net Program (NSNP) in Kenya.

Abbreviations

ASPIRE	Atlas of Social Protection Indicators of Resilience and Equity (database)
CfW	Cash for Work Program of the Youth Employment Support Project (Sierra Leone)
CGE	computable general equilibrium (model)
CSR	corporate social responsibility
GDP	gross domestic product
HIV/AIDS	human immunodeficiency virus and acquired immunodeficiency syndrome
HSNP	Hunger Safety Net Program (Kenya)
IDP	internally displaced person
IMF	International Monetary Fund
LEAP	Livelihood Empowerment against Poverty Program (Ghana)
MASAF PWP	Malawi Social Action Fund Public Works Program
MIS	management information system
NGO	nongovernmental organization
OVC Program	Orphans and Vulnerable Children Program (Kenya)
PIU	project implementation unit
PNBSF	Programme National de Bourses de Sécurité Familiale (National Program of Family Security Transfers) (Senegal)
PPP	purchasing power parity
PSNP	Productive Safety Net Program (Ethiopia)
PSSN	Productive Social Safety Net (Tanzania)
SAGA	semiautonomous government agency (may also refer to a fully autonomous government agency)

SCTP	Social Cash Transfer Program (Malawi)
UNICEF	United Nations Children's Fund
VUP	Vision 2020 Umurenge Program (Rwanda)
WDI	World Development Indicators (World Bank)

All dollar amounts are in U.S. dollars, unless otherwise noted.

Overview

Realizing the Full Potential of Social Safety Nets in Africa

Despite economic growth and improvements in many dimensions of welfare, poverty remains a pervasive and complex phenomenon in Sub-Saharan Africa (Africa hereafter). Approximately two people in five live in poverty, and, because of shocks, many others are vulnerable to falling into poverty. Part of the agenda to tackle poverty in Africa in recent years has been the launch of social safety net programs. Largely absent from the continent until the early 2000s, social safety nets are now included in development strategies in most countries in Africa. The number of social safety net programs has expanded greatly. In several countries, the expansion has arisen concomitantly with significant investment in core instruments of national social safety net systems—such as targeting systems, social registries, and payment mechanisms—that have progressively strengthened the systems and raised their efficiency.

The shift in social policy toward social safety nets reflects a progressive evolution in the understanding of the role that social safety nets can play in the fight against poverty and vulnerability. Evidence shows that these programs can contribute significantly and efficiently to reducing poverty, building resilience, and boosting opportunities among the poorest.

For the full potential of social safety nets to be realized in addressing equity, resilience, and the opportunities available to poor and vulnerable populations in Africa, programs need to be brought to scale and sustained. This involves solving a series of technical issues to identify the parameters, tools, and processes that can deliver maximum benefit to the poor and the vulnerable. However, at least as important, this report argues, is the series of decisive shifts that must occur in three critical areas—political, institutional, and fiscal—as follows:

- First, the political processes that shape the extent and nature of social policy need to be recognized and engaged. This can be done by stimulating the political appetite for social safety nets, choosing politically appropriate

1

parameters, and harnessing the political impacts of social safety nets to promote sustainability.

- Second, social safety net programs must be anchored in strong institutional arrangements to support their expansion, especially because programs are now more frequently implemented through national channels. Expansion requires anchoring in laws and policies, mechanisms for coordination and oversight, and arrangements for program management and delivery.
- Third, in most countries, the level and predictability of the resources devoted to the sector must be expanded so social safety nets can reach the desirable scale. This can be achieved through greater efficiency, more resources, newer sources of financing, and a greater ability to respond effectively to shocks.

This report first presents a snapshot of social safety nets in Africa and the mounting evidence for the effectiveness of these programs in promoting the well-being and productive inclusion of the poorest and most vulnerable. It then focuses on the three areas highlighted above: the political, institutional, and fiscal aspects. It does not systematically discuss technical aspects involved in designing social safety nets (see Grosh et al. 2008 for a thorough treatment). Rather, the report highlights the implications that political, institutional, and fiscal aspects have for program choice and design. It argues that these considerations are crucial to ensuring success in raising social safety nets to scale in Africa and maintaining adequate support. Ignoring these areas could lead to technically sound, but practically impossible, choices and designs.

Reaching the Poor and Vulnerable in Africa through Social Safety Nets (Chapter 1)

Despite Improvements, Poverty and Vulnerability to Shocks Are Widespread

Poverty rates have been falling in Africa. The share of the poor—people living on less than $1.90 a day—declined from 57 percent in 1990 to 41 percent in 2013. However, the decline was not sufficiently rapid to allow Africa to reach the Millennium Development Goal of cutting the poverty rate in half by 2015. Moreover, the number of the poor rose from about 280 million people in 1990 to 390 million people in 2013 because of high population growth. Poverty will remain a challenge in Africa even if macroeconomic growth exceeds expectations. Under a range of economic growth assumptions, global poverty will become increasingly concentrated in Africa and in conflict-affected states (Chandy, Ledlie, and Penciakova 2013; Ravallion 2013; World Bank 2015).

Poverty is not captured solely by monetary measures. Progress has also been made in Africa in nonmonetary well-being. But the rate of progress is leveling off in some places, and there has been an uptick in violent events. The region shows the worst outcomes relative to other regions on most human development indicators. One primary-school-age child in five is not in school, and children in poor households are the least likely to be in school. More than a third of young children are malnourished (appendix table C.1).

Poverty is not a static condition. Among Africa's poor, a small positive shock to incomes could lift many out of poverty, but a small negative shock could drive as many of the vulnerable into poverty. In Africa, two poor households in five are among the transient poor; that is, they are moving into or out of poverty as income fluctuates and they become exposed to shocks (figure O.1).

Figure O.1 Poverty Is Both Chronic and Transient

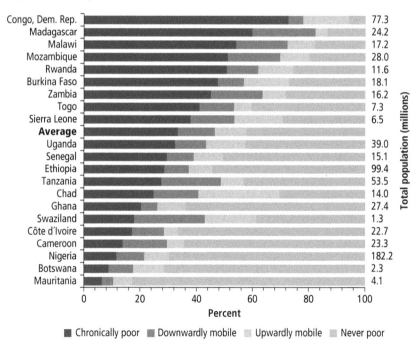

Source: Dang and Dabalen 2017.
Note: Poverty statistics refer to the latest household survey year for each country. The "chronically poor" category includes households that were poor in both periods of the analysis; "downwardly mobile" refers to households that fell into poverty in the second period; "upwardly mobile" includes those who were poor in the first period but not poor in the second period; and "never poor" includes households that were nonpoor in both periods.

Many households in Africa are vulnerable to shocks such as illnesses, weather shocks, and conflict. The nature of shocks is evolving and presenting new challenges. As of mid-2016, Africa accounted for 30 percent of the displaced population worldwide, which represents about 20 million people. Of the top 20 countries in the world in terms of hosting displaced populations, eight are in Africa. Climate change is another obstacle to eradicating poverty in Africa (appendix tables A.1 and C.1). Households in drylands are more likely to be poor than households in other areas (Cervigni and Morris 2016; Hallegatte et al. 2016).

Social Safety Nets Have Been Expanding Rapidly in Africa

Most African countries have recently established social safety net programs as part of a broader strategy to assist the poor and protect the vulnerable (appendix table D.1). In this report, social safety nets—also sometimes called social assistance programs—are defined as noncontributory benefits, provided either in cash or in kind, which are intended to support the poor or the vulnerable. They are a component of the larger social protection system that also includes contributory social insurance, such as pensions and health insurance, as well as labor market policies and programs, and some of the processes analyzed in this report focus more broadly on social protection systems. Programs such as universal child grants or social pensions are included, as they are noncontributory and focus on groups perceived as vulnerable. The definition in this report also includes measures that facilitate access to basic services, such as health care, education, and housing, through targeted fee waivers, scholarships, and lump sum grants to promote productive inclusion. Consumer price subsidies, including energy and food subsidies, are not considered social safety net initiatives in this report. The objectives of social safety nets differ and may range from reducing monetary poverty, food insecurity, and vulnerabilities (such as old age, disability, exposure to natural disasters, and conflict situations) to improving access to basic services among the poor, and to promoting productive inclusion for the poorest.

The average number of new social safety net programs launched in Africa each year rose from 7 in 2001–09 to 14 in 2010–15 (figure O.2). Every African country has at least one social safety net program. The average number of programs per country is 15, ranging from 2 in the Republic of Congo and Gabon to 56 in Burkina Faso and 54 in Chad (appendix tables E.1 and E.2). This trend has also been a global one. By 2015, every country in the world was implementing at least one social safety net program.

There are success stories of rapid expansion in the region that are unique in the developing world (such as in Ghana, Kenya, Senegal, and Tanzania; see figure O.3). However, these remain exceptions in the region, and most programs are implemented on a much smaller scale.

Figure O.2 More Social Safety Net Programs Have Been Launched in Recent Years

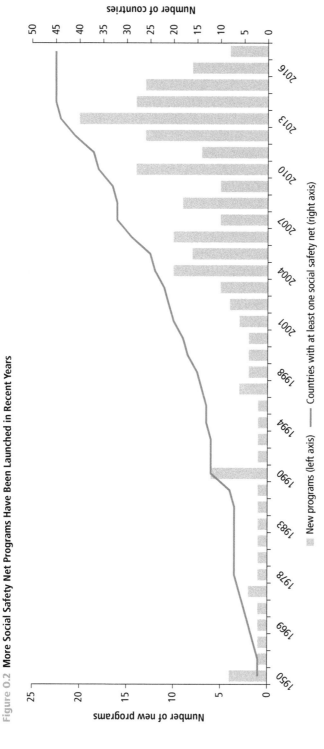

■ New programs (left axis) ── Countries with at least one social safety net (right axis)

Source: ASPIRE (Atlas of Social Protection Indicators of Resilience and Equity) (database), Administrative data, World Bank, Washington, DC, http://www.worldbank.org/aspire.
Note: This figure considers regular programs (not emergency support programs) that are still being implemented and for which information on the year of the launch is available.

Figure O.3 **Flagship Programs in Africa Are among the Most Rapidly Growing**

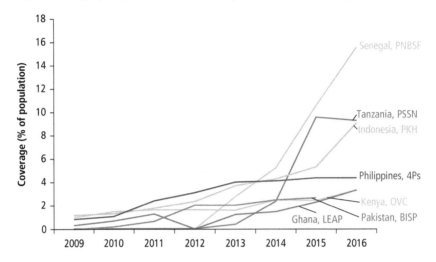

Source: ASPIRE (Atlas of Social Protection Indicators of Resilience and Equity) (database), Administrative data, World Bank, Washington, DC, http://www.worldbank.org/aspire.
Note: 4Ps = Pantawid Pamilyang Pilipino Program; BISP = Benazir Income Support Program; LEAP = Livelihood Empowerment against Poverty; OVC = Orphans and Vulnerable Children; PKH = Program Keluarga Harapan; PNBSF = Programme National de Bourses de Sécurité Familiale; PSSN = Productive Social Safety Net Program.

As programs are created and grow, many countries are also investing in systems to raise efficiency and reduce program duplication. Delivery platforms—such as social registries, interoperable management information systems, and shared payment systems—allow administrative cost savings and facilitate planning and coordination. Social registries are currently being used in 26 countries and are being developed in an additional 16 countries (appendix table D.2). These social registries are systems that identify poor and vulnerable households in a country or region and collect information on socioeconomic situations, thereby providing governments and partners with a central mechanism to identify potential program beneficiaries (Karippacheril, Leite, and Lindert 2017). The stage of development differs, and coverage ranges from 0.1 and 0.3 percent of the population in Zambia and Mozambique; and to 89 and 52 percent of the population in Rwanda and Lesotho, respectively.

The expanding adoption of social safety nets is paralleled by the growing number of national strategies and policies. By 2017, 32 African countries had established national social protection strategies or policies, which include social safety nets as a core pillar, and draft strategies are in the approval process in another 7 countries (appendix table D.1).

The Design of Social Safety Nets Varies across Africa

Figure O.4 highlights the variety in design across the region, as well as patterns observed among groups of countries depending on geographic location, income, fragility, and drought exposure. Cash transfer programs are implemented in almost all countries (46), as well as public works programs (33) and school feeding programs (28) (appendix table E.1). Overall, cash transfers account for 41 percent of total spending, and this share is growing. Social pensions are more prevalent in upper-middle- and high-income countries and in Southern Africa. Public works programs exist in almost all low-income countries and fragile states, especially in West Africa, but are largely absent in middle- and high-income countries. In Central Africa and fragile states, social safety nets are widely used as responses to shocks, and emergency and food-based programs are the most common types of programs.

Social Safety Nets Are Evolving

As programs have grown in number and size, program design features have also evolved. First, there has been a shift toward more use of cash in social safety nets. Second, social safety nets are playing an expanding role in country responses to climate change and human-made shocks. Third, an increasing number of programs are focusing on fostering the productive capacity and resilience of beneficiary households. Similarly, there has been a greater concentration on promoting human capital development, often associated with conditional programs. Because of urbanization and the rising number of the urban poor, recent years have witnessed an increase in social safety nets in urban areas. Finally, countries have gradually been emphasizing the establishment of tools and systems to boost program efficiency and coordination.

Social Safety Nets Are Reaching Some, but Many of the Poor Are Not Covered

The programs with the greatest coverage of age-relevant populations are school feeding and fee waiver programs. With a few exceptions, richer countries tend to run larger programs. The majority of social safety nets in Africa are directly or indirectly targeted to children because they assist households with children. Of all programs, 29 percent directly target children through nutrition interventions, benefits aimed at orphans and other vulnerable children, school feeding programs, the provision of school supplies, and education benefits or fee waivers (appendix table E.3). As a result, the average coverage of children is 15 percent in Africa (appendix table F.2). (Coverages rates of the elderly are around 100 percent in countries with universal old-age social pensions, such as Botswana, Lesotho, Mauritius, Namibia, Seychelles, and Swaziland; appendix table F.1.)

Figure O.4 **The Composition of Social Safety Net Portfolios Is Diverse**

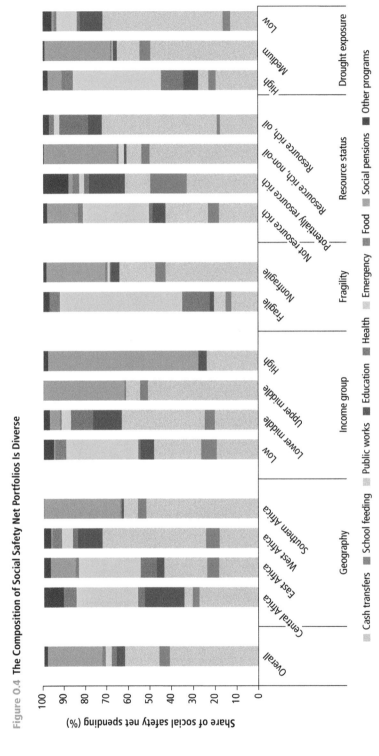

■ Cash transfers ■ School feeding ■ Public works ■ Education ■ Health ■ Emergency ■ Food ■ Social pensions ■ Other programs

Source: ASPIRE (Atlas of Social Protection Indicators of Resilience and Equity) (database), Administrative data, World Bank, Washington, DC, http://www.worldbank.org/aspire.
Note: The figure presents the distribution of all resources deployed by all countries in each group across different program categories. See appendix table G.6.

Though the number of social safety net programs has risen, coverage is often limited. On average, coverage is 10 percent of the African population (appendix tables F.1 and F.2). Poverty rates are higher than coverage rates in most countries (figure O.5). So, even if all existing social safety nets were perfectly targeted to the poor, not all poor households would be reached at the current scale of programs (in addition, benefits are typically low compared to needs). Meanwhile, some programs do not exclusively target the poor, but have broader objectives, such as universal old-age social pensions, school lunch programs for all primary-school students, scholarships for all students in tertiary education, or the targeting of specific categories in the population deemed vulnerable without necessarily taking population welfare characteristics into account.

Notwithstanding the issue of program objectives, the benefit incidence of selected programs that target on the basis of welfare or vulnerability are generally pro-poor, and the performance of programs in Africa is in line with international experience. For instance, more than 60 percent of the households benefiting from the South Africa Child Support Grants program belong to the poorest two quintiles of the national consumption distribution, and over 60 percent of the beneficiaries of the Malawi Social Action Fund are counted among the poor (chapter 1). However, a certain share of resources goes to richer households. Some limitations in targeting are technical: it is difficult and costly to assess the welfare status of households effectively and dynamically. However, the decision to target particular groups is also a political one. Indeed, selecting eligible groups is sometimes driven by the need to generate support among the population and decision makers for social safety net programs (chapter 3).

Low coverage rates are exacerbated by the fact that many programs are small or temporary initiatives implemented in isolation, in narrow geographical areas, or among discrete population groups. Program duplication also occurs, often within a weak institutional environment. This is the situation in Uganda and Zimbabwe, for instance, which implement 39 and 29 social safety net programs, respectively (appendix table E.1). Insufficient coordination among the development partners that often fund such programs exacerbates fragmentation and inefficiencies. Efforts to consolidate and rationalize programs are on the policy agendas of many countries, including the need to focus on a strong institutional framework for social safety nets (chapter 4).

Benefit amounts in social safety net programs are low relative to needs in low-income countries in the region. The highest benefits are usually offered through old-age social pensions or public works, followed by cash transfer programs. Average cash transfers correspond to 10 percent of the national poverty line in low-income countries, versus 57 percent for public works (see chapter 1, table 1.3 and appendix table I.1, for data and assumptions). Greater efficiency in implementation would help support a rise in the value of benefits, but elevating

Figure O.5 **Social Safety Net Coverage Is Not Proportionate to the Extent of Poverty**

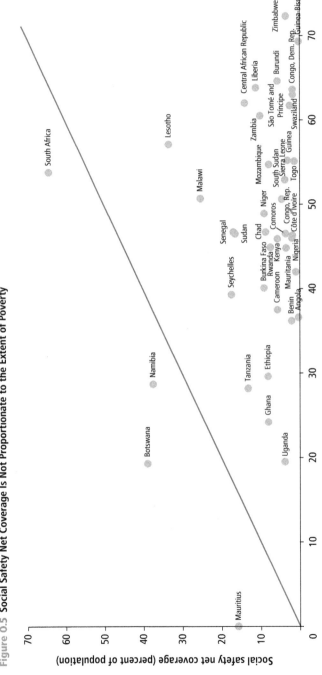

Source: ASPIRE (Atlas of Social Protection Indicators of Resilience and Equity) (database), Administrative data, World Bank, Washington, DC, http://www.worldbank.org/aspire

Note: See methodology in appendixes B.2 and B.3. Social safety net coverage rates are approximated by summing the number of direct and indirect beneficiaries of cash transfers, food-based transfers, and public works programs only. The beneficiaries of the other six program types (social pensions, school feeding, emergency programs, health care and education fee waivers, and other programs) are not included because their beneficiaries are more likely to overlap with those in other programs, which would result in overestimated coverage rates. For more details see appendix tables C.1 and F.1.

these programs to scale would also require a focus on sustainable financing for social safety nets (chapter 5).

Some Countries Spend Heavily, but Programs Must Be Brought to Scale and Sustained

While African countries spend an average 1.2 percent of gross domestic product (GDP) on social safety nets (equivalent to 4.8 percent of total government expenditures), government commitment varies greatly across countries at similar income levels. The average spending in the developing world is comparable, at 1.6 percent of GDP, but the fiscal needs in Africa are greater given the depth of poverty.

Notwithstanding the need to raise domestic resources and grow the economy, government spending on other initiatives that have objectives similar to social safety nets can be large. Spending on energy subsidies, for example, is considerable in some countries. In Central Africa, it is more than three times the spending on social safety nets (chapter 1, figure 1.12 and appendix table G.1). Because these subsidies benefit all consumers and because richer households consume larger quantities of energy, such subsidies are regressive. This points to the political considerations that underpin government spending choices (chapter 3) and to the potential efficiency gains from reallocation.

In many countries, the current stock of social safety net programs lacks fiscal sustainability. Development partners fund more than half the social safety net financing in the majority of African countries. There are large variations, though, and the governments of Angola, Botswana, Gabon, Ghana, Kenya, Mauritania, Mauritius, Senegal, Seychelles, and Sudan finance over 60 percent of their social safety net spending. Humanitarian aid represents the main source of funding in emergency situations, and the role of development partners is critical in many low-income and fragile contexts.

Social Safety Nets Promote Poverty Reduction, Increase Resilience, and Expand Opportunities (Chapter 2)

In parallel with the expansion of social safety net projects in the region, there has also been growing evidence on the impacts of social safety nets on equity (such as through poverty reduction and food security), resilience, and opportunities among the poor and vulnerable. The depth of recent evidence serves as a case for investment in social safety nets, for the effective design of programs, and for bringing programs to scale. A meta-analysis has been undertaken to pool evidence systematically across available studies and to facilitate a robust and consistent comparison of the impacts on key outcomes.

Social Safety Nets Improve Equity

The equity objective of social safety nets—to ensure that the most vulnerable and poorest households are able to reach a minimum level of consumption and cover their basic needs—is often central in low-income settings where poverty is most severe. Social safety nets have been shown to boost consumption and thereby lower poverty. Household consumption rises by an average $0.74 for each $1.00 transferred (figure O.6). In Ethiopia in 2011, the direct effect of transfers to rural households through the Productive Safety Net Program (PSNP) and food aid has been estimated as equivalent to a reduction of 1.6 percentage points in the national poverty rate. If social safety nets are brought to scale, simulation scenarios show that average transfers of $50 a month can reduce the poverty rate by up to 40 percent.

Households do not spend all the cash from social safety nets on consumables; they allocate some to productive investments, lumpy expenditures such as school fees, and savings. The vast majority of evidence shows that households do not use transfers on temptation goods, such as alcohol or tobacco.

Cash from social safety nets can also stimulate the demand for retail goods, services, and agricultural goods in local economies. Through such spillovers, nonbeneficiaries can also gain. For each $1 transferred to beneficiaries, nonbeneficiaries can experience estimated income increases of $0.30 or more. Together with the impacts on beneficiaries, these additional income effects lead to local economy multipliers of 1.08 to 1.84; that is, each dollar transferred through a social safety net to a beneficiary household is projected to add more than a dollar to the local economy (Taylor, Thome, and Filipski 2014; Taylor et al. 2013, 2014; Thome et al. 2014a, 2014b).

Building Resilience through Social Safety Nets

Social safety nets can help build household resilience to shocks. If poor households are able to rely on regular support from safety nets, they can avoid resorting to costly and often irreversible coping strategies, such as selling their most productive assets at deflated prices or taking children out of school.

Social safety net programs also help boost savings and foster the inclusion of beneficiaries in local community networks. Beneficiary households are between 4 and 20 percentage points more likely to be saving relative to comparable nonbeneficiary households. Given the initial low savings rate among such households, this implies an expansion by a factor of almost two in the incidence of savings. Evaluations suggest that households are also using transfers to reduce borrowing and indebtedness. Social safety net programs do not appear to crowd out private transfers (from family and friends), which can be a critical lifeline for poor families.

There is encouraging evidence suggesting that social safety net transfers can successfully boost investment in productive assets, especially livestock holdings,

Figure O.6 Consumption Increases Because of Social Safety Nets

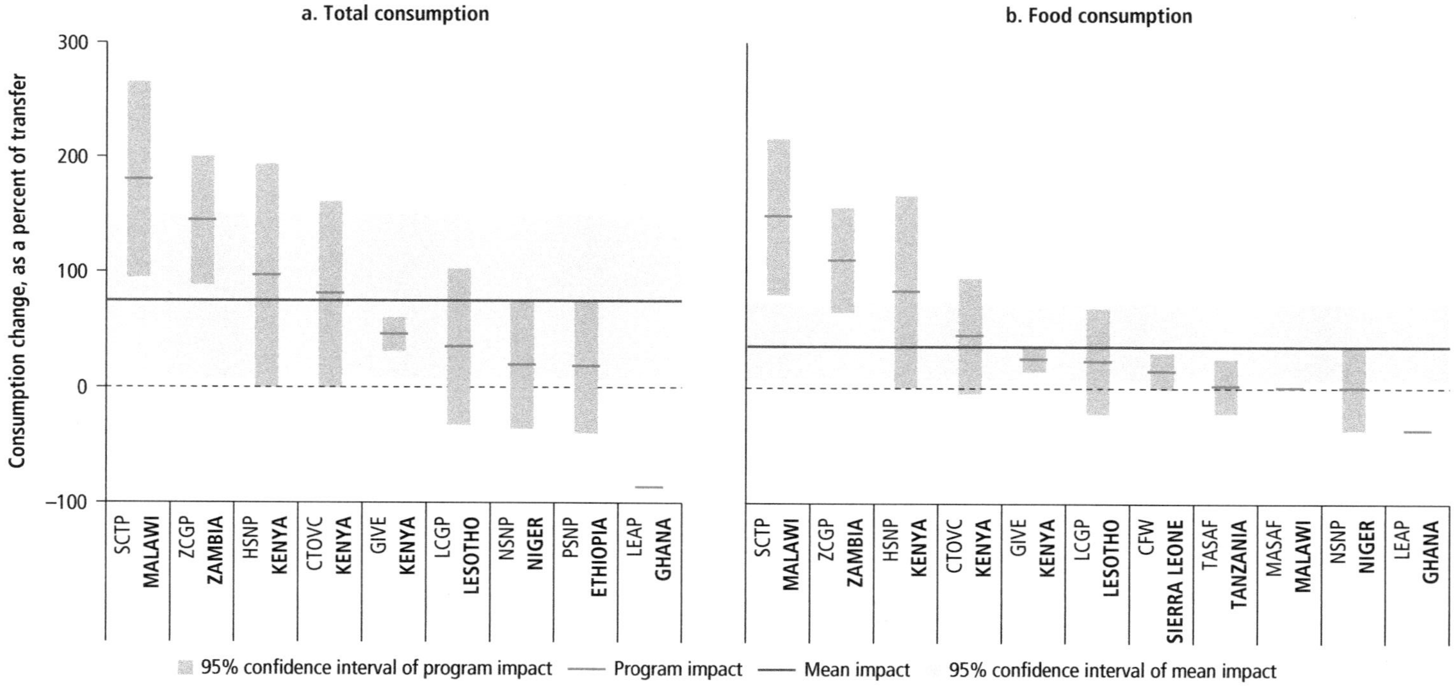

Consumption change, as a percent of transfer

a. Total consumption

b. Food consumption

95% confidence interval of program impact   —— Program impact   —— Mean impact   95% confidence interval of mean impact

a. Total consumption categories: SCTP MALAWI, ZCGP ZAMBIA, HSNP KENYA, CTOVC KENYA, GIVE KENYA, LCGP LESOTHO, NSNP NIGER, PSNP ETHIOPIA, LEAP GHANA

b. Food consumption categories: SCTP MALAWI, ZCGP ZAMBIA, HSNP KENYA, CTOVC KENYA, GIVE KENYA, LCGP LESOTHO, CFW SIERRA LEONE, TASAF TANZANIA, MASAF MALAWI, NSNP NIGER, LEAP GHANA

Source: Based on the meta-analysis described in chapter 2.

which represent an alternate form of savings. For example, livestock ownership rose an average of 34 percent across seven programs reporting on this outcome.

Adverse coping strategies, including the use of child labor, can also be avoided if households have access to social safety nets. Programs specifically targeted at children appear to reduce child labor the most, and strong communication strategies advocating for the rights and well-being of children may help generate these results.

Increasing Opportunities through Social Safety Nets

By fostering opportunities, including through investment in human capital and productive activities, social safety nets grow the incomes of poor households now and for the benefit of the next generation.

Social safety nets promote investments in children's education. In Africa, programs lead to an average 6 percent rise in school attendance and a 7 percent improvement in enrollments relative to baseline rates. These impacts are modest and reflect the high rates of lower-primary enrollment prior to program implementation. Improvements are especially pronounced in upper-primary and secondary school, where the enrollment is lower, though the barriers are also greater. The improvements are consistent with decreased child labor and increases in expenditures on schooling, such as the purchase of uniforms and school supplies, as well as fee payments. There is a lack of evidence on the impacts of social safety nets on skills and learning.

The impact of social safety nets on health care is limited. Several studies report on this outcome, but no significant average effect has been found, reflecting both the demand and supply side constraints and the speed at which program impacts can be realized. Where promising results emerge, they are often related to investments in younger infants, for example, child growth monitoring under South Africa's Child Support Grant Program or exclusive breastfeeding in Niger's Safety Net Project. In both health care and education, simulations indicate that social safety nets will have the largest impact on the poorest households that are most likely to otherwise miss out.

The transformative potential of social safety nets to boost education and health care outcomes hinges on the adequacy of public services. To realize gains, the quantity and quality of basic services must be improved. This is also a principle in agriculture and in water and sanitation.

Social safety net transfers are not handouts. Rather, they promote longer-term opportunities for productive inclusion (figure O.7). The limited evidence shows that the programs typically result in more income opportunities, rather than more idleness. Beneficiaries launch or expand business activities and invest in productive assets, while avoiding labor that may be damaging to their health. More analysis is needed to understand how cash transfer

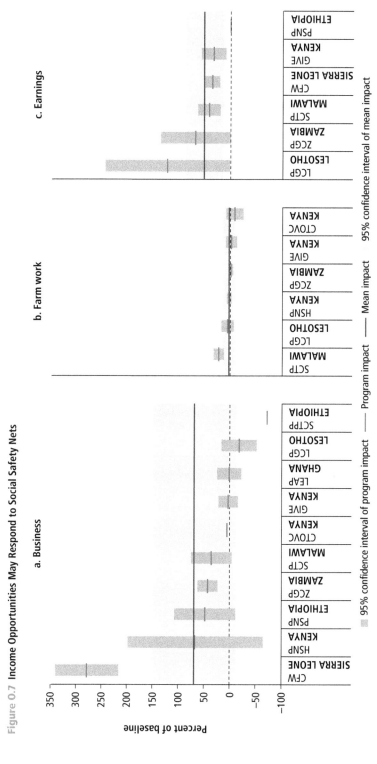

Figure O.7 Income Opportunities May Respond to Social Safety Nets

Source: Based on the meta-analysis described in chapter 2. "Business" refers to the household operating a nonfarm business (almost always small-scale or microenterprise business activities). Specific definitions of "Earnings" vary across studies.

15

programs can become a foundation on which to build engagement in complementary productive programs.

Bringing Social Safety Nets to Scale

Social safety nets in Africa do not yet cover all poor households. What impacts could be realized if programs were expanded to cover all poor households? Using data available from household surveys, alongside the results of the study's meta-analysis, this question is explored through simulations for three countries (Ghana, Liberia, and Niger), which assume that the number of beneficiary households would reach the number of extremely poor households in each country.

The simulations show that even relatively modest transfers ($50 per household per month) would have a sizable impact on consumption among beneficiaries. If transfers were perfectly targeted, consumption among the poor would increase within a range of 12 percent–17 percent. These consumption gains would generate a decline in poverty rates by as much as 40 percent. The most substantial impacts would be realized with perfect targeting, but even imperfect targeting would reduce poverty in all three countries.

The impacts of expansion reach other facets of household life. Simulations indicate that ownership of livestock among the poor would rise. Likewise, well-targeted programs may raise landownership. Both can put households on a pathway out of poverty.

Overall, evidence clearly shows that social safety net programs can contribute significantly and efficiently to reducing poverty, building resilience, and boosting opportunities. For the full potential of social safety nets to be realized, these programs need to be brought up to scale and sustained. While this involves many technical decisions (box O.1), a series of decisive shifts must simultaneously occur in three other critical areas: political, institutional, and fiscal. These are explored in turn in the following chapters.

BOX O.1

Design Lessons in Bringing Social Safety Nets to Scale

A number of lessons emerge from the evaluations of program impacts in chapter 2 with regard to the design of programs and bringing social safety nets to scale:

- First, the value of a cash transfer matters. Ensuring impacts requires sufficiently large transfers.
- Second, the impact of programs relies on predictability. If benefits are not delivered with regularity, households cannot use them as effectively. As programs go to scale,

(continued next page)

Box O.1 (continued)

fiscal sustainability (i.e., regular funding) is needed to ensure that programs reach maximum impact.

- Third, coordination with complementary programs, such as skills training or other employment schemes, is critical for maximizing resilience and promoting productive inclusion. As social safety nets grow, there will be a greater need for a sound institutional framework to tie programs together.

- Fourth, as programs grow, so will the demand for other services, such as schools, health care, and agricultural extension. The access to and quality of services become central instruments in maximizing program impacts. Achieving such impacts will then require institutional coordination as well as more investments in these services.

Recognizing and Leveraging Politics to Expand and Sustain Social Safety Nets (Chapter 3)

The impressive rate of expansion of social safety nets across Africa in the past decade proves that ideas, preferences, and political platforms can change even in places where the political environment might initially be unsupportive. Political dynamics evolve, and windows of opportunity open. These processes represent an opportunity to build sustainable, large-scale social safety net systems. The technical work of designing these systems should not ignore the political dimensions of social policy. Understanding and addressing the political processes and political economy behind social policy are as relevant and necessary as any technical assessment for crafting and implementing ambitious programs.

This study considers three main points of interaction between politics and social safety nets (figure O.8). First, the scope of social safety nets depends on political acceptability and desirability, which depend on social norms, the prevalence of poverty, and ideological factors such as the perceived causes of poverty and preferences for redistribution. Second, the choice of program and design parameters is influenced by political preferences and incentives and in turn influences the commitment to programs. Third, there is a feedback loop: the implementation of social safety net programs shapes the political environment. Politicians and citizens adjust their preferences and incentives and redefine their relationship as social safety net programs are implemented.

The Political Appetite for Adopting and Expanding Social Safety Nets

Political appetite is critical for expanding social safety nets and bringing them to scale, and for shaping social protection policies and programs more broadly. This appetite results from many factors. Here, the focus is on three factors that underpin a country's appetite for the adoption or expansion of social safety net

Figure O.8 **Politics and Social Safety Nets Interact**

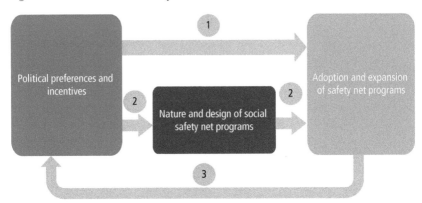

programs: beliefs and perceptions about social assistance, socioeconomic volatility, and the influence of external actors, including development partners.

Preconceptions influence the support for social safety nets. Commonly held preconceptions include the belief that the poor and recipients of social safety net benefits are lazy and undeserving of assistance. This idea is deep-rooted and has played a critical role in shaping policy choices (Seekings 2015). In Zambia, the social safety net agenda was strongly opposed by a minister of finance who claimed that the poor were really only lazy (Pruce and Hickey 2017).

Similarly, some believe that transfers to the poor are wasted resources because social safety net programs do not have productive impacts or may generate a culture of dependency. Both misconceptions can be partly addressed by showing decision makers evidence for such programs, including impact evaluations, direct exposure to successful programs in other countries, or country pilot experiences. Impact evaluations show that beneficiaries do not spend social safety net transfers on temptation goods, such as alcohol or tobacco, but rather on food and investments (chapter 2). The evidence also shows that programs have productive impacts through human capital and productive investments. They also confirm that programs result in more work by offering the opportunity for households to expand their farms and businesses.

Perceptions about social safety nets may shift following study tours and other forms of direct learning from similar programs around the world. In Ethiopia, the integration of social protection objectives in a rural development program partly drew on a study tour by government officials in the 1990s to the Maharashtra Employment Guarantee Scheme, in India (Lavers 2016). Senegal's Programme National de Bourses de Sécurité Familiale (national cash transfer program, PNBSF) reflects the influence of the Brazilian and Mexican experiences to which a senior official had been exposed (Ndiaye 2017). Given the importance of direct exposure to programs, pilot projects can also play a major role in convincing constituencies of the merits of the programs. In Uganda, the promotion of the Senior Citizens Grant Program as a success story through field visits, media story placements, and an evaluation seem to have created the support needed to make the program a political reality (Hickey and Bukenya 2016).

Changing political appetite by changing perceptions of the impact and value of social safety nets is not a quick process. At the other extreme, periods of rapid economic or social change offer a window of opportunity, wherein the political appetite for social safety net programs can evolve quickly. In many cases, emergency response programs established outside the sphere of social safety nets have created the political buy-in and infrastructure from which social safety nets have developed. Various crises have formed the basis of sustained social safety net systems, such as droughts in Botswana and Mauritania or conflicts in Mozambique and Sierra Leone (Albrecht 2017; Buur and Salimo 2017; Seekings 2016). Political crises or a desire to avoid a political crisis can also play a role. In Senegal, rising prices following the 2008–09 financial crisis and weak peanut and fishing sectors contributed to the president's emphasis on social safety nets following the 2012 election (Ndiaye 2017). Health crises have also been influential, for instance, the spread of HIV/AIDS in Botswana, Kenya, Lesotho, and Zambia or the Ebola outbreak in West Africa in 2014 (Granvik 2015; Hamer 2016; Pruce and Hickey 2017; Wanyama and McCord 2017).

Economic reforms—often a response to shocks—may rally political support for social safety nets to compensate those affected by fiscal consolidation and more generally garner support for the reforms. In Mozambique, urban protests spread across the country in 2008 and 2010 in response to the government's removal of subsidies and the rising costs of food and fuel. The protests provided the impetus for the adoption of the Productive Social Action Program in 2013 (Buur and Salimo 2017). Such situations offer an opportunity to rally for change in political appetite and support longer-term social safety net systems. Thus, social safety nets are becoming an explicit part of macroeconomic policy reforms.

In less volatile circumstances, international platforms and development partners can catalyze political support for social safety nets. One such entry point for shifting the policy dialogue is the international community's focus on the responsibility of governments for advancing human rights, as presented in the Universal Declaration of Human Rights, which is often enshrined in legally binding agreements. Except for Botswana, the Comoros, Mozambique, and South Sudan, all countries in the region have ratified the International Covenant on Economic, Social, and Cultural Rights, and all but the Comoros and South Sudan are state parties to the International Covenant on Civil and Political Rights. The core values of human rights are in the constitutions of most countries, which identify particular groups as worthy of support (table O.1).

Table 0.1 **Constitutions Cover Vulnerable Groups**

	Ethiopia	Kenya	Mozambique	Rwanda	Sierra Leone	Uganda	Zambia
Women		X	X				
Elderly	X	X	X	X	X	X	X
Disabled	X	X	X	X	X	X	X
Orphans	X	X	X				
Children	X	X	X				
Youth		X	X		X		
Indigents				X			
Minorities		X				X	
Survivors of conflict			X	X			

Source: World Bank data review.

Most countries are also parties to regional or global organizations that provide a normative framework for social safety nets, and more broadly for social protection systems, including the African Union Social Policy Framework, the Sustainable Development Goals, and the Social Protection Floor Initiative. While rights-based arguments may not have been significant in the adoption or expansion of social safety nets in the region, social safety nets themselves can help governments fulfill their human rights obligations by promoting civil, social, political, and economic rights.

Development partners can influence the political appetite for social safety nets by offering financing and technical assistance to overcome fiscal and capacity hurdles that influence the policy agenda (Chinyoka and Seekings 2016; Siachiwena 2016; Ulriksen 2016). On average, development partners finance 55 percent of program spending (with higher shares in lower-income countries, fragile and conflict-affected states, and humanitarian crises; figure O.9). However, until the dynamics of domestic politics help generate the commitment of key national stakeholders, development partner influence is mostly effective in securing the capacity and commitment of bureaucrats rather than political actors. Development partner pressure alone has not been found to be sufficient to generate substantial political commitment (Hickey and Lavers 2017). The initiative to introduce or expand social safety net programs can usually be traced to the dynamics of domestic politics, and development partners often only engage once the commitment of key stakeholders has been secured. For example, in Ethiopia, various development partners had long voiced concerns about the emergency food system. However, changes were finally adopted only when this coincided with the Ethiopian government's concerns, which were precipitated by a series of crises (Lavers 2016). In general, decisions to expand social safety nets have been made solely within broader government strategies, even when the programs have been largely financed by development partners (Cherrier 2015).

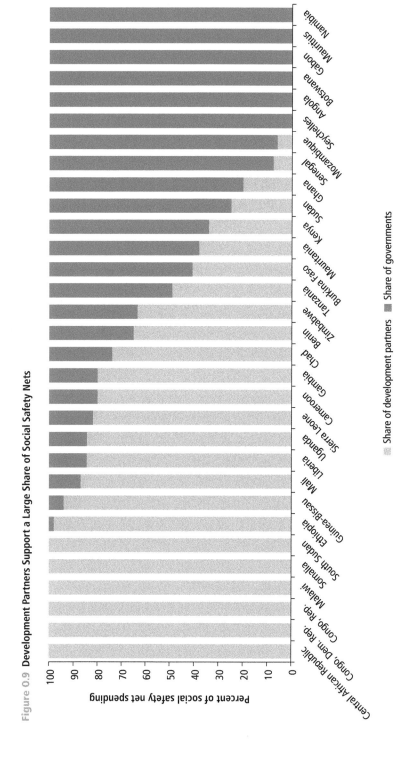

Figure O.9 Development Partners Support a Large Share of Social Safety Nets

Percent of social safety net spending

Countries (top to bottom): Namibia, Mauritius, Gabon, Botswana, Angola, Seychelles, Mozambique, Senegal, Ghana, Sudan, Kenya, Mauritania, Burkina Faso, Tanzania, Zimbabwe, Benin, Chad, Gambia, Cameroon, Sierra Leone, Uganda, Liberia, Mali, Guinea-Bissau, Ethiopia, South Sudan, Somalia, Malawi, Congo, Dem. Rep., Central African Republic, Congo, Rep.

Legend: Share of development partners ■ Share of governments

Source: For Angola, Burkina Faso, Cameroon, the Republic of Congo, the Democratic Republic of Congo, Gabon, Kenya, Liberia, Malawi, Mauritius, Mozambique, Namibia, Senegal, Seychelles, Sierra Leone, Somalia, South Sudan, Sudan, Tanzania, Uganda, and Zimbabwe: ASPIRE (Atlas of Social Protection Indicators of Resilience and Equity) (database), Administrative data, World Bank, Washington, DC http://www.worldbank.org/aspire. For Benin, Botswana, and Mauritania: Monchuk (2014). For the Central African Republic: World Bank (2016d). For Chad: World Bank (2016c). For Ethiopia: World Bank (2016a). For The Gambia: UNICEF (2013). For Ghana: World Bank (2016a). For Guinea Bissau: World Bank (forthcoming a). For Mali: World Bank (forthcoming b).

Program Parameters Are Political

Domestic politics are also crucial for program design. The best designs are those that are technically sound, administratively feasible, and politically savvy. The elements of technical soundness and administrative feasibility are the main focus during program design, while political palatability is often underestimated or dealt with reluctantly (Pritchett 2005). At the extreme, a perfect technical design that ignores the politics of support for social safety nets could eventually be the worst option for those it means to serve. Political obstacles can be overcome to some degree by choosing the characteristics and parameters of programs that factor in political preferences or incentives, albeit sometimes with a technical efficiency trade-off.

Among the features of programs that have a political nature are conditionalities. Conditionalities could be introduced with the technical motivation of boosting the impact of programs. They can also be proposed to address perceptions related to deservingness by requiring beneficiaries to undertake extra efforts (such as sending children to school or taking children for regular health checkups). Often established as a technical option for self-targeting, work requirements may also help overcome concerns about the alleged laziness of recipients (public works programs, for instance). To promote a productive impact and alleviate concerns about dependency, social safety net programs are sometimes cast as part of a larger development program. Complementary initiatives, such as credit and extension programs, provide a potential route toward graduation. In Tanzania, the productive orientation of the Productive Safety Net Program was a major factor in securing political support because it addressed concerns about dependency and the importance of self-reliance (Ulriksen 2016).

The fear of promoting a culture of dependency may also be addressed by including clear time bounds in social safety net programs. Recertification processes may be considered a flexible time limitation. For instance, in Senegal, the PNBSF includes households for five years, after which a recertification process is planned to evaluate whether the households should stay in or exit the program. Recertification does not automatically push beneficiaries out of social safety nets, as in a time-bound design, but it may offer reassurance that the program is based on actual needs.

In some contexts, the response to concerns about deservingness and self-reliance has been to target only those who are thought to be unable to provide for themselves. While most safety net spending is on programs that include poverty, vulnerability, or welfare as targeting criteria (77 percent of total spending on average), in line with national constitutions, some programs in Kenya, Uganda, and Zambia are categorically targeted and, in most cases, means-tested, and target mothers, the elderly, children, and the disabled (see table O.1). Indeed, social safety net spending typically goes to the elderly

Figure O.10 Poverty Targeting Accounts for Most of Social Safety Net Spending, but the Elderly Benefit Most

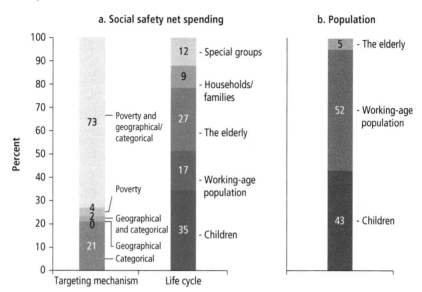

Source: ASPIRE (Atlas of Social Protection Indicators of Resilience and Equity) (database), Administrative data, World Bank, Washington, DC, http://www.worldbank.org/aspire.
Note: The poverty category includes all programs that explicitly target households on the basis of welfare, poverty, or vulnerability, see methodology in appendix A.2.1. To identify households, these programs rely on community targeting, means or income tests, proxy-means tests, pension tests, self-targeting, or a combination of these. The figure presents the distribution of all resources deployed by all countries across different categories. See appendix table G.6.

and children in most of the region, and is not always also conditional on poverty (figure O.10). The elderly tend to be disproportionately supported relative to children (they receive 27 percent of all expenditures but represent only 5 percent of the population), although the impact on poverty reduction would be much larger with universal programs for children than with social pension programs (Guven and Leite 2016).

Political realities may necessitate targeting groups beyond the poorest to attain political support. In some cases, while a focus on specific geographical areas might make sense from a poverty perspective, national coverage might be preferred. For example, in 2016, the Nigerian government decided to cover all six of the country's geographical zones in a pilot project on productive activities. In Uganda, the choice to roll out the Senior Citizen's Grant by targeting the 100 eldest pensioners in new districts arguably reflected a political move to distribute a small transfer as widely as possible, rather than pursue a more impactful technical design. At the end of the spectrum, universal coverage can be the preferred option if the focus is on strict equality in treatment and the avoidance of any form of exclusion.

Similarly, taking political considerations into account in designing a social safety net program may result in technically suboptimal programs. In Rwanda, for example, the emphasis placed on infrastructure development has made ensuring the labor intensity of public works challenging. Political tweaks should be introduced as a last resort, kept to a minimum, and mitigated by a careful focus on program transparency because the tweaks are often added at the expense of technical soundness.

Political Impacts May Favor Social Safety Net Sustainability

While political realities influence program design, the implementation of programs can also change the political landscape. Social safety nets can affect the way households relate to governments, and leveraging this can be a means to promote program sustainability. More generally, social safety nets may induce changes in the discourse on poverty and on the role of the government and public policy. These efforts can help individuals realize that they are rights-holders and governments realize they are duty-bearers. This feedback loop shown in figure O.8 establishing and enhancing social safety nets can, in practice, generate more political appetite for programs, thereby fostering both expansion and sustainability.

Social safety nets may empower and promote social inclusion and the autonomy of beneficiaries within communities (Pavanello et al. 2016). In Kenya, Mozambique, and Zambia, orphans, other vulnerable children, and disabled beneficiaries have reported that cash transfers raised their sense of self-confidence, dignity, ability to be more assertive, and perception of future well-being (Attah et al. 2016; Handa et al. 2014a, 2014b; Haushofer and Shapiro 2013; Jones et al. 2016; Seidenfeld, Handa, and Tembo 2013). Greater social and economic inclusion within communities enhances household social support and resilience to shocks. Greater social cohesion and proximity may increase the support of richer households for social safety net programs, thereby contributing to program sustainability.

Programs may have negative impacts on inclusion and solidarity, however, if, for instance, the selection process among beneficiaries is perceived as unclear or unfair or if poverty rates are high (Ellis 2012). The selection process among beneficiaries must discourage stereotyping and resentment among nonbeneficiaries.

Social safety nets can change communities, and the interventions can result in political mobilization by bringing governments closer to beneficiaries (Jones et al. 2016). Some programs make explicit efforts to establish and promote relationships between the government and beneficiaries. In Cameroon and Mauritania, a contract is signed between beneficiaries and the government during the registration of households for the programs, which highlights the contractual relationship. This is similar to the efforts in some Latin American social safety net programs to reshape the relationships between governments and individuals by signing contracts of co-responsibility, whereby beneficiaries commit to using basic services, while the government commits to ensuring adequate provision of the services, thereby emphasizing a reciprocal relationship (Fiszbein and Schady 2009).

These interventions can reshape the relationship between individuals and the state by increasing the capacity of individuals or groups to access other government processes, for instance, by supporting households in their efforts to obtain national identity numbers or identity cards. Thus, showing a valid birth certificate has been a condition for receiving the child support grant in South Africa. Because this requirement effectively bars access to the program by certain groups, a new procedure was introduced for delivering birth certificates directly to hospitals, thereby giving access to formal identification to new segments of the population (Glassman and Temin 2016).

Social accountability mechanisms may strengthen the political feedback loop by contributing to greater empowerment and voice among beneficiaries. Program features such as grievance redress and community and beneficiary participation may contribute to the social contract (Molyneux 2016; Ringold et al. 2012). However, social accountability mechanisms tend to be deployed most effectively by better-educated, wealthier, and more able-bodied individuals rather than those with less capacity to organize and voice their concerns (Giannozzi and Khan 2011; King and Hickey 2017). In Kenya, for example, the lack of political mobilization behind the Hunger Safety Net Program (HSNP) may be attributed to the fact that beneficiaries were mostly nomadic pastoralists in the north, a marginalized group (Hurrell and MacAuslan 2012). The design of social accountability mechanisms is thus critical in maximizing program potential.

Social safety nets may help establish a relationship between the poor and vulnerable and their government. They have also been shown to exert an impact on the political process. Social safety nets have appeared on political platforms. There is some evidence that elections have played a role in catalyzing a policy focus on social safety nets, such as the introduction of the Livelihood Empowerment against Poverty Program (LEAP) before the 2008 elections in Ghana or the correlation between the 2002 and 2007 elections and spikes in social assistance expenditures in Kenya. In Botswana, Ipelegeng, a public works program, specifically extended the previously rural-only drought relief programs to urban areas where opposition support had been growing (Hamer 2016). The political appetite for expanding social safety nets may also be spurred by concerns around the issues of local government and local politicians. In Kenya and Zambia, for instance, members of Parliament have urged the expansion of small-scale pilot programs to new districts because of perceptions that political advantage may be gained by delivering benefits to their constituent local communities (Pruce and Hickey 2017; Wanyama and McCord 2017).

Evidence for the effect of social safety nets on voting behavior and electoral outcomes is derived mostly from large-scale cash transfer programs in Asia and Latin America. Electoral benefits are generally reaped by members of the incumbent party. Impacts may be lasting, but they eventually pale. Voters tend to reward incumbent parties, rather than the parties that initiated the programs. Adopting the programs of previous policy makers and supporting their expansion can therefore be rewarded politically. Even in national programs, the political gains may be local.

Once they expand beyond a certain size and demonstrate favorable impacts, programs can create long-term commitments that are politically difficult to discontinue. In Brazil, Colombia, and Mexico, for instance, programs that have been established for more than a decade and demonstrated positive impacts have been gradually adopted by parties and elites across the board, although each administration typically adjusts the programs to reflect changing policy objectives or approaches to poverty reduction. The name of a program may even be altered though the core features are retained.

Anchoring in Strong Institutions to Expand and Sustain Social Safety Nets (Chapter 4)

Institutions are central to the delivery of social safety nets and influence all aspects of program effectiveness. If the social safety nets in Africa are to be adequately expanded, institutions must evolve along multiple parameters, including the anchoring in laws and policies, mechanisms for coordination and oversight, and arrangements for management and delivery. Small pilot interventions may show results and contribute to building political support for the expansion of social safety nets, but broadening coverage typically requires some consolidation. Often, over time, as programs mature, program management will be shifted to government ministries or agencies; program designs and processes will become standardized; staffing will be transferred to the civil service or outsourced; and more comprehensive rules for the overall social safety net system will be formalized in policies, strategies, and laws.

Institutions impose the rules of the game that shape all aspects of social safety net policy, design, and implementation, ranging from establishing eligibility criteria and the regulations and procedures that govern the operations of the organizations that deliver the social safety net programs (including mandates and human resource policies) to sectoral laws and regulations. Beyond the formal rules, informal institutions—conventions and customary practices—influence the provision of social safety nets because, for example, they mediate notions of deservingness or support and incentivize civil servants and frontline staff to deliver programs appropriately.

There are multiple paths toward formal and informal rules of the game that enable credible social safety nets in Africa, and many are linked to the development of broader social protection systems. Building a social protection system does not necessarily require a focus on a single entity or agency to manage multiple programs. Instead, it calls for a focus on the institutions, including the processes, that guide the design and delivery of social safety nets within government systems, including both formal and informal structures. There are numerous possible paths in this process. In some countries, such as Ethiopia, the development of a social protection policy took place after significant consolidation of social safety net programs and the achievement of near nationwide coverage. In other countries—such as Chad, Niger, and Sierra Leone—the development of social protection policies occurred early in the evolution of social safety nets and was accompanied by the implementation of small pilot programs. In Latin America, the need for greater coordination among a growing number of social programs encouraged governments to create coherent social safety net systems, usually within social protection policy and legal frameworks.

From Frameworks to Commitments: Emerging National Strategies for Social Safety Nets

Across the region, countries have increasingly focused on establishing an overarching institutional framework to advance social safety nets. Often, the policy commitments are embedded in international conventions and declarations, attesting to the layering of institutions across local, national, and international levels. The presence of these policies and laws or legal frameworks may signal an important step toward the firm anchoring of social safety nets in Africa, but it will not be sufficient to bring social safety nets to scale, as these first need to be matched with political support and financial resources.

There has been widespread adoption across Africa of international treaties related to social safety nets. However, there is variation in the degree to which social safety nets are anchored in national legislation, at times as part of a broader position on social protection. In most countries, legal support is limited to general constitutional provisions for supporting the vulnerable. This is the case in 12 of the 16 countries reviewed (table O.2). In Niger, for example, the constitution explains that "the State sees to the elderly through a policy of social protection."

All countries include social safety nets in their national development strategies. Similarly, social protection policies and strategies have become common across Africa—typically covering both social safety nets and social

Table O.2 **Safety Nets in Most Countries Are Anchored in Laws, Policy, or Constitutions**

Country	Constitutions include support for particular groups	Social safety net interventions in national development strategies and plans	A social protection policy or strategy exists and includes social safety nets	Social safety net entitlements or institutions are enshrined in national laws
Botswana	Yes	Yes	No	Yes
Chad	No	Yes	Yes	No
Congo, Rep.	No	Yes	Yes[a]	No
Ethiopia	Yes	Yes	Yes	No
Ghana	Yes	Yes	Yes	No
Kenya	Yes	Yes	Yes	Yes[b]
Mauritania	No	Yes	Yes	No
Mozambique	Yes	Yes	Yes	Yes
Niger	Yes	Yes	Yes	No
Rwanda	Yes	Yes	Yes	No
Senegal	No	Yes	Yes	No
Sierra Leone	Yes	Yes	Yes	No
South Africa	Yes	Yes	Yes	Yes
Tanzania	Yes	Yes	No[c]	No
Uganda	Yes	Yes	Yes	No
Zambia	Yes	Yes	Yes	No

Source: A review of national documents for 16 countries.
a. MEPATI (2012).
b. However, the Social Assistance Act contains provisions that have not been implemented, and it is expected to be repealed and replaced by a new act.
c. A social protection strategy has been drafted and is awaiting approval.

insurance—but they are often general and not fully implemented. Among the 48 countries in the region, 32 have approved and 7 are in the process of drafting such policies (figure O.11). However, while national strategies and policies may underpin social protection measures by making important statements about a government's ambitions, few of the programs that are guided by these strategies have been brought to scale.

Despite broad commitments in strategies and policies, most governments are reluctant to apply a terminology of entitlements. Basing entitlements or responsibilities firmly in laws could undermine a government's ability to implement social safety nets or to legislate in the future if the legal framework is unwieldy or impractical. However, if it is aligned with political interests and backed by sufficient resources, a legal framework can act as a strong anchor for social safety nets that prevents undue interruptions or suspension of programs. South Africa offers an example of how political incentives may be aligned with a legal framework for social safety nets. Similarly, in Mozambique,

Figure 0.11 **Many Countries Have Adopted Social Protection Strategies**

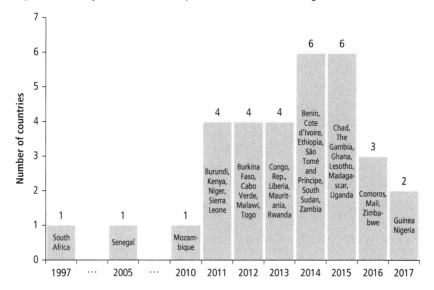

Source: World Bank review of country documents.
Note: More details are presented in appendix D, table D.1.

the development of an appropriate legislative framework—embodied in the Social Protection Law of 2007 and the National Strategy for Basic Social Security in 2009—has been key in realizing a social safety net.

Rooting Social Safety Nets in Organizations for Policy Setting, Oversight, Coordination, and Management

Until recently, there were few ministries responsible for social protection or social safety nets in Africa. The choice of responsibility is often a first step in setting out the institutional arrangements for social safety nets in governments. The criteria for the selection of a ministerial home for a social safety net typically depend on the factors that led to the emergence of the social safety net. In some countries, programs have emerged out of the experience of providing social security among formal sector workers; in others, they have appeared because of a concern about food insecurity or vulnerability to disaster. Typically, this background has determined where programs are housed.

The choice of ministry for policy setting, oversight, and coordination typically also results from considerations about mandates and political power, with initial decisions shaping the evolution of social safety nets in a country. In the region, this responsibility has been vested in a social ministry in 22 of the 38 countries reviewed (figure O.12 and appendix table D.1). This choice may reflect a desire to name a ministry that is already mandated to promote policies

Figure 0.12 Social Ministries Are the Typical—but Not the Only—Policy, Oversight, and Coordination Entities

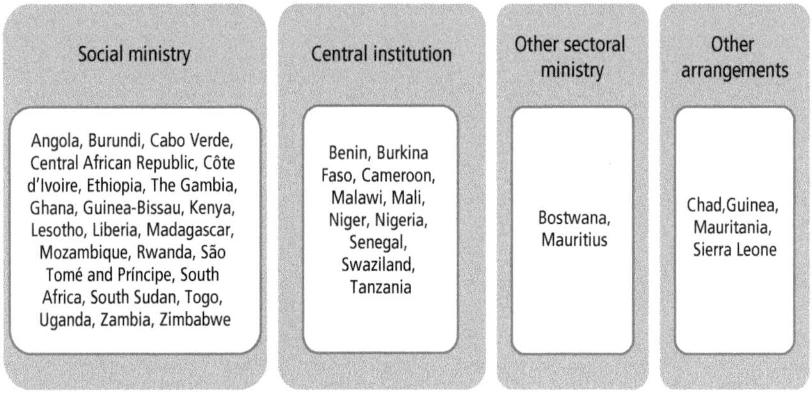

Social ministry	Central institution	Other sectoral ministry	Other arrangements
Angola, Burundi, Cabo Verde, Central African Republic, Côte d'Ivoire, Ethiopia, The Gambia, Ghana, Guinea-Bissau, Kenya, Lesotho, Liberia, Madagascar, Mozambique, Rwanda, São Tomé and Príncipe, South Africa, South Sudan, Togo, Uganda, Zambia, Zimbabwe	Benin, Burkina Faso, Cameroon, Malawi, Mali, Niger, Nigeria, Senegal, Swaziland, Tanzania	Bostwana, Mauritius	Chad, Guinea, Mauritania, Sierra Leone

Source: World Bank review of country documents for 38 countries.
Note: Central institutions include offices of the president or prime minister and ministries of the economy, planning, or finance. Other sectoral ministries include ministries of local government and rural development. See methodology in appendix A.2.2 and more details in appendix table D.1.

that support the poor and vulnerable. However, while social ministries may have the strongest mandate to support the poor, their financial resources and political influence are often limited. Central organizations—the office of the prime minister, the office of the president, or ministries of finance and planning—have been selected in a fourth of the countries. While these organizations may enjoy considerable authority and may have special procedures available that allow them to act more swiftly than technical ministries, the organizational culture may be less sympathetic to the needs of the vulnerable. The relative importance of these factors may change, resulting in shifts in the entity that leads in policy setting, oversight, and coordination.

Ensuring That Organizations Can Effectively Implement Social Safety Nets

The responsibility for the implementation and management of social safety net interventions is frequently housed in an entity separate from the policy-making and oversight entity, and usually in a ministry with a mandate that aligns with the aims of the program. Thus, social safety net programs with a protective focus, such as through unconditional transfers to categorical groups considered vulnerable, tend to be housed in social ministries, while programs that focus on more productive aspects may be assigned to ministries specializing in rural development, agriculture, roads, infrastructure, or water. Programs may shift homes over time. For instance, a program that emerges as a short-term response to an emergency may be in a high-profile agency, such as an office of the president. However, as the program matures, a social ministry or agency with a policy mandate to serve the vulnerable may become a more appropriate home. Because these programs are relatively new in Africa, there are few examples of changes in institutional arrangements, whereas there are examples in countries or regions with more established programs, such as Colombia or Latin America more generally.

The choice of ministerial home shapes the evolution of social safety nets. Thus, a program may conform to the vision and mandate of the responsible organization. For instance, social workers in a social ministry may tend to focus on vulnerable groups with specific needs that are a reflection of the professional mandate and priorities of the social workers. Conversely, the coexistence of multiple views of social safety nets may result in institutional fragmentation. In particular, the preferences of development partners may play a decisive role in the selection of a ministry, and this tendency can lead to decisions to locate similar programs in different organizations, as in Tanzania and Uganda.

While the institutional home is tasked with managing the social safety net program or programs, operations are realized through organizations that manage and deliver interventions. There are five main categories of such entities: a preexisting department, a special-purpose department, a project implementation unit, a semiautonomous government agency, and a nongovernmental organization (NGO) or regional or international institution (United Nations agency and so on). Management arrangements vary by context, and the choice influences effectiveness. For instance, government departments are often hampered by the need to abide by ministerial procedures, and their fiduciary procedures or hiring standards are typically more restrictive than those that apply to a semiautonomous government agency or a project implementation unit. However, project implementation units are not suitable as a management structure in the long run and as programs are expanded. More sustainable solutions include making use of permanent ministerial units and local civil servants.

As programs grow, coordination becomes more critical, not least because of limited fiscal space and the need for efficiency (chapter 5). At this stage, the organizations responsible for delivering social safety nets need to involve multiple sectors and actors depending on design elements. Universal or unconditional programs may be associated with simpler institutional arrangements run broadly through one sectoral entity and local and national representatives. Conditional programs often require the engagement of multiple sectors, such as the ministries of health and education, as well as robust procedures for collecting information from health centers and schools on compliance with the program conditions. Public works programs frequently require the involvement of diverse technical staff. Actors charged with implementation may be located in the private sector or civil society. Responsibility for the payment of transfers is often contracted to payment service providers.

At the higher level, social protection policies often include the creation of interministerial coordination committees, which are frequently expected to be chaired by ministers or cabinet secretaries. Forming such committees and calling meetings once they are formed are rarely prioritized. In Burkina Faso, for instance, the intersectoral national council for social protection only meets once or twice a year and mainly focuses on information sharing, the main output of which is lists of programs and expenditures. In countries where humanitarian programs are prominent or in fragile settings, NGOs and development partners often play critical roles. The coordination and oversight of these large programs implemented outside government are often of practical importance because of the size of the programs and the political nature of the response to shocks. In most Sahelian countries, humanitarian actors have initiated efforts to coordinate interventions, capitalize on good practices, and engage in advocacy.

In most African countries, social safety nets are the responsibility of national governments, but implementation arrangements vary. Most programs are funded centrally through the government budget or development partners, and, in all countries, central entities are tasked with policy setting, coordination, and oversight. Delivery may remain centralized or be deconcentrated or devolved. In some countries, such as the Republic of Congo, a national ministry delivers the social safety net program through frontline workers accountable to the ministry. Typically, if implementation occurs through a project implementation unit, as in Burkina Faso and Cameroon, the delivery is centralized, and project staff are recruited to coordinate local implementation. In other cases, the frontline delivery of programs falls to local services (deconcentration) or local governments (devolution), which are required to follow centralized guidelines and standards.

While standardized guidelines exist for most programs, some delivery choices depend on some local decision making. National standards enable consistent implementation, but some tasks may benefit from devolved decision making so delivery takes local realities into account. This flexibility can result in more effective processes, such as in targeting, and can encourage local buy-in. However, it can also lead to distortions or bias in implementation because local norms and practices may favor particular groups or objectives. In many contexts, in practice, there is variation across locations in the application of guidelines. This can be deliberate or the result of inadequate communication among program implementers.

Creating Incentives to Encourage Individual Actors to Deliver Results

As there are multiple ways to manage social safety nets, there are also various options in staffing. Programs may be delivered by staff who are fully dedicated to the programs or by staff who, besides social safety net activities, are responsible for other programs. Staff may be civil servants or temporary staff on fixed-term contracts. Key functions might also be contracted to private sector providers, such as administering payments, organizing training activities, or even running the program implementation unit. Many programs also make use of voluntary community structures for elements of implementation.

The issue of incentives for civil servants is generally critical for effective implementation, particularly as programs are taken to scale and shift into national systems. In many countries, the perception that civil servants are paid less than their peers working in the private sector (and less than the technical assistance providers paid by development partners in externally funded projects) and that career progression and accompanying pay increases are limited can produce low motivation and job dissatisfaction. The resulting high staff turnover—combined with slow recruitment processes, which may be based on networking rather than expertise—leads to gaps in capacity. Job dissatisfaction and low motivation among staff contribute to poor performance within the civil service. Interagency rivalry and rivalry between permanent and contract staff may also contribute to low capacity and, ultimately, poor performance. While reliance on technical assistance and contracts may deliver results in the short term, longer-term solutions are required to embed social safety nets at the heart of government systems and ensure sustainability.

Harnessing Resources to Expand and Sustain Social Safety Nets (Chapter 5)

Bringing social safety nets to scale has obvious fiscal implications. In light of the current fiscal context in most African countries, expanding the coverage of programs represents a serious challenge. Harnessing resources to expand social safety nets requires a multipronged approach, including achieving operational efficiency in interventions; enhancing the level and sustainability of financial resources; identifying the proper mix of domestic, foreign, public, and nonpublic funding sources; and deploying a flexible financing strategy to respond to shocks and crises.

Spending and Financing for Social Safety Nets: A Snapshot

Africa devotes on average 1.2 percent of GDP to social safety nets, compared with the global average of 1.6 percent. This spending is lower than spending on other sectors such as energy subsidies, health care, education, and, in some cases, the military (figure O.13). In particular, spending on energy subsidies—often cited as a means of supporting vulnerable households, but largely regressive in practice—is greater than spending on social safety nets in the region, with particularly high levels in Central and East Africa and in low-income countries.

Figure O.13 **Spending Is Lower on Social Safety Nets Than on Other Sectors**

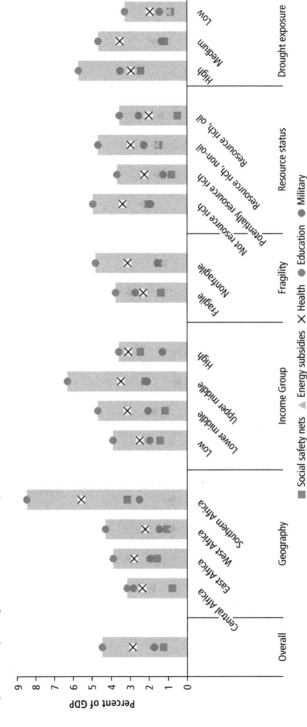

■ Social safety nets ▲ Energy subsidies ✕ Health ● Education ● Military

Sources: Spending data: ASPIRE (Atlas of Social Protection Indicators of Resilience and Equity) (database), Administrative data, World Bank, Washington, DC, http://www.worldbank .org/aspire. Energy subsidies: Coady et al. 2015. Other data: WDI (World Development Indicators) (database), World Bank, Washington, DC, http://databank.worldbank.org/data /reports.aspx?source=world-development-indicators.
Note: See methodology in appendix B.4 and more details in appendix G, table G.1. Data do not reflect recent reductions in subsidies, which have taken place post 2015 in several countries. Social safety net spending estimates are moderately different from those in World Bank (2018) due to data updates in this report and varying treatment of outlier data points.

Spending varies across the region. Africa-wide, upper-middle-income countries spend an average 2.2 percent of GDP, while low-income countries spend 1.4 percent, and lower-middle-income countries spend an average 1.0 percent. Southern Africa, with more upper-middle-income countries, spends an average of five times more than Central Africa and two times more than West and East Africa. Spending on social safety nets is lower in fragile states and resource-rich countries. Countries with greater exposure to natural disasters allocate more resources than those facing a low or medium risk of disaster. Particularly high spending is observed in a few countries (Lesotho, Namibia, and South Africa).

Development partners are critical for the financing of social safety nets (see figure O.9). On average, governments finance 46 percent of program spending, and development partners cover the other 54 percent (appendix table G.8 presents detailed information for selected programs). The share of development partners is higher in lower-income countries, in fragile and conflict-affected states, and in humanitarian crises. Given the fiscal constraints facing many governments, development partner support is likely to be crucial for bringing programs to scale in most countries.

Administrative costs may be high early on, but decline with scale. In terms of efficiency, administrative costs represent an average 17 percent of program spending (appendix table G.9). This reflects both the cost of initial investments in systems and the small size of many programs. While data are limited, the share of administrative costs tends to be lower in public works, school feeding, and social pension programs, possibly because of less costly targeting. Administrative costs tend to fall as programs increase in size. Administrative costs of the Social Safety Net Program in Cameroon also fell, from 65 percent in 2015 to 23 percent in 2016, as the number of beneficiaries quadrupled (figure O.14). In Mali, the administrative cost of the Jigisemejiri Program declined from 42 percent to 12 percent between 2014 to 2016, while the number of beneficiaries expanded from about 30,000 to about 375,000 individuals. The administrative costs of Mozambique's Basic Social Subsidy Program decreased slightly when benefit levels increased. However, expansion does not necessarily immediately lead to savings if programs expand geographically and need to develop new networks and systems, as with the Tanzania flagship program and the Malawi MASAF public works program (appendix table G.9).

Making Better Use of Existing Resources

There is substantial space to improve program efficiency and effectiveness. Effectiveness (defined as the highest coverage possible for a given level of spending) is higher in countries with stronger social safety net systems, with a central institution leading the sector, and with large social registries. On the other hand, the presence of development partners and of a social protection strategy are negatively associated with effectiveness, probably linked to the fact that

Figure 0.14 Administrative Costs Often Decline as Programs Grow, but Not Always

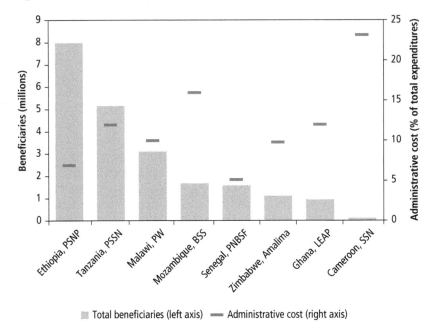

Total beneficiaries (left axis)   ▬ Administrative cost (right axis)

Source: ASPIRE (Atlas of Social Protection Indicators of Resilience and Equity) (database), Administrative data, World Bank, Washington, DC, http://www.worldbank.org/aspire.
Note: See details in appendix G, table G.9; Amalima = Response to Humanitarian Situation; BSS = Basic Social Subsidy Programme; LEAP = Livelihood Empowerment against Poverty; MASAF PWP = Malawi Social Action Fund Public Works Program PNBSF = National Cash Transfer Program; PSNP = Productive Safety Net Program; PSSN = Productive Social Safety Net Program; SSN = Social Safety Net.

effectiveness tends to be lower in countries with lower income levels or fragile countries, where development partners are more present (chapter 5 and table 5.2). Efficiency gains can be sought through enhanced administration (better tools, a systems approach, and improved resource allocation), improved accuracy in beneficiary selection, and the realignment of program objectives with beneficiary selection.

Well-functioning administrative tools are critical for the timely delivery of social safety nets to beneficiaries, but also for lowering the costs of benefit delivery. The Government of South Africa achieved large efficiency gains by overhauling administration, introducing a specialized agency for centralized administration and payments, distributing biometric smart cards, reregistering beneficiaries, and undertaking regular biometric proof-of-life verification (notwithstanding recent controversies surrounding the arrangements regarding the payment systems). Adopting technology can lower administrative costs.

For example, the shift from cash to e-payments removes the complexity of distributing cash and reduces leakage. In Mexico, the integration of e-payments and social assistance—97 percent of 2.6 million pensioners are paid through a centralized system—saves about $900 million in administrative costs annually.

Upgrading administrative processes and introducing technology can be expensive and brings capacity demands in the short term. A review of the use of e-payments for emergency cash transfers in Kenya and Somalia found that e-payments were not immediately cheaper than manual payments because of the higher start-up costs (O'Brien, Hove, and Smith 2013). The existing infrastructure and implementation capacity are critical for the successful introduction of new technology. In Zambia, an innovative mobile technology enumeration and registration system for the Social Cash Transfer Program did not outperform the paper system in a small pilot initiative because of challenges related to the poor network and the lack of compatibility with the management information system (IDinsight 2015). However, the situation may change in the medium to long terms.

Adopting a systems approach can also promote efficiency, especially in contexts with multiple programs. Unifying the tools used across programs to identify and enroll beneficiaries, make payments, and manage information can lead to economies of scale and help tackle fraud and error (chapter 4). The development of information systems and registries can result in significant savings. In Brazil in 2013, by checking data against the National Database of Social Information, which contains records on social security benefits, the unemployment insurance program was able to block approximately $385 million in erroneous payments. In Romania in 2013, using a unique personal identification number in all major national databases (tax administration, social assistance, health care, pensions, disability) allowed cross-checks between social assistance and external data, which led to the recovery of around $1.65 million.

A second avenue for efficiency gains is allocative efficiency, the extent to which programs reach the poor and vulnerable. Reaching the intended target population is not devoid of costs or easy to do (chapters 1 and 3). Programs with an explicit goal to target the poor are generally pro-poor, but some resources still go to the nonpoor. In the eight countries presented in figure O.15, an average 14 percent of social safety net spending is received by the richest 20 percent of the population, and 20 percent is received by the second-richest quintile. While there is scope for improving targeting and while these programs tend to be better targeted than other government interventions, perfect targeting does not exist, and costs vary depending on context. There is always a trade-off between cost savings and precision in reaching the poor. For example, proxy-means testing is costlier than a categorical or universal approach. There are also political considerations in targeting (chapter 3).

Figure 0.15 Social Safety Nets Are Progressive, but Some Benefits Go to Better-Off Households

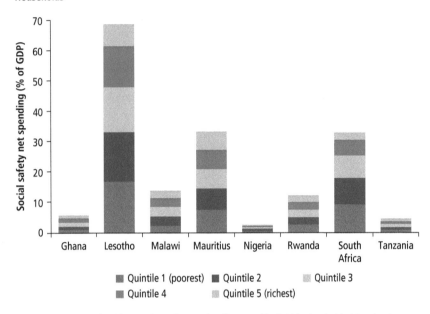

Source: ASPIRE (Atlas of Social Protection Indicators of Resilience and Equity) (database), Administrative data, World Bank, Washington, DC, http://www.worldbank.org/aspire. Incidence is estimated on the basis of household survey data (appendix A, table A.2).
Note: Estimates are based on beneficiary incidence and total spending. For more details, see appendix G, table G.7.

Program choice, scale, and design are important for efficiency in poverty reduction. Programs may have smaller effects on poverty reduction if their coverage of the poor is limited, if they are poorly targeted, if the benefits are not delivered regularly, if the benefit amounts are too small, or if there are other constraints (beyond cash) that impede poverty reduction. Energy subsidies are an example of benefits often put in place with a poverty mandate, but with weak poverty impacts because they tend to favor the better off, given that large shares of the benefits accrue to richer households, which have the highest levels of consumption (Inchauste and Victor 2017). Several countries have phased out or reduced energy subsidies in favor of targeted social safety net programs, thereby achieving stronger poverty impacts and fiscal savings. More generally, evidence on the effectiveness of alternative program choices, design, and implementation arrangements, such as the information provided in chapter 2, can help policy makers make effective choices.

Securing Sustainable Resources to Expand and Sustain Coverage
Improving program efficiency and effectiveness can generate gains, but most countries must still raise social safety net spending to take programs to scale sustainably.

Further compounding this problem is the fact that the need for social safety nets tends to run countercyclical to macroeconomic conditions. Governments thus typically face fiscal pressures precisely when programs are most needed. During these times, social safety net spending should be protected or even increased to prevent long-lasting negative impacts of fiscal consolidation on the poor (IMF 2017).

Strengthening fiscal systems is the most sustainable option for financing sustained social safety nets at scale, given the uncertainties in the global macroeconomic and political environment, the rising costs of borrowing, and the unpredictable nature of external financing (IMF 2015). More generally, improving tax systems is a widely recognized imperative in Africa, where tax revenues stood at an average of about 21 percent of GDP between 2011 and 2014, compared with over 30 percent in high-income countries. Governments have a number of options for boosting tax revenue through quick, short-term wins and deeper long-term reforms. Curtailing illicit financial flows could also free resources for social safety nets. In 2012, almost $1 trillion in illicit financial flows are estimated to have moved out of developing countries, and these flows amounted to almost 10 times the total aid received by developing countries (Kar, Cartwright-Smith, and Hollingshead 2010; Ortiz, Cummins, and Karunanethy 2015).

The increase in domestic revenue is unlikely to be sufficient to meet the financing required to bring social safety nets to scale in the short term. Governments need to also identify alternative funding sources. The financing provided by development partners is an obvious option that is already crucial for financing social safety net spending. It is especially strategic for financing initial investments, for example, establishing the building blocks for delivery. It can also be a catalyst for mobilizing domestic resources for social safety nets. In Mozambique, development partners have been central in advocating for a rise in budget allocations for the social protection strategy and the related plan (Bastagli 2015). Ethiopia's PSNP is an example of the successful integration of government and development partner funding, as well as of development partner harmonization.

Governments could explore more innovative financing options. Development impact bonds could be used to mobilize private sector financing for development objectives, including those of social safety nets. Development impact bonds allow private investors to prefinance social programs. Public sector agencies then pay back investors the principal, plus a return if the financed programs deliver the expected social outcomes (CGD and Social Finance 2013). Thus, the returns to investments are contingent on the achievement of the envisaged development objectives (Coleman 2016). Similarly, diaspora bonds could be used to direct remittances toward development goals. They are debt instruments issued by a government to raise financing from a diaspora and have been successfully introduced in India,

Israel, and Nigeria (Ketkar and Ratha 2007). Relative to other social sectors and regions, corporate social responsibility is an underutilized source for supporting social safety nets in Africa. A few governments have developed strategies and tools to access these resources to fund economic and development strategies. In Mauritius, all firms are requested to spend 2 percent of their profits on corporate social responsibility activities approved by the government or to transfer these funds for the government to invest in social and environmental projects.

Developing a Financing Strategy for Reliable, Effective Emergency Response

To manage the impacts of shocks effectively, ensure timely access to resources, and ultimately mitigate long-term fiscal impacts, governments are adopting a strategic approach to risk financing. In most contexts, disaster risk financing covers only a fraction of disaster losses, often in an unpredictable and untimely fashion. This leaves many of the vulnerable exposed. There are several financial instruments to address varying needs of governments to manage shock-responsive activities with financing that is timely, predictable, and commensurate with the magnitude of the shock.

Contingency or reserve funds can be established to finance relief, rehabilitation, reconstruction, and prevention activities in emergencies. These are used in, for instance, Colombia, Costa Rica, India, Indonesia, the Marshall Islands, Mexico, the Philippines, the Lao People's Democratic Republic, and Vietnam. Several African countries are seeking to establish similar funds. In Kenya, the government is in the final stages of operationalizing a national contingency fund dedicated to drought emergencies. Efforts are also under way to establish such funds in Madagascar and Mozambique. Contingent loans can be used to gain access to liquidity immediately following an exogenous shock. They have been used by multilateral development banks to create lines of credit that can be activated if a shock occurs.

Risk transfer mechanisms, which are financial or insurance instruments, are another option for insuring against shocks. They can be used in the case of risk to specific meteorological or geological events—droughts, hurricanes, earthquakes, and floods—or commodity price shocks. These market-based products use scientific information and actuarial modeling to estimate the losses that would be sustained because of a specific event and then price the risk. Payments are triggered if a prespecified underlying parametric index reaches a certain value (such as a stated level of rainfall, the length and intensity of a drought, or commodity price movements). Examples include the Caribbean Catastrophe Risk Insurance Facility, the Pacific Catastrophe Risk Assessment and Financing Initiative, and African Risk Capacity.

Depending on the frequency and severity of the various risks in a particular country, governments can combine financing instruments. Each instrument is adapted to different needs and has different cost implications. Sovereign insurance may provide cost-effective coverage against extreme events, but it may be inefficient and costly in protecting against recurring low-intensity events. For such frequent events, a dedicated contingency fund may be a more appropriate solution. Combining instruments also enables governments to take into account the evolving needs for funds for emergency response or long-term reconstruction. A government might decide to purchase ex ante rapidly disbursable risk transfer instruments to ensure immediate liquidity in the aftermath of extreme events, but raise the larger sums required to finance reconstruction efforts through ex post budget reallocations or by issuing bonds.

The Road Ahead for Bringing Social Safety Nets to Scale in Africa

Governments in Africa are increasingly positioning social safety nets as a core instrument in their strategies to address poverty and vulnerability. The number of programs has expanded rapidly, and coverage is growing, albeit slowly. Programs are also evolving to integrate a productive focus and adaptability in the face of shocks. Still, in most countries, most of the poor and vulnerable are not yet covered by social safety net systems. A range of rigorous evaluations have demonstrated that such programs can improve equity, resilience, and opportunities for the benefit of the poor and vulnerable. For these systems to play this role, however, they need to be brought to scale and provide effective coverage in a sustainable fashion.

Bringing social safety nets to scale to reach their full potential in Africa—making them sustainable and effective at combating poverty and vulnerability—will require a focus on the political, institutional, and fiscal barriers and opportunities. A strategic approach to engaging in the political process, including choosing politically informed program parameters, can strengthen social safety net systems. Understanding how to anchor social safety nets in institutions for coordination, management, and implementation at scale is critical. Social safety nets require reliable funding, but also efficient spending. In light of the fiscal constraints that many governments face, smarter spending and new sources of funds are needed, as well as a financing strategy that matches the risk profile of the country. Overall, strategic choices need to be made to give social safety nets the place they deserve in Africa's broader national development and poverty reduction strategies.

References

Albrecht, Peter. 2017. "The Political Economy of Social Protection in Sierra Leone." Background paper, *Realizing the Full Potential of Social Safety Nets in Africa*, edited by Kathleen Beegle, Aline Coudouel, and Emma Monsalve, forthcoming. World Bank, Washington, DC.

Attah, Ramlatu, Valentina Barca, Andrew Kardan, Ian MacAuslan, Fred Merttens, and Luca Pellerano. 2016. "Can Social Protection Affect Psychosocial Wellbeing and Why Does This Matter? Lessons from Cash Transfers in Sub-Saharan Africa." *Journal of Development Studies* 52 (8): 1115–31.

Bastagli, Francesca. 2015. "Bringing Taxation into Social Protection Analysis and Planning." ODI Working Paper 421, Overseas Development Institute, London.

Buur, Lars, and Padil Salimo. 2017. "The Political Economy of Social Protection in Mozambique." Background paper, *Realizing the Full Potential of Social Safety Nets in Africa*, edited by Kathleen Beegle, Aline Coudouel, and Emma Monsalve, forthcoming. World Bank, Washington, DC.

Cervigni, Raffaello, and Michael Morris, eds. 2016. *Confronting Drought in Africa's Drylands: Opportunities for Enhancing Resilience*. Africa Development Forum Series. Washington, DC: Agence Française de Développement and World Bank.

CGD (Center for Global Development) and Social Finance. 2013. *Investing in Social Outcomes: Development Impact Bonds; The Report of the Development Impact Bond Working Group*. London: Social Finance Ltd; Washington, DC: CGD.

Chandy, Laurence, Natasha Ledlie, and Veronika Penciakova. 2013. "The Final Countdown: Prospects for Ending Extreme Poverty by 2030." Global Views Policy Paper 2013-04, Brookings Institution, Washington, DC.

Cherrier, Cécile. 2015. "Examining the Catalytic Effect of Aid on Domestic Resource Mobilization for Social Transfers in Low-Income Countries." UNRISD Working Paper 2015-3, United Nations Research Institute for Social Development, Geneva.

Chinyoka, Isaac, and Jeremy Seekings. 2016. "Social Policy Reform under the Government of National Unity in Zimbabwe, 2009–13." CSSR Working Paper 373, Centre for Social Science Research, University of Cape Town, Cape Town.

Coady, David P., Ian W. H. Parry, Louis Sears, and Baoping Shang. 2015. "How Large Are Global Energy Subsidies?" IMF Working Paper 15/105, International Monetary Fund, Washington, DC.

Coleman, David. 2016. "Variations on the Impact Bond Concept: Remittances as a Funding Source for Impact Bonds in Low- and Middle-Income Countries." *Education Plus Development* (blog), September 27.

Dang, Hai-Anh H., and Andrew L. Dabalen. 2017. "Is Poverty in Africa Mostly Chronic or Transient? Evidence from Synthetic Panel Data." Policy Research Working Paper 8033, World Bank, Washington, DC.

Ellis, Frank. 2012. "'We Are All Poor Here': Economic Difference, Social Divisiveness, and Targeting Cash Transfers in Sub-Saharan Africa." *Journal of Development Studies* 48 (2): 201–14.

Fiszbein, Ariel, and Norbert R. Schady. 2009. *Conditional Cash Transfers: Reducing Present and Future Poverty*. With Francisco H. G. Ferreira, Margaret E. Grosh,

Niall Keleher, Pedro Olinto, and Emmanuel Skoufias. World Bank Policy Research Report. Washington, DC: World Bank.

Giannozzi, Sara, and Asmeen Khan. 2011. "Strengthening Governance of Social Safety Nets in East Asia." Social Protection Discussion Paper 1116, World Bank, Washington, DC.

Glassman, Amanda, and Miriam Temin. 2016. *Millions Saved: New Cases of Proven Success in Global Health*. Washington, DC: Center for Global Development and Brookings Institution Press.

Granvik, Mia. 2015. "Policy Diffusion, Domestic Politics, and Social Protection in Lesotho, 1998–2012." CSSR Working Paper 357, Centre for Social Science Research, University of Cape Town, Cape Town.

Grosh, Margaret E., Carlo del Ninno, Emil Tesliuc, and Azedine Ouerghi. 2008. *For Protection and Promotion: The Design and Implementation of Effective Safety Nets*. Washington, DC: World Bank.

Guven, Melis U., and Phillippe G. Leite. 2016. "Benefits and Costs of Social Pensions in Sub-Saharan Africa." Social Protection and Labor Discussion Paper 1607, World Bank, Washington, DC.

Hallegatte, Stéphane, Mook Bangalore, Laura Bonzanigo, Marianne Fay, Tomaro Kane, Ulf Narloch, Julie Rozenberg, David Treguer, and Adrien Vogt-Schilb. 2016. *Shock Waves: Managing the Impacts of Climate Change on Poverty*. Climate Change and Development Series. Washington, DC: World Bank.

Hamer, Sam. 2016. "'Our Father's Programmes': Political Branding around Social Protection in Botswana, 2008–2014." CSSR Working Paper 370, Centre for Social Science Research, University of Cape Town, Cape Town.

Handa, Sudhanshu, Bruno Martorano, Carolyn Tucker Halpern, Audrey Pettifor, and Harsha Thirumurthy. 2014a. "The Government of Kenya's Cash Transfer Program Reduces the Risk of Sexual Debut among Young People Age 15–25." *PLoS ONE* 9 (1).

———. 2014b. "Subjective Well-Being, Risk Perceptions, and Time Discounting: Evidence from a Large-Scale Cash Transfer Programme." Innocenti Working Paper 2014–02, UNICEF Office of Research, Florence.

Haushofer, Johannes, and Jeremy Shapiro. 2013. "Household Response to Income Changes: Evidence from an Unconditional Cash Transfer Program in Kenya." Working paper, Abdul Latif Jameel Poverty Action Lab, Massachusetts Institute of Technology, Cambridge, MA.

Hickey, Samuel, and Badru Bukenya. 2016. "The Politics of Promoting Social Cash Transfers in Uganda." ESID Working Paper 69, Effective States and Inclusive Development Research Centre, Global Development Institute, School of Environment, Education, and Development, University of Manchester, Manchester, U.K.

Hickey, Samuel, and Tom Lavers. 2017. "The Political Economy of the Adoption, Design, and Implementation of Social Protection." Background paper, *Realizing the Full Potential of Social Safety Nets in Africa*, edited by Kathleen Beegle, Aline Coudouel, and Emma Monsalve, forthcoming. World Bank, Washington, DC.

Hurrell, Alex, and Ian MacAuslan. 2012. "The Political Implications of Cash Transfers in Sub-Saharan Africa: Shaking up the Social System." *Public Management Review* 14 (2): 255–72.

IDinsight. 2015. "Evaluation of M-Tech and Paper Enumeration of Social Cash Transfer Beneficiaries in Zambia: Implementation Guide." November 25, IDinsight, New Delhi.

IMF (International Monetary Fund). 2015. *Regional Economic Outlook: Sub-Saharan Africa, Navigating Headwinds*. World Economic and Financial Surveys. Washington, DC: IMF.

———. 2017. *Regional Economic Outlook: Sub-Saharan Africa, Restarting the Growth Engine*. World Economic and Financial Surveys (April 17). Washington, DC: IMF.

Inchauste, Gabriela, and David G. Victor, eds. 2017. *The Political Economy of Energy Subsidy Reform*. Directions in Development: Public Sector Governance Series. Washington, DC: World Bank.

Jones, Nicola, Bassam Abu-Hamad, Paola Pereznieto, and Kerry Sylvester. 2016. "Transforming Cash Transfers: Citizens' Perspectives on the Politics of Programme Implementation." *Journal of Development Studies* 52 (8): 1207–24.

Kar, Dev, Devon Cartwright-Smith, and Ann Hollingshead. 2010. "The Absorption of Illicit Financial Flows from Developing Countries: 2002–2006." Global Financial Integrity, Center for International Policy, Washington, DC.

Karippacheril, Tina George, Phillippe George Leite, and Kathy Lindert. 2017. "Guidance Note and Assessment Tool on Social Registries for Social Assistance and Beyond." Working paper, World Bank, Washington, DC.

Ketkar, Suhas L., and Dilip Ratha. 2007. "Development Finance via Diaspora Bonds: Track Record and Potential." Policy Research Working Paper 4311, World Bank, Washington, DC.

King, Sophie, and Samuel Hickey. 2017. "Building Democracy from Below: Lessons from Western Uganda." *Journal of Development Studies* 53 (10): 1584–99.

Lavers, Tom. 2016. "Social Protection in an Aspiring 'Developmental State': The Political Drivers of Ethiopia's PSNP." WIDER Working Paper 2016/130 (November), United Nations University–World Institute for Development Economics Research, Helsinki.

Molyneux, Maxine. 2016. "Can Cash Transfer Programmes Have 'Transformative' Effects?" With Nicola Jones and Fiona Samuels. *Journal of Development Studies* 52 (8): 1087–98.

Monchuk, Victoria. 2014. *Reducing Poverty and Investing in People: New Role of Safety Nets in Africa*. Directions in Development. Washington, DC: World Bank.

Ndiaye, Alfred. 2017. "The Political Economy of Social Protection in Senegal." Background paper, *Realizing the Full Potential of Social Safety Nets in Africa*, edited by Kathleen Beegle, Aline Coudouel, and Emma Monsalve, forthcoming. World Bank, Washington, DC.

O'Brien, Clare, Fidelis Hove, and Gabrielle Smith. 2013. "Factors Affecting the Cost-Efficiency of Electronic Transfers in Humanitarian Programmes." Oxford Policy Management.

Ortiz, Isabel, Matthew Cummins, and Kalaivani Karunanethy. 2015. "Fiscal Space for Social Protection: Options to Expand Social Investments in 187 Countries." ESS Working Paper 48, Extension of Social Security, International Labour Office, Geneva.

Pavanello, Sara, Carol Watson, W. Onyango-Ouma, and Paul Bukuluki. 2016. "Effects of Cash Transfers on Community Interactions: Emerging Evidence." *Journal of Development Studies* 52 (8): 1147–61.

Pritchett, Lant. 2005. "A Lecture on the Political Economy of Targeted Social Safety Nets." Social Protection Discussion Paper 0501, World Bank, Washington, DC.

Pruce, Kate, and Samuel Hickey. 2017. "The Politics of Promoting Social Protection in Zambia." ESID Working Paper 75, Effective States and Inclusive Development Research Centre, Global Development Institute, School of Environment, Education, and Development, University of Manchester, Manchester, U.K.

Ravallion, Martin. 2013. "How Long Will It Take to Lift One Billion People Out of Poverty?" Policy Research Working Paper 6325, World Bank, Washington, DC.

Ringold, Dena, Alaka Holla, Margaret Koziol, and Santhosh Srinivasan. 2012. *Citizens and Service Delivery: Assessing the Use of Social Accountability Approaches in the Human Development Sectors.* Directions in Development: Human Development Series. Washington, DC: World Bank.

Seekings, Jeremy. 2015. "The 'Developmental' and 'Welfare' State in South Africa: Lessons for the Southern African Region." CSSR Working Paper 358, Centre for Social Science Research, University of Cape Town, Cape Town.

———. 2016. "Drought Relief and the Origins of a Conservative Welfare State in Botswana, 1965–1980." CSSR Working Paper 378, Centre for Social Science Research, University of Cape Town, Cape Town.

Seidenfeld, David, Sudhanshu Handa, and Gelson Tembo. 2013. "24-Month Impact Report for the Child Grant Programme." September, American Institutes for Research, Washington, DC.

Siachiwena, Hangala. 2016. "Social Protection Policy Reform in Zambia during the Sata Presidency, 2011–2014." CSSR Working Paper 380, Centre for Social Science Research, University of Cape Town, Cape Town.

Taylor, J. Edward, Justin Kagin, Mateusz Filipski, and Karen Thome. 2013. "Evaluating General Equilibrium Impacts of Kenya's Cash Transfer Programme for Orphans and Vulnerable Children (CT-OVC)." PtoP, From Protection to Production Series, Food and Agriculture Organization of the United Nations, Rome.

Taylor, J. Edward, Karen Thome, Benjamin Davis, David Seidenfeld, and Sudhanshu Handa. 2014. "Evaluating Local General Equilibrium Impacts of Zimbabwe's Harmonized Social Cash Transfer Programme (HSCT)." PtoP, From Protection to Production Series, Food and Agriculture Organization of the United Nations, Rome.

Taylor, J. Edward, Karen Thome, and Mateusz Filipski. 2014. "Evaluating Local General Equilibrium Impacts of Lesotho's Child Grants Programme." PtoP, From Protection to Production Series, Food and Agriculture Organization of the United Nations, Rome.

Thome, Karen, J. Edward Taylor, Benjamin Davis, Sudhanshu Handa, David Seidenfeld, and Gelson Tembo. 2014a. "Local Economy-Wide Impact Evaluation (LEWIE) of Zambia's Child Grant Programme." PtoP, From Protection to Production Series, Food and Agriculture Organization of the United Nations, Rome.

Thome, Karen, J. Edward Taylor, Justin Kagin, Benjamin Davis, Robert Darko Osei, and Isaac Osei-Akoto. 2014b. "Local Economy-Wide Impact Evaluation (LEWIE) of

Ghana's Livelihood Empowerment against Poverty (LEAP) Programme." PtoP, From Protection to Production Series, Food and Agriculture Organization of the United Nations, Rome.

Ulriksen, Marianne S. 2016. "Ideational and Institutional Drivers of Social Protection in Tanzania." WIDER Working Paper 2016/142, United Nations University–World Institute for Development Economics Research, Helsinki.

UNICEF. 2013. "Moving Towards an Integrated and Equitable Social Protection in The Gambia: Analysis of Social Protection Systems in The Gambia." UNICEF, New York. https://www.unicef.org/gambia/Moving_towards_an_integrated_and_equitable_social _protection_in_the_Gambia.pdf

Wanyama, Fredrick O., and Anna McCord. 2017. "The Politics of Scaling Up Social Protection in Kenya." ESID Working Paper 87, Effective States and Inclusive Development Research Centre, Global Development Institute, School of Environment, Education, and Development, University of Manchester, Manchester, U.K.

World Bank. 2015. *A Measured Approach to Ending Poverty and Boosting Shared Prosperity: Concepts, Data, and the Twin Goals*. Policy Research Report Series. Washington, DC: World Bank.

———. 2016a. "Ethiopia Public Expenditure Review." World Bank, Washington, DC. https://openknowledge.worldbank.org/handle/10986/24370.

———. 2016b. "Ghana Social Protection Assessment and Public Expenditure Review." World Bank, Washington, DC. https://www.openknowledge.worldbank.org /handle/10986/26379.

———. 2016c. "Republic of Chad: Shaping Adaptive Safety Nets to Address Vulnerability." Washington, DC.

———. 2016d. "République centrafricaine Jeter de nouvelles bases pour la stabilité et la croissance." Washington, DC.

———. 2018. *The State of Social Safety Nets 2018*. World Bank, Washington, DC.

———. Forthcoming a. "Guinea-Bissau: Social Safety Net Assessment." Washington, DC.

———. Forthcoming b. "Social Protection Financing Diagnostics for Mali." Washington, DC.

Introduction

In Sub-Saharan Africa (Africa hereafter), despite strong economic growth and improvements in many dimensions of welfare, poverty remains a pervasive and complex phenomenon. The agenda in recent years has included the attempt to tackle poverty through the launch of social safety net programs. The shift in social policy that this represents reflects a progressive evolution in the understanding of the role that social safety nets can play in the fight against poverty and vulnerability.

The expansion of social safety nets has been accompanied by shifts in the design of programs. It has also often been associated with investments in systemic instruments, such as targeting systems, registries, and payment systems, to strengthen the overall system and increase efficiency.

For countries in Africa to fully realize the potential of social safety nets to help the poorest and most vulnerable seize economic opportunities, there is a need to look beyond the technical aspects of social safety net systems.

This report argues that decisive efforts must focus on three areas: the political, the institutional, and the fiscal. First, this ambitious agenda implies a shift in the perception and political economy of social safety nets and their potential in national policies for poverty reduction and growth. Second, expansion calls for a strong anchoring of the sector's programs in institutional arrangements that have the mandate and resources required to deliver these programs as intended. Third, in most countries, more attention to the efficiency, size, and sustainability of resources is necessary if social safety net programs are to reach the desired scale.

The report begins with the identification of gaps by contrasting the levels of poverty and vulnerability and the state of social safety net systems in the various subregions and countries of Africa (chapter 1: *Reaching the poor and vulnerable in Africa through social safety nets*).

The report then presents evidence of the impact of social safety nets on equity and poverty reduction, as well as building resilience and expanding opportunities for the poorest and most vulnerable (chapter 2: *Social safety nets promote poverty reduction, increase resilience, and expand opportunities*).

The study then turns to the three systemic shifts that are needed to unleash the full potential of social safety nets in Africa: the need for a shift in the political economy of social safety nets and their place in society (chapter 3: *Recognizing and leveraging politics to sustain and expand social safety nets*), the need for strong institutional anchoring to expand social safety nets (chapter 4: *Anchoring in strong institutions to expand and sustain social safety nets*), and the need for additional fiscal space and greater predictability in funding (chapter 5: *Harnessing resources to expand and sustain social safety nets*). Throughout these three chapters, the study systematically highlights recommendations for the adoption of good practices in terms of the nuts and bolts of social safety nets, including the adoption of design innovations to facilitate scaling up these programs.

Chapter 1

Reaching the Poor and Vulnerable in Africa through Social Safety Nets

Kathleen Beegle, Maddalena Honorati, and Emma Monsalve

Although there has been progress in improving socioeconomic conditions, poverty and vulnerability remain pervasive in Africa. Because of high population growth, the number of the poor rose from about 280 million to 390 million in the period 1990–2013 despite the falling poverty rate. Many people lack adequate water and sanitation, and many children are in poor health and lack quality education opportunities. Vulnerability to shocks is substantial because numerous households live in risky environments.

To tackle these challenges, every African country has established at least one social safety net program, and many have several. The number of new social safety net programs launched has increased in Africa over the last decade. Some countries, such as Senegal and Tanzania, have rapidly taken their programs to scale.

Program design varies across the region. Programs focused on cash transfers, public works, or school feeding are the most common. As programs have grown in number and size, design features have also evolved. Notable shifts include more use of cash, programs designed to respond to climate change, a concentration on productive capacity and resilience, and programs promoting human capital development. Countries have also been creating tools and systems to boost program efficiency and coordination.

Nonetheless, existing programs fail to cover most of the poor. Even if there were no errors in targeting the poor, not all needs would be met because poverty rates are higher than coverage rates in most countries.

To realize the full potential of social safety nets for addressing problems in equity, resilience, and opportunity for poor and vulnerable populations in Africa, programs need to be brought to scale and maintained at scale.

Despite Improvements, Poverty and Vulnerability to Shocks Are Widespread

Poverty rates have been falling in Africa.[1] The share of the poor declined from 57 percent in 1990 to 41 percent in 2013 (figure 1.1).[2] However, the decline was not sufficiently rapid to reach the target of the Millennium Development Goals of cutting the poverty rate in half by 2015. Moreover, the number of the poor in Africa rose from about 280 million in 1990 to 390 million because of high population growth driven by high fertility rates.

Despite progress, two Africans in five are still living in poverty. These extreme statistics emphasize the critical challenge facing efforts to reduce poverty and share prosperity in Africa. While there is diversity across and within countries, some characteristics dominate the profile of the poor. The majority of the poor reside in rural households and are engaged in smallholder farming (about 80 percent) (World Bank 2016a). The poor are less well educated and live in larger households. Children are significantly more likely than adults to be poor. Almost half of Africa's poor are under 15 years of age, although children represent less than half the total population. People with disabilities exhibit higher poverty rates, largely because of their lower educational attainment (Filmer 2008; Mitra, Posärac, and Vick 2013).

Figure 1.1 **Poverty Rates Are Falling in Africa, but the Number of the Poor Is Rising**

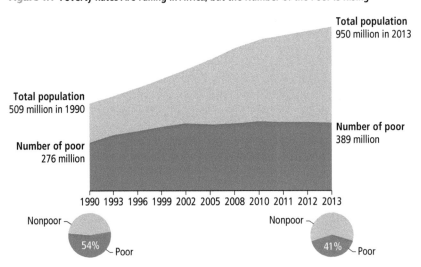

Source: PovcalNet (online analysis tool), World Bank, Washington, DC, http://iresearch.worldbank.org /PovcalNet/.

Income poverty is but one way to assess living standards. Well-being in Africa has also improved by many other dimensions. More children are in school, and the gender gap in schooling has narrowed. Adult literacy rates increased 4 percentage points from 1995 to 2012. Life expectancy at birth rose 6.2 years, and the prevalence of chronic malnutrition among young children fell 6 percentage points. The number of deaths from politically motivated violence declined. Indicators of voice and accountability advanced slightly, and there was a trend toward a greater participation of women in household decision making. Taken together, destitution gauged through a multidimensional poverty approach declined significantly in 18 of 19 African countries with sufficient data to track changes (Alkire and Housseini 2014).

These improvements notwithstanding, Africa shows the worst outcomes relative to other regions on most indicators. Moreover, the rate of progress is leveling off in some areas, including a recent uptick in violent events. The evidence is growing that the quality of education belies the enhancements in enrollment. Multiple deprivations still characterize the lives of a sizable share of African women (data on men are not available) (Beegle et al. 2016).

Likewise, while poverty rates have declined, vulnerability is substantial because households are located in risky environments (Hill and Verwimp 2017). Many of the poor are living only slightly below the poverty line and are thus close to escaping poverty, but others among the nonpoor are vulnerable to falling into poverty (figure 1.2). With the decline in poverty has come an increase in the size of the vulnerable population (Dang and Dabalen 2018). Among Africa's poor, a small positive shock to incomes could lift many out of poverty, but a small negative shock could drive as many of the vulnerable into poverty. A negative shock to household incomes of 16 to 26 percent is estimated to result in a rise in the poverty rate of 5 to 12 percentage points. In Africa, three poor households in five are chronically poor, while an estimated two poor households in five are transiently poor, that is, moving into or out of poverty as their income fluctuates and they are exposed to shocks (Beegle et al. 2016).

In addition, refugees and internally displaced people who have been affected by conflict represent about 2 percent of Africa's population (Maystadt and Verwimp 2015). Globally, the number of people displaced by shocks, including refugees, is at an all-time high. While the war in the Syrian Arab Republic has recently been associated with large numbers of refugees, the majority of the world's refugees are in Africa. These populations are not evenly distributed, but are especially large in several countries (Cameroon, Chad, the Democratic Republic of Congo, Ethiopia, Kenya, Nigeria, Somalia, Sudan, and Uganda) (World Bank 2017; appendix C, table C.1). Rather than international refugees, forced displacement is mostly driven in the region by internal

Figure 1.2 Poverty Is Both Chronic and Transient

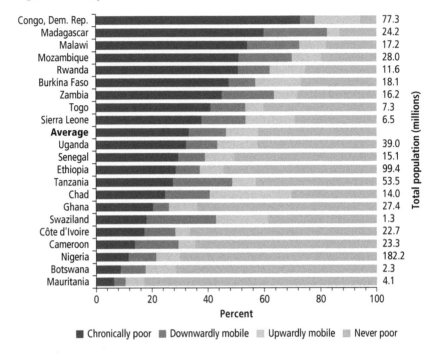

Source: Dang and Dabalen 2018.
Note: Poverty statistics refer to the latest household survey year for each country. The "chronically poor" category includes households that were poor in both periods of the analysis; "downwardly mobile" refers to households that fell into poverty in the second period; "upwardly mobile" includes those who were poor in the first period but not poor in the second period; and "never poor" includes households that were nonpoor in both periods.

displacement and security risks. The displaced face additional hurdles because they find few income-earning opportunities to help them in their efforts to escape poverty.

Poverty will remain a challenge in Africa even if macroeconomic growth exceeds expectations. Under a range of economic growth assumptions, global poverty will become increasingly concentrated in Africa and in conflict-affected countries (Chandy, Ledlie, and Penciakova 2013; Ravallion 2013; World Bank 2015a). The majority of countries most at risk of not reaching the target of a 3 percent poverty rate by 2030 are in Africa (Chandy 2017). The lack of a demographic transition and high fertility will impede poverty reduction, and children will bear a growing burden of poverty (Watkins and Quattri 2016). Climate change will be an additional obstacle to eradicating poverty in Africa, where households in drylands are already more likely to be poor than households in other areas (Cervigni and Morris 2016; Hallegatte et al. 2016).

Social Safety Nets Have Been Expanding Rapidly in Africa

Most African countries have recently established social safety net programs as part of a broader strategy to protect and promote the poor and the vulnerable. In this report, social safety nets—also sometimes known as social assistance programs—are defined as noncontributory benefits provided either in cash or in kind and intended to support the poor and the vulnerable (households and individuals particularly exposed to idiosyncratic and covariate risks and lacking sufficient coping mechanisms or resources to mitigate the impacts). They are a component of the larger social protection systems that also include contributory social insurance, such as pensions and health insurance, as well as labor market policies and programs, and some of the processes analyzed in this report focus more broadly on social protection systems.[3]

Drawing on the 2012–22 World Bank Social Protection Strategy framework, social safety nets have the three broad objectives of improving the resilience, equity, and opportunities of households (World Bank 2012a, 2012b). Resilience is achieved if well-designed and well-implemented social safety nets help individuals insure against risks (such as illness and natural disasters) and avoid negative coping strategies. The equity objective of social safety nets aims to ensure that even the most vulnerable and poorest households reach a minimum level of consumption and cover basic needs. Some social safety net programs have been designed to promote income-generating opportunities and create productive links within local economies. Programs such as universal child grants or social pensions are included, as they are noncontributory and focus on groups perceived as vulnerable. The definition in this report also includes measures that facilitate the poor's access to basic services such as health care, education, and housing through targeted fee waivers and scholarships as well as lump-sum grants to promote livelihoods and productive inclusion. General consumer price subsidies, including energy and food subsidies, are not considered to be among social safety net initiatives in this report. This study divides programs into nine categories based on the type of benefit and the permanent or emergency nature of the programs or transfers (box 1.1).

In recent years, social safety nets have been increasingly deployed in the developing world, especially in Africa. By 2015, every country in the world was implementing at least one social safety net program (World Bank 2015b). Most of the recent surge has occurred in Africa (Cirillo and Tebaldi 2016). Mauritius was the first country in Africa to introduce a social safety net program, in 1950, in the form of disability pensions and basic noncontributory allowances for widows and guardians of orphans. The number had risen to 18 countries by 2000, then to 32 by 2008 at the onset of the economic crisis, to 36 in 2010, and to 45 in 2017. The average number launched each year rose from 7 in 2001–09

BOX 1.1

The Definition of Social Safety Nets and the Typology of Programs

Social safety nets are noncontributory programs targeting the poor or vulnerable. They may be designed, implemented, and supported by governments, international organizations, or nongovernmental organizations (NGOs). Their distinctive feature is their noncontributory nature, that is, beneficiaries do not have to contribute financially to receive the benefits. This differentiates them from contributory forms of social protection, whereby prior contributions and participation in the labor market determine benefit eligibility. To compare effectively across countries and regions, this report classifies social safety net programs into nine groups, building on Grosh et al. (2008), as follows:

1. Cash transfer programs: Cash transfer programs offer periodic monetary transfers to beneficiaries with a view to providing regular, predictable income support. This category includes poverty reduction programs; family and child allowances (including orphan and vulnerable children benefits); public-private charity; disability pensions, allowances, or benefits; war veterans' pensions, allowances, or benefits; noncontributory funeral grants; burial allowances; entrepreneurship support and start-up incentives (grant, loans, training); and other cash programs. Both conditional and unconditional cash transfer programs are included in this category. This category excludes public works, emergency, scholarships, and social pension programs, which are covered in other categories. They are sometimes called "cash transfers" in the report.

2. School feeding programs: This category includes school feeding programs, which supply meals or snacks for children at school to encourage their enrollment and attendance and improve their nutritional status and ability to learn. It also includes take-home food rations for children's families. They are sometimes called "school feeding" in the report.

3. Public works programs: This category includes public works, workfare, and direct job creation programs providing support in cash or food (including food-for-training or food-for-assets programs). Public works programs offer short-term employment at low wages on labor-intensive projects, such as road construction and maintenance, irrigation infrastructure, reforestation, soil conservation, and social services. Support is typically in the form of either cash or food transfers. They are sometimes called "public works" in this report.

4. Education interventions: In our typology, this category includes scholarships and targeted subsidies in education (e.g., OVC bursaries). It excludes general education interventions (e.g., free basic education). Educational fee waivers and scholarships assist households in meeting the cost of educational services. Fee waivers and scholarships may cover the entire fee or only part of it or other, selected expenditures. They are sometimes called "education" in this report.

(continued next page)

Box 1.1 (continued)

5. Health interventions: In our typology, this category includes targeted subsidies and fee waivers in health (e.g., reduced medical fees for vulnerable population). It excludes general health interventions (e.g., free health care/treatments and campaigns). Health fee waivers assist selected households in meeting the cost of health services. They are sometimes called "health" in this report.

6. Emergency programs: This category includes programs providing emergency support in cash and in-kind (including support to refugees/returning migrants). Emergency support programs supply cash or in-kind transfers to individuals or households in case of emergency or in response to shocks. The shocks may encompass weather shocks (drought, floods), pandemics, food insecurity, human-made crises, and economic downturns. The transfers are usually temporary, typically over a period of a few months. They are sometimes called "emergency" in this report.

7. Food-based programs: In our typology, food-based programs include programs providing food stamps and vouchers, food distribution programs, and nutritional programs that involve therapeutic feeding distribution and promote good feeding practices. This category excludes food-for-work programs, emergency in-kind transfer programs, and meals provided at schools, which are classified in other groups. They are sometimes referred to as "food" in this report.

8. Social pensions: This category includes old-age social pensions, allowances, or benefits. Social pensions are regular cash transfers provided exclusively to the elderly. Unlike contributory pensions or social insurance programs, social pensions do not require prior contributions. Social pensions may be universal or targeted to the poor.

9. Other programs: This category includes other noncontributory programs targeting the poor or vulnerable, such as programs distributing school supplies, tax exemptions, social care services, and other programs not included in the other eight categories.

to 14 in 2010–15 (figure 1.3). Chapter 3 explores the factors behind this growth, including various crises and reforms, as well as evolving social contracts, perceptions of the potential of social safety nets, and international influence.

The widespread adoption of social protection in general and social safety nets in particular is paralleled by the growing number of national strategies or policies (table 1.1; appendix D, table D.1). Social protection has been the focus of attention in numerous national poverty reduction and growth strategies. By 2016, 32 African countries had established national social protection strategies or policies, which include social safety nets as a core pillar. Draft strategies are in the approval process in another seven countries.

Figure 1.3 **More Social Safety Net Programs Have Been Launched in Recent Years**

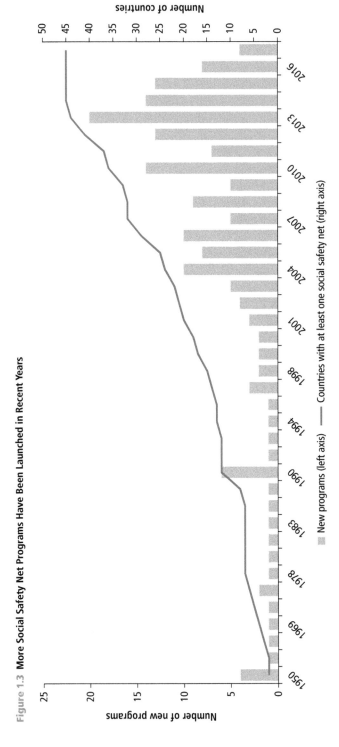

Source: ASPIRE (Atlas of Social Protection Indicators of Resilience and Equity) (database), Administrative data, World Bank, Washington, DC. http://www.worldbank.org/aspire.
Note: This figure considers regular programs (not emergency programs) that are still being implemented and for which information on the year of the launch is available.

56

Table 1.1 **Three of Five African Countries Have Approved a National Social Protection Strategy**
Cumulative numbers

Status	2013	2015	2016
Not present	18	14	9
In progress	18	10	7
Present	12	24	32

Source: World Bank internal monitoring tools.

Social safety nets are varied and numerous in Africa, but are often fragmented within countries. Every African country has at least one social safety net program. The average number of programs per country is 15, ranging from 2 in the Republic of Congo and Gabon to 54 in Chad and 56 in Burkina Faso (appendix E, table E.1). The countries in West Africa and lower-income countries typically implement more programs (appendix E, table E.2). The number and diversity of programs reflect the settings and country contexts. The Central African Republic and Chad are implementing more than 30 programs, but many of these are small or temporary initiatives implemented in isolation in narrow geographical areas or among discrete population groups. Program duplication also occurs, often within a weak institutional environment. This is the situation in Uganda and Zimbabwe, which are conducting 39 and 29 social safety net programs, respectively. Insufficient coordination among the development partners that often fund such programs exacerbates fragmentation and inefficiencies. Efforts to consolidate and rationalize programs are on the policy agendas of many countries.

The Design of Social Safety Nets Varies across Africa

Cash transfer programs, as well as public works programs and school feeding programs, are being implemented in almost all African countries. Using the categories defined in box 1.1, among the 46 countries analyzed, 46 are implementing at least one cash transfer program; 33 are implementing at least one public works program; 20 are implementing education interventions; 15 run health interventions; 28 are implementing at least one school feeding program; 23 are implementing at least one food-based program; 22 countries are implementing emergency programs; and 12 countries are implementing social pensions as stand-alone programs (appendix E, table E.1). (box 1.2 offers more detail on public works programs.)

The composition of the social safety net portfolio varies across countries (appendix E, table E.1). Overall, cash transfers account for almost 41 percent of total spending, and this share is growing. Social pensions are more prevalent in upper-middle- and

BOX 1.2

How Do Public Works Work?

Public works programs have emerged as a critical type of social safety net in low-income settings and fragile states, as well as in middle-income countries (Grosh et al. 2008; Subbarao et al. 2013). These programs typically require that beneficiaries work before they may become eligible to receive a transfer in cash or in kind. The largest public works programs include the PSNP in Ethiopia and the Employment Guarantee Scheme in Maharashtra and the National Rural Employment Guarantee Act in India. In Africa, 29 of the 48 countries implement public works, though not necessarily on a large scale, and 70 programs have been identified. Public works programs may be primarily oriented toward the provision of a social safety net, or they may be primarily oriented toward supplying infrastructure (Subbarao et al. 2013). A a social safety net, the focus of public works are as a means of offering income support to the poor.

Public works programs usually involve labor-intensive activities, tend to operate mostly in rural areas (though some have recently been implemented in urban areas), offer modest wages so the poor self-target into the programs, and are often run off-season, when there are few employment opportunities. They appeal to policy makers and stakeholders because they contribute to a productive economy, create community assets (such as rehabilitated roads, irrigation schemes, and other infrastructure), and are not perceived as supplying handouts, given that they require effort from beneficiaries.

Public works have been widely promoted as tools to protect poor households in the face of large macroeconomic or agroclimatic shocks (Ravallion 1999). They have recently been garnering attention in fragile and conflict-affected situations as tools to restart local economic activity quickly or target the employment of high-risk groups, such as young men (Blattman and Ralston 2015). Public works can also contribute to the development of assets, as in Ethiopia, where the PSNP was found to mitigate the risks of climate change by restoring deforested and depredated land (Jirka et al. 2015). As a result, public works programs may smooth consumption among the poor in the short term, such as other social safety net programs, but also create productive assets that contribute to improving livelihoods over the longer term.

Public works may be adapted to a variety of contexts, but there are challenges. Thus, they are generally more difficult to implement than simple cash transfer programs; they are institutionally more complex to administer because many line ministries are often involved, as in the Kazi Kwa Vijana (work for youth) Program in Kenya; and they require strong checks and balances against possible error, fraud, and corruption (Subbarao et al. 2013).

high-income countries and in Southern Africa. Public works programs exist in almost all low-income countries and fragile states, especially in West Africa, but are largely absent in middle- and high-income countries. In Central Africa and fragile states, social safety nets are widely used as responses to shocks, and emergency and food-based programs are the most common types of programs (figure 1.4).

Figure 1.4 The Composition of Social Safety Net Portfolios Is Diverse

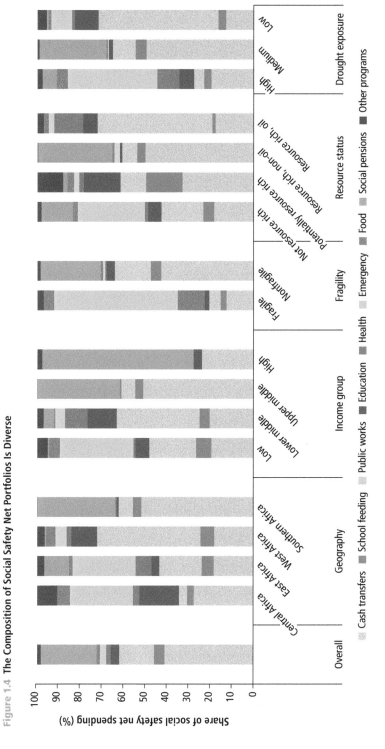

Source: ASPIRE (Atlas of Social Protection Indicators of Resilience and Equity) (database), Administrative data, World Bank, Washington, DC, http://www.worldbank.org/aspire.

The vast majority of social safety nets in Africa are targeted to children, either directly or indirectly by assisting households with children (appendix E, table E.3; appendix G, table G.6, presents data on spending). Among all programs, 29 percent directly target children through nutrition interventions, benefits aimed at orphans and other vulnerable children, school feeding programs, the provision of school supplies, and education benefits or fee waivers. Among all programs, 31 percent target households more broadly; 19 percent target working-age individuals; 6 percent target the elderly; and 14 percent target other population segments, including the disabled, people living with HIV/AIDS, refugees, and internally displaced people. The relative importance of old-age and veterans' social pensions varies from 7 percent of programs in upper-middle-income countries and 9 percent in Southern Africa to less than 1 percent in low-income countries. Programs are often not gender neutral (box 1.3).

Though the number of social safety net programs has increased, coverage is often limited. The combined coverage of programs in Africa is 10 percent of the

---

BOX 1.3

The Links between Social Safety Nets and Gender

The substantial gender inequality in Africa is well documented. Huge gaps exist in many spheres of life. Empowering women and girls is thus a critical aspect of economic development. Social safety nets can be a tool for confronting gender inequality. A growing body of evidence indicates that the impact of these programs is not always gender neutral (World Bank 2014). Social safety nets have been shown to empower women, including by reducing the physical abuse of women by men, increasing women's decision-making power, and curbing risky sexual behavior (Bastagli et al. 2016). Paying cash transfers directly to women has been shown in some contexts to lead to greater household spending on children's needs, a reflection of greater empowerment and differential preferences in spending among men and women. This will not be the case everywhere. The channels through which these impacts occur are complex and depend on gender norms and the roles assigned to women by society (World Bank 2014).

Social safety net programs can be more effective at achieving gender-relevant impacts if they are thoughtfully designed with this aim. Common gender-sensitive provisions in public works programs include more flexible working hours, as in the Tanzania Social Action Fund, quotas on women's participation, less strenuous works for women, and the availability of childcare facilities (Tebaldi 2016). Other gender-sensitive design features include accommodating lower levels of literacy; allowing more flexibility in the requirements for official documents, such as birth and marriage certificates; and locating services near women's homes.

total population (figure 1.5; appendix F, tables F.1 and F.2; appendixes B.2 and B.3 for methodology). Despite the limited number of social pension programs in Africa, these programs exhibit one of the highest coverage rates among those age-eligible, according to the country program criteria, reaching 19 percent of the elderly. School feeding programs reach 15 percent of children ages 5–14. Cash transfers reach 6 percent of the total population. Less-extensive coverage is achieved by public works programs (3 percent of the population), emergency programs (2 percent), food-based transfers, and other social safety nets (1 percent each).

However, these averages mask important variations by type of program. With few exceptions, richer countries tend to run larger programs. Coverage is greater in upper-middle-income countries across all program types, except public works programs and emergency programs, which show greater coverage in lower-middle-income countries (see figure 1.5). This mirrors the composition of program portfolios in lower-income countries, which tend to be geared toward food programs and public works programs. Similarly, food programs and one-time emergency programs are the largest programs in terms of coverage in countries characterized by fragile settings.

Coverage varies across population groups. Programs targeting children—such as school feeding programs, education fee waivers, and nutrition programs—reach an average of 15 percent of children ages 0–14. Social pensions and veterans' benefits reach the equivalent of 16 percent of the elderly population (population older than 64 years) (figure 1.6). These averages are driven up by social pensions in Southern Africa. Some individuals may benefit from multiple programs, which would result in double counting. In addition, survivor pensions and veterans' pensions may also be received by the non-elderly, which artificially increases the coverage estimate. Appendix H shows the largest programs in the region by program typologies based on coverage rates and number of beneficiaries.

Cash transfer programs targeted to households on the basis of well-being are the most rapidly growing type of social safety net programs. Such programs have been steadily expanding in Lesotho, South Africa, and Zambia. There are also success stories of rapid efforts to increase the scale of programs in the region that are unique in the developing world. The Livelihood Empowerment against Poverty Program (LEAP) in Ghana, the cash transfer of the Orphans and Vulnerable Children (OVC) Program in Kenya, the Programme National de Bourses de Sécurité Familiale (National Program of Family Security Transfers, PNBSF) in Senegal, and the Productive Social Safety Net (PSSN) Program in Tanzania have been expanding rapidly in a short time. The annual growth rate in the number of beneficiary households in the Tanzania program is the highest in the world, even relative to mature cash transfer programs in comparator lower-middle-income countries in Asia

Figure 1.5 Program Coverage Varies by Type and Country Group

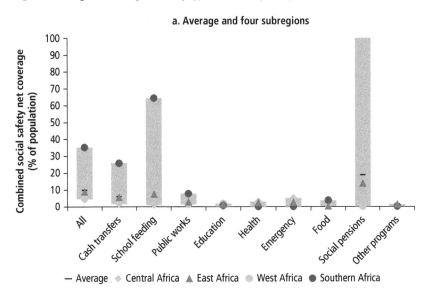

a. Average and four subregions

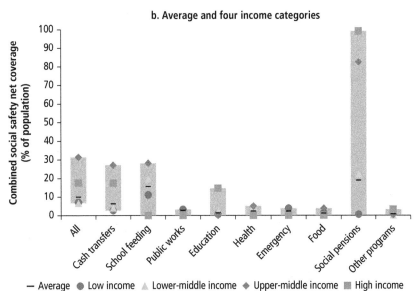

b. Average and four income categories

Source: ASPIRE (Atlas of Social Protection Indicators of Resilience and Equity) (database), Administrative data, World Bank, Washington, DC, http://www.worldbank.org/aspire.
Note: See methodology in appendixes B.2 and B.3 and more details in appendix F, table F.2.

Figure 1.6 **Children and the Elderly Are the Most Covered Groups**

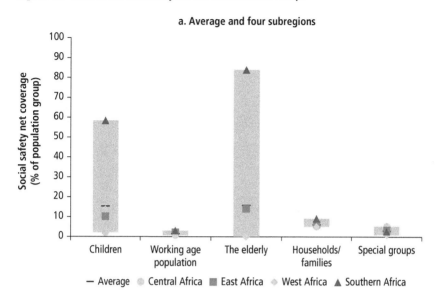

a. Average and four subregions

— Average   Central Africa   ■ East Africa   West Africa   ▲ Southern Africa

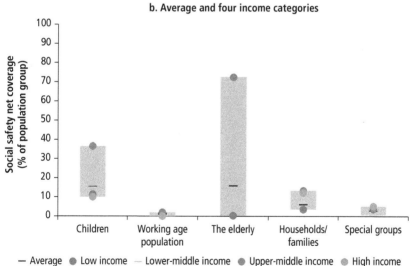

b. Average and four income categories

— Average   ● Low income   — Lower-middle income   ● Upper-middle income   ● High income

Source: ASPIRE (Atlas of Social Protection Indicators of Resilience and Equity) (database), Administrative data, World Bank, Washington, DC, http://www.worldbank.org/aspire.
Note: See methodology in appendixes B.2 and B.3 and more detailed information in appendix F, table F.2.

Figure 1.7 **Flagship Programs in Africa Are among the Most Rapidly Growing**

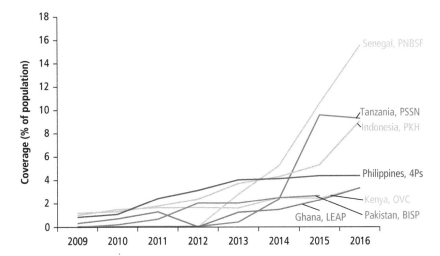

Source: ASPIRE (Atlas of Social Protection Indicators of Resilience and Equity) (database), Administrative data, World Bank, Washington, DC, http://www.worldbank.org/aspire
Note: 4Ps = Pantawid Pamilyang Pilipino Program; BISP = Benazir Income Support Program; LEAP = Livelihood Empowerment against Poverty; OVC = Orphans and Vulnerable Children; PKH = Program Keluarga Harapan; PNBSF = Programme National de Bourses de Sécurité Familiale; PSSN = Productive Social Safety Net Program.

and Latin America (figure 1.7). However, these are exceptions, and programs, even the more mature ones (programs in operation for more than five years), often do not grow beyond particular geographical areas. This is the case among many food distribution, school feeding, and nutrition programs, but also among social pension programs in Southern and East Africa. With the exception of the PSNP in Ethiopia, established public works programs have not expanded much.

Social Safety Nets Are Evolving

There are several other trends in social safety nets in Africa. First, there has been a shift toward the greater use of cash benefits in social safety net programs. Second, program objectives have been evolving; an expanding role is being played by social safety nets in response to climate change and human-made shocks. Third, a rising number of programs are emphasizing building the productive capacity and resilience of beneficiary households. Fourth, there has been an increasing focus on promoting human capital development. Fifth, social safety nets have been appearing in urban areas. Sixth, countries have been gradually concentrating on developing tools and systems to improve program efficiency and coordination.

The progressive shift away from food and in-kind transfers toward cash benefits likely reflects a mix of factors, among which were greater perceived efficiency and less complexity in coordination across institutions. Changes in technology, the greater concentration of people in urban areas, and greater market integration are likewise more conducive to the use of cash transfers (World Bank 2016a, 2016b; Garcia and Moore 2012). Cash benefits are becoming more common in long-running institutional programs, but also in emergency and crisis situations and in wider discussions of humanitarian assistance (Bailey and Harvey 2017; ODI 2015; World Bank 2016b). Cash transfers have become the primary response in support of disaster-affected populations and the preferred option if markets are functioning adequately.

Social safety net programs are increasingly used to respond to climate change and other disasters and shocks (box 1.4). By design and in their delivery

---

BOX 1.4

What Are Shock-Responsive Social Safety Nets?

Shock-responsive social safety nets are systems that are ready to "meet the anticipated needs of vulnerable populations resulting from the impact of endogenous or exogenous shocks which adversely affects livelihoods and labor markets" (McCord 2013). They have traditionally been used to assist the poor and help households manage risks (Grosh et al. 2008). Recently, however, the role of social safety net programs has been expanded to serve as instruments to help cope with covariate shocks, such as natural disasters. These shocks represent special challenges because they affect many large groups of people simultaneously (OPM 2015).

A key feature of shock-responsive social safety net programs is their scalability; that is, the coverage and support they provide may be scaled up rapidly during crises and then scaled back thereafter (Bastagli 2014; Ovadiya 2014a, 2014b; Watson 2016). The rapid expansion can be accomplished in various ways (table B1.4.1).

Several countries have implemented programs with scalable components that allow expansion in response to shocks. While cash transfers are commonly involved in such approaches, food support and public works are also used in shock-responsive social safety net programs. In Ethiopia, for instance, the government has regularly expanded the PSNP to respond to droughts since 2008. Thus, the program was successfully expanded during the Horn of Africa drought in 2011 to support an additional 3.1 million beneficiaries for three months and to extend the duration of transfers for 6.5 million of the existing 7.6 million beneficiaries. This response was credited with preventing the worst impacts of the drought, and emerging evidence shows that the program helped protect households from the effects of drought and enabled them to bounce back more quickly after the shock.

(continued next page)

Box 1.4 (continued)

Table B1.4.1 Options for Expanding Social Safety Nets in Response to Covariate Shocks

Option	Description
Vertical expansion	Increasing the benefit value or duration of an existing program, which may include (a) adjustment of transfer amounts or (b) introduction of extraordinary payments or transfers.
Horizontal expansion	Adding new beneficiaries to an existing program, which may include (a) extension of geographical coverage, (b) an extraordinary enrollment campaign, (c) modifications of entitlement rules, and (d) relaxation of requirements or conditionality.
Piggybacking	Using the administrative framework of a social safety net to deliver benefits, but running the shock-response program separately (as with the extension of the Pantawid Pamilyang Pilipino Program in response to Typhoon Haiyan in 2013 in the Philippines or with the humanitarian response using the National Information System for Social Assistance to target support during the drought in 2015–16 in Lesotho).
Shadow alignment	Developing a parallel system that aligns as best as possible with social safety net programs (as, in Kenya, with the alignment of the value of transfers in the Urban Early Warning Early Action Project).
Refocusing	Refocusing social safety nets by centering them on the people who are most vulnerable to shocks.

Source: OPM 2015; elaboration based on various sources.

In Kenya, the Hunger Safety Net Program (HSNP) preregistered all 374,000 households in the four northernmost counties and opened bank accounts and issued debit cards on their behalf. Among these households, 27 percent are regular program beneficiaries. The others receive one-time payments only in the event of an increased risk of shock for each month they are deemed at risk, depending on the geographical areas identified as most at risk. Payment is triggered automatically by a vegetation condition index derived from satellite data that indicate which subcounties are at risk or extreme risk. Accordingly, the program may temporarily cover 50 percent to 75 percent of the population of these counties (Watson 2016).

A number of factors are important for ensuring successful disaster response, including (1) the existence of an established social safety net system to provide administrative capacity and infrastructure; (2) specific policy features, such as the integration of climate and disaster risk considerations into the planning and design of social safety net programs, links to an established early warning system, and central registries for targeting or verification; (3) strong institutional capacity to ensure effective communication channels, clearly defined roles and responsibilities, possible coordination through a single central agency, and the pooling and smoothing of development partner funds, as discussed in chapter 4; and (4) a targeting mechanism that allows rapid horizontal expansion because the target group of more permanent social safety net programs does not always coincide with emergency initiatives, such as registries that collect information on vulnerable groups beyond existing program beneficiaries (Bastagli 2014; Ovadiya 2014a, 2014b; Watson 2016).

Political factors can affect the design and implementation of shock-responsive social safety net programs, including through the political implications of the vertical and horizontal expansion of social safety nets and of deciding to call for and release emergency funds. These factors need to be taken into consideration in designing shock-responsive features of social safety nets, as discussed in chapter 3.

Source: Based on information in Watson 2016.

systems, shock-responsive social safety nets include mechanisms to address the effects of slow-onset events such as droughts or environmental degradation and rapid-onset events such as floods, cyclones and hurricanes, and pandemics. In some countries, social safety net programs may be modified to respond quickly to predictable shocks or sudden disasters. They may thus combine regular, predictable transfers for the chronically poor and scalable mechanisms that allow the programs to be temporarily expanded to new people or new areas. In other countries, separate programs are set up to be activated in emergencies and then reabsorbed once the crisis is over. In Madagascar, the Intervention Fund for Development was used to deliver cash transfers to people affected by a severe drought in 2016. In the Sahel, Burkina Faso, Mali, Mauritania, Niger, and Senegal are testing mechanisms to reach households affected by shocks with temporary transfers. The PSNP in Ethiopia incorporates several features to respond to climate change, including a contingency budget to help poor households and communities cope with transitory shocks and the use of targeting to identify the communities most vulnerable to climate change.

Social safety net programs were also used to help address the Ebola emergency in West Africa. Despite limitations, governments leveraged modest existing programs and scaled up cash transfers and public works programs. In Sierra Leone, around 5,000 youth participated in public works, and over 10,000 beneficiaries were enrolled in cash transfer programs in 2015. In Liberia, a public works program and a cash transfer program were launched to reach over 10,000 poor youth and 10,000 poor households, respectively. In Guinea, the cash-for-work activity continued operating throughout the epidemic, providing 12,000 temporary jobs. Scalable mechanisms have the potential to reduce the cost of emergency response. If crises are recurrent and predictable, it may be more cost-effective to invest in social safety net programs or components that may be activated as needed than to rely on emergency aid. Social safety nets will not eliminate the need for humanitarian action because the magnitude of some shocks may still require emergency interventions beyond those provided through social safety nets. Social safety nets are also being considered to support forcibly displaced population groups, which face additional challenges of identification, registration, and social inclusion.

A growing number of social safety net programs include additional activities to support beneficiary livelihoods. As chapter 2 shows, social safety nets can promote beneficiaries' income-generation capacity. In addition, various approaches are used to foster the productive inclusion of beneficiaries, such as enrolling beneficiaries in agricultural development projects, extension services, microinsurance schemes, financial services, or skills training programs to help foster income-generating activities. The PSNP in Ethiopia and the Vision 2020 Umurenge Program (VUP) in Rwanda link beneficiaries to financial services, while the HSNP in Kenya and the Rural Development Public Works Program in Mali link beneficiaries to rural development programs. In other contexts, programs offer additional components—such as training, start-up capital, and savings support—to promote productive capacity. Thus, the BRAC approach, which combines social safety net transfers with elements of livelihood development and access to finance through asset transfers, technical skills training, and life skills coaching, has been piloted in several countries (Hashemi and de Montesquiou 2016). This approach is currently being tested in five Sahel countries. Some programs, in particular public works programs, also contribute to the development of community assets to increase resilience to shocks. In some contexts, the productive focus may also respond to political concerns that social safety nets might create dependence among beneficiaries.

Social safety net programs are increasingly being leveraged to promote investments in human capital, especially among children, to reduce the intergenerational transmission of poverty. Programs have demonstrated positive impacts on child health and education, as described in chapter 2. Programs may promote the adoption of good practices in nutrition, early childhood development, hygiene, education, health care, and so on. They may also stimulate the use of specific basic services by encouraging or requiring health care visits, growth monitoring sessions, or school attendance. These mechanisms or conditionalities used to promote positive behavior or service use include requirements to participate in promotion sessions and to conform with a particular desirable behavior, with or without any verification of compliance, and with or without sanctions for noncompliance. Efforts to encourage human capital investments have become more frequent, especially in West Africa, including in Burkina Faso, Cameroon, the Republic of Congo, The Gambia, Mali, Mauritania, Niger, São Tomé and Príncipe, Senegal, Sierra Leone, and Togo. At least 22 countries in Africa now have programs that use some mechanism to promote human capital investments (32 if scholarships are included). Table 1.2 presents a few examples, and box 1.5 discusses these mechanisms in more detail.

As Africa becomes increasingly urbanized, more attention is being given to the introduction or adaptation of social safety net programs to support the urban poor. Urban poverty involves diverse issues, opportunities, and challenges (World Bank 2015b). With the exception of fee waivers and universal social pensions, most social safety nets in Africa have typically been designed with a rural focus. There is a need to create innovative social safety nets to fit the urban context. Following the 2007–08 food price rises, however, a few programs were launched in urban areas, such as the voucher system in Burkina Faso, the urban cash-for-work program in Mali, the PNBSF cash transfer program in Senegal, and the program to supply free access to water in urban Madagascar. Governments are now considering adjustments in design and implementation arrangements to identify and cover the urban poor more effectively. Ethiopia and Tanzania are beginning to implement urban programs, while Mali and Nigeria are planning to do so. Nuts-and-bolts challenges include the

Table 1.2 **Mechanisms to Encourage Human Capital Investments in Selected Cash Transfer Programs**

Mechanism	Country	Program	Description
Participation in promotion sessions	Burkina Faso	Burkin-Nong-Saya	The program requires participation in social and behavioral change communication activities related to nutrition and early childhood development.
	Mauritania	Tekavoul (national social transfer program)	The program requires participation in sessions of social promotion, with a focus on early childhood development, education, health care, and civil registration.
	Niger	Social Safety Net Project	The program requires participation in social and behavioral change communication activities related to nutrition and early childhood development.
	Togo	Cash Transfer for Vulnerable Children	The main transfer is not conditional. A bonus transfer is provided for those attending information sessions.
	Sierra Leone	Social Safety Net Program	The program encourages participation in quarterly workshops focused on human capital, particularly maternal and child health (by organizing these workshops around the payment of transfers). Workshop participation is not mandatory to receive the transfer.
Adoption of particular behaviors: Compliance is not monitored	Ghana	Livelihood Empowerment against Poverty (LEAP)	Beneficiaries are entitled to free registration for the national health insurance scheme and should register and use pre- and postnatal care, skilled delivery, newborn and child health care, full vaccination, and birth registration. Fulfillment of these activities is not monitored.
	Senegal	Programme National de Bourses de Sécurité Familiale (PNBSF)	The program explicitly specifies three conditions around school attendance, vaccination, and birth registration. However, these are not monitored. Instead, the program uses the participation in promotion sessions as a condition for the receipt of transfers. (The program falls between this category and the category above.)
	Kenya	Cash transfer of the Orphans and Vulnerable Children (OVC) Program	The program encourages orphans and vulnerable children's attendance in primary school and visits to health centers for immunizations and other interventions. It encourages compliance, but does not apply penalties for noncompliance. However, despite the absence of penalties, 84 percent of beneficiaries believe they must follow rules to continue receiving payments.
Adoption of particular behaviors: Compliance monitored, and penalties assessed	Guinea	Cash Transfer for nutrition and girls education	The transfers for nutrition are expected to be spent on nutrition, particularly for children. If, after the third transfer, the children's health status does not show improvement because of willful neglect, the grant is suspended. Reintegration after suspension is possible if the children show improvement in weight-to-height measurements. The transfers for health care are conditional on quarterly health checkups among children ages under 6. Cash transfers for education require 90 percent school attendance among children ages 7–14.
	Tanzania	Productive Social Safety Net (PSSN) Program	The program imposes conditions on the use of health care and education services. To monitor compliance, data from health centers and schools are entered into the program management information system every two months. Payments are made every two months. Compliance is tracked after the first payment cycle. Penalties are deducted from the subsequent payment cycle.

BOX 1.5

Cash Transfer Programs: Mechanisms to Promote Investment in Human Capital

Conditional cash transfer programs have become popular in developing countries over the past two decades. First introduced in Latin America, they were subsequently expanded to Africa, Asia, and the Middle East. Starting with Bolsa Família in Brazil and Prospera in Mexico in 1997, the number of conditional cash transfer programs in the developing world had risen to 27 by 2008 and 64 by 2014. While there are important differences in implementation across countries and regions, the programs share one important feature: they encourage beneficiaries to adopt positive behaviors. Globally, they typically aim to promote school attendance, improve nutrition practices, or encourage regular immunization and health care visits. Some programs in Africa also focus on civil registration, early childhood development, hygiene, sanitation, and water use.

In Africa, the nature and intensity of the mechanisms deployed to encourage investment in human capital vary greatly, often depending on the supply of basic services and monitoring capacity in a country. Cash transfer programs may be classified along two dimensions: first, depending on the type of action that is required (participate in a promotion session; comply with a simple, punctual behavior; adopt a more complex, continuous behavior; and so on) and, second, depending on the extent to which compliance is compulsory, verified, and associated with the imposition of penalties. In addition to actual program design, the perception of beneficiaries is also important. Some programs do not impose strict conditions, but communicate strongly around specific behaviors. As a result, beneficiaries perceive a conditionality. Evaluations of the Lesotho Child Grants Program and the Malawi Social Cash Transfer Program highlight the strong messaging and social marketing of the programs on the need to use transfers for the welfare of children, which are perceived by many beneficiaries as actual conditions (see chapter 2). For each dimension, there is a range of alternative program options. A few examples include the following:

- *Programs that foster the adoption of certain behaviors through promotion sessions.* This category includes Burkina Faso's Burkin-Nong-Saya Program, Chad's cash program for households in food deficit, Mauritania's Tekavoul Program, Niger's Social Safety Net Project, and Sierra Leone's Social Safety Net Program. A social safety net program in Togo conditions a bonus transfer on attendance at information sessions as an addition to its main unconditioned cash transfer for pregnant women and mothers of children under age 2. Sessions often cover prenatal and postnatal care, nutrition, early childhood development, child health, education, civil registration, and hygiene. Some programs make participation in these sessions compulsory (for instance, in Mauritania), while others simply encourage participation (Sierra Leone). In practice, even if participation is officially compulsory, it is not always rigorously monitored. Evaluations show that, even in the absence of active monitoring,

(continued next page)

Box 1.5 (continued)

attendance rates tend to be high. In Cameroon and Niger, for instance, 95 percent of beneficiaries attend the sessions even though there is no rigorous verification.

- *Programs that formally require the adoption of certain behaviors, but do not monitor compliance.* These programs typically announce that beneficiaries must adopt certain behaviors, usually linked to the use of basic services to improve children's education, nutrition, and health status. In the cash transfer program in Cameroon, heads of beneficiary households sign moral contracts that lay out specific actions in 15 areas, including health care, schooling, nutrition, civic action, participation in community public works, and training in income-generating activities. Other programs clearly identify and inform beneficiaries that they need to adopt a set of behaviors—such as school enrollment and attendance, vaccination, and birth registration in the case of Senegal's PNBSF—but do not monitor compliance. (The PNBSF has also recently made participation in promotion sessions compulsory.) In Ghana, LEAP formally lays out certain expectations of beneficiaries in the program operations manual for households with under-15-year-olds. (It does not specify these for poor elderly or disabled beneficiaries.) However, it does not monitor the adoption of these behaviors and actions.

- *Programs that require the adoption of certain behaviors, monitor compliance, and impose penalties for noncompliance.* In Guinea, cash transfers are conditioned on quarterly health checkups for children under the age of 6 and on 90 percent school attendance among primary-school children. If, after reception of the third cash transfer, a child's health status has shown no improvement, the grant is suspended. In Kenya, a small pilot intervention among a subset of households benefiting from the cash transfer of the OVC Program involved monitoring and the application of penalties for noncompliance with conditions on primary-school attendance, immunizations, and health checkups among children. This pilot was, however, discontinued in 2017 due to a number of operational challenges related to implementing the pilot. The Madagascar Human Development Cash Transfer Program requires beneficiaries to ensure a minimum of 80 percent attendance by at least two of their children of primary-school age. If households do not comply with the condition, they are penalized through the removal of part of the benefit. The Tanzania PSSN Program verifies compliance with school attendance and visits to health clinics. It fully enforces the conditionalities, and beneficiaries lose the corresponding benefit if they fail to comply.

A few regional patterns emerge. In West Africa, programs tend to encourage participation in promotion sessions, and compliance with requirements is often not monitored (or penalized). In East and Southern Africa, programs tend to be closer to the Latin American model, wherein conditions are monitored and penalties are enforced for noncompliance.

Sources: Aline Coudouel, based in part on Baird et al. 2014; Fiszbein and Shady 2009; World Bank 2015b.

identification and targeting of the poor in informal urban settlements, communication campaigns, and high population mobility, which could result in low program uptake and enrollment.

Enhancing the efficiency and coordination of social safety net programs has become a central pillar of national strategies in many countries. Many governments aspire to improve the impact of the programs by strengthening coordination and investing in shared systems to reduce cost-inefficiencies and the duplication of effort. Delivery platforms such as social registries, interoperable management information systems, and shared payment systems allow administrative cost savings and facilitate planning. Social registries can help improve the identification and targeting of beneficiaries within social safety net systems. These systems support outreach, the collection and processing of needs assessment data, and registration and eligibility information for social safety net programs. These registries also represent a platform so individuals or households may be considered across various programs (Karippacheril, Leite, and Lindert 2017).

Registries are currently used in 26 countries and are being developed in an additional 16 countries (see appendix D, table D.2). The stage of development and the scale of the registries differ. Coverage ranges from 89 percent and 52 percent of the population in Rwanda and Lesotho to 0.1 and 0.3 percent in Zambia and Mozambique, respectively (figure 1.8). Many countries use social registries as a gateway for coordinating registration and eligibility assessments

Figure 1.8 Social Registries Are Often Small

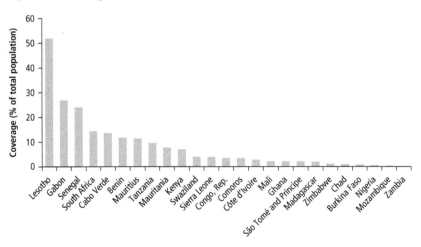

Note: See appendix table D.2.

across social programs, including social safety nets, health care, and other social programs. The national household registry being developed in Ghana is intended to replace existing systems to identify the beneficiaries of the LEAP cash transfer program and the indigent beneficiaries of the National Health Insurance Scheme, among other programs. Similarly, in Senegal, the registry of poor households is used by social safety net programs and the subsidized health insurance program. In Rwanda, the Ubuehe social registry update was completed in 2017, and the registry covers 2.4 million households and 10.4 million people (almost the entire population). Key building blocks of social safety net delivery systems—especially targeting mechanisms, social registries, and payment systems—are also critical to the development of shock-responsive programs.

Social Safety Nets Are Reaching Some, but Many of the Poor Are Not Covered

Although programs have been expanded, most of the poor in Africa are still not covered by social safety nets. Even if all existing social safety nets were perfectly targeted to the poor, not all poor households would be reached at the current scale of programs (in addition, benefits are typically low compared to needs). This is because poverty rates are higher than coverage rates in most countries (figure 1.9; appendix C, table C.1, and appendix F, table F.1). In practice, in addition, some programs might not target the poor exclusively and may have broader objectives, such as universal social pensions, school feeding programs for all primary-school students, scholarships for all students in tertiary education, or programs that target specific categories deemed vulnerable without necessarily taking into account welfare characteristics.

In addition, benefit leakage contributes to limited coverage of the poor. The benefit incidence of selected programs that target on the basis of poverty, welfare, or vulnerability are generally pro-poor, and the performance of programs in Africa is in line with international experience. For instance, more than 60 percent of the households benefiting from the South Africa child support grants programs belong to the poorest two consumption quintiles, and over 60 percent of beneficiaries of the Malawi MASAF Public Works Program (PWP) are among the poor (figure 1.10). However, a certain share of resources goes to richer households. Some limitations in targeting are technical because it is hard and costly to assess the welfare status of households effectively and dynamically. However, the decision to target particular groups is also a political one. Indeed, selecting eligible groups is sometimes driven by the need to generate support among the population and decision makers for social safety net programs.

Figure 1.9 Social Safety Net Coverage Is Not Proportionate to the Extent of Poverty

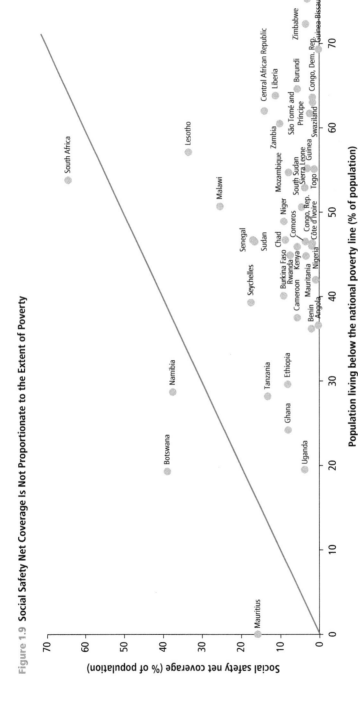

Social safety net coverage (% of population)

Population living below the national poverty line (% of population)

Sources: ASPIRE (Atlas of Social Protection Indicators of Resilience and Equity) (database), Administrative data, World Bank, Washington, DC, http://www.worldbank.org/aspire; PovcalNet (online analysis tool), World Bank, Washington, DC, http://iresearch.worldbank.org/PovcalNet/.
Note: See methodology in appendixes B.2 and B.3. Social safety net coverage rates are approximated by summing the number of direct and indirect beneficiaries of cash transfers, food-based transfers, and public works programs only. The beneficiaries of the other six program types (social pensions, school feeding, emergency programs, health care and education fee waivers, and other programs) are not included because their beneficiaries are more likely to overlap with those in other programs, which would result in overestimated coverage rates. For more details see appendix tables C.1 and F.1.

Figure 1.10 Flagship Programs Benefit the Poor, but also the Nonpoor

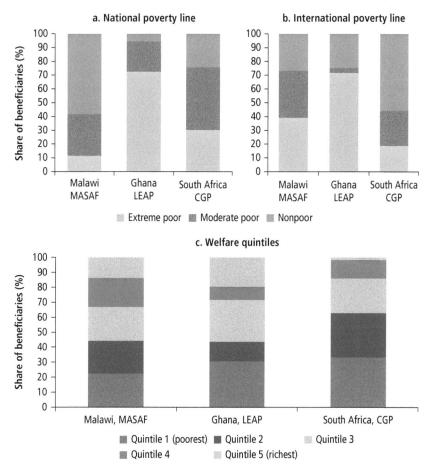

Source: ASPIRE (Atlas of Social Protection Indicators of Resilience and Equity) (database), World Bank, Washington, DC, http://www.worldbank.org/aspire. Based on household survey data (appendix A, table A.2).
Note: CGP = Child Grant Program; CSG = Child Support Grant; MASAF PWP = Malawi Social Action Fund Public Works Program; PSNP = Productive Safety Net Program; VUP = Vision 2020 Umurenge Program.

Within Africa, some groups have particularly large unmet needs. In rural areas, coverage is a little higher, because of the rural focus of many programs; but higher poverty rates relative to urban areas imply that the coverage is still largely inadequate. Similarly, the number of people living in drylands in East Africa and West Africa who are exposed to droughts and other shocks is projected to grow by 15 percent to 100 percent by 2030, suggesting increasing future needs (Cervigni and Morris 2016). Coverage among internally displaced people and refugees is also limited (World Bank 2017).

Benefit amounts are low relative to the needs in low-income countries. Average benefits from cash transfer programs—food, in-kind, and fee waiver programs are not included because the value of the transfers is not directly measurable—vary by program and country groups (table 1.3). Benefits usually take into account the cost of basic food items, services, and, sometimes, household size, and are often adjusted for urban or rural settings. The highest benefits are usually offered through public works or social pensions. The latter reach $299 and $84 a month in upper-middle-income countries such as Mauritius and South Africa, representing about 5 percent and 2 percent of per capita gross domestic product (GDP) in these countries, respectively (2011 purchasing power parity [PPP] U.S. dollars; appendix I, table I.3). Public works benefits are usually paid per day or per week and are seasonal. Assuming that rotation would allow the same beneficiary to work 24 days, monthly amounts would be equivalent to $73 in the Malawi MASAF public works program, $155 in the Ethiopia UPSNP, and $153 in the Youth Employment and Skills Development Project in Burkina Faso (in 2011 PPP U.S. dollars; appendix I, table I.2). The daily wage is generally similar to the minimum wage. In Ghana, the compensation paid in 2015 by the Labor-Intensive Public Works Program for a six-hour working day averaged $5 in 2011 PPP U.S. dollars, similar to the minimum wage for an eight-hour working day. In low-income countries, cash transfer programs targeted to the poor provide an average of about $30 in 2011 PPP U.S. dollars a month, equivalent to around 4 percent of per capita GDP and 10 percent of the national poverty line in these countries (table 1.3 and appendix I, table I.1). About $20 in 2011 PPP U.S. dollars a month is provided in Tanzania and Uganda. The South Africa child support grant program is among the most generous large cash transfer programs, supplying an average of $84 in 2011 PPP U.S. dollars a month, equivalent to 2 percent of per capita GDP. Inflation will reduce the value, though few programs index benefits to price indexes, the minimum wage, or other anchors.

Some Countries Spend Heavily, but Programs Need to Be Brought to Scale and Sustained

African countries spend an average of around 1.2 percent of GDP on social safety nets, compared with a global average of 1.6 percent in the developing world (appendix G, table G.3; World Bank 2015b). This represents about 4.6 percent of total government spending. While richer countries invest more on social safety nets on average, the level of government commitment varies across countries with similar GDPs. Indeed, spending may be high even in

Table 1.3 Benefit Amounts Are Low Relative to Needs in Low-Income Countries

Country group	Program type	Number of programs (countries)	Monthly benefit ($, 2011 PPP)	As a share, %					Minimum wage
				GDP per capita	National poverty line	National poverty gap	$1.90 a day poverty line	$1.90 a day poverty gap	
Low income	Cash transfer	20 (13)	30	4	10	1	9	1	
	Public works	16 (13)	141	23	57	5	47	4	210
Lower-middle income	Cash transfer	12 (8)	63	5	12	1	22	3	
	Public works	4 (3)	227	18	37	3	83	11	153
	Social pension	5 (5)	25	2	7	1	10	1	
Upper-middle income	Cash transfer	14 (3)	196	5	29	5	92	284	
	Public works	2 (2)	235	6	62	5	112	22	142
	Social pension	4 (4)	133	3	30	3	63	340	

Source: ASPIRE (Atlas of Social Protection Indicators of Resilience and Equity) (database), World Bank, Washington, DC, http://www.worldbank.org/aspire.
Note: Monthly amounts are in constant 2011 international dollars. Amounts are converted to international dollars using PPP rates based on the International Comparison Program 2011 round. Monthly amounts for public works programs are estimated on the assumption of 24 days of work in a month. The benefit per capita is estimated by dividing the total benefit level by the average household size.

countries with low GDP per capita (figure 1.11). Chapter 5 argues that expanding the scale of social safety nets to cover all the poor and vulnerable requires a strong commitment to prioritize social safety nets in national budgets to realize allocative and administrative efficiency gains.

Spending levels vary greatly across the region and program type. Upper-middle-income countries in Africa spend an average of 2.2 percent of GDP (6.9 percent of total government expenditures), while low-income countries spend 1.4 percent of GDP (4.8 percent of total government expenditures). Southern Africa spends five times more than Central Africa and two times more than East Africa and West Africa. Non–resource-rich countries devote more than seven times as much to social safety nets (2.1 percent of GDP, or 5.4 percent of government expenditures) as oil-rich countries (0.3 percent of GDP, or 1.8 percent of total government expenditures). Countries with higher exposure to droughts allocate more resources to these programs than countries with low or medium exposure (appendix G, table G.3). When considering all spending going to social safety nets in Africa, the largest category of programs are cash transfer programs, which account for 41 percent of all spending (followed by social pensions, with 26 percent, and public works, with 16 percent), though there are significant regional variations (appendix G, table G.6). Also, the bulk of overall spending is channeled through programs that are targeted according to the poverty, vulnerability, or well-being status of beneficiaries (77 percent), once again with significant variations across country groups (appendix G, table G.6).

Social safety net spending is low relative to government spending on energy subsidies (figure 1.12; appendix G, table G.1). For instance, in Central Africa, the spending on energy subsidies is more than three times the spending on social safety nets. The equivalent of almost 2.20 percent of GDP in Cameroon is spent on subsidies compared with the 0.10 percent of GDP spent on social safety nets. About 1.90 percent of GDP in the Democratic Republic of Congo is spent on subsidies, compared with 0.7 percent of GDP on social safety nets. In oil-rich countries, energy subsidies are sometimes used as policy instruments to distribute oil revenues among the population. Energy subsidies benefit all population groups, but are often regressive because richer households consume larger quantities of energy.

Humanitarian assistance represents the main source of funding in emergency situations, and development partners remain critical in many low-income and fragile contexts. The average amount of humanitarian assistance flowing to fragile countries (3.9 percent of GDP) is larger than the social safety net spending of the governments of these countries (1.4 percent of GDP). The Central African Republic and South Sudan are the largest recipients of humanitarian aid (21.6 and 11.3 percent of GDP, respectively), followed by Burundi, Chad, the Democratic Republic of Congo, Liberia, Mali, Niger, and Sierra Leone (appendix G, table G.1). In these countries, humanitarian action provides

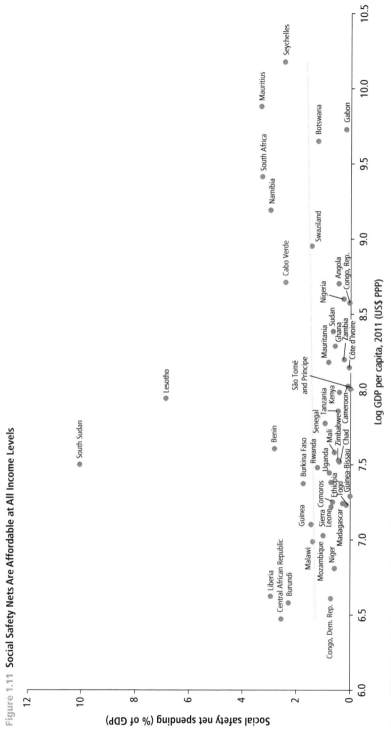

Figure 1.11 Social Safety Nets Are Affordable at All Income Levels

Social safety net spending (% of GDP)

Log GDP per capita, 2011 (US$ PPP)

Source: ASPIRE (Atlas of Social Protection Indicators of Resilience and Equity) (database), Administrative data, World Bank, Washington, DC, http://www.worldbank.org/aspire.
Note: See methodology in appendix B.4 and more details in appendix G, tables G.1 and G.2. Social safety net spending estimates are moderately different than those in World Bank (2018) due to data updates in this report and different treatments of outlier data points. PPP = purchasing power parity.

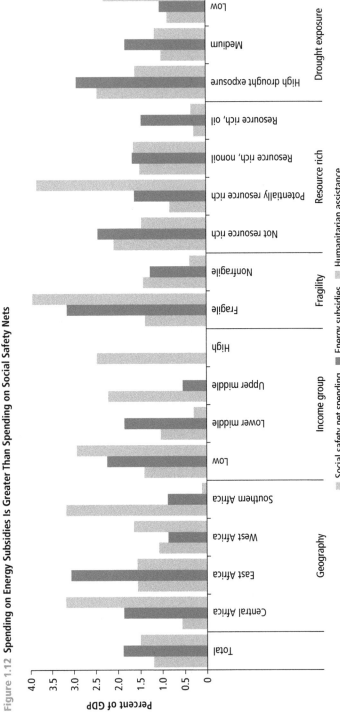

Figure 1.12 Spending on Energy Subsidies Is Greater Than Spending on Social Safety Nets

Legend: Social safety net spending; Energy subsidies; Humanitarian assistance

Categories (x-axis groupings): Total; Central Africa, East Africa, West Africa, Southern Africa (Geography); Low, Lower middle, Upper middle, High (Income group); Fragile, Nonfragile (Fragility); Not resource rich, Potentially resource rich, Resource rich, nonoil, Resource rich, oil (Resource rich); High drought exposure, Medium, Low (Drought exposure)

Y-axis: Percent of GDP (0, 0.5, 1.0, 1.5, 2.0, 2.5, 3.0, 3.5, 4.0)

Sources: Spending on social safety nets: ASPIRE (Atlas of Social Protection Indicators of Resilience and Equity) (database), Administrative data, World Bank, Washington, DC, http://www .worldbank.org/aspire. Spending on subsidies: Coady et al. 2015. Humanitarian aid: Development Initiatives 2017.
Note: See methodology in appendix B.4 and more details in appendix G, table G.1. Data do not reflect reductions in subsidies which have taken place since 2015. Social safety nets spending estimates are moderately different than those in World Bank (2018) due to data updates in this report and different treatment of outlier data points.

the core of support to beneficiaries, and social safety nets play a smaller role. While social safety net spending is channeled through government budgets and government agencies, the resources for humanitarian aid are provided through more diverse channels. Humanitarian aid tends to be supplied through dedicated streams flowing from development partners or the United Nations system, which typically involves operational humanitarian agencies, not governments. In an effort to integrate humanitarian aid through short-term emergency interventions and regular, predictable, long-term social safety net programs, the resources are sometimes distributed from official government delivery platforms if social safety net programs have been established.

The role of development partners in expanding social safety nets is critical because they are the main funders of social safety nets in Africa. Development assistance through bilateral and multilateral organizations represents more than half the social safety net financing in the majority of African countries. Some of the important multilateral institutions are the European Union, the United Nations Children's Fund, the World Bank, the World Food Programme, and several bilateral organizations. Dependence on external financing can jeopardize sustainability if programs are 100 percent funded by development partners, though some programs have transitioned from full funding by development partners at inception to gradually increasing support by domestic resources. For instance, Kenya has undertaken a long-term commitment to support safety net programs with domestic resources through its National Safety Net Program, which fully funds some programs and covers more than half the cost of others. Still, in several countries, social safety nets are mostly funded by external financing (the PSNP in Ethiopia and the PSSN in Tanzania) and emergency social safety nets in the Central African Republic (appendix G, table G.5).

Despite progress in reducing poverty in recent decades, the cost of eliminating poverty in Africa will still be high. One way to approximate the resources needed to eliminate poverty is to estimate the aggregate poverty gap, which is the monetary value of the gap between the consumption level of the poor and the poverty line. In Africa, the average poverty gap is about 15 percent of GDP among people living below the national poverty line. The poverty gap has been falling as the poverty rate has declined. Still, the average poverty gap as a share of domestic resources (GDP) is large, indicating that domestic resources in most countries are unlikely to be sufficient to end poverty.[4]

Notes

1. Throughout this report, "Africa" refers to the 48 countries in Sub-Saharan Africa.
2. The poverty rate is computed as the share of the population living on less than $1.90 a day, the international threshold for global poverty estimates. The most recent

benchmark year for cross-country comparisons is 2013. See PovcalNet (online analysis tool), World Bank, Washington, DC, http://iresearch.worldbank.org /PovcalNet/.

3. Definitions of social protection vary, but the term generally refers to policies and programs aimed at preventing or protecting individuals against poverty, vulnerability, and social exclusion throughout the life cycle, with a particular focus on vulnerable groups. Social protection seeks to build human capital, productive assets, and access to productive jobs. The definition in this report is consistent with the World Bank Social Protection Strategy 2012–22 and the World Bank Africa Social Protection Strategy (World Bank 2012a, 2012b).

4. The gap between need and spending is highly underestimated here because this simple calculation ignores administrative costs and leakages or insufficient targeting to reach the poor.

References

Alkire, Sabina, and Bouba Housseini. 2014. "Multidimensional Poverty in Sub-Saharan Africa: Levels and Trends." OPHI Working Paper 81, Oxford Poverty and Human Development Initiative, University of Oxford, Oxford.

Bailey, Sarah, and Paul Harvey. 2017. "Time for Change: Harnessing the Potential of Humanitarian Cash Transfers." ODI Report, Overseas Development Institute, London.

Baird, Sarah, Francisco H.G. Ferreira, Berk Özler, and Michael Woolcock. 2014. "Conditional, Unconditional, and Everything in Between: A Systematic Review of the Effects of Cash Transfer Programmes on Schooling Outcomes." *Journal of Development Effectiveness* 6: 1–43.

Bastagli, Francesca. 2014. "Responding to a Crisis: The Design and Delivery of Social Protection." ODI Briefing 90, Overseas Development Institute, London.

Bastagli, Francesca, Jessica Hagen-Zanker, Luke Harman, Valentina Barca, Georgina Sturge, and Tanja Schmidt. 2016. *Cash Transfers: What Does the Evidence Say? A Rigorous Review of Programme Impact and of the Role of Design and Implementation Features*. With Luca Pellerano. London: Overseas Development Institute.

Beegle, Kathleen, Luc Christiaensen, Andrew Dabalen, and Isis Gaddis. 2016. *Poverty in a Rising Africa*. Africa Poverty Report. Washington, DC: World Bank.

Blattman, Christopher, and Laura Ralston. 2015. "Generating Employment in Poor and Fragile States: Evidence from Labor Market and Entrepreneurship Programs." Working paper, Columbia University, New York.

Cervigni, Raffaello, and Michael Morris, eds. 2016. *Confronting Drought in Africa's Drylands: Opportunities for Enhancing Resilience*. Africa Development Forum Series. Washington, DC: Agence Française de Développement and World Bank.

Chandy, Laurence. 2017. "No Country Left Behind: The Case for Focusing Greater Attention on the World's Poorest Countries." Global Economy and Development, Brookings Institution, Washington, DC.

Chandy, Laurence, Natasha Ledlie, and Veronika Penciakova. 2013. "The Final Countdown: Prospects for Ending Extreme Poverty by 2030." Global Views Policy Paper 2013–04, Brookings Institution, Washington, DC.

Cirillo, Cristina, and Raquel Tebaldi. 2016. *Social Protection in Africa: Inventory of Non-contributory Programmes*. Brasília: International Policy Center for Inclusive Growth, United Nations Development Programme.

Coady, David P., Ian W. H. Parry, Louis Sears, and Baoping Shang. 2015. "How Large Are Global Energy Subsidies?" IMF Working Paper 15/105, International Monetary Fund, Washington, DC.

Dang, Hai-Anh H., and Andrew L. Dabalen. 2018. "Is Poverty in Africa Mostly Chronic or Transient? Evidence from Synthetic Panel Data." *Journal of Development Studies*.

Development Initiatives. 2017. "Global Humanitarian Assistance Report 2017." Development Initiatives, Bristol, U.K.

Filmer, Deon. 2008. "Disability, Poverty, and Schooling in Developing Countries: Results from 14 Household Surveys." *World Bank Economic Review* 22 (1): 141–63.

Fiszbein, Ariel, and Norbert R. Schady. 2009. *Conditional Cash Transfers: Reducing Present and Future Poverty*. With Francisco H. G. Ferreira, Margaret E. Grosh, Niall Keleher, Pedro Olinto, and Emmanuel Skoufias. World Bank Policy Research Report. Washington, DC: World Bank.

Garcia, Marito H., and Charity M. T. Moore. 2012. *The Cash Dividend: The Rise of Cash Transfer Programs in Sub-Saharan Africa*. Directions in Development: Human Development Series. Washington, DC: World Bank.

Grosh, Margaret E., Carlo del Ninno, Emil Tesliuc, and Azedine Ouerghi. 2008. *For Protection and Promotion: The Design and Implementation of Effective Safety Nets*. Washington, DC: World Bank.

Hallegatte, Stéphane, Mook Bangalore, Laura Bonzanigo, Marianne Fay, Tomaro Kane, Ulf Narloch, Julie Rozenberg, David Treguer, and Adrien Vogt-Schilb. 2016. *Shock Waves: Managing the Impacts of Climate Change on Poverty*. Climate Change and Development Series. Washington, DC: World Bank.

Hashemi, Syed M., and Aude de Montesquiou. 2016. "Graduation Pathways: Increasing Income and Resilience for the Extreme Poor." With Katharine McKee. CGAP Brief, Consultative Group to Assist the Poor, World Bank, Washington, DC.

Hill, Ruth, and Philip Verwimp. 2017. "Managing Risk and Conflict." In *Accelerating Poverty Reduction in Africa*, edited by Kathleen Beegle and Luc Christiaensen, chapter 4. Washington, DC: World Bank.

Jirka, Stefan, Dominic Woolf, Dawit Solomon, and Johannes Lehmann. 2015. "Climate Finance for Ethiopia's Productive Safety Net Programme (PSNP): Comprehensive Report on Accessing Climate Finance and Carbon Markets to Promote Socially and Environmentally Sustainable Public Works Social Safety Net Programs." World Bank Climate Smart Initiative Report, Cornell University, Ithaca, NY.

Karippacheril, Tina George, Phillippe George Leite, and Kathy Lindert. 2017. "Guidance Note and Assessment Tool on Social Registries for Social Assistance and Beyond." Working paper, World Bank, Washington, DC.

Maystadt, Jean-François, and Philip Verwimp. 2015. "Forced Displacement and Refugees in Sub-Saharan Africa: An Economic Inquiry." Policy Research Working Paper 7517, World Bank, Washington, DC.

McCord, Anna. 2013. "Shockwatch and Social Protection: Shock Response Readiness Appraisal Toolkit." June, Overseas Development Institute, London.

Mitra, Sophie, Aleksandra Posärac, and Brandon Vick. 2013. "Disability and Poverty in Developing Countries: A Multidimensional Study." World Development 41 (1): 1–18.

ODI (Overseas Development Institute). 2015. "Doing Cash Differently: How Cash Transfers Can Transform Humanitarian Aid; Report of the High Level Panel on Humanitarian Cash Transfers." September, Center for Global Development, ODI, London.

OPM (Oxford Policy Management). 2015. "Conceptualising Shock-Responsive Social Protection." Shock-Responsive Social Protection Systems Research Working Paper 1 (October), OPM, Oxford.

Ovadiya, Mirey. 2014a. "Building Flexible and Scalable Social Protection Programs That Can Respond to Disasters." Social Protection and Labor Technical Note 1, World Bank, Washington, DC.

———. 2014b. "Adapting Benefit Transfer Mechanisms to Respond to Disasters and Climate Change-Related Events." Social Protection and Labor Technical Note 3, World Bank, Washington, DC.

Ravallion, Martin. 1999. "Appraising Workfare." World Bank Research Observer 14 (1): 31–48.

———. 2013. "How Long Will It Take to Lift One Billion People out of Poverty?" Policy Research Working Paper 6325, World Bank, Washington, DC.

Subbarao, Kalanidhi, Carlo del Ninno, Colin Andrews, and Claudia Rodríguez-Alas. 2013. Public Works as a Safety Net: Design, Evidence, and Implementation. Directions in Development: Human Development Series. Washington, DC: World Bank.

Tebaldi, Raquel. 2016. "Gender and Social Protection in Sub-Saharan Africa: A General Assessment of Program Design." Policy Research Brief 58, International Policy Centre for Inclusive Growth, United Nations Development Programme, Brasília.

Watkins, Kevin, and Maria Quattri. 2016. "Child Poverty, Inequality, and Demography: Why Sub-Saharan Africa Matters for the Sustainable Development Goals." Overseas Development Institute, London.

Watson, Carol. 2016. "Shock-Responsive Social Protection in the Sahel: Community Perspectives." Shock-Responsive Social Protection Systems Research Working Paper 3, OPM, Oxford.

World Bank. 2012a. World Bank 2012–2022 Social Protection and Labor Strategy: Resilience, Equity, and Opportunity. Washington, DC: World Bank.

———. 2012b. Managing Risk, Promoting Growth: Developing Systems for Social Protection in Africa—The World Bank's Africa Social Protection Strategy 2012–2022. World Bank, Washington, DC.

———. 2014. The State of Social Safety Nets 2014. World Bank, Washington, DC.

———. 2015a. *A Measured Approach to Ending Poverty and Boosting Shared Prosperity: Concepts, Data, and the Twin Goals*. Policy Research Report Series. Washington, DC: World Bank.

———. 2015b. *The State of Social Safety Nets 2015*. Washington, DC: World Bank.

———. 2016a. *Poverty and Shared Prosperity 2016: Taking On Inequality*. Washington, DC: World Bank.

———. 2016b. "Strategic Note: Cash Transfers in Humanitarian Contexts—Final Draft Prepared for the Principals of the Inter-Agency Standing Committee." June, World Bank, Washington, DC.

———. 2017. *Forcibly Displaced: Toward a Development Approach Supporting Refugees, the Internally Displaced, and Their Hosts*. World Bank, Washington, DC.

———. 2018. *The State of Social Safety Nets 2018*. World Bank, Washington, DC.

Chapter **2**

Social Safety Nets Promote Poverty Reduction, Increase Resilience, and Expand Opportunities

Colin Andrews, Allan Hsiao, and Laura Ralston

There is growing evidence on the impacts of social safety nets on equity, resilience, and opportunities among the poor and vulnerable in Africa. The depth of recent evidence serves to make a case for investment in social safety nets, for the effective design of programs, and for bringing programs to scale.

The equity objective of social safety nets involves ensuring that the most vulnerable and poorest households reach a minimum level of consumption and are able to cover basic needs. Numerous studies have demonstrated that social safety nets boost consumption and reduce poverty. The vast majority of evidence indicates that households do not use transfers on temptation goods such as alcohol or tobacco. The associated consumption patterns have spillover effects in local economies. Social safety nets have been shown to stimulate the demand for retail, services, and agricultural goods.

Social safety nets also help build household resilience to economic shocks through increased savings and investments in productive assets, especially livestock holdings. They also limit adverse coping strategies among households, including the use of child labor.

Social safety net transfers are not handouts. Instead, they promote longer-term opportunities for productive inclusion. They foster opportunities through investment in human capital: In Africa, programs have been shown to increase school attendance substantially. Their impact on health care is more limited and reflects the demand-side and supply-side constraints to improved health and the speed at which program impacts can be realized. Social safety nets also foster opportunities through investments in productive activities: they lead to the launch or expansion of business activities and more time spent on household farms.

Social safety nets are among the most frequently evaluated social policy interventions in Africa. The depth of evidence has been critical in motivating a a consensus on the need to invest in social safety nets, and the evaluations have informed design. As programs mature and coverage is expanded, the diversity in the evaluations can help gauge the likely impacts of bringing social safety nets to scale.

The impacts of the related programs can be framed around the broad objectives of social safety nets, which are distilled here into a simplified framework that focuses on equity, resilience, and opportunity.[1]

First, the equity objective of social safety nets is often the most central in low-income settings because it involves seeking to ensure that the most vulnerable and poorest households reach a minimum level of consumption and are able to cover basic needs. Typical outcomes of interest include measures of consumption, food security, and poverty among beneficiary households (figure 2.1). In some cases, strong social safety nets can also help remove incumbent redistributive programs that are inefficient and costly, or they can support macroeconomic reforms that boost long-run economic growth by compensating immediate losers (Inchauste and Victor 2017) (see chapters 3 and 5).

Second, the resilience objective is underpinned by the insurance function of well-implemented social safety nets. If poor households can rely on regular support from social safety nets, they can avoid resorting to costly and often irreversible coping strategies, such as selling their most productive assets at deflated prices. From an ex ante perspective, programs can help households diversify into higher-return, but also higher-risk, income activities that may boost households out of poverty.

Third, the opportunity objective of social safety nets aims to allow households to make investments they would otherwise miss. Typically, the outcomes of interest associated with this objective are investments in education, nutrition, and health care among children and in the increased earnings of income providers within the households.

Figure 2.1 Conceptual Framework for Considering the Impacts of Social Safety Nets

Equity	Resilience	Opportunity
Consumption	Savings	Human capital investments:
Food security	Private transfers	Education
Poverty	Reduced negative coping	Health
	mechanism	Nutrition
	Livelihood strenghtening	Productive inclusion
	Productive assets	Income and earnings potential

Beyond these three objectives of social safety nets, recent discussions have considered the extent to which social safety nets may contribute to economic growth (Alderman and Yemtsov 2013; Barrientos 2012). Channels for growth principally focus on the extent to which social safety nets enable investments and better risk management among beneficiary households and their communities: pathways that are aligned with the resilience and opportunity objectives.

There is an impressive evidence base, including rigorous impact evaluations and a growing literature, much of which is specific to the Africa region.[2] Since 2005, 55 impact evaluations, examining 27 social safety net programs in 14 African countries, have been conducted (annex 2A). These studies cover national flagship social safety net programs in Ethiopia, Ghana, Kenya, Malawi, South Africa, Tanzania, and others. There is also a recent array of literature that aggregates evaluation findings, including systematic reviews of the global evidence on various social safety net programs; systematic reviews of specific interventions, such as cash transfers; systematic reviews of specific outcomes, for example, in education; and comparative country studies (Baird et al. 2013; Bastagli et al. 2016; Davis et al. 2016; Hagen-Zanker, McCord, and Holmes 2011; IEG 2011; Kabeer, Piza, and Taylor 2012; Saavedra and Garcia 2012). One caveat to the recent literature is that Africa-specific findings can be difficult to glean within global studies, and there are no studies that combine comparable cross-country evidence from Africa to develop the average size of effects.

To address these shortcomings, a meta-analysis has been conducted and is presented here. The objective of the meta-analysis is to pool evidence across African studies in a systematic way to facilitate a robust and consistent comparison of impacts on key outcomes. Underpinning the meta-analysis are several important methodological decisions (see annex 2B; Ralston, Andrews, and Hsiao 2017). Conducting a meta-analysis based on a range of impact evaluations necessarily focuses on the outcomes of those studies. Some outcomes of interest that are inherently difficult to measure are not covered, for instance, the incidence of gender-based violence, social cohesion, and political economy indicators such as trust in government and willingness to accept reforms. A second caveat to this approach is that many impact evaluations are done during early phases of program development, rather than when programs are fully mature and at scale. To speak to this second point, the meta-analysis discussion has been extended to explore the potential impact if programs are brought to scale. Simulations are developed for three countries—Ghana, Liberia, and Niger—to show the scope for poverty reduction, consumption increases, human development improvements, and greater investments in productive assets. A general equilibrium analysis has also been carried out to assess the relative value of social safety net interventions done alone versus those done alongside complementary supply-side interventions that may boost aggregate demand.

While the focus of this analysis is an examination of program impacts on socioeconomic well-being, a number of the studies reflected on critical design features to maximize the impact of bringing programs to scale. Four broad lessons emerge. First, the value of a cash transfer is important. Ensuring impacts requires sufficiently large transfers. Benefits need to be updated over time to account for inflation, which reduces purchasing power. Second, the impact of programs relies on predictability. If benefits are not delivered with regularity, households cannot use them as effectively. As programs are brought to scale, fiscal sustainability, that is, regular funding, is needed to ensure that they reach maximum impact (see chapter 5). Third, coordination with complementary programs, such as skills training or other employment schemes, is crucial in maximizing resilience and promoting productive inclusion. As social safety nets grow, there will be a greater need for a sound institutional framework to tie programs together (see chapter 4). Fourth, as programs grow, so will the demand for key public services, such as schools, health care, and agricultural extension. The access to and quality of services can be central factors in maximizing program impacts.

Social Safety Nets Improve Equity

In examining the evidence on equity, the analysis focuses on the impact of social safety net programs on raising household consumption. One of the fundamental purposes of social safety nets is to improve the well-being of the poorest or most vulnerable and lay a foundation for equality of opportunity by allowing families to meet basic needs (World Bank 2012). Household consumption is one of the main channels of the impact of a social safety net intervention because poor households are expected to use the social safety net to satisfy basic household needs, including for food and nonfood staple goods. Hence, in addition to overall household consumption, food consumption is specifically examined as a more immediate indicator of impact because food typically constitutes more than half of household consumption among poorer households. Several studies assess food security measures, although the set of indicators is not sufficiently consistent for the pooled meta-analysis.

The literature provides valuable details on individual programs' impacts on equity. Of 35 cash transfer studies reviewed, including 12 in Africa, 25 (9 in Africa) were found to have a significant impact on raising household consumption (Bastagli et al. 2016). Social safety net programs more generally have also been shown to boost consumption, but also to increase frequency and diversity in consumption patterns (Davis et al. 2016).

For the meta-analysis, results from nine programs in Africa were analyzed for impacts on total household consumption.[3] On average, total consumption increases by an average $0.74 for each $1.00 transferred, and this result is significant (box 2.1; figure 2.2).[4] In most programs, there is an increase in household consumption. However, there is considerable heterogeneity across countries in the size of impacts and the precision of estimates. Five programs result in significant increases: the Social Cash Transfer Program (SCTP) in Malawi, the Child Grant Program in Zambia, and Kenya's Hunger Safety Net Program (HSNP), Orphans and Vulnerable Children (OVC) Program, and

---

BOX 2.1

Unpacking the Findings of the Meta-analysis

Figures 2.2–2.7 show the results of the meta-analysis. Each figure is divided into two panels.

The top panel shows the average size of the effect (the orange horizontal line) and individual program impacts (purple horizontal dashes) expressed in percentage change (to facilitate comparability). The shaded grey bars show the 95 percent confidence interval for each estimate. The overall confidence interval is indicated by the yellow shaded area.

The second panel shows the impact of these programs on beneficiaries. The light blue bar reports baseline measures of the outcome in a standardized way, and the dark blue bars show the incremental change that is attributed to the social safety net program. The data presented here reflect more closely what is typically reported in individual evaluations, but the outcome measures have been converted to comparable units, such as monthly household expenditures or net enrollment rates. All dollar amounts report 2011 purchasing power parity (PPP) U.S. dollars, a price-adjusted comparable unit across countries.

By way of an illustrative example, consider the findings presented on Kenya's OVC program (fourth from left) regarding the impacts of total consumption in figure 2.2. The top panel reports that household consumption rose by 80 percent of the value of the transfer (at a confidence interval of 1 percent–160 percent). The second panel reports that the transfer increased total consumption from $346 to $404.

Scanning across programs, as reported in the figure note, one may see that monthly transfers varied between $21 and $79, or 8 percent–50 percent of baseline consumption (panel B), and the impacts on consumption varied between reducing consumption by $0.86 per $1.00 transferred (the Livelihood Empowerment against Poverty Program [LEAP] in Ghana) and increasing it by $1.79 per $1.00 transferred (SCTP in Malawi).

GiveDirectly. Beneficiary households experience the greatest rise in consumption in Malawi with the SCTP, 179 percent of the value of the transfers. The Zambia Child Grant Program also exhibits large positive effects on total consumption and by subcategories of consumption: 76 percent of the transfer is spent on food, followed by health care and hygiene (7 percent), clothing (6 percent), and communication and transportation (6 percent), demonstrating that the transfers are used to meet basic needs. Both the Malawi and Zambia

Figure 2.2 Consumption Increases Because of Social Safety Nets

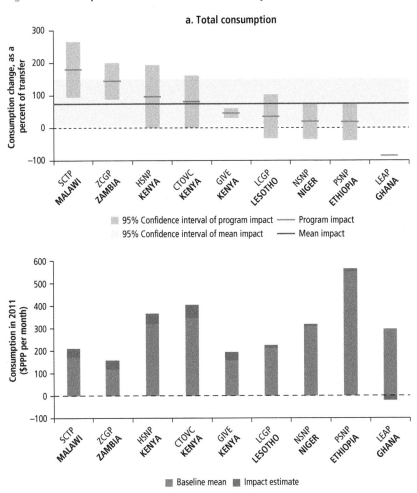

(continued next page)

Figure 2.2 Continued

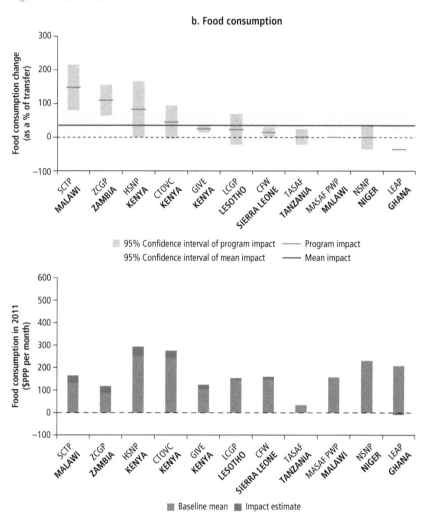

b. Food consumption

Source: World Bank meta-analysis.
Note: The mean value of the household transfer (in 2011 US$, purchasing power parity) is $65 for Ethiopia PSNP (12 percent of total consumption); $24 for Ghana LEAP (8 percent and 12 percent of total and food consumption); $47 for Kenya HSNP (15 percent and 19 percent of total and food consumption); $71 for Kenya CTOVC (21 percent and 29 percent of total and food consumption); $79 for Kenya GIVE (50 percent and 75 percent of total and food consumption); $34 for Lesotho LCGP (16 percent and 24 percent of total and food consumption); $21 for Malawi SCTP (13 percent and 16 percent of total and food consumption); $44 for Malawi MASAF PWP (28 percent of food consumption); $44 for Niger NSNP (14 percent and 19 percent of total and food consumption); $83 for Sierra Leone CFW (56 percent of food consumption); $48 for Tanzania TASAF (146 percent of total and food consumption); and $27 for Zambia ZCGP (23 percent and 31 percent of total and food consumption).

programs highlight the multiplier potential of social safety nets, given that the resulting increases in consumption exceed the total transfer received. Overall, the impact as a share of household consumption before the intervention ranges between 0 percent and 33 percent, while the value of the transfer varies between 8 percent and 50 percent of the baseline household consumption.

The programs with the largest impact on consumption per dollar targeted poor households on the basis of indicators of household welfare, such as the SCTP in Malawi and the Zambia Child Grant Program. Households in these programs show the lowest levels of baseline consumption, at $172 and $119 per month, respectively (figure 2.2, lower panel of a). The size of these transfers was modest in relative terms (11 percent to 23 percent of baseline consumption) and absolute terms ($21–$27 per month). This finding is quite logical: the poorest live on the tightest household budgets, and the extra dollar is likely to have a greater impact on their standards of living. GiveDirectly in Kenya also targets poor households—those living on $157 per month—and realizes robustly positive consumption gains, although at a slightly lower range: about 45 percent of the transfer is spent on consumption. One explanation is that, because the program has large transfers, ranging from $45 to $160 (a mean of $79) per month, this encouraged greater spending on durable assets (such as roofs), which tend to cost more, rather than daily consumption expenditures. The program also explored delivering transfers as a single lump sum rather than monthly and found that this promoted investment over consumption.

The effects on food consumption were also strong for most programs, with a significant average effect of $0.36 per $1.00 transferred. Of the programs, 10 of the 11 available (in eight countries) were associated with rises in food consumption, among which four were significant. Across the programs, food consumption rose by up to 148 percent of the size of the transfers and up to 34 percent of food consumption prior to the program (baseline food consumption). The small increase found in the Malawi Social Action Fund public works program (MASAF PWP) appears to reflect a blend of poor design (low transfer value, limited days of employment) and weak implementation (irregular project delivery, low asset creation) (Beegle, Galasso, and Goldberg 2015).

The vast majority of the evidence suggests that households do not use the transfers to raise expenditures on temptation goods such as alcohol or tobacco (Evans and Popova 2014; Handa et al. 2017). Even where the findings point to such consumption, it is on a small scale, such as in the Cash for Work Program of the Youth Employment Support Project (CfW) in Sierra Leone (Rosas and Sabarwal 2016).

After household welfare and food consumption, a third category of equity measurement is food security. Several impact evaluations, especially those in which the program transfer is in kind rather than cash, study the impact on food security either as a complement to or in place of consumption measures. Because of the lack of coverage and consistency in measurement, the meta-analysis does not include food security. In some cases, the evaluations show increases in food security, such as in the Productive Safety Net Program (PSNP) and the Social Cash Transfer Pilot Program in Ethiopia, the Niger Safety Net Project, and the Food and Unconditional Cash Transfer Program and the AIDS Support Organization in Uganda. Yet, they find no significant consumption impacts. Generally, the food security increases are captured through expanded dietary diversity, higher food scores, improved anthropometric measures among children, and a reduction in reported food insecurity. All of which can be consistent with no change in the overall consumption value. Ethiopia's PSNP provides a striking example of the long-term impacts on food security outcomes using the food gap (number of months a household reports food shortages), which represents a broader focus than standardized consumption measures based on shorter recall periods. Between 2006 and 2014, there was substantial improvement in food security, reflected in a fall in the mean food gap from 3.0 months to 1.9 months (Berhane, Hirvonen, and Hoddinott 2015). The improvement was the most substantial among households with greater initial food insecurity. The immediate direct effect of the transfer to rural households through the PSNP in 2011 has been estimated at a 1.6 percentage point reduction in the national poverty rate (World Bank 2015).

Social safety net programs affect not only beneficiary households but, through local economy effects and spillovers, also nonbeneficiary households. Thus, evaluations find sizable consumption effects among nonbeneficiaries. Based on a combination of survey data collected among households and businesses within local communities, projections indicate that, for each $1.00 equivalent transferred to beneficiaries, nonbeneficiaries also see real income increases: $0.26–$0.83 in the Ethiopia Social Cash Transfer Pilot Program, $0.39 in LEAP in Ghana, $0.03–$0.16 in the OVC program in Kenya, $0.33 in the Lesotho Child Grants Program, $0.30 in the Zambia Child Grant Program, and $0.36 in the Zimbabwe Harmonized Social Cash Transfer Program (Taylor, Thome, and Filipski 2014; Taylor et al. 2013, 2014; Thome et al. 2014a, 2014b). These income increases are mainly mediated through greater demand for goods and services in the retail and agriculture sectors of local economies in which other households are also involved. Together with the impacts on beneficiaries, these additional income effects lead to local economy multipliers of 1.08 to 1.84. So, each dollar transferred to a poor household is projected to add more than a dollar to the local economy. These findings are especially relevant in a low-income setting because they highlight the links between social safety nets and the rural economy. However, it is unclear whether these impressive outcomes can be sustained as interventions are implemented at full scale nationally. For example, the models used for the local economy projections assume fixed input prices for goods produced outside communities; but if programs are brought to scale, these prices may adjust upward in response to greater demand, moderating the multiplier effects.

Building Resilience through Social Safety Nets

Resilience has become a key focus of social safety nets and within the broader development arena. Resilience in this case is "the ability of countries, communities, and households to manage change by maintaining or transforming living standards in the face of shocks or stress" (DFID 2011, 6). Thanks to resilience, shocks or stresses—such as earthquakes, droughts, or violent conflict—can be confronted without compromising long-term prospects (Alfani et al. 2015). Resilience is linked to the concept of consumption smoothing, whereby individuals prefer a stable level of consumption despite variations in income and will therefore borrow or save to preserve continuity in consumption. The focus on resilience stems from the recognition that households in developing countries live in risky environments and that the risk is greatest among the poor (Hallegatte et al. 2016; Hill and Verwimp 2017). The emerging emphasis on resilience is also reflected in attempts to strengthen coordination between social safety nets and humanitarian interventions (Clarke and Dercon 2016; Slater, Bailey, and Harvey 2015; see chapters 3 and 5).

Resilience is analyzed through the lens of livelihood strengthening, improved coping strategies, and risk management. Outcomes include the ownership of productive assets for livelihood strengthening, decreases in informal wage work and child labor as indicators of less harmful coping strategies, and savings and private transfers for risk management. In terms of productive assets, because many studies are conducted in rural areas and because smallholder farming is the main livelihood, assets include those associated with agriculture. These outcomes are interconnected with equity and opportunity: the ability to save can improve the ability to send children to school, and more productive assets may lead to higher incomes and then greater consumption and less poverty. A challenge in the analysis of resilience revolves around the fact that impact evaluations are not usually devised to capture the direct responses of beneficiaries to shocks, given the unexpected time-varying nature of shocks and the lack of high-frequency longitudinal studies. Instead, this study focuses on measurable outcomes hypothesized to improve household resilience.

Encouraging evidence suggests that social safety net transfers can successfully boost investment in productive assets, especially livestock holdings. For most of the poor, livestock holdings, agricultural tools, and other household assets represent a store of value and a form of savings, besides their effect in strengthening livelihood activities.

One of the most striking results is the significant rise in livestock ownership, which indicates an average improvement of 34 percent across seven programs relative to baseline levels (figure 2.3). Across programs, four studies report significant impacts. Studies reporting on this outcome typically find investments in small livestock, such as chickens, ducks, and goats. Cattle ownership tends to show smaller increases if they are at all significant. The case of Malawi's SCTP is illustrative; limited cattle ownership is attributed to the large expense of purchasing cattle, the relative rarity of this activity among smallholders, and a perception among beneficiaries that

Figure 2.3 **A Range of Productive Assets Respond to Social Safety Net Transfers**

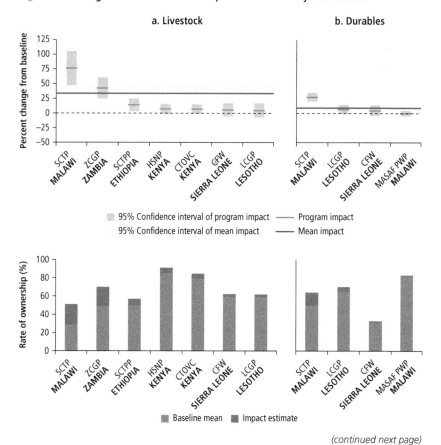

(continued next page)

Figure 2.3 **Continued**

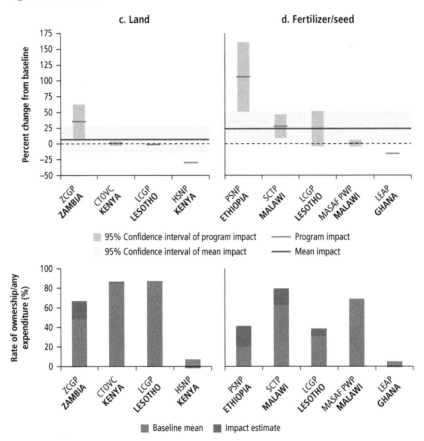

Source: World Bank meta-analysis.
Note: The mean value of the household transfer (in 2011 US$, purchasing power parity) is Malawi SCTP $21, Zambia ZCGP $27, Ethiopia SCTPP $60, Kenya HSNP $47, Kenya CTOVC $71, Sierra Leone CFW $83, Lesotho LCGP $34, Malawi MASAF PWP $44, Ethiopia PSNP $65, and Ghana LEAP $24.

investments in large livestock may compromise their program eligibility (Covarrubias, Davis, and Winters 2012). In Niger, recipients of cash transfers had lasting increases in livestock assets (Stoeffler, Mills, and Premand 2016). Expenditures on durables (tools and other equipment for farms and businesses) exhibited a smaller, but still significant, improvement: a 10 percent increase relative to the baseline. Durables include investments in agricultural tools, as in Ethiopia's Social Cash Transfer Pilot Program, Malawi's SCTP, and Zambia's Child Grant Program (Berhane et al. 2015; Boone et al. 2013; Seidenfeld, Handa, and Tembo 2013).

Resilience is partly captured through ownership of certain types of durable goods. Across programs, the definition of durables varies (see Ralston, Andrews, and Hsiao 2017 for details), but they tend to include expenditures for home improvements and sometimes productive tools for farming). We find modest impacts, although in the case of SCTP in Malawi, the definition is any durable good. There is additional evidence of social safety nets leading to increases in expenditures for home improvements specifically, such as on metal or plastic sheeting for roofs and walls in GiveDirectly in Kenya, the Lesotho Child Grants Program, and the CfW in Sierra Leone (Haushofer and Shapiro 2016; Pellerano et al. 2014; Rosas and Sabarwal 2016).

Two programs are associated with an expansion in the application of fertilizers or seeds (as measured by any expenditure on either), and only one program finds an increase in land ownership. Neither outcome is significantly impacted on average across the programs that report on them. Evidence for improved fertilizer and seed use comes from the PSNP in Ethiopia and the SCTP in Malawi, which may demonstrate a shift to higher-risk, higher-return agricultural practices. The Ethiopia findings are important for an understanding of mediating factors because this intervention was coupled with an initiative to support household agricultural productivity, namely, the Household Asset Building Program. Only the Zambia Child Grant Program reports a substantial positive impact on outcomes in land ownership: beneficiaries expanded the area of land they worked by 18 percent (34 percentage points relative to the baseline).

Another indicator of resilience is reduced reliance on child labor as a coping strategy (figure 2.4). Child labor can inhibit school attendance, thereby negatively affecting the future earnings potential of children. Overall, social safety net programs that report on this outcome find no average effect. However, some of the programs specifically targeted at children show a reduction, including the Burkina Faso Take-Home Rations Program among girls, the Kenya OVC program, and the Lesotho Child Grants Program. These programs are associated with strong communication strategies advocating for the rights and well-being of children, such as encouraging school attendance, which may help generate these results because, if children are in school, they also have less time to work. Results of programs in Latin America support these findings. Meta-analyses focusing on the impacts of conditional cash transfer programs in Brazil, Colombia, Mexico, Nicaragua, and Uruguay show promising results, particularly among children with the highest returns to work, such as young adolescent boys (Kabeer, Piza, and Taylor 2012).

Another possible sign of resilience is reduced reliance on wage work. Poor rural households often sell more than the optimal amount of labor off their farms to obtain an immediate income source. In Malawi, this type of work is known as *ganyu*, is generally low-wage and casual, and may lead to poverty traps (Devereux 1997). Along with significant reductions in such informal wage work associated with the SCTP in Malawi, wage work fell substantially among

Figure 2.4   Social Safety Nets May Reduce the Reliance on Child Labor

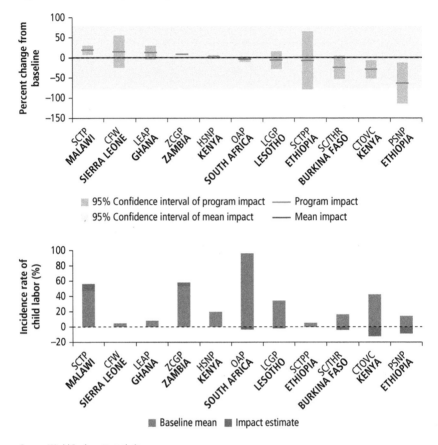

Source: World Bank meta-analysis.
Note: The mean value of the household transfer (in 2011 US$, purchasing power parity) is Sierra Leone CFW
$83. Ghana LEAP $24, Zambia ZCGP $27, Kenya HSNP $47, South Africa OAP $100, Lesotho LCGP $34,
Ethiopia SCTPP $60, Burkina Faso SC/THR $27, Kenya CTOVC $71, and Ethiopia PSNP $82.

beneficiaries of Ethiopia's Social Cash Transfer Pilot Program and the child
grant programs in Lesotho and Zambia.

Social safety net programs can also help improve the ability of households to
manage risk through, for example, increased savings. The average increase was 92
percent in the incidence of savings relative to the baseline (figure 2.5). Typically,
savings rates are low among populations targeted by social safety net programs
because these populations are struggling to cover day-to-day necessities rather
than saving to confront adversity. The studies included in the meta-analysis find,
for instance, that only 5 percent to 35 percent of beneficiaries were saving previous

to the programs, but, under the programs, are 4 percent to 20 percent more likely than comparable nonbeneficiary households to be saving. The value of savings rose significantly, by, for example, 9 percent in the CfW in Sierra Leone and 92 percent in Kenya's GiveDirectly (Haushofer and Shapiro 2016; Rosas and Sabarwal 2016). Furthermore, most economic models predict that means-tested social safety nets lead to lower precautionary savings if, for instance, beneficiaries expect that social safety nets will respond with higher transfers to unanticipated shocks, thereby reducing the need or even the incentive to self-insure (Aiyagari 1994; Hubbard, Skinner, and Zeldes 1995). However, in the cash transfer pilot implemented by the Tanzania Social Action Fund, the poorest households were most likely to begin saving under the program, although these new savings were quickly exhausted during a subsequent drought. This may be taken as evidence that social safety nets

Figure 2.5 The Impact of Social Safety Nets on Savings and Private Transfers

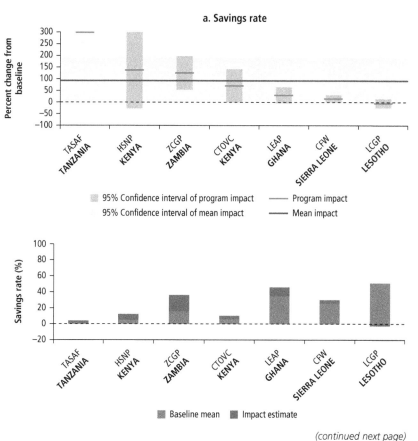

(continued next page)

Figure 2.5 Continued

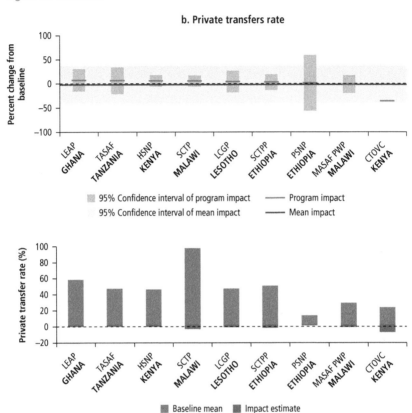

Source: World Bank meta-analysis.
Note: The mean value of the household transfer (in 2011 US$, purchasing power parity) is Tanzania TASAF $48, Kenya HSNP $47, Zambia ZCGP $27, Kenya CTOVC $71, Ghana LEAP $24, Sierra Leone CFW $83, Lesotho LCGP $34, Malawi SCTP $21, Ethiopia SCTP $60, Ethiopia PSNP $65, and Malawi MASAF PWP $44.

are not perceived by individuals as sufficient to reduce exposure to income uncertainty, but rather, through consistent social safety net support, beneficiaries are more able to build up their own precautionary savings.

The crowding out of remittances to households (that is, private transfers from family and friends) is very modest and mostly not statistically significant (see figure 2.5). Moreover, evaluations show that households are using program transfers to reduce borrowing and indebtedness (not measured in the meta-analysis). This is the case of LEAP in Ghana and the Malawi SCTP, in which beneficiaries report less need to make purchases on credit because of the transfers (CPC 2016; Handa et al. 2013). The evidence on credit access is less clear: evaluations reflect on the increased creditworthiness of households receiving transfers in, for instance, Ghana LEAP and Kenya HSNP, but there is little evidence that more credit has been forthcoming (Handa et al. 2013; Merttens et al. 2013). In the Ghana LEAP and the Zambia Child Grant Program, the social safety nets help beneficiaries realign social networks and, in some cases, improve the bargaining power of women (Handa et al. 2013; Seidenfeld, Handa, and Tembo 2013).

Overall, the policy implication is that social safety nets may have a major impact in boosting savings for improved risk management, but they are not sufficient for households to buffer completely against shocks independently. Nonetheless, social safety net programs are not significantly crowding out private transfers and are not likely to impact adversely or substitute for other risk management strategies.

Increasing Opportunities through Social Safety Nets

Human capital development and productive inclusion are two important dimensions of the effort to foster opportunity. The dimension of human capital development involves the recognition that social safety nets have long been viewed as a tool for promoting investments in education and health care among children. Well-established conditional cash transfer programs in Latin America, such as Bolsa Família in Brazil and Prospera in Mexico, have the core objective of enabling poor families in rural and urban communities to invest in the human capital of their children by improving outcomes in education, health, and nutrition (Fiszbein and Schady 2009). Compelling evidence documents the positive impacts of these programs, including their longer-term effects, which vary from positive to more mixed (Baez and Camacho 2011; Behrman, Parker, and Todd 2011; Gertler, Martinez, and Rubio-Codina 2012). The dimension of productive inclusion revolves around the effectiveness of social safety nets in promoting a sustained exit out of poverty. Such an exit may be fostered by engaging households in more productive activities that lead to higher income trajectories. The previous section touched on this by considering the degree to which social safety nets encourage investments in productive assets. This section investigates whether social safety net programs have led to higher incomes and earning opportunities among beneficiaries.

Social Safety Nets Are Investments in Education
The literature focuses extensively on the impacts of cash transfer programs on education, though largely outside Africa. Evidence on 19 conditional cash transfer programs in 15 developing countries, including one in Africa (Malawi), finds significant impacts on primary-school enrollment and

attendance (Saavedra and Garcia 2012). The increase in enrollment was 5.5 percentage points relative to the mean baseline of 84.0 percent, and the increase in attendance was 2.5 percentage points relative to a baseline of 80.0 percent. Conditional and unconditional cash transfer programs have been shown to improve school enrollment and attendance across 25 countries (five of which are in Africa) (Baird et al. 2013). There is no statistical difference in the impact on enrollment and attendance between conditional and unconditional cash transfer programs. But programs in which the conditionality is explicitly monitored and in which the associated penalties are enforced show substantially larger effects, about a 35 percent improvement in the odds of enrollment relative to programs without any schooling conditions. A review of the impacts on attendance and cognition of 27 cash transfer programs in 20 countries, half of which are in Africa, finds an impact on attendance, but a less clear-cut pattern in learning outcomes (Bastagli et al. 2016). The evidence base is not sufficient to make any generalizations on the impacts of cash transfers on ultimate outcomes such as learning (as measured by test scores) or cognitive development. The policy implications of this work highlight the need to complement cash transfer delivery with a variety of other interventions, such as nutritional support, educational outreach, and supply-side grants.

The impacts in Africa are consistent with the international literature, showing promising potential to realize improvements in short-term outcomes such as attendance and enrollment. Of the 27 programs covered in the meta-analysis, 13 reported on school enrollment rates and 15 reported on school attendance rates. Although the mean effect is not statistically significant (6 percent rise in attendance and 7 percent improvement in enrollment), the impact of programs specifically targeting children as beneficiaries is significant (see the second cluster of results in figure 2.6, which presents the results according to the population targeted by the programs). One of the most striking enrollment results includes Burkina Faso's Nahouri Cash Transfers Pilot Project, which increased enrollment from 49 percent to 57 percent and attendance from 46 percent to 56 percent, which represent 17 percent and 22 percent increases, respectively, relative to the baseline (Akresh, de Walque, and Kazianga 2013).

Improvements in enrollment and school attendance are consistent with other positive impacts detected on educational expenditures on shoes, uniforms, and blankets, the lack of which represent key barriers to enrollment and attendance, especially in secondary school. Education-related expenditures are reported to increase by 16 percent in the Malawi SCTP, 23 percent in Kenya GiveDirectly, and 16 percent in the Lesotho Child Grants Program (CPC 2016; Haushofer and Shapiro 2016; Pellerano et al. 2014). Similarly, in Kenya's Child Sponsorship Program, giving out uniforms reduced school absenteeism by 6.4 percentage points (43.0 percent) from a base of 15.0 percent (Evans, Kremer, and Ngatia 2009). It is notable that programs targeting poor and vulnerable households more generally appear to be accompanied by greater enrollment rather than attendance outcomes in, for example, the Ghana LEAP, the Malawi SCTP, and the Tanzania TASAF (CPC 2016; Evans et al. 2014; Handa et al. 2013). This may also be tied to the importance of messaging and communications among beneficiaries on the intended goal of a transfer.

Figure 2.6 **School Attendance Is Boosted by Social Safety Nets**

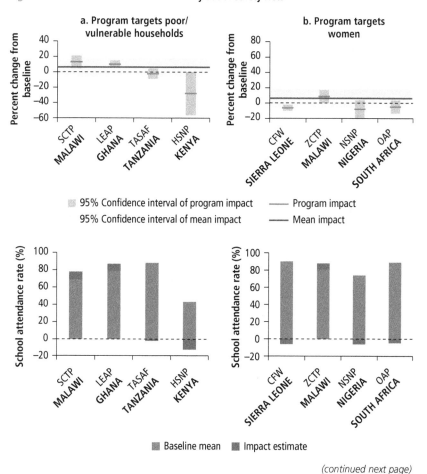

(continued next page)

Figure 2.6 Continued

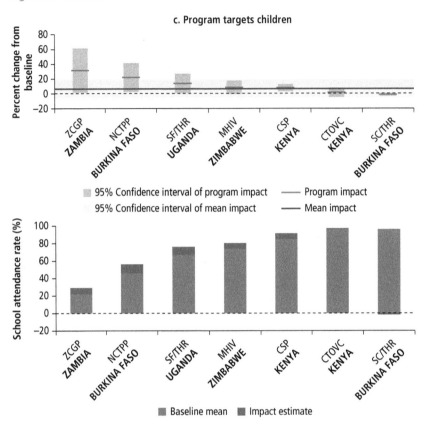

Source: World Bank meta-analysis.
Note: The mean value of the household transfer (in 2011 US$ purchasing power parity) is Malawi SCTP $21, Ghana LEAP $24, Tanzania TASAF $48, Kenya HSNP $47, Zambia ZCGP $27, Burkina Faso NCTPP $14, Uganda SF/THR $65, Zimbabwe MHIV $30, Kenya CSP $37, Kenya CTOVC $71, Burkina Faso SC/THR $27, Sierra Leone CFW $83, Malawi ZCTP $25, Niger NSNP $44, and South Africa OAP $100.

A closer look at individual evaluations indicates that gains in education are especially pronounced in upper-primary and secondary school, where dropout rates rise. Adolescents ages 15–19 were 15 percent more likely to complete higher education in Tanzania, and enrollment rates among children ages 13–17 were 10 percent higher in the Lesotho Child Grants Program (Evans et al. 2014; Pellerano et al. 2014). Many evaluations reporting no impacts among younger children show strong outcomes among older children. For instance, secondary-school enrollment increased by 6 percent to 7 percent in the Kenya HSNP and the OVC program (Ward et al. 2010).

In South Africa, adolescents in households currently receiving the Child Support Grant among younger children in the household were absent from school 2.2 fewer days than adolescents in households receiving no grants (DSD, SASSA, and UNICEF 2012). Nonetheless, poor quality and availability of schools and high financial barriers are considerable constraints on the progression through secondary school, an issue noted even in countries that have achieved positive impacts, such as the Lesotho Child Grants Program (DSD, SASSA, and UNICEF 2012).

Two widely cited evaluations look at the specific role of school feeding by comparing different modalities of at-school meals versus take-home rations, but do not find consistent effects. In the two main interventions of food for education programs in Uganda, neither intervention had a significant impact on primary enrollments, but both programs showed impacts on attendance and on upper-primary school (grades 6 and 7). The take-home rations intervention showed substantially larger impacts than the in-school feeding intervention (Alderman, Gilligan, and Lehrer 2008). The latter, however, exhibited an impact in cognitive gains among preschool children. In Burkina Faso, the school canteens and take-home rations interventions both raised enrollments among girls by 5 percent, but had variable impacts on attendance depending on the labor constraints within families (Kazianga, de Walque, and Alderman 2009). Absenteeism decreased only among families with a relatively large child labor supply. In addition, take-home rations enhanced anthropometric measures among the younger siblings of beneficiaries (those ages 1–5). Beyond these evaluations, the literature on the impacts of in-kind transfers on education in Africa is thin (for a discussion, including the mixed global evidence see Gentilini 2014).

Globally and within Africa, the evidence suggests that conditions can strengthen the educational impacts of social safety net programs, but that unconditional programs are also effective at improving school attendance and enrollment. Programs in which the conditionality is explicitly monitored and enforced have larger impacts than programs without any schooling conditions, but programs that do not monitor and enforce conditionality perform comparably with those with no conditions (Baird et al. 2013). Within the meta-analysis, 4 programs have conditions associated with schooling; 8 have no conditions; and 3 have both conditional and unconditional components.[5] Conditions associated with schooling seem to result in larger impacts. Of the programs with conditions on schooling, 5 of 7 report significant, impacts on attendance, and 3 of 6 report significant impacts on enrollment. Of the programs without schooling conditions, 7 of 11 report significant impacts on attendance, and 3 of 9 report significant impacts on enrollment. In the Malawi Zomba Cash Transfer Program, the strongly enforced conditional cash transfer arm achieved a large gain in enrollment and a modest, yet significant, advantage in learning. The Burkina Faso Nahouri Cash Transfers Pilot Project found that conditional cash transfers had a greater impact than unconditional cash transfers in targeting marginal children not already enrolled in school or less likely to enroll and a greater impact on attendance among all children (Akresh, de Walque, and Kazianga 2013; Baird, McIntosh, and Özler 2011). Meanwhile, Zimbabwe's Manicaland HIV/STD Prevention Program found similar positive significant impacts on school attendance associated with both unconditional and conditional cash transfers.

However, even if they might yield larger impacts, conditions may not always be appropriate in programs in Africa, particularly if access to education is limited or if monitoring and enforcement would be inefficiently expensive. In these situations, programs with implicit conditionality may be more suitable (Pellerano et al. 2014; Schüring 2010). There is evidence that perceptions of conditions and encouraging service use and certain behaviors can influence program outcomes (Benhassine et al. 2013; Schady and Araujo 2006; for more mixed results from behavior change in Nigeria, see Premand, Barry, and Smitz 2016 and Barry, Maidoka, and Premand 2017). Evidence from the programs covered in this review appear to strongly support this conclusion. Of 17 programs covered in the meta-analysis, 3 have such implicit (unmonitored/unenforced) conditions related to child schooling that are associated with forceful messaging and social marketing: Lesotho's Child Grants Program, Malawi's SCTP, and Zambia's Child Grant Program. These programs increased enrollment or attendance. Unlike the programs with enforced conditions, each of these programs has advanced toward cash transfers that have been brought to scale nationwide.

Evidence of Health Impacts of Social Safety Nets Is Limited

The evidence on health outcomes in Africa is more limited. The meta-analysis found nine studies that reported on health care expenditures, but the mean impact on monthly spending was not significant (CPC 2016; Evans et al. 2014; Haushofer and Shapiro 2016; Merttens et al. 2013; Pellerano et al. 2014; Premand and del Ninno 2016; Rosas and Sabarwal 2016; Seidenfeld, Handa, and Tembo 2013; Ward et al. 2010). Studies finding positive impacts include those examining Kenya's HSNP and Zambia's Child Grant Program. In Kenya's HSNP, households spent more on health per capita without negative impacts on food consumption or asset retention. In Zambia, approximately 5 percent of transfers were related to health and hygiene, and there is some evidence of impact on young children through improved feeding and reductions in wasting. This evidence suggests that transfers have the potential to improve health outcomes, consistent with the impacts on food security and dietary diversity. However, the meta-analysis shows that the results so far in health expenditures are not statistically significant, and, where positive impacts are obtained, determining why is difficult.

The impact of social safety nets on early childhood development is an emerging area of focus in programs and the accompanying evaluations. The results to date have been mixed, however. In Kenya's HSNP and OVC programs, there is little evidence on child nutritional status, and, in both cases, the outcomes are presented with considerable caution. Anthropometric status reflects multiple complex influences and take time to appear, while other outcomes occur more quickly. The quality of the anthropometric data gathered—which are widely acknowledged to be challenging, time-varying external factors—and the small sample sizes mean that significant effects are difficult to detect (Merttens et al. 2013). Several impact evaluations have not involved the collection of anthropometric information, for example, Tanzania's TASAF (Pellerano et al. 2014).

Despite the challenges and difficulties, recent evaluations and the broader literature show some promising early childhood outcomes. The potential to realize improved childhood outcomes is clear in studies of cash transfer programs in Latin America. Evidence on Nicaragua's Red de Protección Social and Atención a Crisis programs—a conditional cash transfer program—shows improved nutrition and health outcomes for young children (Barham, Macours, and Maluccio 2013; Macours, Schady, and Vakis 2012). While the evidence in Africa is nascent on this theme, some countries point to potential impacts. A long-term evaluation of South Africa's Child Support Grant Program shows that the grant raises the likelihood that the growth of children in recipient households will be monitored and that height-for-age scores will improve (DSD, SASSA, and UNICEF 2012). A recent impact evaluation of the Niger Safety Net Project shows that accompanying measures can lead to changes in nutrition practices related to exclusive breastfeeding and complementary feeding, which contribute to improve food security among children (Premand and del Ninno 2016).

Social Safety Nets Foster Productive Inclusion

Focusing on social safety nets and productive inclusion addresses the critical issue of graduating beneficiaries from poverty. Specifically, it responds to the debate about whether these programs result in investments in productive activities and whether they create work disincentives among beneficiaries. Several influential studies have recently begun to key on the debate. Thus, Blattman, Fiala, and Martinez (2013) conclude that, in Uganda, cash grants targeted on groups of youth can lead to enhanced employment opportunities. Banerjee et al. (2015) find that a multifaceted approach aimed at raising the incomes of the poor can achieve sustainable outcomes cost effectively. Such an approach, adopted in several countries, provides a productive asset grant (often livestock), training and support, life skills coaching, temporary cash support for consumption, and, typically, access to savings accounts and health information or services, at a total PPP equivalent cost of $437 to $1,228 per household. A similar program in rural Bangladesh has had large and permanent impacts on the occupational choices and earnings of beneficiaries (Bandiera et al. 2013).

Among 10 studies in the meta-analysis that reported on whether the household was operating a nonfarm business (almost always small-scale or microenterprise business activities), six find significant positive impacts (figure 2.7): Ethiopia's PSNP (during the months when no public works activities were carried out), Kenya's HSNP and OVC programs (for woman-headed households), Malawi's SCTP, Sierra Leone's CfW program, and Zambia's Child Grant

Figure 2.7 Income Opportunities May Respond to Social Safety Nets

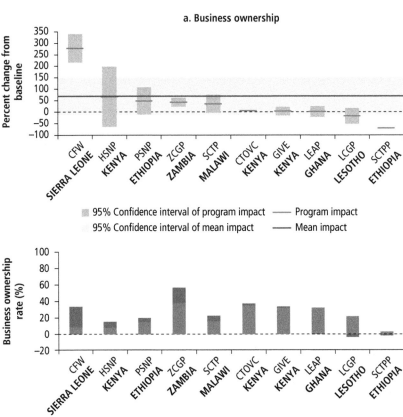

(continued next page)

Figure 2.7 Continued

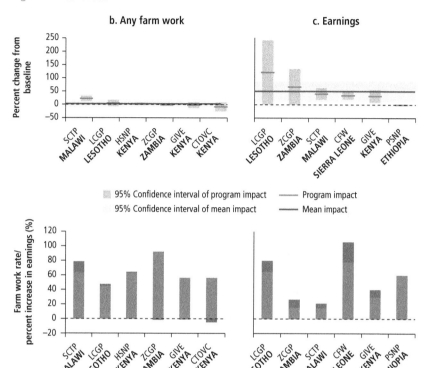

Source: World Bank meta-analysis.
Note: "Business" refers to the household operating a nonfarm business (almost always small-scale or microenterprise business activities). Specific definitions of "Earnings" vary across studies. The mean value of the household transfer (in 2011 US$ purchasing power parity) is Sierra Leone CFW $83, Kenya HSNP $47, Ethiopia PSNP $65, Zambia ZCGP $27, Malawi SCTP $21, Kenya CTOVC $71, Kenya GIVE $79, Ghana LEAP $24, Lesotho LCGP $34, and Ethiopia SCTPP $60.

Program (further studied by Asfaw et al. 2014; CPC 2016; Gilligan et al. 2009; Merttens et al. 2013; Rosas and Sabarwal 2016; and Seidenfeld, Handa, and Tembo 2013).

Expanding income opportunities compliments resilience. Many of the programs associated with more business activities are also associated with household investments in productive assets, as shown in figure 2.3. In some instances, the increase in incidence of having a household business is accompanied by a decrease in off-farm wage work. The Zambia Child Grant Program reduced the share of households in which an adult member is engaged in wage labor by 9 percentage points, an impact that is stronger among working-age women, while the share of beneficiary households operating an enterprise increased by 17 percentage points (Seidenfeld, Handa, and Tembo 2013). Another resilience-related finding is that, under the Old-Age Pension scheme in South Africa, pension-recipient households were more likely to include prime-age adult members who had migrated from the household and were working (Ardington, Case, and Hosegood 2009). Social safety nets have been shown in some programs to facilitate out-migration, in the Sierra Leone CfW and in the Concern International program in the Democratic Republic of Congo, that may generate important new sources of income for households in the form of remittances (Aker 2013; Rosas and Sabarwal 2016).

Turing to work on household farms, these programs generally do not increase or decrease the likelihood of working on the household farm (figure 2.7b). The one exception is the SCTP in Malawi, which raised the probability of working on the farm. This is not to say that these programs do not increase the intensity of farming, as shown by the increase in inputs resulting from some programs (in figure 2.3). These programs do not create dependency in terms of beneficiaries stopping their work activities once they get social safety net benefits.

Finally, the meta-analysis examines the impact of these programs on household earnings, with the caveat that the specific definition of earnings (in terms of what it covers) varies across studies (see details in Ralston, Andrews, and Hsiao 2017). Household income earnings increase as a result of program participation. This reflects the combination of an increase in households having a business as well as greater farm productivity or participation. Among the six studies with an earnings outcome, the meta-analysis finds a significant positive impact, with a 51 percent rise in monthly earnings. The Lesotho Child Grants Program found higher earnings consistent with increased use of purchased seeds and fertilizers reported earlier. Increases in agricultural harvest yields and the value of sales were found in the Ethiopia Social Cash Transfer Pilot Program, the Malawi SCTP, and the Zambia Child Grant Program (Berhane et al. 2015; CPC 2016; Seidenfeld, Handa, and Tembo 2013).

Bringing Social Safety Nets to Scale

At the time of their evaluation, most of the programs captured in the review were operating at a scale that is too small to cover all poor households in a population. A logical next question is therefore focused on the impacts that might be realized if the programs were brought to scale to cover all poor households. From a general equilibrium perspective, bringing programs to scale would not only reduce poverty but might also produce economy-wide impacts (box 2.2).

BOX 2.2

Measuring Spillover and Feedback Effects: The Ghana Case Study

If they are brought to scale, social safety nets have the potential to affect the overall macroeconomy. The relevant spillover effects have been explored through a computable general equilibrium model. Taking Ghana as a case study, the impact of expanding LEAP to cover all extremely poor households in the country (as defined by the national extreme poverty line)—about 400,000 rural and 43,000 urban households— is modeled with the generous assumption of perfect targeting.[a] The LEAP transfers vary by household size and represent 12 percent of the extreme poverty line or 36 percent of mean consumption among the extremely poor.[b] Administrative costs are assumed to be add 25 percent to transfer costs. The total cost of the increase is thus 0.6 percent of the 2013 gross domestic product. The model examines outcomes when the program is funded through either a foreign aid grant or domestic tax revenues.

Expanding at current transfer values would reduce the extreme poverty rate in Ghana from 8.2 percent to an estimated 4.2 percent. Agriculture and manufacturing would experience a rise in demand for domestically produced staples and finished products as a result of the LEAP being brought to scale. This would lead to modest output increases in these sectors. This is also likely to generate higher incomes among beneficiaries and other rural households dependent on agriculture, which is labor intensive and is a substantial employer, especially among the poorest households. However, given that the program is small relative to the size of the economy, the percent changes in total consumption or output would be small from the perspective of the national economy. Likewise, the employment expansion would be small.

The source of program financing—grant aid (externally financed) or taxes—has a notable effect on program impacts, including on income distribution and the exchange rate. The source of funding has some effect on the distributional impacts of the program. If the program is externally financed, nonbeneficiary households would be expected to experience modest consumption gains, on the order of 0.1 percent to 0.2 percent, through the spillover effects of the greater demand and the positive impact of real exchange rate appreciation. In the internally financed program simulations, there are modest consumption losses for nonbeneficiaries, on the order of 0.2 percent to 1.0 percent, reflecting the net redistribution effect of tax-funded programs that, in this context, outweighs any consumption spillover effects. The wealthiest households in the economy would experience the largest consumption losses. In total, this leads to about a 0.8 percent rise in private consumption in the externally financed scenario and a 0.1 percent decline in the internally financed scenario. However, there are other implications to consider in comparing these two financing scenarios. For example, if the program is financed through foreign aid, there would be an influx of foreign currency into the country, which would lead to real exchange rate appreciation, and this would have a negative impact on exports, namely, the cocoa and mining sectors, which would experience respective projected output declines of 1.5 percent and

(continued next page)

Box 2.2 (continued)

0.4 percent, with labor moving to other, expanding sectors and the combination of less exports and more imports leading to higher consumption at home. These effects would not arise in the tax financing scenario.

Additional aggregate output and consumption gains are possible if the social safety net programs are coupled with complementary sectorwide investment projects. Under the complementary scenarios, aggregate output would expand more, reaching around 0.1 percent of gross domestic product.

Source: Levy and Lofgren 2017; annex 2C.
a. This leads to an overestimation of the poverty reduction impact because perfect targeting has not been achieved.
b. The LEAP transfer is approximately twice the transfer explored in the partial equilibrium simulations.

The partial equilibrium impacts of expanding programs are explored through simulations for three countries—Ghana, Liberia, and Niger—based on data available from household surveys, alongside the meta-analysis results (see annex 2C). These countries offer contrasting starting points in terms of social safety net coverage and show diversity in size, the sources of fragility, livelihood vulnerability, sectoral composition, and level of economic development.[6] To ensure comparability, the simulations have been conducted based on assumed monthly transfers to households of $50 (at 2011 PPP prices), equivalent to the median amount transferred in programs included in the meta-analysis. Recognizing that perfect targeting may not be achieved, the simulations assume perfect targeting, imperfect targeting (60 percent inclusion accuracy), and no targeting, whereby all households have an equal chance of being covered regardless of their poverty level.

Even relatively modest transfers would have a sizable impact on consumption. If transfers were perfectly targeted, consumption among the extremely poor would increase in the range of 12 percent to 17 percent. Under imperfect targeting, the consumption gains would be 7 percent to 10 percent. With no targeting, the gains would be between 0.0 percent and 2.7 percent.

These consumption gains would generate a decline in extreme poverty rates by as much as 40 percent (figure 2.8). The most substantial impacts on the extreme poverty rate would be realized with perfect targeting: from 8.2 percent to 6.7 percent in Ghana, from 18.2 to 11.6 percent in Liberia, and from 17.0 percent to 12.3 percent in Niger. The extreme poverty gap—the mean relative distance of extremely poor households to the extreme poverty line—would fall from 2.2 percent to 1.7 percent in Ghana, from 4.2 percent to

Figure 2.8 **Bringing Programs to Scale May Reduce Poverty**

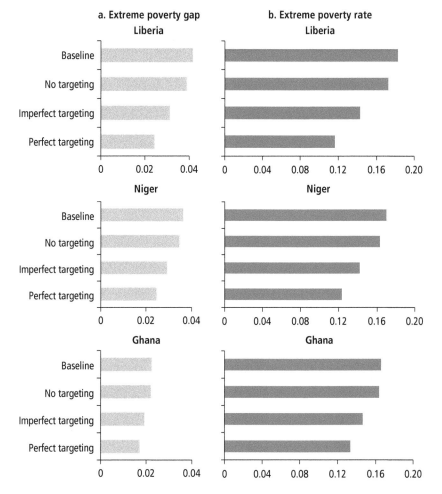

Source: Calculations drawing on household surveys in Ghana 2012/13, Liberia 2014, and Niger 2014.
Note: Shows estimated impact of $50 transfer per month (in 2011 purchasing poverty parity terms).

2.4 percent in Liberia, and from 3.6 percent to 2.5 percent in Niger, highlighting the extent of the reduction in extreme poverty achieved through well-designed, successfully implemented social safety nets. With imperfect targeting, the declines in extreme poverty would be less by about a third. These reductions in poverty represent one way to characterize the gains to society from expanding social safety nets, but other approaches may also be considered (box 2.3).

BOX 2.3

How Does Society Gain When a Poor Household Gains?

An underlying premise of studies on the impact of the provision of support to poor households is that society also gains if poor households experience welfare gains. This is consistent with the assignment of greater weight to the incomes of the poor over the incomes of the wealthy, which is an altruistic approach as well as a utilitarian approach: the notion that the value of an extra dollar of income is relatively higher for a poor household than for a wealthy household (Chenery et al. 1974). A third approach models the trade-off between more or fewer social safety nets for the poor based on assumptions about the extent to which people have an aversion to inequality (Eden 2017). This aversion may arise because people worry about the downside risk of their own future income status—they want to know a program exists in the event they become poor themselves—or because they value less inequality for other personal reasons. Incorporating an inequality risk aversion approach is another way to assess the social welfare gains of social safety nets. It incorporates the administrative costs and other economic costs of programs, such as the distortionary effects of taxation (including labor-supply effects) if programs are financed through additional taxation.

Under even highly conservative assumptions, there are social welfare gains from social safety nets that are financed through a uniform increase in taxes on labor incomes (Eden 2017). A greater degree of targeting enhances the estimates of this gain in social welfare. This research is extended to compare these gains with the gains one might obtain through alternative government spending (such as building a road). Here, the evidence is more mixed and sensitive to the assumed parameter values. The optimality of diverting funds from government investment projects to redistributive programs such as social safety nets depends on the rate of return to other government investments, the administrative cost of transfers, the elasticity of labor supply to taxation, and the social aversion to inequality.

Agriculture is prevalent in the livelihoods of the extremely poor, and many of the poor already own agricultural assets. Assuming effective targeting, simulations find that programs could expand the ownership of mid- and large-size quantities of livestock among the extremely poor to 51 percent–62 percent in Ghana and to 22 percent–28 percent in Liberia (table 2.1). Similarly, poultry ownership, often the first type of livestock acquired by the extremely poor, would increase to 57 percent–69 percent in Ghana and to 53 percent–67 percent in Liberia. Likewise, well-targeted programs may raise land ownership to 89 percent–92 percent in Ghana and to 100 percent in Niger.

Although social safety net programs are important in helping younger children living in extremely poor households catch up in schooling, the initial

Table 2.1 **Bringing Social Safety Nets to Scale Can Have Large Impacts on Well-Being**
Percent

Simulated outcome measures	Liberia	Niger	Ghana
Extreme poverty rate	8.2–18.1	9.0–16.8	5.7–8.2
Incidence of livestock ownership among the extremely poor	20.4–28.1	—	—
Incidence of land ownership among the extremely poor	—	98.1–100.0	85.7–92.3
School enrollment rate, 5- to 11-year-olds	97.1–99.0	95.9–96.2	—
School enrollment rate, 12- to 18-year-olds	22.3–22.8	18.3–18.7	—

Source: Calculations drawing on household surveys in Ghana 2012/13, Liberia 2014, and Niger 2014.
Note: Estimates for the impacts of well-targeted, imperfectly targeted, and nontargeted programs. — = not available.

enrollment rates in primary education are already high. In Liberia and Niger, enrollment rates among 5- to 11-year-olds at the baseline stood at 96.2 percent and 95.5 percent, respectively. Simulations suggest that enrollment rates may rise to between 97.1 percent and 99.0 percent and to between 95.9 percent and 96.2 percent in Liberia and Niger, respectively. Among older children (12- to 18-year-olds), simulations suggest similar patterns, though at a much lower magnitude, given the low baseline enrollment rates (22.2 percent in Liberia and 18.2 percent in Niger), particularly among children living in extreme poverty (8.5 percent in Liberia and 16.8 percent in Niger). Even if social safety net programs achieve sustained and accumulated impacts on education among 12- to 18-year-olds, it would be many years before substantial improvements in enrollment rates would appear, given the low starting points; and such improvements would be conditional on significant enhancements on the supply side.

Annex 2A: Programs Included in the Meta-analysis

Table 2A.1 Evaluation Studies Included in the Meta-analysis

Country	Program	Reference	Program end year	Target group	Benefit type	Evaluation method	Exposure, years
Burkina Faso	School Canteens and Take-Home Rations Program	Kazianga, de Walque, and Alderman 2009	2007	Poor rural households with children ages 7–15	Food	E	1
Burkina Faso	Nahouri Cash Transfers Pilot Project	Akresh, de Walque, and Kazianga 2012	2010	Poor rural households with children ages < 16	Cash	E	2
Burkina Faso	School Canteens and Take-Home Rations Program	Kazianga, de Walque, and Alderman 2014	2007	Poor rural households with children ages 7–15	Food	E	1
Burkina Faso	Nahouri Cash Transfers Pilot Project	Akresh, de Walque, and Kazianga 2013	2010	Poor rural households with children ages 7–15	Cash	E	2
Ethiopia	Productive Safety Net Program	Gilligan, Hoddinott, and Taffesse 2008	Ongoing	Able-bodied individuals, labor-constrained households	Cash, food, training	QE	1
Ethiopia	Productive Safety Net Program	Andersson, Mekonnen, and Stage 2011	Ongoing	Able-bodied individuals, labor-constrained households	Cash, food, training	QE	2.5
Ethiopia	Productive Safety Net Program	Gilligan et al. 2009	Ongoing	Able-bodied individuals, labor-constrained households	Cash, food, training	QE	2
Ethiopia	Productive Safety Net Program	Sabates-Wheeler and Devereux 2010	Ongoing	Able-bodied individuals, labor-constrained households	Cash, food, training	QE	2
Ethiopia	Productive Safety Net Program	Berhane et al. 2011	Ongoing	Able-bodied individuals, labor-constrained households	Cash, food, training	QE	4
Ethiopia	Productive Safety Net Program	Rodrigo 2012	Ongoing	Able-bodied individuals, labor-constrained households	Cash, food, training	QE	5
Ethiopia	Productive Safety Net Program	Hoddinott et al. 2012	Ongoing	Able-bodied individuals, labor-constrained households	Cash, food, training	QE	5
Ethiopia	Productive Safety Net Program	Weldegebriel and Prowse 2013	Ongoing	Able-bodied individuals, labor-constrained households	Cash, food, training	QE	Not reported

(continued next page)

Table 2A.1 Continued

Country	Program	Reference	Program end year	Target group	Benefit type	Evaluation method	Exposure, years
Ethiopia	Social Cash Transfer Pilot Program	Kagin et al. 2014	2014	Able-bodied individuals, labor-constrained households	Cash	QE	2
Ethiopia	Social Cash Transfer Pilot Program	Berhane et al. 2015	2014	Able-bodied individuals, labor-constrained households	Cash	QE	2
Ghana	Livelihood Empowerment against Poverty Program	Handa et al. 2013	Ongoing	Poverty and demographic status	Cash	QE	2.5
Ghana	Livelihood Empowerment against Poverty Program	Thome et al. 2014b	Ongoing	Poverty and demographic status	Cash	QE	2.5
Kenya	Child Sponsorship Program	Evans, Kremer, and Ngatia 2009	Ongoing	Schoolchildren ages 5–14	In kind	E	2.5
Kenya	Cash Transfer for Orphans and Vulnerable Children	Ward et al. 2010	Ongoing	Ultrapoor rural households with orphans and vulnerable children ages 0–17	Cash	E	2
Kenya	Cash Transfer for Orphans and Vulnerable Children	Taylor et al. 2013	Ongoing	Ultrapoor labor-constrained households with children	Cash	QE	2
Kenya	Hunger Social Safety Net Program	Merttens et al. 2013	Ongoing	Income poor	Cash	E	2
Kenya	GiveDirectly	Haushofer and Shapiro 2016	Ongoing	Poor households	Cash	E	1
Kenya	Cash Transfer for Orphans and Vulnerable Children	Asfaw et al. 2014	Ongoing	Ultrapoor rural households with orphans and vulnerable children ages 0–17	Cash	E	4
Kenya, Malawi	Cash Transfer for Orphans and Vulnerable Children, Social Cash Transfer Program	Zezza, de la Brière, and Davis 2010	Ongoing	Orphans, ultrapoor	Cash	QE	KEN: 2, MWI: 1

(continued next page)

Table 2A.1 Continued

Country	Program	Reference	Program end year	Target group	Benefit type	Evaluation method	Exposure, years
Lesotho	Lesotho Child Grants Program	Pellerano et al. 2014	Ongoing	Poorest households with child	Cash	E	2
Lesotho	Lesotho Child Grants Program	Taylor, Thome, and Filipski 2014	Ongoing	Poorest households with child	Cash	QE	—
Lesotho	Lesotho Child Grants Program	Daidone et al. 2014	Ongoing	Poorest households with child	Cash	E	2
Malawi	Zomba Cash Transfer Program	Baird et al. 2013	2009	Poorest households with one child	Cash	E	2
Malawi	Zomba Cash Transfer Program	Baird et al. 2012	2009	Women who have never married, ages 13–22 and in school at baseline	Cash	E	1.5
Malawi	Social Cash Transfer Program	Covarrubias, Davis, and Winters 2012	Ongoing	Ultrapoor labor-constrained households	Cash	E	1
Malawi	Social Cash Transfer Program	Boone et al. 2013	Ongoing	Ultrapoor labor-constrained households	Cash	E	1
Malawi	Malawi Social Action Fund public works program	Beegle, Galasso, and Goldberg 2015	Ongoing	Able-bodied poor	Cash	E	0.13
Malawi	Zomba Cash Transfer Program	Baird et al. 2015	2009	Women who have never married, ages 13–22 and in school at baseline	Cash	E	4
Malawi	Social Cash Transfer Program	CPC 2015	Ongoing	Ultrapoor labor-constrained households	Cash	E	1
Malawi	Zomba Cash Transfer Program	Baird, McIntosh, and Özler 2009	2009	Women who have never married, ages 13–22 and in school at baseline	Cash	E	1

(continued next page)

Table 2A.1 Continued

Country	Program	Reference	Program end year	Target group	Benefit type	Evaluation method	Exposure, years
Malawi	Zomba Cash Transfer Program	Baird, McIntosh, and Özler 2009	2009	Women who have never married, ages 13–22 and in school at baseline	Cash	E	1
Malawi	Zomba Cash Transfer Program	Baird, McIntosh, and Özler 2011	2009	Women who have never married, ages 13–22 and in school at baseline	Cash	E	2
Niger	Niger Social Safety Net Project	Premand and del Ninno 2016	Ongoing	Extremely poor women in chronically poor households	Cash	E	3
Sierra Leone	Cash for Work Program	Rosas and Sabarwal 2016	2015	Young people ages 15–35 in poor communities	Cash	E	0.33
South Africa	Old-Age Pension	Hamoudi and Thomas 2005	Ongoing	Elderly people	Cash	QE	Not discussed
South Africa	Old-Age Pension	Edmonds 2006	Ongoing	Elderly people	Cash	QE	1
South Africa	Child Support Grant Program	Agüero, Carter, and Woolard 2007	Ongoing	Women with children	Cash	QE	1.2
South Africa	Old-Age Pension	Ardington, Case, and Hosegood 2009	Ongoing	Elderly people	Cash	QE	2.5
South Africa	Chile Support Grant Program	DSD, SASSA, and UNICEF 2012	Ongoing	Women with children	Cash	QE	?
Tanzania	RESPECT	Packel et al. 2012	2010	Demographic, 18–30 years	Cash; health services	E	1
Tanzania	RESPECT	Akresh, de Walque, and Kazianga 2012	2010	Demographic, 18–30 years	Cash; health services	E	1
Tanzania	Pilot cash transfer program implemented by the Tanzania Social Action Fund	Evans et al. 2014	2012	Poor vulnerable households	Cash	E	2.7
Uganda	School Feeding Program and Take-Home Rations Program	Alderman, Gilligan, and Lehrer 2008	2007	Children ages 6–17 enrolled in primary school	Food	E	0.8

(continued next page)

Table 2A.1 Continued

Country	Program	Reference	Program end year	Target group	Benefit type	Evaluation method	Exposure, years
Uganda	School Feeding Program and Take-Home Rations Program	Alderman, Gilligan, and Lehrer 2008	2007	Children ages 6–17 enrolled in primary school	Food	E	0.8
Uganda	School Feeding Program and Take-Home Rations Program	Alderman, Gilligan, and Lehrer 2008	2007	Children ages 6–17 enrolled in primary school	Food	E	0.8
Uganda	Youth Opportunities Program	Blattman, Fiala, and Martinez 2012	Ongoing	Youth groups, roughly ages 16–35	Cash	E	2.25
Uganda	AIDS Support Organization and World Food Programme	Rawat et al. 2014	Ongoing	Registered HIV-positive AIDS Support Organization clients	Food	QE	1
Uganda	Food and Unconditional Cash Transfer Program in Uganda	Gilligan and Roy 2016	2012	Households with a child ages 3–5 at an early childhood development center	Cash, in kind	E	1
Zambia	Zambia Child Grant Program	Thome et al. 2014a	Ongoing	Households with children under age 5 living in program districts	Cash	QE	3
Zambia	Zambia Child Grant Program	AIR 2014	Ongoing	Households with children under age 5 living in program districts	Cash	E	2
Zambia	Zambia Child Grant Program	Seidenfeld, Handa, and Tembo 2013	Ongoing	Households with children under age 5 living in program districts	Cash	E	2
Zimbabwe	Manicaland HIV/Sexually Transmitted Disease Prevention Project	Robertson et al. 2013	2011	Poor households with children	Cash	E	1
Zimbabwe	Harmonized Social Cash Transfer Program	Taylor et al. 2014	Ongoing	Poor labor-constrained households	Cash	QE	Maximum of 2

Note: Evaluation Method is either a quantitative impact evaluation (E) or a qualitative evaluation (QE). — = not available.

122

Table 2A.2 **Program Acronyms**

Country	Acronym	Program
Burkina Faso	NCTPP	Nahouri Cash Transfers Pilot Project
Burkina Faso	SC/THR	School Canteens and Take-Home Rations
Ethiopia	PSNP	Productive Safety Net Program
Ethiopia	SCTPP	Social Cash Transfer Pilot Program
Ghana	LEAP	Livelihood Empowerment against Poverty Program
Kenya	CSP	Child Sponsorship Program
Kenya	OVC program	Cash Transfer for Orphans and Vulnerable Children
Kenya	HSNP	Hunger Safety Net Program
Kenya	GIVE	GiveDirectly
Lesotho	LCGP	Lesotho Child Grants Program
Malawi	ZCTP	Zomba Cash Transfer Program
Malawi	MASAF PWP	Malawi Social Action Fund Public Works Program
Malawi	SCTP	Social Cash Transfer Program
Niger	NSNP	Niger Safety Net Project
Sierra Leone	CfW	Cash for Work Program of the Youth Employment Support Project
South Africa	CSG	Child Support Grant
South Africa	OAP	Old-Age Pension
Tanzania	TASAF	Pilot cash transfer program implemented through the Tanzania Social Action Fund
Tanzania	RESPECT	Rewarding Sexually Transmitted Infection Prevention and Control in Tanzania
Uganda	SF and THR	School Feeding Program and Take-Home Rations Program: food for education programs
Uganda	FUU	Food and Unconditional Cash Transfer in Uganda
Zambia	ZCGP	Zambia Child Grant Program
Zimbabwe	HSCTP	Harmonized Social Cash Transfer Program
Zimbabwe	MHIV	Manicaland HIV/STD Prevention Program

Annex 2B: Meta-analysis Methodology

This annex provides technical details on the methodology of the meta-analysis. (Additional information is available in Ralston, Andrews, and Hsiao 2017.) The meta-analysis draws estimates from 55 studies of 27 social safety net programs in 14 countries. The final data presented in this chapter draw on 35 studies to generate 199 estimates of impacts across 16 outcomes. We focus on outcomes reported in studies of at least two programs. For each estimated impact, data are extracted on point estimates, standard errors, baseline means of the outcome, transfer sizes, and numbers of observations in the study. The approach builds on the methodology of the Independent Evaluation Group (IEG 2011).

Selection of Impact Evaluations to Be Included in the Meta-Analysis

Social safety net evaluations have been surveyed in the World Bank's impact evaluation databases, academic journals, and institutions involved directly in impact evaluations. The databases of the Africa Impact Evaluation Initiative, Development Impact Evaluation, Spanish Impact Evaluation Fund, and Social Protection Publication Database have been covered.[7] The institutions surveyed include the Abdul Latif Jameel Poverty Action Lab, the Innovations for Poverty Action Lab, and the International Initiative for Impact Evaluation.[8] The process of updating the sample for more recent evaluations also involved cross-checks with more recent reviews, including Bastagli et al. (2016) and Davis et al. (2016).

The criteria for including an impact evaluation follows the approach of the Independent Evaluation Group (IEG 2011). Four filters have been applied, as follows:

- *Development focus:* The evaluated programs have been implemented in developing or transition countries and explicitly evaluated the social safety net component.
- *Use of objective methods:* Evaluations construct a counterfactual and use standard statistical methods to estimate impact.
- *Robustness of findings:* Studies address plausible sources of bias and show that results are convincingly robust to a variety of confounding factors. The final studies have been published.
- *Final inspection:* Only studies that demonstrate relevance, technical rigor, and robust findings are included in the sample. To avoid duplication, only the most recent versions of evaluations are retained.

There are limitations inherent in the search criteria applied to select impact evaluations to include in the meta-analysis. First, the inclusion of published rather than unpublished impact evaluations may bias the sample toward more positive results. Second, the analysis focuses only on impact evaluation studies and may not fully capture information covered through routine monitoring and process evaluation assessments. This information can provide valuable details on program implementation. Third, the approach does not focus on comparing or rating the quality of individual methodological approaches.

The dataset is generated from the final set of 55 selected impact evaluations of 27 social safety net programs in 14 countries in Africa. These evaluations were published between 2005 and 2016. Some outcome impacts are estimated multiple times for the same program. In these cases, the estimate generated under the most credible identification strategy is chosen. For example, among the two child labor estimates for the Lesotho Child Grants Program, the estimate that is calculated with control variables is retained. Multiple estimates for an outcome from a given paper are recorded only in cases where there are multiple treatment arms (for example, if treatment is conditional or unconditional or involves vouchers versus cash). In the statistical analysis, these arms are averaged to obtain a single point estimate and confidence band per outcome in a given paper.

In the case of household consumption, the households in the studies benefited from the programs for between four months and three years. Eight impact evaluations cover an exposure period of two or more years; two evaluations cover one year; and three cover shorter seasonal interventions (Kenya GiveDirectly, the Malawi MASAF PWP, and the CfW in Sierra Leone). The meta-analysis requires that estimates cover outcomes across at least two programs. Several well-known results in the impact evaluation literature are omitted from the meta-analysis because of this requirement. The meta-analysis also requires that raw estimates be sufficiently comparable to allow for comparison across studies. Specifically, the meta-analysis requires consistency in how outcomes are defined. It is not appropriate to combine estimates that test fundamentally different outcomes. For example, the food consumption meta-analysis focuses on food expenditures; estimates for food security—on which indicators are constructed differently across studies—and caloric intake are omitted.

Standardization across Studies

Converting social safety net transfers into monthly household transfers in 2011 PPP U.S. dollars. The size of the social safety net program transfer is recorded in local currency units whenever it is reported in this way in the original evaluations. Otherwise, it is reported in U.S. dollars. First, these figures are converted into monthly household transfers. Reported annual transfers are divided by 12, and reported workday transfers are multiplied by 20. Reported per capita transfers are multiplied by the average household size. Second, exchange rates are applied so that all transfers are measured in local currency units in the baseline year. If a given evaluation reports the size of the transfer in both local currency units and U.S. dollars, the local currency units are used, and an exchange-rate conversion does not need to be carried out in this case. Third, country- and year-specific inflation rates are applied to convert the size of all transfers into 2011 terms. Fourth, PPP U.S. dollar conversion factors are applied to convert the size of all transfers to 2011 PPP U.S. dollars. Exchange rates, inflation rates, and PPP U.S. dollar conversion factors are all taken from World Development Indicators data.[9]

Standardization of baseline means, impact estimates, and standard errors. For the conversion of baseline means, impact estimates, and impact standard errors into comparable units, a similar methodology is applied. The harmonization is required for outcomes measured in monetary terms (consumption, food consumption, and earnings). Per capita, annual, and daily measures are converted to monthly household measures, and the necessary exchange, inflation, and PPP adjustments are applied.

Assumptions. A linear-scaling assumption underlies the aforementioned conversions. The time-period and household-size conversions applied to transfer sizes assume that transfer sizes scale linearly. The same assumption underlies the conversions of baseline means, impact estimates, and standard errors. This assumption is likely to be the least robust in the case of impact estimates. Thus, it is conceivable that a transfer of $10 for two weeks of work is worth half as much as a transfer of $20 for one month of work, but it is less certain that a household spending $10 over two weeks in response to treatment is equally likely to spend $20 over one month in response to a treatment that is twice as large. One might conclude that the household will focus the additional treatment funds on other areas of spending.

Reporting the Impacts on Outcomes

For consumption and food consumption, the household propensity to consume the amount of the social safety net transfer is reported. This is calculated simply by dividing the impact estimates by the transfer sizes. For other outcomes, percentage point increases are calculated relative to baseline means of the outcome by dividing the impact estimates by baseline means. The meta-analysis involves plotting these quantities for each outcome and calculating an aggregate mean effect. The aggregate effect weights each estimate by the number of observations used to generate the estimate.

Annex 2C: Partial and General Equilibrium Methodology

Partial and general equilibrium analyses were undertaken to explore the potential impact of programs if they are brought to scale. This is a relatively nascent area of analysis for social safety nets in Africa, despite the numerous impact evaluation studies available.

The partial equilibrium approach presented measures the aggregate impact on poverty rates, school enrollment rates, and household investment if the most successful interventions are brought to scale and their impacts, as measured in the meta-analysis, are experienced among a larger population of vulnerable households. This takes into account only direct effects, and it is considered a partial equilibrium approach because it does not attempt to capture feedback or spillover effects that program expansion might entail. Baseline details and parameters are shown in table 2C.1.

The simulations allow for a 10 percent to 40 percent increase in the incidence of livestock ownership and a 5 percent to 10 percent increase in the incidence of land ownership; the meta-evaluation revealed average increases of 34 percent

Table 2C.1 **Country Information and Simulation Parameters**

Indicator	Liberia	Niger	Ghana
Transfer information			
Monthly transfer (2011 PPP U.S. dollars)	50	50	50
Value of transfer per household per year (2016 U.S. dollars)	360	307	332
Value of transfer (% of national extreme poverty line)	8.0	7.6	6.2
Value of transfer (% of mean consumption of the extremely poor)	18.3	14.9	14.2
Number of households covered at baseline	4,000	37,000	70,000
Number of extremely poor households	87,000	322,000	215,000
Total cost of transfers per year (2016 U.S. dollars, millions)	31.3	98.8	71.4
Baseline outcome measures			
Baseline extreme poverty rate (%)	18.2	16.9	8.3
Baseline incidence of livestock ownership of extremely poor (%)	20.0	—	46.8
Baseline incidence of land ownership of extremely poor (%)	—	97.5	85.5
Baseline school enrollment rate, 5- to 11-year-olds (%)	96.2	95.5	—
Baseline school enrollment rate, 12- to 18-year-olds (%)	22.2	18.2	—
Simulation parameters			
Propensity to consume (consumption per dollar transferred)		0.74	
Impact on livestock ownership		10%–40% increase	
Impact on land ownership		5%–10% increase	
Impact on school enrollment		5%–15% increase	

Source: Calculations drawing on household surveys in Ghana 2012/13, Liberia 2014, and Niger 2014.
Note: — = not available.

and 8 percent, respectively. On school enrollments, the simulations allowed for a 5 percent to 15 percent rise in enrollment among beneficiary populations. This reflects the positive results seen in the most successful programs (such as the Burkina Faso Nahouri Cash Transfers Pilot Project and the Malawi SCTP), but also the more modest results achieved in many programs. For example, the meta-analysis found mean increases of 7 percent in school enrollments (95 percent confidence interval: −2 percent to 16 percent).

The general equilibrium modeling presented in box 2.2 takes into account the indirect effects of expanding social safety net programs; the details are described in Levy and Lofgren (2017). This approach accounts for spillovers and feedback effects; these are indirect or second-order outcomes that may arise as programs expand and reach their full scale. They are specifically considered in terms of the net total consumption and incomes of beneficiaries and nonbeneficiaries, prices, and labor participation. Macroeconomic indicators include total domestic demand, exports, imports, gross domestic product, and production in aggregate sectors. There is a related literature that focuses on the impacts on local economies, but not the effects of expansions (see Taylor, Thome, and Filipski 2014; Taylor et al. 2013, 2014; Thome et al. 2014b).

The general equilibrium modeling is done using a computable general equilibrium model that sets out a fully articulated system of demand and supply functions for each sector of an economy. Such a model also facilitates an analysis of the impacts of alternative policy packages (such as complementary interventions that may be designed to raise productivity) and the consequences of various avenues of program funding (such as bilateral aid versus domestic tax revenues). While computable general equilibrium models allow greater modeling detail and can capture more effectively the short-run spillover and feedback effects, they are also static and are not well suited to modeling the intergenerational impacts of investments in the human capital of children that may arise if beneficiaries are covered by social safety net programs.

These two approaches—the partial equilibrium approach and the general equilibrium approach—have advantages and disadvantages. The partial equilibrium estimates translate impact evaluation findings into an aggregate impact of bringing programs to scale and is considered the immediate impact of programs prior to household and producer responses (Caldés, Coady, and Maluccio 2006). Its appeal is that it is a fairly simple and straightforward calculation. However, if the scale of the program is sufficiently large, the effects of the program cannot be fully understood without considering the impact on and the feedback from the broader economy. On the other hand, the general equilibrium approach relies on a complex set of equations and assumptions about macroeconomic responses, which often are simplifications of how the real world works.

Notes

1. For further discussion of frameworks for the study of social safety nets, see Bastagli et al. (2016); Devereux and Sebastes-Wheeler (2004); Grosh et al. (2008); Tirivayi, Knowles, and Davis (2013); and World Bank (2012).
2. Impact evaluations are defined as studies that derive the impact of a social safety net program by using robust counterfactual data. They include randomized controlled trials, as well as difference-in-differences and regression discontinuity methods.
3. Consumption refers to food and a wide range of recurrent nonfood expenditures, but excludes consumer durables (such as a new roof or a car), productive investments (such as farming equipment), or annual expenditure items.
4. The two extreme outliers—the Livelihood Empowerment against Poverty Program (LEAP) in Ghana and the Social Cash Transfer Program (SCTP) in Malawi—have

been dropped from the meta-estimate of $0.74 per $1.00 equivalent transferred. Including them would increase the meta-estimate to $0.92.

5. Programs with conditions are the food-for-education programs (the School Canteens Program and the Take-Home Rations Program) in Burkina Faso, the OVC program in Kenya, the Tanzania TASAF, and the food for education programs (the School Feeding Program and the Take-Hone Rations Program) in Uganda. Unconditional programs are LEAP in Ghana, the Child Sponsorship Program and the HSNP in Kenya, the Lesotho Child Grants Program, the Niger Safety Net Project, the CfW in Sierra Leone, the Old-Age Pension in South Africa, and the Zambia Child Grant Program. Programs with components with and without conditions are the Nahouri Cash Transfers Pilot Project in Burkina Faso, the Malawi SCTP, and the Manicaland HIV/STD Prevention Program in Zimbabwe.

6. The baseline coverage used in these simulations matches the level of coverage of social safety net programs at the time of the most recent household survey. Since then, the size of social safety nets has grown in Ghana and Niger.

7. See AIM (Africa Impact Evaluation Initiative) (database), Africa Region, World Bank, Washington, DC, http://go.worldbank.org/E70Y4QHZW0; DIME (Development Impact Evaluation) (database), World Bank, Washington, DC, http://www.worldbank.org/en/research/dime; SIEF (Spanish Impact Evaluation Fund) (database), World Bank, Washington, DC, http://web.worldbank.org/WBSITE/EXTERNAL/EXTABOUTUS/ORGANIZATION/EXTHDNETWORK/EXTHDOFFICE/0,,contentMDK:23150708~menuPK:8535092~pagePK:64168445~piPK:64168309~theSitePK:5485727,00.html; Social Development Publications Database, World Bank, Washington, DC, http://www-esd.worldbank.org/sdvpubs/.

8. See J-PAL (Abdul Latif Jameel Poverty Action Lab), Massachusetts Institute of Technology, Cambridge, MA, https://www.povertyactionlab.org/; IPA (Innovations for Poverty Action), New Haven, CT, https://www.poverty-action.org/; 3ie (International Initiative for Impact Evaluation), New Delhi, http://www.3ieimpact.org/en/.

9. See WDI (World Development Indicators) (database), World Bank, Washington, DC, http://data.worldbank.org/products/wdi.

References

Agüero, Jorge M., Michael R. Carter, and Ingrid Woolard. 2007. "The Impact of Unconditional Cash Transfers on Nutrition: The South African Child Support Grant." Working Paper 39, International Poverty Centre, United Nations Development Programme, Brasília.

Aiyagari, S. Rao. 1994. "Uninsured Idiosyncratic Risk and Aggregate Saving." *Quarterly Journal of Economics* 109 (3): 659–84.

AIR (American Institutes for Research). 2014. "Zambia's Multiple Category Targeting Grant: 36-Month Impact Report." Draft, AIR, Washington, DC.

Aker, Jenny C. 2013. "Cash or Coupons? Testing the Impacts of Cash versus Vouchers in the Democratic Republic of Congo." Working Paper 320, Center for Global Development, Washington, DC.

Akresh, Richard, Damien de Walque, and Harounan Kazianga. 2012. "Alternative Cash Transfer Delivery Mechanisms: Impacts on Routine Preventative Health Clinic Visits in Burkina Faso." Policy Research Working Paper 5958, World Bank, Washington, DC.

———. 2013. "Cash Transfers and Child Schooling: Evidence from a Randomized Evaluation of the Role of Conditionality." Policy Research Working Paper 6340, World Bank, Washington, DC.

Alderman, Harold, Daniel O. Gilligan, and Kim Lehrer. 2008. "The Impact of Alternative Food for Education Programs on School Participation and Education Attainment in Northern Uganda." Working paper, International Food Policy Research Institute, Washington, DC.

Alderman, Harold, and Ruslan Yemtsov. 2013. "How Can Safety Nets Contribute to Economic Growth?" Policy Research Working Paper 6437, World Bank, Washington, DC.

Alfani, Federica, Andrew Dabalen, Peter Fisker, and Vasco Molini. 2015. "Can We Measure Resilience? A Proposed Method and Evidence from Countries in the Sahel." Policy Research Working Paper 7170, World Bank, Washington, DC.

Andersson, Camilla, Alemu Mekonnen, and Jesper Stage. 2011. "Impacts of the Productive Safety Net Program in Ethiopia on Livestock and Tree Holdings of Rural Households." Journal of Development Economics 94 (1): 119–26.

Ardington, Cally, Anne Case, and Victoria Hosegood. 2009. "Labor Supply Responses to Large Social Transfers: Longitudinal Evidence from South Africa." American Economic Journal: Applied Economics 1 (1): 22–48.

Asfaw, Solomon, Benjamin Davis, Josh Dewbre, Sudhanshu Handa, and Paul Winters. 2014. "Cash Transfer Programme, Productive Activities, and Labour Supply: Evidence from a Randomized Experiment in Kenya." Journal of Development Studies 50 (8): 1172–96.

Baez, Javier E., and Adriana Camacho. 2011. "Assessing the Long-Term Effects of Conditional Cash Transfers on Human Capital: Evidence from Colombia." Policy Research Working Paper 5681, World Bank, Washington, DC.

Baird, Sarah Jane, Ephraim Chirwa, Craig T. McIntosh, and Berk Özler. 2015. "What Happens Once the Intervention Ends? The Medium-Term Impacts of a Cash Transfer Experiment in Malawi." 3ie Impact Evaluation Report 27, International Initiative for Impact Evaluation, New Delhi.

Baird, Sarah Jane, Francisco H. G. Ferreira, Berk Özler, and Michael Woolcock. 2013. "Relative Effectiveness of Conditional and Unconditional Cash Transfers for Schooling Outcomes in Developing Countries: A Systematic Review." Campbell Systematic Reviews 8 (September), Campbell Collaboration, Oslo.

Baird, Sarah, Richard S. Garfein, Craig T. McIntosh, and Berk Özler. 2012. "Effect of a Cash Transfer Program for Schooling on Prevalence of HIV and Herpes Simplex Type 2 in Malawi: A Cluster Randomized Trial." Lancet 379 (9823): 1320–29.

Baird, Sarah Jane, Craig T. McIntosh, and Berk Özler. 2009. "Designing Cost-Effective Cash Transfer Programs to Boost Schooling among Young Women in Sub-Saharan Africa." Policy Research Working Paper 5090, World Bank, Washington, DC.

———. 2011. "Cash or Condition? Evidence from a Cash Transfer Experiment." Quarterly Journal of Economics 126 (4): 1709–53.

Bandiera, Oriana, Robin Burgess, Narayan Das, Selim Gulesci, Imran Rasul, and Munshi Sulaiman. 2013. "Can Basic Entrepreneurship Transform the Economic Lives of the Poor?" IZA Discussion Paper 7386, Institute for the Study of Labor, Bonn.

Banerjee, Abhijit, Esther Duflo, Nathanael Goldberg, Dean Karlan, Robert Osei, William Parienté, Jeremy Shapiro, Bram Thuysbaert, and Christopher Udry. 2015. "A Multifaceted Program Causes Lasting Progress for the Very Poor: Evidence from Six Countries." *Science* 348 (6236): 772–89.

Barham, Tania, Karen Macours, and John A. Maluccio. 2013. "More Schooling and More Learning? Effects of a Three-Year Conditional Cash Transfer Program in Nicaragua after 10 Years." IDB Working Paper IDB-WP-42, Inter-American Development Bank, Washington, DC.

Barrientos, Armando. 2012. "Social Transfers and Growth: What Do We Know? What Do We Need to Find Out?" *World Development* 40 (1): 11–20.

Barry, Oumar, Ali Mory Maidoka, and Patrick Premand. 2017. "Promoting Positive Parenting Practices in Niger through a Cash Transfer Programme." *Early Childhood Matters*.

Bastagli, Francesca, Jessica Hagen-Zanker, Luke Harman, Valentina Barca, Georgina Sturge, and Tanja Schmidt. 2016. *Cash Transfers: What Does the Evidence Say? A Rigorous Review of Programme Impact and of the Role of Design and Implementation Features*. With Luca Pellerano. London: Overseas Development Institute.

Beegle, Kathleen, Emanuela Galasso, and Jessica Goldberg. 2015. "Direct and Indirect Effects of Malawi's Public Works Program on Food Security." Policy Research Working Paper 7505, World Bank, Washington, DC.

Behrman, Jere R., Susan W. Parker, and Petra E. Todd. 2011. "Do Conditional Cash Transfers for Schooling Generate Lasting Benefits? A Five-Year Followup of PROGRESA/Oportunidades." *Journal of Human Resources* 46 (1): 93–122.

Benhassine, Najy, Florencia Devoto, Esther Duflo, Pascaline Dupas, and Victor Pouliquen. 2013. "Turning a Shove into a Nudge? A 'Labeled Cash Transfer' for Education." NBER Working Paper 19227, National Bureau of Economic Research, Cambridge, MA.

Berhane, Guush, Stephen Devereux, John F. Hoddinott, Jessica B. Hoel, Keetie Roelen, Kibrewossen Abay, Martha Kimmel, Natasha Ledlie, and Thomas Woldu Assefa. 2015. *Evaluation of the Social Cash Transfer Pilot Programme, Tigray Region, Ethiopia: Endline Report*. Washington, DC: International Food Policy Research Institute.

Berhane, Guush, Kalle Hirvonen, and John F. Hoddinott. 2015. "The Implementation of the Productive Safety Nets Programme, 2014: Highlands Outcomes Report." International Food Policy Research Institute, Washington, DC.

Berhane, Guush, John F. Hoddinott, Neha Kumar, and Alemayehu Seyoum Taffesse. 2011. "The Impact of Ethiopia's Productive Safety Nets and Household Asset Building Programme: 2006–2010." Report, International Food Policy Research Institute, Washington, DC.

Blattman, Christopher, Nathan Fiala, and Sebastian Martinez. 2012. "Employment Generation in Rural Africa: Mid-term Results from an Experimental Evaluation of the Youth Opportunities Program in Northern Uganda." DIW Discussion Paper 1201, German Institute for Economic Research, Berlin.

———. 2013. "The Economic and Social Returns to Cash Transfers: Evidence from a Ugandan Aid Program." Working paper, Department of Political Science and Department of International and Public Affairs, Columbia University, New York.

Boone, Ryan, Katia Covarrubias, Benjamin Davis, and Paul Winters. 2013. "Cash Transfer Programs and Agricultural Production: The Case of Malawi." *Agricultural Economics* 44 (3): 365–78.

Caldés, Natàlia, David Coady, and John A. Maluccio. 2006. "The Cost of Poverty Alleviation Transfer Programs: A Comparative Analysis of Three Programs in Latin America." *World Development* 34 (5): 818–37.

Chenery, Hollis B., Montek S. Ahluwalia, C. L. G. Bell, John H. Daly, and Richard Jolly. 1974. *Redistribution with Growth: Policies to Improve Income Distribution in Developing Countries in the Context of Economic Growth.* London: Oxford University Press.

Clarke, Daniel J., and Stefan Dercon. 2016. *Dull Disasters? How Planning Ahead Will Make a Difference.* Washington, DC: World Bank; Oxford Oxford University Press.

Covarrubias, Katia, Benjamin Davis, and Paul Winters. 2012. "From Protection to Production: Productive Impacts of the Malawi Social Cash Transfer Scheme." *Journal of Development Effectiveness* 4 (1): 50–77.

CPC (Carolina Population Center). 2015. *Malawi Social Cash Transfer Program: Midline Impact Evaluation Report.* Chapel Hill, NC: CPC, University of North Carolina at Chapel Hill.

———. 2016. *Malawi Social Cash Transfer Programme: Endline Impact Evaluation Report.* Chapel Hill, NC: CPC, University of North Carolina at Chapel Hill.

Daidone, Silvio, Benjamin Davis, Joshua Dewbre, and Katia Covarrubias. 2014. "Lesotho's Child Grant Programme: 24-Month Impact Report on Productive Activities and Labour Allocation; Lesotho Country Case Study Report." PtoP, From Protection to Production Series, Food and Agriculture Organization of the United Nations, Rome.

Davis, Benjamin, Sudhanshu Handa, Nicola Hypher, Natalia Winder Rossi, Paul Winters, and Jennifer Yablonski, eds. 2016. *From Evidence to Action: The Story of Cash Transfers and Impact Evaluation in Sub-Saharan Africa.* Oxford, UK: Oxford University Press.

Devereux, Stephen. 1997. "Household Food Security in Malawi." IDS Discussion Paper 362 (December), Institute of Development Studies, Brighton, UK.

Devereux, Stephen, and Rachel Sebastes-Wheeler. 2004. "Transformative Social Protection." IDS Working Paper 232, Institute of Development Studies, Brighton, UK.

DFID (UK Department for International Development). 2011. "Defining Disaster Resilience: A DFID Approach Paper." Department for International Development, London.

DSD (South Africa, Department of Social Development), SASSA (South African Social Security Agency), and UNICEF (United Nations Children's Fund–South Africa). 2012. "The South African Child Support Grant Impact Assessment: Evidence from a Survey of Children, Adolescents, and Their Households." UNICEF–South Africa, Pretoria.

Eden, Maya. 2017. "Is There Enough Redistribution?" Policy Research Working Paper 8003, World Bank, Washington, DC.

Edmonds, Eric V. 2006. "Child Labor and Schooling Responses to Anticipated Income in South Africa." *Journal of Development Economics* 81 (2): 386–414.

Evans, David K., Stephanie Hausladen, Katrina Kosec, and Natasha Reese. 2014. *Community-Based Conditional Cash Transfers in Tanzania: Results from a Randomized Trial.* World Bank Study Series. Washington, DC: World Bank.

Evans, David K., Michael Kremer, and Mūthoni Ngatia. 2009. "The Impact of Distributing School Uniforms on Children's Education in Kenya." Working paper, World Bank, Washington, DC.

Evans, David K., and Anna Popova. 2014. "Cash Transfers and Temptation Goods: A Review of Global Evidence." Policy Research Working Paper 6886, World Bank, Washington, DC.

Fiszbein, Ariel, and Norbert R. Schady. 2009. *Conditional Cash Transfers: Reducing Present and Future Poverty.* With Francisco H. G. Ferreira, Margaret E. Grosh, Niall Keleher, Pedro Olinto, and Emmanuel Skoufias. World Bank Policy Research Report. Washington, DC: World Bank.

Gentilini, Ugo. 2014. "Our Daily Bread: What Is the Evidence on Comparing Cash versus Food Transfers?" Social Protection and Labor Discussion Paper 1420, World Bank, Washington, DC.

Gertler, Paul J., Sebastian Martinez, and Marta Rubio-Codina. 2012. "Investing Cash Transfers to Raise Long-Term Living Standards." *American Economic Journal: Applied Economics* 4 (1): 164–92.

Gilligan, Daniel O., John F. Hoddinott, Neha Kumar, and Alemayehu Seyoum Taffesse. 2009. "Can Social Protection Work in Africa? Evidence on the Impact of Ethiopia's Productive Safety Net Program on Food Security, Assets, and Incentives." Working paper, International Food Policy Research Institute, Washington, DC.

Gilligan, Daniel O., John F. Hoddinott, and Alemayehu Seyoum Taffesse. 2008. "The Impact of Ethiopia's Productive Safety Net Programme and Its Linkages." IFPRI Discussion Paper 00839, International Food Policy Research Institute, Washington, DC.

Gilligan, Daniel O., and Shalini Roy. 2016. "The Effect of Transfers and Preschool on Children's Cognitive Development in Uganda." 3ie Impact Evaluation Report 32 (March), International Initiative for Impact Evaluation, New Delhi.

Grosh, Margaret E., Carlo del Ninno, Emil Tesliuc, and Azedine Ouerghi. 2008. *For Protection and Promotion: The Design and Implementation of Effective Safety Nets.* Washington, DC: World Bank.

Hagen-Zanker, Jessica, Anna McCord, and Rebecca Holmes. 2011. "Systematic Review of the Impact of Employment Guarantee Schemes and Cash Transfers on the Poor." With Francesca Booker and Elizabeth Molinari. ODI Systematic Review, Overseas Development Institute, London.

Hallegatte, Stéphane, Mook Bangalore, Laura Bonzanigo, Marianne Fay, Tomaro Kane, Ulf Narloch, Julie Rozenberg, David Treguer, and Adrien Vogt-Schilb. 2016. *Shock Waves: Managing the Impacts of Climate Change on Poverty.* Climate Change and Development Series. Washington, DC: World Bank.

Hamoudi, Amar, and Duncan Thomas. 2005. "Pension Income and the Well-Being of Children and Grandchildren: New Evidence from South Africa." On-Line Working

Paper CCPR 043-05 \ California Center for Population Research, University of California, Los Angeles.

Handa, Sudhanshu, Silvio Daidone, Amber Peterman, Benjamin Davis, Audrey Pereira, Tia Palermo, and Jennifer Yablonski. 2017. "Myth Busting? Confronting Six Common Perceptions about Unconditional Cash Transfers as a Poverty Reduction Strategy in Africa." Innocenti Working Paper 2017-11, Office of Research, United Nations Children's Fund, Florence.

Handa, Sudhanshu, Michael Park, Robert Osei Darko, Isaac Osei-Akoto, Benjamin Davis, and Silvio Daidone. 2013. "Livelihood Empowerment against Poverty Program: Impact Evaluation." Report, Carolina Population Center, University of North Carolina at Chapel Hill, Chapel Hill.

Haushofer, Johannes, and Jeremy Shapiro. 2016. "The Short-Term Impact of Unconditional Cash Transfers to the Poor: Experimental Evidence from Kenya." *Quarterly Journal of Economics* 131 (4): 1973–2042.

Hill, Ruth, and Philip Verwimp. 2017. "Managing Risk and Conflict." In *Accelerating Poverty Reduction in Africa*, edited by Kathleen Beegle and Luc Christiaensen, chapter 4. Washington, DC: World Bank.

Hoddinott, John F., Guush Berhane, Daniel O. Gilligan, Neha Kumar, and Alemayehu Seyoum Taffesse. 2012. "The Impact of Ethiopia's Productive Safety Net Programme and Related Transfers on Agricultural Productivity." *Journal of African Economies* 21 (5): 761–86.

Hubbard, R. Glenn, Jonathan Skinner, and Stephen P. Zeldes. 1995. "Precautionary Saving and Social Insurance." *Journal of Political Economy* 103 (2): 360–99.

IEG (Independent Evaluation Group). 2011. *Evidence and Lessons Learned from Impact Evaluations on Social Safety Nets*. Washington, DC: World Bank.

Inchauste, Gabriela, and David G. Victor, eds. 2017. *The Political Economy of Energy Subsidy Reform*. Directions in Development: Public Sector Governance Series. Washington, DC: World Bank.

Kabeer, Naila, Caio Piza, and Linnet Taylor. 2012. "What Are the Economic Impacts of Conditional Cash Transfer Programmes? A Systematic Review of the Evidence." Technical report (December), EPPI-Center, Social Science Research Unit, Institute of Education, University of London, London.

Kagin, Justin, J. Edward Taylor, Federica Alfani, and Benjamin Davis. 2014. "Local Economy-Wide Impact Evaluation (LEWIE) of Ethiopia's Social Cash Transfer Pilot Programme." PtoP, From Protection to Production Series, Food and Agriculture Organization of the United Nations, Rome.

Kazianga, Harounan, Damien de Walque, and Harold Alderman. 2009. "Educational and Health Impacts of Two School Feeding Schemes: Evidence from a Randomized Trial in Rural Burkina Faso." Policy Research Working Paper 4976, World Bank, Washington, DC.

———. 2014 "School Feeding Programs, Intrahousehold Allocation, and the Nutrition of Siblings: Evidence from a Randomized Trial in Rural Burkina Faso." *Journal of Development Economics* 106: 15–34.

Levy, Stéphanie, and Hans Lofgren. 2017. "General Equilibrium Effects of Social Safety Nets: The Case of Ghana's LEAP Program." Working paper, World Bank, Washington, DC.

Macours, Karen, Norbert R. Schady, and Renos Vakis. 2012. "Cash Transfers, Behavioral Changes, and Cognitive Development in Early Childhood: Evidence from a Randomized Experiment." *American Economic Journal: Applied Economics* 4 (2): 247–73.

Merttens, Fred, Alex Hurrell, Marta Marzi, Ramla Attah, Maham Farhat, Andrew Kardan, and Ian MacAuslan. 2013. *Kenya Hunger Social Safety Net Programme, Monitoring and Evaluation Component: Impact Evaluation, Final Report, 2009 to 2012.* Oxford: Oxford Policy Management.

Packel, Laura, William H. Dow, Damien de Walque, Zachary Isdahl, and Albert Majura. 2012. "Sexual Behavior Change Intentions and Actions in the Context of a Randomized Trial of a Conditional Cash Transfer for HIV Prevention in Tanzania." Policy Research Working Paper 5997, World Bank, Washington, DC.

Pellerano, Luca, Marta Moratti, Maja Jakobsen, Matěj Bajgar, and Valentina Barca. 2014. *Child Grants Programme Impact Evaluation: Follow-up Report.* Oxford: Oxford Policy Management.

Premand, Patrick, Oumar Barry, and Marc Smitz. 2016. "Transferts Monétaires, Valeur Ajoutée de Mesures d'Accompagnement Comportemental, et Développement de la Petite Enfance au Niger. Rapport Descriptif de l'Évaluation d'Impact à Court Terme du Projet Filets Sociaux." Report No: ACS18664. Washington, DC: World Bank, 2016.

Premand, Patrick, and Carlo del Ninno. 2016. "Cash Transfers, Behavioral Accompanying Measures, and Child Development in Niger." Working paper, World Bank, Washington, DC.

Ralston, Laura, Colin Andrews, and Allan Hsiao. 2017. "A Meta-Analysis of Social Safety Net Programs in Africa." Policy Research Working Paper 8255, World Bank, Washington, DC.

Rawat, Rahul, Elizabeth Faust, John A. Maluccio, and Suneetha Kadiyala. 2014. "The Impact of a Food Assistance Program on Nutritional Status, Disease Progression, and Food Security among People Living with HIV in Uganda." 3ie Grantee Final Report, International Initiative for Impact Evaluation, New Delhi.

Robertson, Laura, Phyllis Mushati, Jeffrey W. Eaton, Lovemore Dumba, Gideon Mavise, Jeremiah Makoni, Christina Schumacher, et al. 2013. "Effects of Unconditional and Conditional Cash Transfers on Child Health and Development in Zimbabwe: A Cluster-Randomised Trial." *Lancet* 381 (9874): 1283–92.

Rodrigo, María F. 2012. "Impact Evaluation of the Productive Safety Nets Program in Ethiopia." Paper presented at the 2013 Agricultural and Applied Economics Association and Canadian Agricultural Economics Society Joint Annual Meeting, Washington, DC, August 4–6.

Rosas, Nina, and Shwetlena Sabarwal. 2016. "Can You Work It? Evidence on the Productive Potential of Public Works from a Youth Employment Program in Sierra Leone." Policy Research Working Paper 7580, World Bank, Washington, DC.

Saavedra, Juan Esteban, and Sandra Garcia. 2012. "Impacts of Conditional Cash Transfer Programs on Educational Outcomes in Developing Countries: A Meta-analysis." Labor and Population Working Paper WR-921-1, RAND Corporation, Santa Monica, CA.

Sabates-Wheeler, Rachel, and Stephen Devereux. 2010. "Cash Transfers and High Food Prices: Explaining Outcomes on Ethiopia's Productive Safety Net Program." FAC Working Paper 004, Future Agricultures Consortium, University of Sussex, Brighton, UK.

Schady, Norbert R., and María Caridad Araujo. 2006. "Cash Transfers, Conditions, School Enrollment, and Child Work: Evidence from a Randomized Experiment in Ecuador." Policy Research Working Paper 3930, World Bank, Washington, DC.

Schüring, Esther. 2010. "Conditions, Conditionality, Conditionalities, Responsibilities: Finding Common Ground." Working Paper 2010WP014, Maastricht Graduate School of Governance, Maastricht University, Maastricht, the Netherlands.

Seidenfeld, David, Sudhanshu Handa, and Gelson Tembo. 2013. "Social Cash Transfer Scheme: 24-Month Impact Report for the Child Grant Programme." September, American Institutes for Research, Washington, DC.

Slater, Rachel, Sarah Bailey, and Paul Harvey. 2015. "Can Emergency Cash Transfers 'Piggyback' on Existing Social Protection Programmes?" Background note, Overseas Development Institute, London.

Stoeffler, Quentin, Bradford Mills, and Patrick Premand. 2016. "Poor Households' Productive Investments of Cash Transfers: Quasi-Experimental Evidence from Niger." Policy Research Working Paper 7839, World Bank, Washington, DC.

Taylor, J. Edward, Justin Kagin, Mateusz Filipski, and Karen Thome. 2013. "Evaluating General Equilibrium Impacts of Kenya's Cash Transfer Programme for Orphans and Vulnerable Children (CT-OVC)." PtoP, From Protection to Production Series, Food and Agriculture Organization of the United Nations, Rome.

Taylor, J. Edward, Karen Thome, Benjamin Davis, David Seidenfeld, and Sudhanshu Handa. 2014. "Evaluating Local General Equilibrium Impacts of Zimbabwe's Harmonized Social Cash Transfer Programme (HSCT)." PtoP, From Protection to Production Series, Food and Agriculture Organization of the United Nations, Rome.

Taylor, J. Edward, Karen Thome, and Mateusz Filipski. 2014. "Evaluating Local General Equilibrium Impacts of Lesotho's Child Grants Programme." PtoP, From Protection to Production Series, Food and Agriculture Organization of the United Nations, Rome.

Thome, Karen, J. Edward Taylor, Benjamin Davis, Sudhanshu Handa, David Seidenfeld, and Gelson Tembo. 2014a. "Local Economy-Wide Impact Evaluation (LEWIE) of Zambia's Child Grant Programme." PtoP, From Protection to Production Series, Food and Agriculture Organization of the United Nations, Rome.

Thome, Karen, J. Edward Taylor, Justin Kagin, Benjamin Davis, Robert Darko Osei, and Isaac Osei-Akoto. 2014b. "Local Economy-Wide Impact Evaluation (LEWIE) of Ghana's Livelihood Empowerment against Poverty (LEAP) Programme." PtoP, From Protection to Production Series, Food and Agriculture Organization of the United Nations, Rome.

Tirivayi, Nyasha, Marco Knowles, and Benjamin Davis. 2013. "The Interaction between Social Protection and Agriculture: A Review of Evidence." PtoP, From Protection to Production Series, Food and Agriculture Organization of the United Nations, Rome.

Ward, Patrick, Alex Hurrell, Aly Visram, Nils Riemenschneider, Luca Pellerano, Clare O'Brien, Ian MacAuslan, and Jack Willis. 2010. "Cash Transfer Programme for Orphans and Vulnerable Children (CT-OVC), Kenya: Operational and Impact Evaluation, 2007–2009, Final Report." Oxford Policy Management, Oxford.

Weldegebriel, Zerihune Berhane, and Martin Prowse. 2013. "Climate Change Adaptation in Ethiopia: To What Extent Does Social Protection Influence Livelihood Diversification?" IOB Working Paper 2012.11, Institute of Development Policy and Management, Universiteit Antwerpen, Antwerp.

World Bank. 2012. *World Bank 2012–2022 Social Protection and Labor Strategy: Resilience, Equity, and Opportunity.* Washington, DC: World Bank.

————. 2015. *Ethiopia Poverty Assessment 2014*. Report AUS6744. Washington, DC: World Bank.

Zezza, Alberto, Bénédicte de la Brière, and Benjamin Davis. 2010. "The Impact of SCTs on Household Economic Decision-Making and Development in Kenya and Malawi." Paper presented at the Fifth African Economic Conference, "Setting the Agenda for Africa's Economic Recovery and Long-Term Growth," Tunis, October 27–29.

Chapter **3**

Recognizing and Leveraging Politics to Expand and Sustain Social Safety Nets

Thomas Bossuroy and Aline Coudouel

Social policy is shaped by politics, but it also influences politics. Social safety nets are no exception: the political dimensions of policies need to be considered in conjunction with technical decisions.

The scope of social safety nets depends on political appetite, that is, acceptability and desirability, which depends on social norms and ideological factors, such as the perceived causes of poverty and the preferences for redistribution. Evidence on the impact of programs can be harnessed to change political appetite. Periods of rapid economic or social change offer a window of opportunity, wherein the political appetite for social safety net programs can evolve quickly. International platforms and development partners can catalyze the political support for social safety nets.

The choice of program and design parameters is political. Program design features, such as conditionalities, recertification processes, or a productivity focus, may be important in rallying program support. Political realities may require the targeting of groups beyond the poorest to attain political support. In some cases, while a focus on specific geographical areas may make sense from a poverty perspective, nationwide coverage may be preferred.

There is also a feedback loop: the implementation of social safety net programs shapes the political environment. Politicians and citizens adjust their preferences and incentives and redefine their relationships as social safety net programs are implemented. Social accountability mechanisms can strengthen this political feedback loop. Grievance redress and community and beneficiary participation can help maximize program potential by contributing to greater empowerment and voice among beneficiaries.

Political processes shape the extent and nature of social policy. Decisions about the scale of social safety nets and other forms of redistribution toward the vulnerable are the subject of debates and struggles between competing interests with different incentives.

The staggering expansion of social safety nets across Africa in the past decade demonstrates that ideas, preferences, and political platforms change, even in places where the political environment was initially unsuitable (see chapter 1). Political dynamics evolve, and windows of opportunity open and close. Unpacking and learning from these processes represents a chance to build sustainable social safety net systems. The technical work of designing these systems should also engage with the political dimensions of social policy. Understanding and addressing the political processes and political economy behind social policy are as relevant and necessary as any technical assessment in crafting and implementing ambitious programs.

Bringing social safety nets to scale should encompass recognizing and leveraging the associated politics. Beyond the theoretical or historical discussions on the multiple ways in which political, social, and cultural factors determine social policy (on which there is a large literature), specific examples across Africa of ways political processes have shifted to shape, expand, and sustain social safety net programs can help provide guidance to social policy practitioners and advocates.

There are three main points of interaction between politics and social safety nets (figure 3.1). First, the scope of social safety nets is contingent on political acceptability and desirability, which depend on social norms, the prevalence of poverty, and ideological factors, such as the perceived causes of poverty and the preferences for redistribution. It is important to examine the conditions under which political preferences may shift to reveal space for greater commitment to redistributive policies. Second, the choice of program and design parameters is a mediating factor.

Figure 3.1 Politics and Social Safety Nets Interact

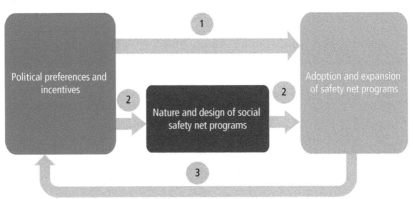

Often influenced by political preferences and incentives, it may influence the level of commitment to social safety net programs. The design process should be a factor in these preferences to maximize buy-in without undermining program impacts. Third, there is a feedback loop. The implementation of social safety net programs shapes the political environment. Politicians and citizens adjust their preferences and incentives and redefine their relationships in the presence of social transfers.

The politics of social policy is often analyzed in terms of social contracts rather than political regimes (box 3.1). The adoption and expansion of social safety nets are not highly correlated with the nature of political regimes. While democratization may promote the greater participation of the poor in the political process, the voice of the poor may be distorted because of narrow electoral participation among vulnerable citizens, low expectations, limited information on government policies, vote buying or patronage, and the salient role of non-economic issues such as ethnicity or religion (Roemer 1998; van de Walle 2014; Weyland 1996). Meanwhile, because they face the threat of popular uprisings or divisions in ruling coalitions, autocratic regimes also have incentives to secure support from and stability for the majority of the population (Lavers and Hickey 2016). Understanding political commitment to the poor is not as simplistic as

---

BOX 3.1

Social Contracts and Social Safety Nets

A social contract involves the interplay between a society's expectations that the state will provide services to and secure revenue from the population, backed by the will of policy makers to direct public resources and the capacity of governments to fulfill social expectations (OECD 2009; Rousseau 1968). The deployment of social safety net programs, similar to other government interventions, depends on the social contract between the government and citizens (Hickey 2011). In most African countries, the social contract is mostly founded on intragroup solidarity rather than on the government-led provision of benefits. Support for the poor and vulnerable is predominantly provided through private solidarity networks shaped by kinship (Hill and Verwimp 2017).

Social contracts evolve as a result of changing contexts. During the period of strong economic growth in the 2000s, social contracts in many Latin American countries changed and led to increased social spending. Public resources were used to promote education and health care spending, as well as transfers to the poorest population groups (Breceda, Rigolini, and Saavedra 2008). Social contracts also shifted rapidly in the Arab world in the early 2010s as a result of growing discontent over limited political accountability and voice from a burgeoning middle class, especially youth, whose aspirations were not being met (Silva, Levin, and Morgandi 2013; World Bank 2015).

Social safety nets have emerged in response to changing social contracts, but their existence also likely modifies the social contract as a growing number of individuals become familiar with the programs and as the programs demonstrate effectiveness.

---

differentiating between democratic and autocratic institutions, even though the progress of democracy in Africa opens space for greater representation of the interest of the poor (World Bank 2016).

The political economy of social safety nets in Africa is evolving, and policy has a big role to play in changing political preferences and incentives. By recognizing this process, stakeholders may harness rather than lament the politics of building and sustaining social safety net systems.

The Political Appetite for Adopting and Expanding Social Safety Nets

Analysis of the evolution of social safety nets in many African countries suggests that the appetite for the adoption or expansion of social safety net programs evolves in response to three main factors: beliefs and perceptions about redistribution, a volatile socioeconomic environment and shocks, and the influence of external actors, including development and humanitarian partners.

Shape the Policy Dialogue to Change Misconceptions

Preconceived ideas on social safety nets may constitute a barrier to political buy-in and adoption. Commonly held preconceptions include the belief that the poor and recipients in social safety nets are undeserving of assistance and may become dependent on handouts and that social safety net programs do not have productive impacts and are therefore a waste of public resources. This reflects a general lack of understanding of social programs that, in the long run, should be addressed through the introduction of relevant curricula in tertiary education. Thus, dealing with concerns carefully in the process of policy dialogue is critical to promoting the adoption of social safety nets (box 3.2).

The belief that government support is likely to make people lazy and dependent on assistance is deep-rooted. Analysis in the United Kingdom and the United States suggests that attitudes toward people who are poor influence the support for programs (Alesina, Glaeser, and Sacerdote 2001; Baumberg 2014; Graham 2002). According to van Oorschot (2000, 43), "whether people in need can be blamed or can be held responsible for their neediness seems to be a general and central criterion for deservingness." This holds true in Africa, too. Ideas about deserving groups have played a critical role in shaping domestic political imperatives and have often proven more significant than programmatic platforms or external pressure (Seekings 2015). In Zambia, for instance, the social safety net agenda was opposed most strongly by a minister of finance who denied the existence of poverty in the country by claiming that the poor were really only lazy (Pruce and Hickey 2017). Government officials in Mozambique raised concerns

BOX 3.2

Changing Beliefs Are Part of Changing the Governance Landscape

Governance—the process of designing and implementing policy—underlies every aspect of how countries develop and how their institutions function. However, quite often, the governance process fails to deliver. Though they are armed with national development strategies, governments may fail to adopt pro-growth or pro-poor policies, or, if these are adopted, the policies may fail to achieve their intended goals. Putting governance front and center in the development debate is essential to fostering sustained economic growth and encouraging more equitable and peaceful societies. It is also critical to successfully bring social safety nets to scale.

Despite the sizable challenges, countries have succeeded in enhancing rules, institutions, and processes that have helped them approach development goals. Change occurs not only by reshaping the preferences and beliefs of the powerful, but also by altering incentives and taking into account the interests of previously excluded participants, thereby increasing contestability.

The *preferences and beliefs* of decision makers are critical in determining whether the outcome of the bargain will enhance welfare and whether the system will be responsive to the interests of those who have less influence. Changes in preferences can help jump-start coordination to reach a result that is better for all. Accumulating evidence on the positive impact of social safety nets can change the views of decision makers on social safety nets.

Incentives are fundamental to encouraging commitment in the policy arena, including policies that benefit the poor. The low quality of public services, such as schools and health centers, may prompt the more well-off to utilize private services, which weakens the willingness and the incentives of these individuals to contribute fiscally to supporting public services. Appropriate incentives can spur change: The first antipoverty programs in England and Wales in the 19th century were promoted by wealthy landed gentry who were eager to keep labor in rural areas, against the backdrop of the Industrial Revolution, which was drawing labor to the cities, as well as the threat represented by the French Revolution.

Contestability—who is included or excluded from the policy arena—is determined by the relative power of actors and the barriers to entry. If the procedures for selecting and implementing policies are more contestable, the policies are perceived as fair and induce cooperation more effectively—that is, they are considered legitimate. Participation and ownership in the design of rules can also increase voluntary compliance. However, entrenched social norms may make the participation of poor and disadvantaged groups in policy discussions and policy formulation more difficult; participants in civic activities tend to be wealthier and better educated.

Source: World Bank 2017.

about social safety nets in light of what they argued was an absence of a work ethic and a prevalence of lazybones in the country (Buur and Salimo 2017).

The distance between decision makers and the poor may account for these and other enduring preconceptions. Economic and social distance between groups can undermine support for social policies, while proximity results in greater support for redistribution (Graham 2002; Luttmer 2001; Pritchett 2005). African societies are highly unequal. The urban/rural divide and educational gaps represent the largest and most persistent sources of inequality (Beegle et al. 2016; Bossuroy and Cogneau 2013). Decision makers are socially, geographically, and psychologically distant from the poor, and they are less likely to make social safety nets a priority. Sen (1995, 21) makes an analogy with infectious diseases, which receive greater attention than noninfectious diseases because of the risk of contagion. "I sometimes wonder whether there is any way of making poverty terribly infectious," he writes. "If that were to happen, its general elimination would be, I am certain, remarkably rapid."

The emphasis on self-reliance and individual responsibility may fuel this perception of the poor and depress the interest in social safety nets. The ability to provide for the needs of one's family is usually considered an aspect of human dignity. In countries where relevant data exist, a majority of the population declares that it is humiliating to receive money without having to work for it (figure 3.2). This notion may be even more prevalent among well-educated

Figure 3.2 **Receiving Money without Working for It Is Considered Humiliating in Africa**

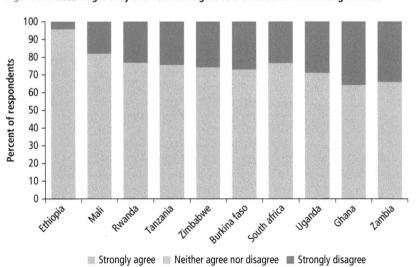

Source: Data of waves 4 (Tanzania, Uganda, Zimbabwe) and 5 (Burkina Faso, Ethiopia, Ghana, Mali, Rwanda, South Africa, Zambia) of the WVS (World Values Survey) (database), King's College, Old Aberdeen, United Kingdom, http://www.worldvaluessurvey.org/wvs.jsp.

segments of the population who were trained in the fundamentals of neoclassical economics, which emphasizes individual endeavor much more than the structural conditions that underpin poverty and vulnerability.

There are also widespread concerns that transfers to the poor are wasted resources. Even though most social safety net programs represent a very small percentage of gross domestic product (GDP, chapters 1 and 5), governments tend to use affordability as an argument against adopting or expanding such programs. This is usually accompanied by a stated preference for investing in programs that are perceived as more productive or better aligned with the small government model, which is focused on producing public goods, fixing market failures, and regulating free competition. The low-cost criterion of social safety net programs is thus associated with political, normative, and ideological factors rather than simply an assessment of the available fiscal space (Seekings 2016a).

Fears of dependency on social safety nets can be partly addressed through the dissemination of rigorous evidence (see chapter 2). There is growing experience with the positive impact of social safety nets on a range of indicators. The claim that social safety nets may represent a work disincentive among beneficiaries has been largely disproven (Banerjee et al. 2015a, 2015b). Similarly, it has been found that beneficiaries do not tend to use social transfers to purchase temptation goods, such as alcohol and tobacco, but rather to smooth consumption and raise human capital expenditures (Evans and Popova 2014; Handa et al. 2017).

Growing evidence also shows that cash transfers have productive impacts. These impacts mostly become manifest through investments in human capital through greater expenditures on nutrition and education among children (Alderman and Yemtsov 2013). Social safety nets may be considered an investment in future generations, with potentially large impacts on productivity and growth (Gertler et al. 2014). The strong productivity impacts of combinations of cash transfers and productive interventions—such as training, savings, and insurance—have been demonstrated (Argent, Augsburg, and Rasul 2014; Banerjee et al. 2015a, 2015b; Blattman, Fiala, and Martinez 2014; Premand and del Ninno 2016). This accumulating evidence is shifting the policy dialogue away from the preconception that social safety nets promote an alleged culture of dependency and is helping make the case that social safety nets foster poverty reduction and economic advancement.

The evidence should be presented in the policy dialogue early in the design stage, with particular attention to the relevance and relatability of the programs discussed. Evidence gathered within the country or neighboring countries carries more weight because decision makers may question the validity of results drawn from distant contexts. The results of randomized controlled trials are often easier to convey to a nonexpert audience and may be better received if one assumes the audience has a more general background in experimental methods of evaluating social programs. The capacity to bring forth meaningful, contextualized, and robust information is a key factor in fostering evidence-based policy making.

Perceptions of social safety nets may shift dramatically following study tours and other forms of direct learning from similar programs around the world. In Ethiopia, the integration of social protection objectives in a rural development program partly drew on a 1990s study tour by government officials to the Maharashtra Employment Guarantee Scheme, in India, for inspiration (Lavers 2016a). Senegal's Programme National de Bourses de Sécurité Familiale (national conditional cash transfer program) reflects the influence of the Brazilian and Mexican experiences, to which a senior official had been exposed in a previous position (Ndiaye 2017). Study tours by government officials from Kenya and Uganda to a pilot social cash transfer scheme in Zambia helped spread the model of cash transfers stripped of conditionalities (Hickey and Bukenya 2016; Pruce and Hickey 2017; Wanyama and McCord 2017). Visits to Ethiopia by government delegations from Mozambique, Rwanda, and Tanzania convinced key decision makers of the appeal of the Productive Social Safety Net (PSSN) (Buur and Salimo 2017; Lavers 2016b; Ulriksen 2016). Study tours have helped persuade some erstwhile opponents, as in the case of Uganda (Hickey and Bukenya 2016). In Mozambique, one of the key turning points in the government's decision to embrace social safety nets was a study tour to South Africa, where key officials realized that social safety nets would be a useful means of maintaining stability (Buur and Salimo 2017).

Given the importance of direct exposure to programs, pilot projects can help convince constituencies of the merits of a social safety net program. In Zambia, the main mechanism of fresh awareness has been rigorous evaluations of the effects of cash transfers at the pilot stage, which created a viable evidence base that civil servants could use later, once a political opening arose. In Uganda, an important factor in stimulating political support for the social safety net agenda has been the rollout of the Senior Citizens Grant Program. The promotion of the program as a success story through field visits, media story placements, and an evaluation seems to have created sufficient support to make the program a political reality that can no longer be challenged (Hickey and Bukenya 2016).

The importance of evidence and exposure to programs has stimulated the creation of groups of practitioners across countries that serve as sustainable platforms for sharing experiences and knowledge. Communities of practice on social safety nets have emerged across Africa, often facilitated by a development partner or an international agency. They have proved meaningful and efficient in promoting learning across programs, disseminating study results, and establishing a stable regional coalition of skilled technicians and advocates.

Carefully countering misconceptions and shifting beliefs is critical in shaping the policy dialogue around social safety nets. There is accumulating evidence that addresses the main causes of resistance, such as the notions that social safety nets may represent work disincentives and promote a culture of dependency, or that they do not have productive effects and should therefore be allocated a minimal share of public resources. Monitoring, disseminating the resulting evidence, and supplying direct exposure to existing social safety net programs may be fruitful in confronting misconceptions and demonstrating that social safety nets generally do not discourage, but rather promote, productive behavior.

Identify Windows of Opportunity in Rapidly Changing Environments

While transforming perceptions and priorities is a long process, crises and shocks have often provided momentum for the establishment of social safety net programs. The political appetite for social safety net programs may evolve quickly during periods of rapid economic or social change or crises (climate shocks, economic downturns, social conflicts), especially if the ruling coalition perceives the evolution as a potential threat to power. Incentives to create or strengthen social safety nets arise not only from the need to assist the vulnerable households most affected by the change or crises, but also from the political need to defuse the risk of political unrest and broaden support.

The appetite for expanding social safety nets evolves quickly during looming political crises. In Senegal, rising fuel and food prices following the 2008–09 financial crisis, alongside the decline in the key peanut and fishing economies, contributed to political demands for regime change and President Macky Sall's emphasis on social programs following his 2012 election (Ndiaye 2017). The 2005 electoral crisis and subsequent large-scale urban protests in Ethiopia alerted the ruling coalition to the threat posed by urban unemployment and poverty and were a major driver of the urban PSNP launched in 2016. A second impetus emerged after the 2007 elections, when the program came to be viewed as a means of resolving the political crisis associated with postelection violence.

A similar political mechanism also contributes to shaping responses to humanitarian crises. Emergency responses to conflicts or famines have become the basis of sustained social safety net systems in many countries across Africa. In Ethiopia, a major food crisis in 2002–03 exposed the limitations of the prevailing agricultural development strategy and led to the adoption of the PSNP (Lavers 2016a). A large number of programs were launched or expanded in the wake of the food, fuel, and financial crises of 2008–09. Droughts, such as in Botswana or Mauritania, and conflicts, such as in Mozambique and Sierra Leone, have spurred governments to establish emergency programs and lay the foundations of social safety net systems. Social funds, such as the social action funds in Malawi and Tanzania, were initially launched to provide community infrastructure in response to economic crises, but evolved into social safety net programs.

Similarly, major health crises have played a significant role in raising interest in improving social safety nets. The disruption of solidarity and protection mechanisms caused by the spread of HIV/AIDS, which led to the incapacity or death of many parents, was an important driver of the establishment of social safety nets in Botswana, Kenya, Lesotho, and Zambia (Granvik 2015; Hamer 2016; Pruce and Hickey 2017; Wanyama and McCord 2017). The impact on family structures shaped the design of social safety net programs. There was a shared emphasis on supporting the elderly, given their additional care burdens, and sometimes also orphans and vulnerable children. Rapidly expanding social safety nets involving cash transfers also formed a key pillar of the response of the government of Sierra Leone to the widespread socioeconomic impacts of the Ebola outbreak in 2014. A cash transfer program was being introduced at the time of the outbreak. Other social safety net programs were limited to labor-intensive public works. As the epidemic unfolded, the authorities became concerned that the disruptions in economic production and the potential for a drop-off in agricultural outputs would result in food shortages and other adverse socioeconomic impacts. In response, the rollout of the cash transfer program was accelerated and expanded to cover four times more beneficiaries; the benefit level was doubled; and the targeting mechanisms were rendered more agile and adapted to confront the vulnerabilities associated with the Ebola virus. The urgency of the situation also prompted the government to strengthen the quality of program implementation and harmonize delivery by governmental and nongovernmental institutions through the adoption of standard operating procedures. The expansion and consolidation of the program have been partially sustained since the Ebola epidemic, and the government has devoted a line to social safety nets in the domestic budget for the first time.

In many cases, emergency response programs established outside the sphere of social safety nets have created the political buy-in and delivery infrastructure on which programs have been developed. Food aid programs have often been the foundation of social safety net programs. Social safety nets in Botswana, Ethiopia, and Zimbabwe have been built directly on long-standing emergency drought relief programs involving public works and food aid components (Chinyoka and Seekings 2016; Hamer 2016). In Mozambique, the development partner promotion of social safety nets sought to build on an existing government program, the Food Subsidy Program. In such cases, governments and development partners have leveraged the continuity in public provisioning. This has not only helped secure political support for new initiatives, but has also facilitated implementation by enabling programs to build on existing delivery mechanisms and administrative systems. In some contexts, however, strong opposition has developed between stakeholders in humanitarian responses and supporters of social safety nets, resulting in duplication.

The links between crisis response mechanisms and social safety nets are also manifest in the recent development of adaptive social protection programs. These programs strive to embed mechanisms for rapidly expanding the coverage of social safety nets to include households or geographical areas as soon as they are hit by a shock, as in the multicountry Sahel Adaptive Social Protection Program launched in 2014. By building on social safety net delivery systems, these mechanisms boost the efficacy of emergency programs.

Economic reforms, which are often a response to shocks, may also raise the political support for social safety nets if there is an anticipated need for compensation among certain categories of people and more generally for garnering support for the reform. In Mozambique, the urban protests and riots that began in Maputo and spread across the country in 2008 and 2010 focused on the government's removal of subsidies under pressure from development partners and the rising costs of food and fuel. The disturbances constituted existential threats to the Mozambique Liberation Front, the dominant political party. The protests provided the impetus for the adoption of social safety net policies, notably the Productive Social Action Program launched in 2013 (Buur and Salimo 2017).

Social safety nets are becoming an explicit part of macroeconomic policy reforms. In the current context of fiscal tightening, many countries are looking for ways to rationalize and target schemes more effectively. Terminating universal subsidies—often regressive and expensive programs—may save public resources, but also negatively affects segments of the population. In Sierra Leone, the first wave of a removal of subsidies in October 2016 resulted in a price rise that would be potentially harmful to the poor. This prompted the government and the International Monetary Fund to discuss linking any further wave of subsidy removal to additional expansion of the social safety net program. In some countries in Asia, programs have also been broadened as part of an effort to stimulate economic growth. Examples include the enlargement of social pension systems in China and Thailand during the global financial crisis (ADB 2009; Kidd and Damerau 2016; Suwanrada and Wesumperuma 2012).

If they are established or expanded to respond to a particular crisis or source of tension, social safety nets generally have a broader range of objectives than merely poverty reduction. In addition to providing support to the poor, programs may aim at containing migration flows, preserving social peace, or temporarily mitigating the impact of a shock on population groups beyond the poor. For example, an objective of Ethiopian government policy has been to limit the rate of urban migration because of concerns that uncontrolled migration, in the absence of adequate urban employment opportunities, is likely to lead to social and political instability. Faced with a direct threat to its power, the ruling coalition attempted to use the PSNP to slow out-migration from rural areas, while augmenting the urban PSNP to provide greater incentives for people to move to or stay in small towns and cities, rather than migrate to Addis Ababa (Lavers 2013, 2016a).

Thus, because the political incentives to adopt or expand social safety nets may shift during periods of rapid change, especially if there is a perceived threat to the ruling coalition, stakeholders should monitor windows of opportunity to bring programs to scale. The rapid change may be caused by any one of numerous factors: climate stress, natural disasters, social tensions, economic crises and reforms, or political conflicts. In providing a clear rationale for direct support to populations, stakeholders may alter the incentives facing decision makers and open the space for shifts in the status quo. It is critical that the decision and policy makers involved in responding to crises or shocks have a good understanding of the potential of social safety net systems to help achieve policy and political objectives.

The Role of International Platforms and Partners

Regional and global organizations in which the large majority of African countries participate provide a normative framework for social safety nets and social protection more generally. The growing enthusiasm for social safety nets throughout the world has resulted in initiatives such as the African Union's Social Policy Framework, the United Nations' Sustainable Development Goals and associated targets, and the United Nations–wide Social Protection Floor Initiative. Social safety nets figure prominently in the Sustainable Development Goals. Goal 1.3 calls for the implementation of "nationally appropriate social protection systems and measures for all, including floors" and, by 2030, the achievement of "substantial coverage of the poor and vulnerable."[1] In 2006, the African Union issued the Livingstone Call for Action on Social Protection in Africa, which notes that "the guarantee of basic social protection strengthens the social contract between the state and citizens, enhancing social cohesion" and appeals for the expansion of social transfer programs.[2]

Most governments have signed agreements to advance human rights, as presented in the universal declaration of human rights, among which are the right to an adequate standard of living and the right to security and protection in case of shocks. Except for Botswana, the Comoros, Mozambique, and South Sudan, all countries in the region have ratified the International Covenant on Economic, Social, and Cultural Rights. As of February 2017, the African

Charter had been ratified by all countries, except South Sudan. The core values of human rights are enshrined in the constitutions of most countries, which identify particular groups as worthy of support (chapter 4; table 3.1). Most countries are also parties to regional or global organizations that provide a normative framework for social safety nets, including the African Union's Social Policy Framework, the Social Protection Floor Initiative, and the Sustainable Development Goals. While rights-based arguments may not have been a significant incentive in the adoption or expansion of social safety nets in the region, social safety nets can help governments fulfill their human rights missions by promoting social and economic rights and broader political rights. Human rights principles can also help promote the sustainability of programs (box 3.3).

It is unclear whether regional organizations and the related commitments of their members contribute to shifting incentives among policy makers. The various rights agreements are not mentioned in most case studies, and, for example, decision makers behind the Vision 2020 Umurenge Program (VUP) in Rwanda were unaware of the African Union framework, although Rwanda is a signatory (Lavers 2016b). On the other hand, this framework was mentioned as a factor in the expansion of social safety nets in Mozambique (Buur and Salimo 2017).

Development partners may influence the adoption and expansion of social safety nets through financing, but also by providing technical assistance, funding study tours and training, amassing and sharing knowledge, and piloting interventions (Chinyoka and Seekings 2016; Siachiwena 2016; Ulriksen 2016).

Table 3.1 **Constitutions Cover Vulnerable Groups**

	Ethiopia	Kenya	Mozambique	Rwanda	Sierra Leone	Uganda	Zambia
Women		X	X				
Elderly	X	X	X	X	X	X	X
Disabled	X	X	X	X	X	X	X
Orphans	X	X	X				
Children	X	X	X				
Youth		X	X		X		
Indigents				X			
Minorities		X				X	
Survivors of conflict			X	X			

Source: World Bank data review.

BOX 3.3

Social Safety Nets and Human Rights Reinforce Each Other

Social safety nets can help ensure the social and economic rights of the poor. They are anchored in international standards, particularly the African Charter on Human and Peoples' Rights; the International Covenant on Economic, Social, and Cultural Rights; and the Universal Declaration of Human Rights.[a] Under these standards, states are obligated to work toward the realization of a series of rights, including the right to an adequate standard of living, the right to security in case of shocks, and the right to health care and education. In this framework, individuals are rights-holders who may make legitimate claims, and states and other actors are duty-bearers that are responsible and can be held accountable for acts or omissions.

Laws and covenants recognize that governments may require time to safeguard these rights among entire populations, and they provide for the progressive realization of the rights. They highlight the special importance of safeguarding the rights of the most disadvantaged and marginalized groups and prohibit retrogressive measures.

Social safety nets may be central to recognizing these rights. Indeed, in practice, many governments face challenges in reaching the poorest population groups and supplying them with basic health care, nutrition, and education services. Because they usually cover groups, including those living in remote areas, characterized by limited contact with government programs, social safety nets may offer a way for governments to bring these people into the realm of public policy and thus help the most marginalized gain access to health care, education, and markets, in addition to providing them directly with support. This underlines the need to enhance the coverage and outreach of programs among the poorest and to respect the fundamental principle of equality in service delivery: establishing interventions among the poorest that are equal in quality to services and interventions among other population groups.

Social safety nets can promote other rights among the poor and, in particular, empower the poor to participate more broadly in societies and to demand other rights. By bringing the poor into the realm of public policies, offering them benefits, and covering them through public services, including identification systems, social safety nets may help the poorest realize other social, economic, and political rights. In small but significant ways, social safety net programs not only protect the poor and vulnerable; they also build democracy from the bottom up by strengthening political rights and contributing to the achievement of social justice.

Human rights also provide guiding principles for the implementation of programs, especially through the principles of equality, participation, and accountability. The principles of equality and nondiscrimination call for designs that avoid discrimination based on criteria other than poverty or vulnerability. They also demand a proactive

(continued next page)

Box 3.3 (continued)

approach in addressing obstacles that individuals or groups may face, for instance, by deploying outreach. Meaningful and effective participation requires an engagement with civil society in program design and implementation. Transparency and accountability can be realized only through mechanisms to promote adequate public awareness and options for expressing grievances and seeking redress. In practice, following these key principles fosters program support in civil society because the principles are fair and well understood, and failures and omissions can be challenged. This ultimately contributes to program expansion and long-term sustainability.

Source: Prepared by Eva Kloeve.
Note: For a detailed discussion of relevant issues, see Sepúlveda and Nyst (2012).
a. See "African Charter on Human and Peoples' Rights," African Commission on Human and Peoples' Rights, Banjul, The Gambia, http://www.achpr.org/instruments/achpr/; "International Covenant on Economic, Social, and Cultural Rights," Office of the United Nations High Commissioner for Human Rights, Geneva, http://www.ohchr.org/EN/ProfessionalInterest/Pages/CESCR.aspx; "Universal Declaration of Human Rights," United Nations, New York, http://www.un.org/en/universal-declaration-human-rights/.

Development partners finance an average 55 percent of program spending; the shares are typically higher in lower-income countries, fragile and conflict-affected states, and nations experiencing humanitarian crises (figure 3.3; appendix G, table G.8). Analysis of programs in Ethiopia, Ghana, Kenya, Lesotho, Mozambique, and Zambia suggests that international development partners tend to assign weight to existing national civil society and public sector proponents of social safety nets, help strengthen institutions entrusted with the delivery of programs, and encourage the adoption of mechanisms for more transparent and accountable delivery systems (Cherrier 2015). However, the multiplicity of partners and programs with distinct agendas and priorities may also create fragmentation and prevent the formation of a coherent policy framework (see chapter 4).

Development partners have been shown to influence the policy agenda through the dissemination of high-level strategic reports and normative frameworks, along with the policy dialogue and technical assistance provided to recipient countries. In many countries, these initiatives have been critical in developing the policy frameworks and instruments for social protection that have been adopted among bureaucrats and advocates in civil and political society.

Development partner involvement alone is not sufficient to achieve a shift toward the political adoption of social safety nets, which often results from attempts to secure or expand existing power in the face of changing

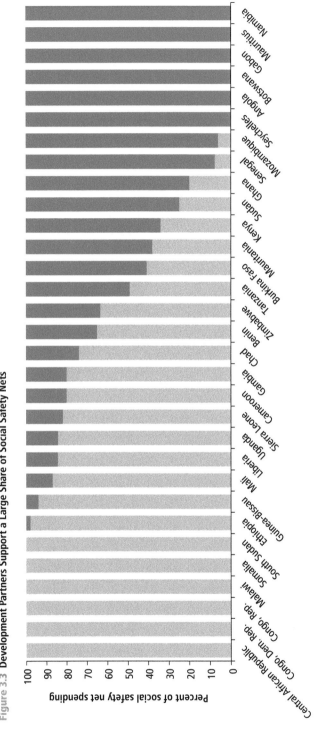

Figure 3.3 Development Partners Support a Large Share of Social Safety Nets

■ Share of development partners ■ Share of governments

Source: ASPIRE (Atlas of Social Protection Indicators of Resilience and Equity) (database), Administrative data, World Bank, Washington, DC, http://datatopics.worldbank.org/aspire/.
Note: AFD = Agence Française de Développement; CERF = Central Emergency Response Fund; CGAP = Consultative Group to Assist the Poor; DFID = UK Department for International Development; ECHO = European Community Humanitarian Aid Office; Enabel = Belgian development agency; ICRC = International Committee of the Red Cross; IFAD = International Fund for Agricultural Development; KOICA = Korea International Cooperation Agency; OFDA = Office of US Foreign Disaster Assistance; SHF = Somalia Humanitarian Fund; SIDA = Swedish International Development Cooperation Authority; UNDP = United Nations Development Programme; UNTF = UN Trust Fund to End Violence against Women; USAID = US Agency for International Development; WFP = World Food Programme.

circumstances (Hickey and Lavers 2017). For example, in Rwanda, the VUP originated in internal government debates over the Poverty Reduction Strategy Paper and the identification of a need for a poverty reduction program, for which the government later approached partners for support (Lavers 2016b). Similarly, in Ethiopia, various development partners had long voiced their concerns about the dysfunctional emergency food system constructed beginning in the 1980s and proposed a shift to cash and longer-term, predictable support. The policy agenda was set at a technical level. However, only when this coincided with government concerns precipitated by a series of crises did the government begin to take development partner proposals seriously (Lavers 2016a). In Senegal, while development partners had been involved in social protection for some time, the adoption of the national conditional cash transfer program appears to have been an internal decision by the Sall administration—notably, on the recommendation of a key adviser who had been exposed to the Brazilian and Mexican conditional cash transfer schemes (Ndiaye 2017). In general, decisions to expand social safety nets have tended to occur within broader government strategies, even if they are largely financed by development partners (Cherrier 2015).

Program Parameters Are Political

Politics is important in program design. Program parameters must take prevailing preferences, incentives, and perceptions into account. The best designs are those that are technically sound, administratively feasible, and politically savvy as they increase political buy-in while maximizing impacts. The elements of technical soundness and administrative feasibility are often addressed during program design, but the politically palatable aspect is frequently underestimated or dealt with reluctantly (Pritchett 2005). At the extreme, a perfect technical design that ignores the politics of support for social safety nets could eventually be the worst option for those it means to serve. In the words of Pritchett (2005, 5–6), policy makers who "ignored electoral politics would not just not do the 'optimal' thing for the poor, but would do the 'pessimal' thing for the group they were trying to protect," as becomes clear if support for the program decreases and the budget shrinks accordingly.

Political obstacles can be overcome to some degree by, for instance, choosing the characteristics and parameters of the programs so as to factor in political preferences or adapting targeting to make it compatible with political incentives. However, political tweaks need to be introduced as a last resort, kept to a minimum, and mitigated by a careful focus on inclusiveness and program transparency to avoid risks of capture.

Prevailing Preferences Should Be Factored In during the Selection of Programs

Several types of programs can be implemented as social safety nets, and various parameters can be included in the design. These encompass public works, cash transfers with or without conditionalities, accompanying measures, program duration, and graduation criteria. Decision making about these parameters is primarily technical and is taken to maximize the anticipated impact, but political considerations often come into play to maximize buy-in.

Among the features of programs that have a political nature are conditionalities. Conditionalities could be introduced with the technical motivation of boosting the impact of programs. They can also be proposed to address perceptions related to deservingness by requiring beneficiaries to undertake extra efforts. To promote investments in the human capital of household members, especially children, some programs condition the receipt of benefits on participation in information sessions on good practice behaviors or on actual behavioral changes, such as school registration and attendance or regular visits to health care facilities. These conditions, in addition to contributing to investments, can help address perceptions related to deservingness by requiring beneficiaries to undertake extra effort (see chapter 1, box 1.5).

Work requirements may help overcome concerns about the alleged laziness of transfer recipients. Labor-intensive public works are used for a range of reasons, including the embedded self-targeting mechanism or the need for community infrastructure (see chapter 1, box 1.2). For example, in Rwanda, the VUP officially has two objectives: to provide support for the poorest, and to make an economic contribution by building community infrastructure (health care and education facilities and roads). But work requirements also ensure that beneficiaries exert visible effort to receive benefits. Concerns about dependency have been dealt with in Ethiopia and Rwanda through a strong focus on public works carried out by all able-bodied beneficiaries, while unconditional support is provided only to those beneficiaries who cannot work.

To promote a productive impact, social safety net programs are sometimes cast as a component of a larger productive or developmental program. In several cases, complementary initiatives, such as credit and extension programs, supply a potential route toward graduation (box 3.4). The emphasis on self-reliance shows that social safety nets are expected to make an economic contribution or, at least, limit future government financial exposure. Ethiopia's PSNP and Rwanda's VUP are intended to be much more than transfer programs, but are explicitly framed as rural development programs, linking protective and

BOX 3.4

Graduation in Social Safety Net Programs

Social safety nets are designed to support the poor and vulnerable, but usually not on a permanent basis. Ideally, as households acquire resources and improve their ability to provide for themselves, they should graduate from the programs. To complement modest transfers, programs sometimes offer expanded social safety nets to enhance livelihoods, strengthen resilience, and lift people out of poverty (Daidone et al. 2015). The graduation components often include skills training, coaching, asset transfers, and the promotion of savings, in addition to the basic cash transfers. Evidence on the impacts of pilot interventions of a graduation model in six countries shows positive results, and many programs have incorporated elements of graduation in their design (Banerjee et al. 2015a, 2015b).

The VUP in Rwanda provides an example of a coordinated graduation system. The program design allows for (a) a reduction of income poverty through direct support involving cash transfers and public works wages; (b) facilitation of access to basic services for all beneficiary households, together with access to vocational training; and (c) streams of income generated from livelihood projects supported through financial services and other means (Gahamanyi and Kettlewell 2015). Participants along each of these pathways are expected to graduate to another pathway or exit the program after receiving one or a combination of these benefits over a significant period of time.

---

productive functions through transfers, credit, extension programs, and public works. As a result, while development partners framed the PSNP as the largest social safety net program in Africa, the government continued to describe it as a food security and agricultural program, omitting social protection entirely from national development strategies in 2006 and 2010. In Tanzania, the productive orientation of the PSSN was a major factor in convincing the government and securing political support because it linked the program to general concerns about dependency and the importance of self-reliance, an idea that goes back to Nyerere, but also to the vision of development advocated by contemporary governments (Ulriksen 2016). Having a broader productive focus can help a larger range of stakeholders relate to programs and appreciate their value. Similarly, humanitarian interventions are increasingly complemented by resilience-building programs, which focus on helping households raise their ability to face future shocks through increased productivity and diversity in income-generating activities.

The fear of promoting a culture of dependency may also be addressed by including clear time bounds in social safety net programs. In some cases, beneficiaries are only eligible to receive benefits for a fixed period (typically between 2 and 5 years). The main rationale is generally that, within a restricted budget, limiting duration is a condition for expanding coverage and therefore maximizing the impact and fairness of the program. However, imposing a clear time limit has also been used as a way to reassure decision makers nervous about encouraging long-term reliance on government-provided support. For example, in 2010, a combination of these reasons led Ethiopian development strategists to adopt the very ambitious target of graduating approximately 80 percent of PSNP participants by 2015 (Lavers 2016a). Recertification processes can be considered a flexible time limitation. For instance, in Senegal, the national conditional cash transfer program covers households for five years, after which a recertification process is planned to evaluate whether households should stay in or exit the program. Recertification does not automatically push beneficiaries out of social safety nets, as in a time-bound design, but it may offer reassurance that the program is based on actual needs.

Adjust Targeting to Garner Support for Social Safety Nets

Political preferences and incentives shape the selection criteria for social safety net beneficiaries, and targeting methods often reflect a balance between programmatic and political objectives.

In many contexts, the response to concerns about deservingness and self-reliance has been to target only those who are clearly unable to provide for themselves. For instance, programs in Kenya, Uganda, and Zambia are categorically targeted, as well as means-tested in most cases, to focus on groups that are considered deserving of support, most notably mothers and the elderly, but also children and the disabled. While overall poverty-targeted programs account for the majority of spending in the region, most of the social safety net spending in Central Africa and West Africa goes to categorically targeted programs (figure 3.4; appendix G, table G.6).

Low-income countries and fragile states also allocate a large share of spending to categorically targeted programs in terms of the life-cycle. In Southern Africa and upper-middle- or high-income countries, significant shares of social safety net spending go to programs focused on the elderly (figure 3.5; appendix G, table G.6). Central Africa, East Africa, and fragile states allocate more of their social safety net spending than other country groups to special groups through emergency interventions directed at refugees and returning migrants.

The need to support the most vulnerable is sometimes enshrined in legal systems. Constitutions often single out categorical groups as worthy of public support, rather than the poor in general (see table 3.1). Of course, programs with objectives different or additional to poverty reduction warrant a categorical approach, for example, programs focused on children or pregnant women. And selecting beneficiaries based on categories that are collectively perceived as vulnerable can also help in advocating for higher levels of resources dedicated to social safety nets.

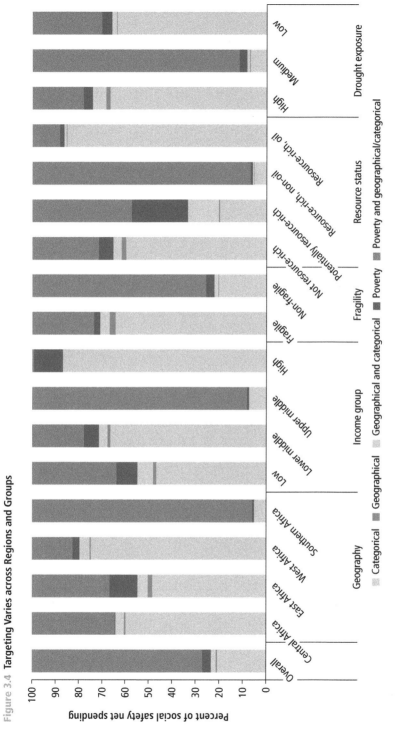

Figure 3.4 Targeting Varies across Regions and Groups

Legend: ▨ Categorical ▤ Geographical ▥ Geographical and categorical ▦ Poverty ▨ Poverty and geographical/categorical

Percent of social safety net spending

Geography: Central Africa, East Africa, West Africa, Southern Africa

Income group: Low, Lower middle, Upper middle, High

Fragility: Fragile, Non-fragile

Resource status: Not resource-rich, Potentially resource-rich, Resource-rich, Resource-rich, non-oil, Resource-rich, oil

Drought exposure: High, Medium, Low

Overall

Source: ASPIRE (Atlas of Social Protection Indicators of Resilience and Equity) (database), World Bank, Washington, DC, http://www.worldbank.org/aspire.
Note: The poverty category includes all programs that explicitly target households on the basis of welfare, poverty, or vulnerability. To identify households, these programs rely on community targeting, means or income tests, proxy-means tests, pension tests, self-targeting, or a combination of these. See methodology in appendices A and B.

Figure 3.5 The Elderly and Children Benefit Most From Social Safety Nets

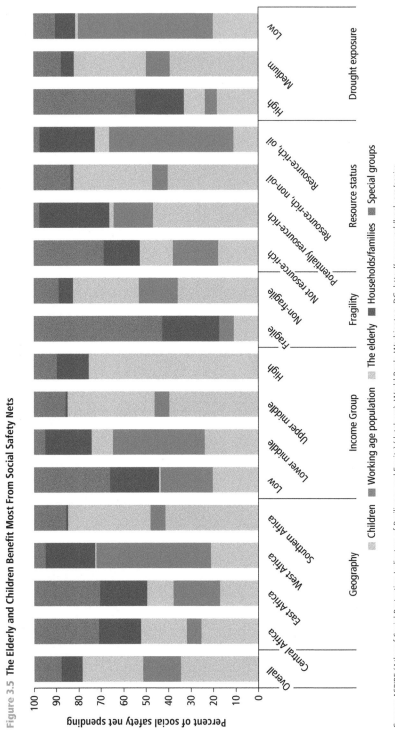

Source: ASPIRE (Atlas of Social Protection Indicators of Resilience and Equity) (database), World Bank, Washington, DC, http://www.worldbank.org/aspire.
Note: See methodology in appendices A and B.

Political incentives may also lead to the targeting of groups besides the poorest to expand support for the program. In some cases, while focusing on specific geographical areas would make sense from a poverty perspective, national coverage might be necessary to secure support (Gelbach and Pritchett 2002; Moene and Wallerstein 2001; van de Walle 1998). This may stem from concerns about equity and universality or the fear of alienating powerful constituents by excluding them. For example, while designing a new national social protection program in 2016, the Nigerian government determined that, for political reasons, all six geographical zones had to be covered by a pilot program on productive activities, which led to an adjustment of the targeting protocol. In Kenya, the consensus reached by members of parliament was to deliver about 30 percent of all transfers to all constituencies regardless of need (in line with political incentives), while allocating the rest according to the local prevalence of poverty, thereby maintaining pro-poor targeting, while ensuring political support. In Uganda, the choice to roll out the Senior Citizen's Grant Program by targeting the 100 eldest pensioners in new districts arguably reflects a political consideration to distribute a small transfer as widely as possible, rather than pursue a more technically informed and pro-poor design. At the end of the spectrum, universal coverage may be the preferred option if the focus is on strict equality of treatment and the avoidance of any form of exclusion. That is, "the beneficiaries of thoroughly targeted poverty alleviation programs are often quite weak politically and may lack the clout to sustain the programs and maintain the quality of the services offered," writes Sen (1995, 14). "Benefits meant exclusively for the poor often end up being poor benefits."

Similarly, politically influential groups may receive more benefits than their economic situation would require. For instance, the elderly tend to be disproportionately supported relative to children, even though universal programs for children would have a much larger impact on poverty reduction than social pension programs (Guven and Leite 2016). This may be because the elderly can be relatively powerful voters, while children's voices are not taken into account. Indeed, in Ghana, Nigeria, Rwanda, South Africa, and Zimbabwe, between 60 percent and 70 percent of individuals believe that the elderly enjoy too much political influence.[3]

Even if programs are targeted to poverty, the targeting methodology should be chosen with consideration for the consequences for voice and agency across communities. Targeting based on independent data collection, such as the proxy means test, offers some guarantees of independence and minimizes the risks of capture, but it may be viewed negatively as an exogenous technical process with little community involvement. Conversely, community-based targeting generally fosters ownership and buy-in by communities or local leaders, but exposes programs to risk of local capture if the program is not run properly. Beyond the various statistical properties that distinguish both methodologies, choosing to use either one or to combine them may also respond to a need to adapt to political constraints or foster buy-in among certain groups.

A Possible Trade-Off between Political and Technical Imperatives

Taking political considerations into account in designing a social safety net program may result in a technically suboptimal program. In Rwanda, for example, the emphasis placed on infrastructure development has made ensuring the labor intensity of public works challenging. Indeed, faced with strong incentives to meet infrastructure targets, local officials have tended to resort to capital-intensive production techniques, thereby reducing the proportion of resources available to wages and favoring strong, able-bodied participants, who might not be the poorest (Lavers 2016a, 2016b). Similarly, imposing conditionalities might result in greater impact; but enforcement can be costly and resource intensive. Meanwhile, imposing time limits or predetermined targets in terms of the number of households expected to graduate from a program can conflict with the objective of poverty reduction. For instance, the decision by the Ethiopian government to graduate a large share of PSNP beneficiaries is said to have resulted in a significant drop in PSNP enrollment after regional governments instructed local administrations to exit participants regardless of the state of food security (Lavers 2016a).

If political considerations inform the choice of target groups, transparency and effectiveness are paramount in protecting programs from capture. The competing tensions between political incentives and more technical approaches to the design of pro-poor programs are particularly evident for the issue of targeting and the selection of beneficiaries and districts. For example, the selection of program participants in Kenya was initially conducted by local committees and reflected the preferences of tribal chiefs, with subsequent validation by the national social protection secretariat. This process has been revised subsequently through the creation of social assistance committees as a result of demands by members of parliament to allow greater involvement in program management in their constituencies, but the number of political appointees on these new committees has triggered fears of patronage (Wanyama and McCord 2017). If this process becomes politicized, the need arises for delivery agencies to become (as far as possible) pockets of bureaucratic effectiveness that are not only well led and managed but are also freer of political pressures (Roll 2014).

It is therefore critical to resort to political tweaks to program design only if resistance cannot be addressed through evidence-based dialogue and to impose strict safeguards. Strengthening the foundations of programs can prevent distortionary use of programs for political gain. Clear operational manuals, information campaigns, and accountability mechanisms can help promote the faithful implementation of programs. While program parameters should not be set too firmly, for they may require adjustment as conditions evolve, basic rights and principles might be institutionalized to discourage manipulation for political gain (chapter 4).

Political Impacts May Favor Social Safety Net Sustainability

The political environment is not an exogenous, unalterable factor that overdetermines policy choices. Politics and policies have a two-way relationship. By promoting the empowerment of their beneficiaries and changing the way beneficiaries relate to governments, social safety nets can shift the incentives faced by decision makers and promote program sustainability.

Social Safety Nets May Foster Empowerment

Social safety net programs may increase power and promote autonomy among beneficiary households. In addition to their broader impact on well-being (chapter 2), cash transfer programs enhance self-esteem among individuals. Positive impacts on psychosocial well-being lead to positive impacts on educational performance, participation in social life, and empowerment for decision making. In Kenya, Mozambique, and Zambia, orphans, other vulnerable children, and disabled beneficiaries report that the cash transfers have boosted their self-confidence, sense of dignity, ability to be more assertive, and expectation of future well-being (Attah et al. 2016; Handa et al. 2014a, 2014b; Haushofer and Shapiro 2013; Jones et al. 2016; Seidenfeld, Handa, and Tembo 2013). However, social safety net programs can also be associated with stereotype threat or stigma because their beneficiaries are labeled as extremely poor (Molyneux 2016). Programs can also have negative side effects, such as feelings of shame because of reliance on program support. Any program that requires people to be identified as poor and unable to provide for themselves would, Sen (1995, 12) warns, "tend to have some effects on their self-respect as well as on the respect accorded them by others."

Social safety nets may also promote greater cohesion and empowerment in recipient communities. By improving the living conditions of their beneficiaries, programs promote greater inclusion by reducing the stigma of helplessness among people with disabilities in Ghana, ensuring that children can go to school well dressed and clean in Lesotho and Zimbabwe, and, more generally, by raising the social status of the poorest, thereby promoting a greater willingness to befriend recipients of cash transfers in Malawi (Attah et al. 2016; MacAuslan and Riemenschneider 2011; Oduro 2014). Greater inclusion is also realized if beneficiaries meet their social obligations and engage in relations of reciprocity, such as paying church tithes or funeral group fees, contributing to savings groups, and attending weddings (chapter 2; Pavanello et al. 2016).

Households in Ghana, Lesotho, and Zimbabwe were able to reenter risk-sharing networks (Attah et al. 2016). Investing in these risk-sharing networks improves household social support and resilience to shocks. Cohesion and proximity increase the support of richer households for social safety net programs, thereby contributing to program sustainability.

However, the impact on social cohesion depends on the acceptability of the selection process for nonbeneficiaries. Indeed, programs may also have negative impacts on inclusion and solidarity, for instance, if the process of selecting beneficiaries is perceived as unclear or unfair or if poverty is significant (Ellis 2012). In Lesotho, tensions between transfer recipients and nonrecipients grew because of a lack of knowledge about selection criteria and the perception that deserving households had been excluded from the program (Attah et al. 2016). Social safety net programs can also alter patterns of informal support within communities, eroding traditional moral obligations toward the poor. In Zimbabwe, nonrecipients were more reluctant to share agricultural inputs or participate in community work to build shared assets; and in Ghana, beneficiaries expressed fears about the consequences they would face if the program ended, in light of eroding traditional support practices (MacAuslan and Riemenschneider 2011; Oduro 2014).

Introducing social safety nets may therefore affect the local political economy. If the selection process is handled in a way that minimizes stereotype threats and the resentment of nonbeneficiaries, social safety net programs may promote greater empowerment among individual beneficiaries and greater cohesion in communities. In African countries, as elsewhere, cultural norms are not static and can be influenced by policies.

Shifting the Public's Expectations of Governments

Social safety net programs can bring governments closer to beneficiaries by showing how governments can effectively respond to needs. New programs can offer important entry points for shifting interactions between governments and individuals (Jones et al. 2016). In South Africa, social safety net programs reportedly made citizens proud of their country (Plagerson, Harpham, and Kielmann 2012). Programs can shape this relationship by providing space for regular interaction between representatives of the government and individuals. In Ghana, beneficiary forums and payment cards helped encourage a contract between the government and beneficiaries and provided a means for beneficiaries to make claims and access social services (Oduro 2014). In South Africa, the affidavit required as proof of a beneficiary's income was considered a direct channel of communication with the government (Plagerson, Harpham, and Kielmann 2012). In Mauritania, a contract is signed between beneficiaries and the government as households are registered, which highlights the contractual basis of the program.

Decentralizing program administration may help foster this local political dynamic. The Tanzania pilot cash transfer program run by TASAF empowered local elected committees in targeting and distributing cash transfers. Compared with the centrally run program, this substantially increased trust in leaders and elected members of local government organizations, boosted voter turnout in local elections, and fostered informal solidarity networks among community members (Evans, Holtemeyer, and Kosec 2017). If programs are centralized and frontline service providers have limited authority to respond to specific queries or complaints, the connection between a program and its beneficiaries is likely to be reduced (Ayliffe, Aslam, and Schjødt 2016; Jones and Samuels 2013). Decentralization is associated, however, with risks of looser oversight and local capture that need to be carefully managed (see chapter 4).

Social safety nets can help reshape the relationship between individuals and the state by expanding the capacity of individuals or groups to access other government processes, for instance, by supporting households in their efforts to obtain national identity documentation (see box 3.3). For example, showing a valid birth certificate has been a condition for receiving the Child Support Grant in South Africa. Because this requirement effectively barred access to the program by certain groups, a new procedure was introduced for delivering birth certificates directly at hospitals, thereby facilitating the acquisition of formal identification among new segments of the population (Glassman and Temin 2016). This not only allows full participation in the program by the poorest or most vulnerable, but it may also have additional benefits for recipients (Hurrell and MacAuslen 2012).

Social safety nets may induce changes in the discourse on poverty and the role of the government and public policy, including perceptions of the obligations of the government to recognize rights. These efforts help individuals understand they are rights-holders and governments realize they are duty-bearers. A sentiment analysis in Tanzania shows that the media is becoming supportive of the PSSN as an instrument that contributes to reducing poverty and inequality (box 3.5).

Social Accountability Mechanisms May Strengthen the Political Feedback Loop

Social accountability mechanisms may further empower beneficiaries. Accountability elements have been increasingly included in social safety net programs in recent years to limit exclusion and to promote voice and rights. Program features such as grievance redress and community and beneficiary participation may be contributing to the development of social contracts (Ringold et al. 2012). Molyneux (2016, 4) argues that social accountability mechanisms can create "some of the embryonic forms of citizenship that can emerge when recipients of welfare begin not only to 'see the state' (Corbridge et al. 2005), but also engage with it and challenge it where it falls short of expectations."

BOX 3.5

The Media Eventually Became Favorable toward the Social Safety Net in Tanzania

A rigorous analysis of the media coverage of Tanzania's PSSN shows that coverage intensified as the program was expanded.[a] The PSSN was designed in 2011 after the successful pilot launch of a conditional cash transfer targeting 6,000 beneficiaries. This developed into a program that provided a combination of labor-intensive public works, conditional cash transfer interventions, and productive activities, including basic skills and awareness training, savings promotion, productive grants, and coaching. During the first stage of the PSSN (2012–13), expansion was modest. A full expansion started in stage 2 (2014–16), and the program was reaching 400,000 beneficiaries by 2014 and more than 1 million households by 2015. Media coverage was almost nonexistent in the early stages and increased along with program coverage during the first stage of the expansion (figure B3.5.1). In 2015, media coverage stabilized, even though the number of beneficiaries tripled.

A sentiment analysis has shown that the media has gradually become more supportive of the PSSN as an instrument that helps reduce poverty and narrow inequality. The overall perception of the program in 2010–15 was positive; 76 percent of relevant media articles had a tone that was favorable. Examples of positive coverage included praise for the program as "a vital vehicle for government to eradicate poverty in the country" (2015), "helping people to get out of poverty and improving social and economic welfare" (2014), and "promoting health and boosting education in the country's poorest households" (2014). The average positive tone became markedly more evident as the program was expanded.

Beyond the poverty impacts of the program, the media highlighted coverage, targeting, conditionalities, and productive activities. The direct beneficiaries are people living below the

Figure B3.5.1 Press Coverage Increased with the Expansion of the PSSN

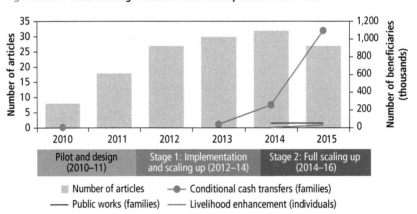

Source: Number of beneficiaries: ASPIRE (Atlas of Social Protection Indicators of Resilience and Equity) (database), World Bank, Washington, DC, http://www.worldbank.org/aspire.

(continued next page)

Box 3.5 (continued)

poverty line and people temporarily affected by short-term shocks. During the first years of the program, news articles focused on the need to expand the program to "cover every poor person in the targeted areas" (2013) and expressed worry that "the poorest families tend to be left behind" (2014). In general, conditionalities and productive activities were praised as a way to motivate beneficiaries to participate and commit to the program. For example, the program "helped poor households to engage in economic activities, thus improving their

Figure B3.5.2 The Media Became More Favorable during Program Expansion

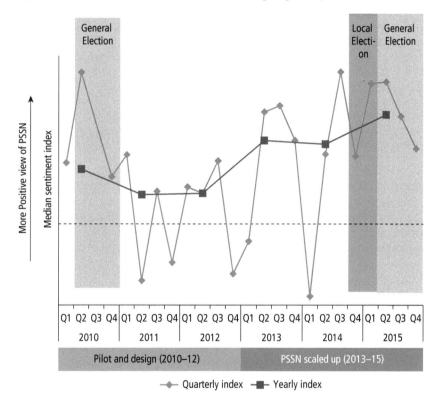

Source: The analysis was based on 142 newspaper articles published in English in 2010–15. The list of articles was built from the Factiva database using search-constructs related to PSSN and TASAF and includes articles from Arusha Times, Business Daily, Citizen, East Africa Business Week, Nation, New Times, Observer, and Tanzania Daily. However, Tanzania Daily News accounts for more than 85 percent of the articles. The sentiment analysis indicates the general perception (positive or negative) of the selected articles. It relies on a simple counting methodology of negative and positive words, the list of which is provided in the sentiment dictionary created by Hu and Liu (2004). The method assigns values of 1 to positive words and –1 to negative words. The sentiment index for every article is the normalized sum of positive and negative values. Words such as "poverty" and "poor" that are included in the Hu and Liu negative words list, but do not have this connotation in the context of social safety net programs, have been excluded. For the database, see Factiva (database), Dow Jones and Company, New York, https://www.dowjones.com/products/factiva/.

(continued next page)

Box 3.5 (continued)

welfare" and "helped to improve academic performance of children from poor households" through an "increase in school enrollment" (2013). Several news outlets examined the graduation strategy and urged beneficiaries to make proper use of the training and resources supplied through the program to establish income-generating activities, thereby linking the impacts of the program to the values of self-reliance. It was claimed that the program had been "requested by poor households . . . to provide them with training on entrepreneurship and financial management so they would be self-dependent" (2014).

In line with international experience, press coverage of the program was influenced by elections (figure B3.5.2). In the run-up to the 2010 and 2015 general elections, the media emphasized the president's achievements during his term. The positive perception of the PSSN rose initially, but decreased as the election drew closer. As in the case for similar programs elsewhere, including in Latin America, some media articles raised questions about the perceived political use of the PSSN before elections. For instance, by the end of 2014, news articles were reporting that "politicians have been warned to stop utilizing the projects implemented under the Tanzania Social Action Fund (TASAF) programs for their political advantages" (2014). Although these reports were not substantiated, and whether the incumbent party or the opposition was seeking to benefit is unclear, the evidence demonstrates the potential for the politicization of cash transfers.

They can stimulate a greater awareness of entitlement and encourage the capacity to make claims (Harland 2014). Osofian (2011), for instance, finds that the Hunger Safety Net Program (HSNP) in northern Kenya, which includes a grievance mechanism and a rights education component, has helped communities hold local government to account. In Sierra Leone, confidence in the social safety net program has reportedly been greatly enhanced since the independent Anticorruption Commission began handling grievance redress and audits and using technology to shorten the response time.

Social accountability may not function equally in all programs or for all types of beneficiaries. Social accountability mechanisms tend to be deployed most effectively by better-educated, wealthier, and more able-bodied citizens rather than poorer and more vulnerable groups with less capacity to organize and voice their concerns (Giannozzi and Khan 2011; King and Hickey 2017). The low political mobilization around the HSNP may be attributed to the fact that beneficiaries were mostly nomadic pastoralists in northern Kenya, a marginalized group "that has tended to stay outside most domestic politics and has little leverage to make large demands" (Hurrell and MacAuslan 2012, 268). The poor might also not be part of networks that are critical to distribute information and convey concerns or may have limited agency to raise their concerns (Grandvoinnet, Aslam, and Raha 2015). Programs that are time bound also likely limit the development of a broader sense of rights and entitlement to benefits.

The design of appropriate social accountability mechanisms is therefore crucial to maximizing programs' potential. The composition of oversight committees appears to be an influential determinant of the effectiveness and impact on beneficiaries. Grievance or redress offices must therefore be independent of the program implementation system so they can rectify errors rather than strengthen the position of program officers (Hurrell and MacAuslan 2012). Social accountability mechanisms may have greater potential if programs facilitate the formation of groups of beneficiaries that can leverage collective action, despite the private nature of the good involved and the individual level of targeting. Efforts to broaden bottom-up accountability mechanisms might be reinforced through stronger incentives for frontline providers (hierarchical discipline associated with top-down governance) (Brett 2003).

Social accountability mechanisms may require time to deliver impacts on power relationships. At early stages, the effectiveness of social accountability mechanisms in Africa is likely to be influenced by local power dynamics and social norms (Tembo 2012). It takes significant time to build an environment that promotes voice and accountability, and progress is not linear (Grandvoinnet, Aslam, and Raha 2015). In settings where patron-client relations are pervasive, maintaining good relations with powerful individuals is the rational choice for the poor (Cornwall, Robins, and Von Lieres 2011). Social accountability mechanisms in social safety nets in Zambia have so far not challenged patron-client networks, although this may partly reflect the weak effort to incorporate such mechanisms within the cash transfer program there (Harland 2014).

Even if their impact is mostly felt in the longer term, feedback loops may be critical at the outset of a program. Indeed, much of the institutionalist literature argues that policy feedback may be particularly influential at nascent stages of social policy development in establishing patterns of path dependence (Pierson 1993).

Closing the Loop: The Risks and Opportunities of Politicization

Introducing or expanding social safety nets affects the relationship between the poor and vulnerable and their government. It also modifies incentives among politicians. Evidence is building that direct support for the poor can become a significant topic in electoral processes and the focus of the campaigns of competing parties or candidates. Because of the growing number of closely fought elections across Africa, the ground is becoming more fertile.

Indeed, social safety net programs may be adopted or expanded to strengthen electoral support. There is some evidence that elections have helped catalyze a policy focus on social safety nets, such as the correlation between the 2002 and 2007 elections and spikes in social safety net expenditures in Kenya or the introduction of the Livelihood Empowerment against Poverty Program (LEAP) before the 2008 elections in Ghana. In Botswana, the Ipelegeng Public Works Program was used specifically to extend rural drought relief programs to urban areas where opposition support had been growing (Hamer 2016). In Uganda, pilot initiatives and the subsequent rollout of social safety nets have been shaped by the need of the ruling National Resistance Movement to secure support in the previously opposition-leaning north, especially in the run-up to the 2016 elections (Hickey and Bukenya 2016). In Senegal, President Abdoulaye Wade proposed the Plan Sésame the year before elections in 2007, which may have contributed to his electoral victory, though the plan failed to materialize in the absence of funding and sustained political commitment (Ndiaye 2017).

The political appetite for expanding social safety nets may also derive from more local governments and local politicians. Pressure from local members of parliament to expand programs in their districts suggests that they realize the potential rewards that could be produced through social safety net programs. For instance, in Kenya and Zambia, there has been pressure from members of parliament to expand small-scale pilot initiatives to new districts as a result of positive perceptions about the programs and the sense that political benefits can be gained from delivering programs to communities (Pruce and Hickey 2017; Wanyama and McCord 2017).

As they gain prominence and visibility, social safety nets become more central as a topic for political branding and electoral campaigns. In many cases, individual leaders seek to become associated with particular programs. Prime Minister Bethuel Pakalitha Mosisili was a key figure pushing for the adoption of the Old-Age Pension in Lesotho, to the point that pensioners regularly talked of collecting their Mosisili (Granvik 2015). Similarly, President Ian Khama of Botswana portrayed expanded public employment programs as his direct contribution, leading to the frequent reference to "our father's programs" (Hamer 2016). To some degree, this mirrors the common reference to the VUP in Rwanda as a gift from President Paul Kagame.

Social safety nets have become an integral part of political debate and electoral promises. In competitive settings, such as Malawi and Sierra Leone, social safety net programs have been used by some presidential candidates as a brand to help differentiate themselves from political rivals during election campaigns (Albrecht 2017; Hamer 2016). In Lesotho, the Old-Age Pension became an electoral issue in 2007, when the main opposition party pledged to raise the monthly payment by a factor of more than three. Ultimately, the incumbent won the election, potentially partly as a result of the introduction of the pension; but, in the process, the opposition also increased support for the program, helping to consolidate the program's sustainability (Devereux and White 2010; Granvik 2015).

Voters tend to reward politicians for social safety net programs if these are well implemented. Evidence on the effect of social safety nets on voting behavior and electoral outcomes is derived mostly from large-scale cash transfer programs in Asia and Latin America (box 3.6). At the national level, electoral benefits generally extend to members of the incumbent party. Impacts are lasting, but eventually taper off. Voters typically reward incumbent parties, rather than the parties that initiated the programs, suggesting that adopting and

BOX 3.6

Electoral Impacts of Social Safety Net Programs in Asia and Latin America

Cash transfers produce electoral benefits for incumbents. In Brazil, Bolsa Família, a cash transfer program, greatly increased the vote share of the incumbents in the three presidential elections from 2002 to 2010, boosting the probability that the poorest voters chose the incumbent by a margin of 32 percent in 2006 and by 21 percent in 2010 (Zucco 2013). In Colombia, beneficiaries of the Familias en Acción conditional cash transfer program were more likely to register, cast a ballot, and vote for the incumbent party in the 2010 presidential election (Báez et al. 2012). A 12.5 percent increase in the beneficiary rate in a municipality led to a 1 percent increase in the incumbent's vote share (Nupia 2011). In Mexico, the cash transfer program led to a 7 percent increase in voter turnout and a 9 percent rise in the vote share among beneficiaries for the incumbents during the 2000 presidential elections (De La O 2013). In 2006, the candidate of the incumbent party led among beneficiaries by double digits, while he was even with the opposition candidate among nonbeneficiaries (Díaz-Cayeros, Estévez, and Magaloni 2009). In Uruguay, beneficiaries of a temporary cash transfer program were 11–13 percent more likely to express support for the incumbent compared with people slightly above the program cutoff (Manacorda, Miguel, and Vigorito 2011).

The political gains endure for a while, but seem to decline eventually. Indeed, parties that originally initiate programs do not receive the same electoral benefits as incumbents. The existence of the cash transfers may also push nonbeneficiaries to defect from the incumbent, especially in countries with large, visible programs (Díaz-Cayeros, Estévez, and Magaloni 2009; Linos 2013). Antiprogram voters may continue to defect for several years, and the pro-incumbent effects also diminish as voters mobilize less (Corrêa and Cheibub 2016).

Cash transfers produce electoral returns for local officials. A field experiment in the Philippines found that the vote share of incumbent mayors was 26 percent higher in competitive elections in municipalities where a cash transfer program was implemented in all villages, compared with municipalities in which the program was only implemented in half the villages (Labonne 2013). In Honduras, the Programa de Asignación Familiar, a household transfer program, raised an incumbent mayor's probability of reelection by 39 percent, but did not influence voting in the presidential election (Linos 2013). A program in Indonesia that targeted benefits to villages boosted vote shares among legislative candidates from the incumbent president's party in the 2009 elections, but did not increase the votes for the incumbent president and had no effect on village politics (Tobias, Sumarto, and Moody 2014).

Voters often seem unclear about whom or which government administration to credit for social safety net programs. The program in the Philippines boosted the reelection chances of mayors, although the program had been implemented by the central government with no input or influence from the mayors (Labonne 2013). Similarly, in Honduras, the mayor and local government played no role in determining whether

(continued next page)

Box 3.6 (continued)

municipalities were selected for the cash transfer program (Linos 2013). A state-level program in Brazil significantly increased support for incumbent mayors (Corrêa 2015). In Uruguay, however, beneficiaries seemed able to differentiate between government entities, showing greater approval only for institutions that supported their cash transfers (Manacorda, Miguel, and Vigorito 2011).

Source: Based on a literature review by Jennifer Turner.

---

supporting the expansion of the programs of the previous government can generate political rewards. In the Latin American and Asian studies, local leaders also seem to benefit, even from nationwide programs. Electoral returns are reported among local officials, sometimes in place of the returns for the elected national officials, as voters often seem unclear about whom to credit for social safety net programs. This support does not stop newly elected officials from holding the government accountable for poor performance (Pavão 2016).

The higher the political stakes, the more program manipulation and capture become attractive. As programs increase in the potential to help secure political support, they begin to fall into the grey area between promising to satisfy the demands of the electorate and vote buying (box 3.7). This can encourage the targeting of programs on the basis of patronage rather than need (Lippert-Rasmussen 2011; Stokes 2007). For instance, in Uganda and Zambia, programs that were once relatively well protected are now reportedly being politicized because members of parliament are pressuring technocrats to include their districts in the rollout. Targeting could also be manipulated to reward supporters of a political party and punish opponents.

A strict respect for the guiding principles of human rights, equity, and clear and transparent operating procedures is paramount in avoiding any suspicion of politically motivated fraud or abuse. The Benin government pushed for the highly decentralized delivery of benefits under the Youth Employment Project, including a cash grant. Nationwide, mayors and local elected officials actively mobilized their services and were keen to showcase participation to their constituencies in the hope that this would reap electoral and political benefits. To avoid the associated risks of clientelism, the government decided to organize a transparent, random selection of beneficiaries. Scratch cards showing random numbers were handed out to each applicant at the time of registration, and beneficiaries were drawn after the end of the registration process through a high-profile public lottery broadcast on national television. This process protected the project from any accusation of fraud and eased the pressure on mayors, most of whom expressed relief because they were thus also being protected from local demands for patronage.

Distinguishing Electoral Accountability and Clientelism in Theory and Practice

Politicians who make promises about the policies and programs they will support once in office are a given of democratic electoral competition. The promises provide voters with information to evaluate the platforms of the various parties and decide how they will vote, but they also enable voters to hold politicians to account for success or failure in delivering on their promises. A functioning competitive democracy depends on the aspiration of politicians to reap electoral benefit by enacting programs that enhance the welfare of their constituencies.

Clientelism is different. While voter mobilization involves politicians promising and then delivering goods to gain and retain support, regardless of whether the support comes from individuals who voted for the candidate, political clientelism involves an unequal exchange, whereby the patron trades the distribution of money or other resources for votes and other kinds of support (Kitschelt 2000; Stokes 2007; van de Walle 2007). The fundamental difference between the two is whether the promises and provision of support are impersonal or personal.

Political clientelism and vote buying are problematic for two main reasons. First, patronage can undermine democratic processes by enabling political elites to secure the political support of the poor, who are likely to be willing to sell their votes at a lower price, while ignoring the interests of the poor (Stokes 2007). Second, social protection benefits delivered as patronage would be distributed based on the political importance rather than the needs of would-be recipients and would therefore likely undermine the objectives of the program.

Individual vote buying is rendered difficult by secret ballots, which limit the ability of political parties to monitor individual votes effectively. Argentina's Peronist party strove to assess individual votes indirectly through the deployment of local agents to monitor people's attendance at party events or at the polls, but this requires a capacity and manpower that the majority of political parties in Africa lack (Stokes 2007; van de Walle 2014). Moreover, the design of cash transfer programs, which increasingly rely on electronic transfers (rather than programs handing cash directly) and contain oversight mechanisms, present logistical challenges to the use of social safety nets to promote clientelism.

However, in practice, there is a grey area between electoral accountability and vote buying (Lippert-Rasmussen 2011; Stokes 2007). Political parties may reward or punish entire communities based on aggregate votes within a particular district. In some cases, the promises of candidates and the distribution of resources may be viewed as a gift of munificence or legislative pork (van de Walle 2007). In contexts in which patronage is deeply embedded in social and political relations, the distribution of benefits, though not strictly conditional, may be interpreted by recipients as an obligation to provide political support.

Once they are expanded sufficiently and have demonstrated their value, programs create long-term commitments that are politically difficult to discontinue. In Brazil, Colombia, and Mexico, for instance, programs have been established for more than a decade and have demonstrated their impacts. They have progressively been adopted by parties across the board, even if each new administration typically adjusts the program to reflect changes in focus on particular policies or approaches to poverty reduction, often altering the name of the intervention, while maintaining core features. Thus, in the 2006 Brazilian elections, the four main presidential candidates, despite the great differences in their political persuasions, all called for expanding Bolsa Família, which occurred. During the following election, no major candidate called for eliminating the program (Zucco 2013).

Notes

1. See "Sustainable Development Goals: 17 Goals to Transform Our World," United Nations, New York, http://www.un.org/sustainabledevelopment/.
2. See "Zambia: Social Protection Conference Issues Call to Action," *Pambazuka News*, April 12, 2006, https://www.pambazuka.org/resources/zambia-social-protection-conference-issues-call-action.
3. WVS (World Values Survey), Wave 6 (2010–2014) (database), King's College, Old Aberdeen, United Kingdom, http://www.worldvaluessurvey.org/WVSDocumentation WV6.jsp.

References

ADB (Asian Development Bank). 2009. "Reforming the Rural Pension System in the People's Republic of China." Social Protection Project Brief, ADB, Manila.

Albrecht, Peter. 2017. "The Political Economy of Social Protection in Sierra Leone." Background paper for *Realizing the Full Potential of Social Safety Nets in Africa*, edited by Kathleen Beegle, Aline Coudouel, and Emma Monsalve. Washington, DC: World Bank.

Alderman, Harold, and Ruslan Yemtsov. 2013. "How Can Social Safety Nets Contribute to Economic Growth?" Policy Research Working Paper 6437, World Bank, Washington, DC.

Alesina, Alberto F., Edward Glaeser, and Bruce I. Sacerdote. 2011. "Why Doesn't the United States Have a European-Style Welfare State?" *Brookings Papers on Economic Activity* 2: 187–254.

Argent, Jonathan, Britta Augsburg, and Imran Rasul. 2014. "Livestock Asset Transfers with and without Training: Evidence from Rwanda." *Journal of Economic Behavior and Organization* 108: 19–39.

Attah, Ramlatu, Valentina Barca, Andrew Kardan, Ian MacAuslan, Fred Merttens, and Luca Pellerano. 2016. "Can Social Protection Affect Psychosocial Wellbeing and Why Does This Matter? Lessons from Cash Transfers in Sub-Saharan Africa." *Journal of Development Studies* 52 (8): 1115–31.

Ayliffe, Tamsin, Ghazia Aslam, and Rasmus Schjødt. 2016. "Social Accountability in the Delivery of Social Protection: Literature Review." Working Paper, Development Pathways, Orpington, UK.

Báez, Javier E., Adriana Camacho, Emily Conover, and Román A. Zárate. 2012. "Conditional Cash Transfers, Political Participation, and Voting Behavior." Policy Research Working Paper 6215, World Bank, Washington, DC.

Banerjee, Abhijit, Esther Duflo, Nathanael Goldberg, Dean Karlan, Robert Osei, William Parienté, Jeremy Shapiro, Bram Thuysbaert, and Christopher Udry. 2015a. "A Multifaceted Program Causes Lasting Progress for the Very Poor: Evidence from Six Countries." *Science* 348 (6236): 772–89.

Banerjee, Abhijit, Rema Hanna, Gabriel Kreindler and Benjamin A. Olken. 2015b. "Debunking the Stereotype of the Lazy Welfare Recipient: Evidence from Cash Transfer Programs Worldwide." HKS Faculty Working Paper 076, Harvard Kennedy School, Cambridge, MA.

Baumberg, Ben. 2014. "Benefits and the Cost of Living: Pressures on the Cost of Living and Attitudes to Benefit Claiming." In *British Social Attitudes: The 31st Report*, edited by Alison Park, Caroline Bryson, and John Curtice, 95–122. London: NatCen Social Research.

Beegle, Kathleen, Luc Christiaensen, Andrew Dabalen, and Isis Gaddis. 2016. *Poverty in a Rising Africa*. Africa Poverty Report. Washington, DC: World Bank.

Blattman, Christopher, Nathan Vincent Fiala, and Sebastian Martinez. 2014. "Generating Skilled Self-Employment in Developing Countries: Experimental Evidence from Uganda." *Quarterly Journal of Economics* 129 (2): 697–752.

Bossuroy, Thomas, and Denis Cogneau. 2013. "Social Mobility in Five African Countries." *Review of Income and Wealth* 59 (S1): S84–S110.

Breceda, Karla, Jamele Rigolini, and Jaime Saavedra. 2008. "Latin America and the Social Contract: Patterns of Social Spending and Taxation." Policy Research Working Paper 4604, World Bank, Washington, DC.

Brett, E. A. 2003. "Participation and Accountability in Development Management." *Journal of Development Studies* 40 (2): 1–29.

Buur, Lars, and Padil Salimo. 2017. "The Political Economy of Social Protection in Mozambique." Background paper for *Realizing the Full Potential of Social Safety Nets in Africa*, edited by Kathleen Beegle, Aline Coudouel, and Emma Monsalve. Washington, DC: World Bank.

Cherrier, Cécile. 2015. "Examining the Catalytic Effect of Aid on Domestic Resource Mobilization for Social Transfers in Low-Income Countries." UNRISD Working Paper 2015-3 (February), United Nations Research Institute for Social Development, Geneva.

Chinyoka, Isaac, and Jeremy Seekings. 2016. "Social Policy Reform under the Government of National Unity in Zimbabwe, 2009–13." CSSR Working Paper 373 (April), Centre for Social Science Research, University of Cape Town, Cape Town.

Corbridge, Stuart, Glyn Williams, Manoj Srivastava, and René Véron. 2005. *Seeing the State: Governance and Governmentality in India.* Cambridge: Cambridge University Press.

Cornwall, Andrea, Steven Robins, and Bettina Von Lieres. 2011. "States of Citizenship: Contexts and Cultures of Public Engagement and Citizen Action." IDS Working Paper 363 (March), Institute of Development Studies, University of Sussex, Brighton, UK.

Corrêa, Diego Sanches. 2015. "Cash Transfers and Mayoral Elections: The Case of Sao Paulo's Renda Mínima." *Brazilian Political Science Review* 9 (2): 109–20.

Corrêa, Diego Sanches, and José Antonio Cheibub. 2016. "The Anti-Incumbent Effects of Conditional Cash Transfer Programs." *Latin American Politics and Society* 58 (1): 49–71.

Daidone, Silvio, Luca Pellerano, Sudhanshu Handa, and Benjamin Davis. 2015. "Is Graduation from Social Safety Nets Possible? Evidence from Sub-Saharan Africa." *IDS Bulletin* 46 (2): 93–102.

De La O, Ana L. 2013. "Do Conditional Cash Transfers Affect Electoral Behavior? Evidence from a Randomized Experiment in Mexico." *American Journal of Political Science* 57 (1): 1–14.

Devereux, Stephen, and Philip White. 2010. "Social Protection in Africa: Evidence, Politics, and Rights." *Poverty and Public Policy* 2 (3): 53–77.

Díaz-Cayeros, Alberto, Federico Estévez, and Beatriz Magaloni. 2009. "Welfare Benefits, Canvassing, and Campaign Handouts." In *Consolidating Mexico's Democracy: The 2006 Presidential Campaign in Comparative Perspective*, edited by Jorge I. Domínguez, Chappell Lawson, and Alejandro Moreno, 229–45. Baltimore: Johns Hopkins University Press.

Ellis, Frank. 2012. "'We Are All Poor Here': Economic Difference, Social Divisiveness, and Targeting Cash Transfers in Sub-Saharan Africa." *Journal of Development Studies* 48 (2): 201–14.

Evans, David K., Brian Holtemeyer, and Katrina Kosec. 2017. "If You Give It, Trust Will Come: The Impacts of Community-Managed Cash Transfers in Tanzania." Working paper, Development Strategy and Governance Division, International Food Policy Research Institute, Washington, DC.

Evans, David K., and Anna Popova. 2014. "Cash Transfers and Temptation Goods: A Review of Global Evidence." Policy Research Working Paper 6886, World Bank, Washington, DC.

Gahamanyi, Vincent, and Andrew Kettlewell. 2015. "Evaluating Graduation: Insights from the Vision 2020 Umurenge Programme in Rwanda." *IDS Bulletin* 46 (2): 48–63.

Gelbach, Jonah B., and Lant Pritchett. 2002. "Is More for the Poor Less for the Poor? The Politics of Means-Tested Targeting." *B.E. Journal of Economic Analysis and Policy* 2 (1): 1–28.

Gertler, Paul J., James J. Heckman, Rodrigo Pinto, Arianna Zanolini, Christel Vermeersch, Susan P. Walker, Susan M. Chang, and Sally M. Grantham-McGregor. 2014. "Labor Market Returns to an Early Childhood Stimulation Intervention in Jamaica." *Science* 344 (6187): 998–1001.

Giannozzi, Sara, and Asmeen Khan. 2011. "Strengthening Governance of Social Safety Nets in East Asia." Social Protection Discussion Paper 1116, World Bank, Washington, DC.

Glassman, Amanda, and Miriam Temin. 2016. *Millions Saved: New Cases of Proven Success in Global Health*. Washington, DC: Center for Global Development and Brookings Institution Press.

Graham, Carol. 2002. "Public Attitudes Matter: A Conceptual Frame for Accounting for Political Economy in Social Safety Nets and Social Assistance Policies." Social Protection Discussion Paper 0233, World Bank, Washington, DC.

Grandvoinnet, Helene, Ghazia Aslam, and Shomikho Raha. 2015. *Opening the Black Box: The Contextual Drivers of Social Accountability*. New Frontiers of Social Policy Series. Washington, DC: World Bank.

Granvik, Mia. 2015. "Policy Diffusion, Domestic Politics, and Social Protection in Lesotho, 1998–2012." CSSR Working Paper 357, Centre for Social Science Research, University of Cape Town, Cape Town.

Guven, Melis U., and Phillippe G. Leite. 2016. "Benefits and Costs of Social Pensions in Sub-Saharan Africa." Social Protection and Labor Discussion Paper 1607, World Bank, Washington, DC.

Hamer, Sam. 2016. "'Our Father's Programmes': Political Branding around Social Protection in Botswana, 2008–2014." CSSR Working Paper 370, Centre for Social Science Research, University of Cape Town, Cape Town.

Handa, Sudhanshu, Silvio Daidone, Amber Peterman, Benjamin Davis, Audrey Pereira, Tia Palermo, and Jennifer Yablonski. 2017. "Myth Busting? Confronting Six Common Perceptions about Unconditional Cash Transfers as a Poverty Reduction Strategy in Africa." Innocenti Working Paper 2017–11, Office of Research, United Nations Children's Fund, Florence.

Handa, Sudhanshu, Bruno Martorano, Carolyn Tucker Halpern, Audrey Pettifor, and Harsha Thirumurthy. 2014a. "The Government of Kenya's Cash Transfer Program Reduces the Risk of Sexual Debut among Young People Age 15–25." *PLoS ONE* 9 (1): e85473.

———. 2014b. "Subjective Well-Being, Risk Perceptions, and Time Discounting: Evidence from a Large-Scale Cash Transfer Programme." Innocenti Working Paper 2014–02, Office of Research, United Nations Children's Fund, Florence.

Harland, Charlotte. 2014. "Can the Expansion of Social Protection Bring about Social Transformation in African Countries? The Case of Zambia." *European Journal of Development Research* 26 (3): 370–86.

Haushofer, Johannes, and Jeremy Shapiro. 2013. "Household Response to Income Changes: Evidence from an Unconditional Cash Transfer Program in Kenya." Working paper, Abdul Latif Jameel Poverty Action Lab, Massachusetts Institute of Technology, Cambridge, MA.

Hickey, Samuel. 2011. "The Politics of Social Protection: What Do We Get from a 'Social Contract' Approach?" *Canadian Journal of Development Studies* 32 (4): 426–38.

Hickey, Samuel, and Badru Bukenya. 2016. "The Politics of Promoting Social Cash Transfers in Uganda." ESID Working Paper 69, Effective States and Inclusive Development Research Centre, Global Development Institute, School of Environment, Education, and Development, University of Manchester, Manchester.

Hickey, Samuel, and Tom Lavers. 2017. "The Political Economy of the Adoption, Design, and Implementation of Social Protection." Background paper for *Realizing the Full*

Potential of Social Safety Nets in Africa, edited by Kathleen Beegle, Aline Coudouel, and Emma Monsalve. Washington, DC: World Bank.

Hill, Ruth, and Philip Verwimp. 2017. "Managing Risk and Conflict." In *Accelerating Poverty Reduction in Africa*, edited by Kathleen Beegle and Luc Christiaensen, chapter 4. Washington, DC: World Bank.

Hu, Minqing, and Bing Liu. 2004. "Mining and Summarizing Customer Reviews." In *KDD '04: Proceedings of the ACM SIGKDD International Conference on Knowledge Discovery and Data Mining*, edited by Special Interest Group on Knowledge Discovery in Data, 168–77. New York: Association for Computing Machinery.

Hurrell, Alex, and Ian MacAuslan. 2012. "The Political Implications of Cash Transfers in Sub-Saharan Africa: Shaking Up the Social System." *Public Management Review* 14 (2): 255–72.

Jones, Nicola, Bassam Abu-Hamad, Paola Pereznieto, and Kerry Sylvester. 2016. "Transforming Cash Transfers: Citizens' Perspectives on the Politics of Programme Implementation." *Journal of Development Studies* 52 (8): 1207–24.

Jones, Nicola, and Fiona Samuels. 2013. "Holding Cash Transfers to Account: Beneficiary and Community Perspectives." With Agnieszka Malachowska. Transforming Cash Transfers Series, Overseas Development Institute, London.

Kidd, Stephen, and Verena Damerau. 2016. "The Political Economy of Social Protection for Informal Economy Workers in Asia." In *Social Protection for Information Workers in Asia*, edited by Sri Wening Handayani, 120–71. Manila: Asian Development Bank.

King, Sophie, and Samuel Hickey. 2017. "Building Democracy from Below: Lessons from Western Uganda." *Journal of Development Studies* 53 (10): 1584–99.

Kitschelt, Herbert. 2000. "Linkages between Citizens and Politicians in Democratic Polities." *Comparative Political Studies* 33 (6–7): 845–79.

Labonne, Julien. 2013. "The Local Electoral Impacts of Conditional Cash Transfers: Evidence from a Field Experiment." *Journal of Development Economics* 104: 73–88.

Lavers, Tom. 2013. "Food Security and Social Protection in Highland Ethiopia: Linking the Productive Social Safety Net to the Land Question." *Journal of Modern African Studies* 51 (03): 459–85.

———. 2016a. "Social Protection in an Aspiring 'Developmental State': The Political Drivers of Ethiopia's PSNP." WIDER Working Paper 2016/130, United Nations University–World Institute for Development Economics Research, Helsinki.

———. 2016b. "Understanding Elite Commitment to Social Protection: Rwanda's Vision 2020 Umurenge Programme." WIDER Working Paper 2016/093, United Nations University–World Institute for Development Economics Research, Helsinki.

Lavers, Samuel, and Tom Hickey. 2016. "Conceptualising the Politics of Social Protection Expansion in Low Income Countries: The Intersection of Transnational Ideas and Domestic Politics." *International Journal of Social Welfare* 25 (4): 388–98.

Linos, Elizabeth. 2013. "Do Conditional Cash Transfer Programs Shift Votes? Evidence from the Honduran PRAF." *Electoral Studies* 32 (4): 864–74.

Lippert-Rasmussen, Kasper. 2011. "Vote Buying and Election Promises: Should Democrats Care about the Difference?" *Journal of Political Philosophy* 19 (2): 125–44.

Luttmer, Erzo F. P. 2001. "Group Loyalty and the Taste for Redistribution." *Journal of Political Economy* 109 (3): 500–28.

MacAuslan, Ian, and Nils Riemenschneider. 2011. "Richer but Resented: What Do Cash Transfers Do to Social Relations?" *IDS Bulletin* 42 (6): 60–66.

Manacorda, Marco, Edward Miguel, and Andrea Vigorito. 2011. "Government Transfers and Political Support." *American Economic Journal: Applied Economics* 3 (3): 1–28.

Moene, Karl Ove, and Michael Wallerstein. 2001. "Targeting and Political Support for Welfare Spending." *Economics of Governance* 2 (1): 3–24.

Molyneux, Maxine. 2016. "Can Cash Transfer Programmes Have 'Transformative' Effects?" With Nicola Jones and Fiona Samuels. *Journal of Development Studies* 52 (8): 1087–98.

Ndiaye, Alfred. 2017. "The Political Economy of Social Protection in Senegal." Background paper for *Realizing the Full Potential of Social Safety Nets in Africa*, edited by Kathleen Beegle, Aline Coudouel, and Emma Monsalve. Washington, DC: World Bank.

Nupia, Oskar. 2011. "Anti-Poverty Programs and Presidential Election Outcomes: *Familias en Acción* in Colombia." Documentos CEDE 14, Centro de Estudios sobre Desarrollo Económico, Bogotá.

Oduro, Razak. 2014. "Beyond Poverty Reduction: Conditional Cash Transfers and Citizenship in Ghana." *International Journal of Social Welfare* 24 (1): 27–36.

OECD (Organisation for Economic Co-operation and Development). 2009. "Concepts and Dilemmas of State-Building in Fragile Situations: From Fragility to Resilience." *OECD Journal on Development* 9 (3): 64–152.

Osofian, Wale. 2011. "Towards Strengthening State-Citizen Relationship in Fragile States and Environments: The Role of Cash Transfer Programmes." Paper presented at the International Conference "Social Protection for Social Justice," Institute of Development Studies, Brighton, UK, April 13–15.

Pavanello, Sara, Carol Watson, W. Onyango-Ouma, and Paul Bukuluki. 2016. "Effects of Cash Transfers on Community Interactions: Emerging Evidence." *Journal of Development Studies* 52 (8): 1147–61.

Pavão, Nara. 2016. "Conditional Cash Transfer Programs and Electoral Accountability: Evidence from Latin America." *Latin American Politics and Society* 58 (2): 74–99.

Pierson, Paul. 1993. "When Effect Becomes Cause: Policy Feedback and Political Change." *World Politics* 45 (4): 595–628.

Plagerson, Sophie, Trudy Harpham, and Karina Kielmann. 2012. "Cash Transfers and Citizenship: Evidence from South Africa." *Journal of Development Studies* 48 (7): 969–82.

Premand, Patrick, and Carlo del Ninno. 2016. "Cash Transfers, Behavioral Accompanying Measures, and Child Development in Niger." Working paper, World Bank, Washington, DC.

Pritchett, Lant. 2005. "A Lecture on the Political Economy of Targeted Social Safety Nets." Social Protection Discussion Paper 0501, World Bank, Washington, DC.

Pruce, Kate, and Samuel Hickey. 2017. "The Politics of Promoting Social Protection in Zambia." ESID Working Paper 75, Effective States and Inclusive Development

Research Centre, Global Development Institute, School of Environment, Education, and Development, University of Manchester, Manchester.

Ringold, Dena, Alaka Holla, Margaret Koziol, and Santhosh Srinivasan. 2012. *Citizens and Service Delivery: Assessing the Use of Social Accountability Approaches in the Human Development Sectors.* Directions in Development: Human Development Series. Washington, DC: World Bank.

Roemer, John. 1998. "Why the Poor Do Not Expropriate the Rich: An Old Argument in New Garb." *Journal of Public Economics* 70 (3): 399–424.

Roll, Michael, ed. 2014. *The Politics of Public Sector Performance: Pockets of Effectiveness in Developing Countries.* Abingdon, UK: Routledge.

Rousseau, Jean-Jacques. 1968. *The Social Contract.* Translated by Maurice Cranston. Penguin Books for Philosophy Series. London: Penguin Books. First published 1762.

Seekings, Jeremy. 2015. "The 'Developmental' and 'Welfare' State in South Africa: Lessons for the Southern African Region." CSSR Working Paper 358, Centre for Social Science Research, University of Cape Town, Cape Town.

———. 2016a. "'Affordability' and the Political Economy of Social Protection in Contemporary Africa." CSSR Working Paper 389, Centre for Social Science Research, University of Cape Town, Cape Town.

———. 2016b. "Drought Relief and the Origins of a Conservative Welfare State in Botswana, 1965–1980." CSSR Working Paper 378, Centre for Social Science Research, University of Cape Town, Cape Town.

Seidenfeld, David, Sudhanshu Handa, and Gelson Tembo. 2013. "Social Cash Transfer Scheme: 24-Month Impact Report for the Child Grant Programme." September, American Institutes for Research, Washington, DC.

Sen, Amartya. 1995. "The Political Economy of Targeting." In *Public Spending and the Poor: Theory and Evidence,* edited by Dominique van de Walle and Kimberly Nead, 11–24. Washington, DC: World Bank; Baltimore: Johns Hopkins University Press.

Sepúlveda, Magdalena, and Carly Nyst. 2012. "The Human Rights Approach to Social Protection." Elements for Discussion Series, Unit for Development Communications, Ministry for Foreign Affairs, Helsinki.

Siachiwena, Hangala. 2016. "Social Protection Policy Reform in Zambia during the Sata Presidency, 2011–2014." CSSR Working Paper 380, Centre for Social Science Research, University of Cape Town, Cape Town.

Silva, Joana, Victoria Levin, and Matteo Morgandi. 2013. *Inclusion and Resilience: The Way Forward for Social Safety Nets in the Middle East and North Africa.* MENA Development Report. Washington, DC: World Bank.

Stokes, Susan C. 2007. "Is Vote Buying Undemocratic?" In *Elections for Sale: The Causes and Consequences of Vote Buying,* edited by Frederic Charles Schaffer, 81–99. Boulder, CO: Lynne Rienner.

Suwanrada, Worawet, and Dharmapriya Wesumperuma. 2012. "Development of the Old-Age Allowance System in Thailand: Challenges and Policy Implications." In *Social Protection for Older Persons: Social Pensions in Asia,* edited by Sri Wening Handayani and Babken Babajanian, 153–67. Manila: Asian Development Bank.

Tembo, Fletcher. 2012. "Citizen Voice and State Accountability: Towards Theories of Change That Embrace Contextual Dynamics." Working Paper 343, Overseas Development Institute, London.

Tobias, Julia E., Sudarno Sumarto, and Habib Moody. 2014. "Assessing the Political Impacts of a Conditional Cash Transfer: Evidence from a Randomized Policy Experiment in Indonesia." Working Paper, SMERU Research Institute, Jakarta.

Ulriksen, Marianne S. 2016. "Ideational and Institutional Drivers of Social Protection in Tanzania." WIDER Working Paper 2016/142, United Nations University–World Institute for Development Economics Research, Helsinki.

van de Walle, Dominique. 1998. "Targeting Revisited." *World Bank Research Observer* 13 (2): 231–48.

van de Walle, Nicolas. 2007. "Meet the Boss, Same as the Old Boss? The Evolution of Political Clientelism in Africa." In *Patrons, Clients, and Policies: Patterns of Democratic Accountability and Political Competition*, edited by Herbert Kitschelt and Steven I. Wilkinson, 50–67. New York: Cambridge University Press.

———. 2014. "The Democratization of Clientelism in Sub-Saharan Africa." In *Clientelism, Social Policy, and the Quality of Democracy*, edited by Diego Abente Brun and Larry Diamond, 230–52. Baltimore: Johns Hopkins University Press.

van Oorschot, Wim. 2000. "Who Should Get What, and Why? On Deservingness Criteria and the Conditionality of Solidarity among the Public." *Policy and Politics* 28 (1): 33–48.

Wanyama, Fredrick O., and Anna McCord. 2017. "The Politics of Scaling Up Social Protection in Kenya." ESID Working Paper 87, Effective States and Inclusive Development Research Centre, Global Development Institute, School of Environment, Education, and Development, University of Manchester, Manchester.

Weyland, Kurt. 1996. *Democracy without Equity: Failures of Reform in Brazil*. Pittsburgh: University of Pittsburgh Press.

World Bank. 2015. "Towards a New Social Contract." MENA Economic Monitor, Middle East and North Africa Region, World Bank, Washington, DC.

———. 2016. *Making Politics Work for Development: Harnessing Transparency and Citizen Engagement*. Policy Research Report. Washington, DC: World Bank.

———. 2017. *World Development Report 2017: Governance and the Law*. Washington, DC: World Bank.

Zucco, Cesar, Jr. 2013. "When Payouts Pay Off: Conditional Cash Transfers and Voting Behavior in Brazil 2002–10." *American Journal of Political Science* 57 (4): 810–22.

Chapter 4

Anchoring in Strong Institutions to Expand and Sustain Social Safety Nets

Sarah Coll-Black, Victoria Monchuk, and Judith Sandford

Institutions—defined as laws, policies, and strategies—are the backbone of the delivery of effective social safety nets. Often understood or defined as the rules of the game, institutions will need to evolve in several dimensions to anchor the expansion of social safety nets in Africa.

For policy setting, oversight, and the coordination of social safety nets, there is no single path. The choice of ministerial home typically depends on the factors that led to the emergence of the programs. More than half of the countries reviewed task the social ministry with these responsibilities. Implementation may be located in other agencies separate from the one tasked with policy setting, oversight, and coordination. The approaches are varied; but as programs evolve, coordination becomes more critical, not least because of limited fiscal space.

Local frontline workers in countries with decentralized or devolved systems may not be accountable to central agencies. National standards need to be balanced with devolved decision making to account for local realities.

While reliance on technical assistance and contracts may deliver results in the short term, longer-term solutions are required to embed programs in government systems to promote sustainability. Generally, incentives available to civil servants are critical for effective implementation, particularly as programs are taken to scale and become nationwide systems. Poor incentives can result in high staff turnover. Combined with slow recruitment, this can lead to gaps in capacity.

Institutions—defined as laws, policies, and strategies—shape human behavior and human interaction and are therefore central to the delivery of social safety nets. Often understood or defined as the rules of the game, institutions shape all aspects of social safety nets, ranging from establishing the benefit eligibility criteria to the rules that govern the organization that delivers the social safety net program (including its mandate and human resource policies) and the laws that govern the sector (box 4.1). Beyond the formal rules, informal institutions—routines, conventions, and customary practices—influence the provision of social safety nets in diverse ways, from mediating notions of deservingness to encourage public support among populations to incentivizing civil servants and frontline staff to deliver programs.

If the social safety nets in Africa are to be expanded to the required scale, governments must make serious investments in strong institutions. The institutions supporting the social safety nets in Africa are evolving as programs are launched, deliver benefits, and become an everyday part of the political and social landscape. These processes can take considerable time and are influenced by many factors, including political and fiscal aspects (chapters 3 and 5). More immediately, if the social safety nets are to be brought to scale, institutions that support their operation and help build their legitimacy are required. These institutions may be of many types, embody international best practices or homegrown solutions, and entail both formal and informal rules. These rules of the game will also evolve because they reflect changing behaviors, beliefs, and power relations within countries.

The institutional anchors of social safety nets must be strong, credible, and produce results. The anchoring institutions must fulfill the following three functions if social safety nets are to become sustainable at scale: (1) commitment, that is, the assurance that policies will remain consistent beyond the political cycle; (2) coordination, the ability to convince numerous actors to take coordinated action in pursuit of a common good; and (3) cooperation, the ability to prevent free riding or to convince actors to take steps they may consider in their interest (World Bank 2017). This chapter explores these aspects of a strong institutional anchoring for social safety nets by considering the policy and legislative context and the organizations that oversee, coordinate, manage, and implement social safety net programs in Africa.

There are multiple paths in the evolution of the rules of the game for social safety nets in Africa, and many are linked to the development of broader social protection systems. Building a social protection system does not necessarily mean focusing on a single entity or agency to manage multiple programs (Robalino, Rawlings, and Walker. 2012). Indeed, Mathauer (2004) explains that, given the multidimensional nature of poverty, social safety nets are naturally multisectoral, thereby requiring the coordination and management of interorganizational and intergovernmental relations. Similarly, by design, social safety

BOX 4.1

Defining Institutions

Often understood as the rules of the game in society, institutions foster stable and predictable human interactions (North 1989; Ostrom 1990). They represent "durable social rules and procedures, formal or informal, which structure the social, economic, and political relations and interactions of those affected by them" (Leftwich 2006, 2). Institutions do, however, create different incentives that focus on different behaviors and enforcement mechanisms that may lead to different outcomes (Bridges and Woolcock 2017).

The best-studied rules are those that are regulatory, that are viewed as laws or practices monitored and enforced by third parties, and that promise reward or punishment. These differ from normative rules, which are the norms and values that set out what is socially acceptable and thus intrinsically influence behavior through feelings of honor and shame. An additional type of rule is one that is cultural-cognitive. This type involves frameworks through which the world may be interpreted, "structuring the way information is received, processed, and given meaning," and thus biasing decisions, irrespective of other incentives or regulatory mechanisms (Andrews 2013, 42–43).

While these various types of rules may each be referred to separately, Scott (2008, 48) argues that they are all distinct aspects of institutions. "Institutions are comprised of regulatory, normative, and cultural-cognitive elements that, together with associated activities and resources, provide stability and meaning to life," he writes.

Thus, each institution has formal and informal aspects. Any attempt to introduce a new rule or to change a rule must consider both sorts of aspects. The informal aspects are frequently invisible (Bridges and Woolcock 2017). The formal aspects are regulatory and visible. Andrews (2013) calls them the tip of the iceberg. According to him, if one only reproduces the visible parts, but not the cultural cognitive and normative foundations, one will obtain an iceberg without foundation, the kind that sinks.

Often, "institution" is used interchangeably with "agency" or "organization," and thus, frequently, the institutions supporting social safety nets are equated with the organizations that are responsible for the design, delivery, management, and oversight of the programs. In an effort to distinguish between institutions and organizations, this chapter defines organizations as "the formally or informally coordinated vehicles for the promotion or protection of a mix of individual and shared interests and ideas" (Leftwich and Sen 2010, 18). Thus, if institutions are the rules of the game, then organizations are the players.[a] Each organization is governed by internal rules, which apply only to the members of the organization, who develop unique systems to monitor and enforce these rules.

a. The political aspects of institutions, which tend also to reflect informal rules, are discussed in chapter 3. This chapter focuses on formal organizations and agencies.

nets require a plurality of providers comprising public (local, regional, and national), private, and voluntary agencies. Finally, the decentralized nature of service delivery interplays with the decentralization process and the nature of communities and their structures.

Countries follow different paths in this process, and progress along one parameter is neither a precondition for progress along another parameter nor sufficient in itself (table 4.1). In some countries, such as Ethiopia, the development of a social protection policy took place after significant consolidation of social safety net programs and the achievement of near nationwide coverage. In other countries, such as Niger and Sierra Leone, the development of social protection policies took place quite early in the evolution of social safety nets and encouraged the implementation of small pilot programs. Figure 4.1 provides a snapshot of these elements across Africa. In Latin America, the need for greater coordination among a growing number of social programs encouraged governments to bring these into a coherent social safety net system, usually guided by a social protection policy. By contrast, the formalization of social safety nets through politics and laws can be counterproductive if these are introduced while space for experimentation is still required to build political support or to gain experience with the delivery of different design features. The necessary space may exist within institutions that operate outside governments. Indeed, creating policies and laws through technically driven processes, often with the support of development partners, can delink these policies and laws from national social norms or political processes and produce inadequate frameworks (Bridges 2016). Despite these various paths, a common feature across countries is the search for institutions that deliver commitment, coordination, and cooperation.

This chapter illustrates the critical role of institutions in bringing social safety nets to scale in Africa. It builds on a desk review of program documents and a series of country case studies for a discussion of four main areas, as follows (box 4.2):

- First, the chapter considers the laws, policies, and strategies that are increasingly being deployed to anchor social safety nets in Africa. It reviews the progress in establishing these frameworks, while emphasizing that more efforts are required if these policies, strategies, and laws are to become rooted in national policy making and supported by political will and financing. The policies, strategies, and laws must remain consistent, thereby providing the committed foundation required by well-functioning institutions.

- Second, the chapter discusses the options for selecting organizations to be responsible for the oversight, coordination, and management of social safety nets. A successful selection will result from a balance between the mandates of the organization and the organization's access to political

Table 4.1 **Bringing Social Safety Nets to Scale Requires an Evolution of Institutions and Organizations**

Time →

	Low coverage, scattered geographically, pilot programs	Expanding coverage, still geographically focused, programs financed and influenced by partners	National or near national coverage among eligible groups, greater government ownership and operation	National coverage among eligible groups, government owned and operated
National strategies	Poverty reduction strategies and constitutional rights	Development of national social safety net or social protection policy, strategy		Statutes or laws defining entitlements and responsible parties
Policy setting, oversight, coordination, and management	Multiple ad hoc, often NGO-led programs	One to three government programs supported by development partners	Consolidation, clarifying who implements which program	Formalizing programs into core governmental services
Implementation	NGOs, contract staff	Government managed, use of project implementation units (PIUs), contract staff, or additional workload for existing government staff	Government managed, more full-time civil servants involved	Government managed, government department or agency, staffed by civil servants

Note: NGO = nongovernmental organization.

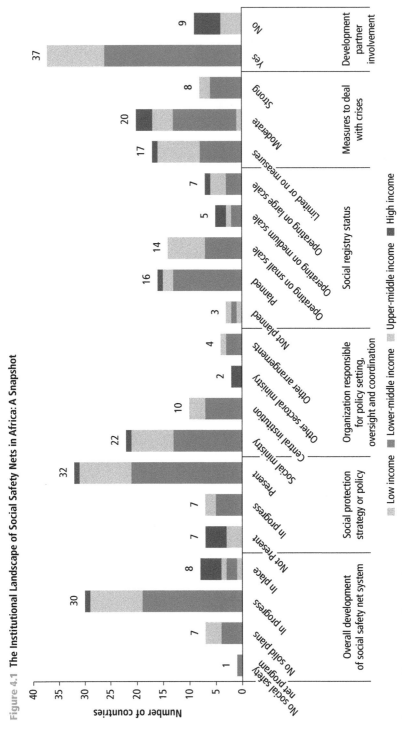

Figure 4.1 The Institutional Landscape of Social Safety Nets in Africa: A Snapshot

Source: World Bank review of country documents.
Note: Typologies described in appendix A. For more details see appendix table D.1 and D.2.

Legend: Low income · Lower-middle income · Upper-middle income · High income

Number of countries

Overall development of social safety net system
- No social safety net program: 1
- No solid plans
- In progress: 7
- In place: 30

Social protection strategy or policy
- Not Present: 8
- In progress: 7
- Present: 7, 32

Organization responsible for policy setting, oversight and coordination
- Social ministry: 22
- Central institution: 10
- Other sectoral ministry: 2
- Other arrangements: 4
- Not planned: 3

Social registry status
- Planned: 16
- Operating on small scale: 14
- Operating on medium scale: 5
- Operating on large scale: 7
- Limited or no measures

Measures to deal with crises
- Limited or no measures: 17
- Moderate: 20
- Strong: 8

Development partner involvement
- Yes: 37
- No: 9

BOX 4.2

Methodology and Case Study Selection

The chapter analyzes the role of social safety net institutions through a review of program documentation in 31 African countries, 16 country case studies, and 8 special country case studies on the legal framework. The case studies were selected to represent a spectrum of contexts, stages of development and expansion of social safety nets, legal frameworks, and historical institutional heritage across Africa.

The countries span from Chad and Mauritania, which, until recently, had limited social safety net programs, to Ethiopia and South Africa, which have more deep-rooted programs. The countries range from the large (Ethiopia, Kenya, South Africa) and the small (Sierra Leone), to francophone (Côte d'Ivoire, the Republic of Congo, Senegal), lusophone (Mozambique), and anglophone (Tanzania, Uganda, Zambia).

The chapter also draws on examples of programs in countries in other regions— such as Brazil, Colombia, Indonesia, and Pakistan—to benchmark and compare with the trends in Africa and benefit from a wider body of knowledge and research on institutions and public sector management.

authority. The initial selections are important because incentives and norms within the responsible organizations will shape the development of social safety nets within a country. For social safety nets, the selections are central to establishing institutions that have the ability to ensure coordination and cooperation across the relevant sectors, thereby encouraging the commitment of organizations to achieving policy objectives.

- Third, the chapter considers the elements that determine the effectiveness of organizations in managing, coordinating, and delivering social safety nets. It shows how various management arrangements can create incentives for organizations to achieve program objectives. It considers how programs may span multiple ministries and agencies and the effects of decentralization or deconcentration on the functioning of these organizations.

- Fourth, the chapter offers reflections on how organizational structures incentivize or constrain staff. It highlights that, as social safety nets become embedded in national systems, the dynamics of civil service participation will come to the fore, with important implications for the commitment and the ability of staff to ensure coordination and cooperation.

From Frameworks to Commitments: Emerging National Strategies for Social Safety Nets

Across the region, governments are now focusing on creating an institutional framework to advance social safety nets. In addition to establishing the formal rules of implementation for individual programs, many governments are identifying the wider policy context for social safety nets, often within a broader framework for social protection. Because, according to the World Bank (2017, 171), "effective policies tend to have long-term objectives (extending beyond the political cycle), matching resources and well-aligned incentives for the actors involved," the elaboration of these policies or strategies can contribute to fostering political interest and support for social safety nets.[1] Often, the policy commitments are embedded in international conventions and declarations, attesting to the layering of institutions across local, national, and international activity spaces (Mehta et al. 1999). While the presence of these policies, laws, and legal frameworks signals an important step forward toward the establishment of a stable anchor for social safety nets in Africa, the legitimacy of these formal institutions rests on whether they will be enforced, which is a function of support for them politically and the will to implement them (World Bank 2017).

Laws, policies, and strategies are largely formal, but informal rules are critical to ensuring credibility. Informal elements "can undermine, reinforce, or even substitute for the functioning of formal institutions" (Leftwich and Sen 2010, 25). This interplay between formal and informal rules implies that setting up formal institutions is more than a technical exercise focused on getting the laws right. It requires understanding the politics of social safety nets, including how policies, strategies, and laws reflect or change cultural understandings of poverty and entitlements (chapter 3). The alignment of formal and informal rules creates the belief that laws and policies will be enforced. The focus here is on the evolution of the formal rules for social safety nets.

Across many countries in Africa, international and regional commitments have provided a springboard for the mobilization of support for social safety nets among politicians and technocrats, thus influencing national policies on social safety nets. Most African countries are signatories of international agreements and declarations that encompass social safety nets (chapter 3). The Universal Declaration of Human Rights commits governments to recognizing and fulfilling the right to social protection, which is also articulated in article 9 of the International Covenant on Economic, Social, and Cultural Rights.[2] This commitment has been translated into law through treaties, customary international law, general principles, regional agreements, and domestic law that express and guarantee human rights. The African Charter on Human and Peoples' Rights reinforces the relevant covenants.[3] More specific commitments are implied in other regional and international declarations. Recommendation R202 of the International

Labour Organization provides guidance on extending and adapting social protection floors to national circumstances.[4] The Ouagadougou Declaration and Plan of Action (2004), the Livingstone Call for Action (2006), the Social Policy Framework for Africa (2008), and the Yaoundé Declaration (2011) all include commitments by African governments to improve the living conditions of vulnerable people through better social protection services.[5] While soft and nonbinding, such international commitments can be evoked in securing the commitment of governments to social safety nets, an approach that has proven useful across countries in Africa in advancing social safety nets. Such international commitments can potentially build momentum at the national level for bringing social safety nets to scale (Kaltenborn et al. 2017).

Despite the widespread adoption of international treaties across Africa, there is significant variation in the degree to which social safety nets are anchored in national legislation—at times as part of a broader position on social protection (table 4.2). Constitutions have recognized the right to social safety nets in some countries, while the constitutions in others offer general provisions for basic rights or the protection of vulnerable groups. The Constitution of Kenya stipulates the "right for every person . . . to social security and binds the State to provide appropriate social security to individuals who are unable to support themselves and their dependents." In Niger, the Constitution explains that everyone "has the right to life, to health, to physical and moral integrity, to a healthy and sufficient food supply, to potable water, to education and instruction in the conditions specified by the law;" and "the State sees to the elderly through a policy of social protection." In Rwanda, "The State shall, within the limits of its capacity, take special measures for the welfare of survivors of genocide who were rendered destitute by genocide committed in Rwanda from October 1, 1990 to December 31st, 1994, the disabled, the indigent, and the elderly as well as other vulnerable groups."[6] Embedding social safety nets in national development strategies or plans is an opportunity to create cross-sectoral synergies in order to improve well-being (Carroll 2011).

Social protection policies and strategies have become common among Africa countries, but they are often quite general, which may undermine their credibility. Among the 48 countries in the region, 39 have approved or are in the process of drafting such policies (see chapter 1, table 1.1, appendix table D.1). In most counties, the strategies or policies are quite recent. Except for South Africa (1997), they date from 2005 or later (figure 4.2). They typically present the overarching principles that govern social safety net programs nationwide. These set out a vision for programs, the main target groups, and the types of benefits. These are agreed upon across various government agencies and development partners. While national strategies and policies make important statements about a government's ambitions, the generic nature of the provisions, which also tend to be quite ambitious in prevailing contexts,

Table 4.2 Social Safety Nets in Most Countries Are Anchored in Law, Policy, or Constitutions

Country	Constitutions include support for particular groups	Social safety net interventions in national development strategies and plans	A social protection policy or strategy exists and includes social safety nets	Social safety net entitlements or institutions are enshrined in national laws
Botswana	Yes	Yes	No	Yes
Chad	No	Yes	Yes	No
Congo, Rep.	No	Yes	Yes[a]	No
Ethiopia	Yes	Yes	Yes	No
Ghana	Yes	Yes	Yes	No
Kenya	Yes	Yes	Yes	Yes[b]
Mauritania	No	Yes	Yes	No
Mozambique	Yes	Yes	Yes	Yes
Niger	Yes	Yes	Yes	No
Rwanda	Yes	Yes	Yes	No
Senegal	No	Yes	Yes	No
Sierra Leone	Yes	Yes	Yes	No
South Africa	Yes	Yes	Yes	Yes
Tanzania	Yes	Yes	No[c]	No
Uganda	Yes	Yes	Yes	No
Zambia	Yes	Yes	Yes	No

Source: A review of national documents for 16 countries.
a. MEPATI (2012).
b. However, the Social Assistance Act contains provisions that have not been implemented and is expected to be repealed and replaced by a new act.
c. A social protection strategy has been drafted and is awaiting approval.

may inadvertently undermine the credibility of these strategies. General statements may be reinterpreted or redefined, thereby opening up the possibility for these policies and strategies to be altered during each political cycle; and even if policy aims are sustained, generic provisions may be difficult to enforce and thus deliver.

The broad, general nature of national policies and strategies may partly derive from the influence of development partners. This influence results in strategies that do not necessarily reflect the political priorities of the government, but rather a tendency toward the application of international best practice (Bridges and Woolcock 2017; Brinkerhoff and Brinkerhoff 2015). In countries in which the development of social safety net strategies has been supported by development partners—such as the Republic of Congo, Mauritania, and Uganda—these generally outline an overall vision of social protection and list programs by target population groups, but do not indicate

Figure 4.2 Many Countries Have Adopted Social Protection Strategies

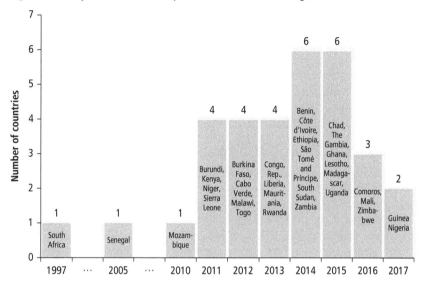

Source: World Bank review of country documents.
Note: More details are presented in appendix D, table D.1.

how these should be prioritized or operationalized. Commonalities among policies and strategies across countries may reflect a broader trend among development partners toward promoting the adoption of external policies and programs that have been deemed to work elsewhere. (Pritchett, Woolcock, and Andrews 2013 set out a critique of this approach.) Others have explained that this approach has arisen from external pressures, which result in countries adopting "the visible trappings of reform . . . without actually implementing them to achieve their intended function" (Brinkerhoff and Brinkerhoff 2015, 224, who also cite Krause 2013).

In establishing policy objectives, most governments are reluctant to use the terminology of entitlements for social safety nets. The governments of Cameroon and Uganda, for instance, expressed concern about creating a legal entitlement to social safety nets that they may find difficult to realize.[7] Identifying the commitment to social safety nets with entitlements introduces the means to enforce the policies, which strengthens the credibility of the programs. Except for Botswana, Mozambique, and South Africa, social safety net programs in the countries reviewed are based largely on strategies or operational manuals without legal authority (see table 4.2). Thus, even if benefits are clearly listed and grievance procedures are described in such documents, the lack of legislation means they are not legally enforceable. This implies that there is no legal obligation to address complaints that arise if the programs are not delivered as intended.

The introduction of legal frameworks for social safety nets can assure greater commitment to the sector, but only if the frameworks build policy objectives that are widely supported (World Bank 2017). For instance, in 2012, the Kenyan Parliament passed a private member's social assistance bill. However, the resulting Act was informed neither by the benefits or the targeting criteria of existing social safety net programs, nor by existing or planned institutional arrangements. Thus, the Act was not enforceable because the government's social safety nets could not deliver on the objectives of the policy, and the policy did not reflect the aims of the ministers responsible for social safety nets. To correct this, the ministry responsible for social protection is currently trying to codify existing social assistance provisions into law, but will need to repeal the 2012 Act before passing a new bill, a more complex and time-consuming process than passing a bill for the first time. Meanwhile, the existing bill has created a misunderstanding. Potential beneficiaries of existing social safety net programs are unable to understand the rationing and poverty targeting that are part of the eligibility assessment process.

Legal frameworks for social safety nets can generate sustained political commitment to delivery on their objectives if they are enforced. South Africa offers an example of how political incentives are aligned with a legal framework for social safety nets, thereby resulting in credible enforcement of the laws. There, the Constitution includes a Bill of Rights that guarantees the right of all South Africans "to have access to social security, including if they are unable to support themselves and their dependents" (Black Sash 2010, 2). This right has been formally recognized in the Social Assistance Act of 2004, which defines eligibility criteria and other parameters of the social grant system. The ability to realize these entitlements derives from the Independent Tribunal for Social Assistance Appeals, which allows citizens to mount a legal challenge if they believe they have been denied benefits to which they feel entitled or if they feel they have been treated unfairly by the South African Social Security Agency. Such examples are rare in Africa, however. Other means of enforcing commitments to social safety nets are apparent in Africa, where there are examples of political commitments that have been translated into increased budgetary allocations and enhanced capacity to deliver programs. In Mozambique, the development of an appropriate legislative framework has been key to establishing social safety nets. The Social Protection Law of 2007 and the National Strategy for Basic Social Security in 2009 resulted in wider coverage and government financing; between 2012 and 2015, budget allocations increased from 0.22 percent to 0.56 percent of gross domestic product (GDP) (ILO, UNICEF, and WFP 2015). Political and social forces can similarly incentivize the enforcement of commitments to delivering social safety nets (chapter 3).

Rooting Social Safety Nets in Organizations for Policy Setting, Oversight, Coordination, and Management

The organizational landscape for social safety nets in Africa has evolved as the responsibilities for policies and programs have become more firmly vested in government ministries. Unlike other sectors, such as health and education, few ministries were responsible for social protection or social safety nets in Africa until recently. Selecting the home for social safety nets is often thus a first step in strengthening the institutional anchoring because these organizations are central to coordinating multiple actors toward the achievement of common objectives and ensuring compliance and decision making that support and reinforce the commitments to social safety nets, even if these decisions are not in the interests of politicians, managers, or technocrats (World Bank 2017). The choice typically depends on the factors that led to the emergence of social safety nets because there is no blank slate (Andrews 2013; chapter 3). In some countries, social safety nets have emerged out of the experience with the provision of social security for formal sector workers; in others, they have emerged out of a concern for food insecurity or vulnerability to disasters. Typically, this origin leads governments to build social safety net programs within sectoral ministries or on the foundations of existing programs. This is critical to success because organizations are more likely to be successful if they "identify, tap into, and build on preexisting capacity" (Barma, Huybens, and Viñuela 2014, 5).

Choice of Home for Policy Setting, Oversight, and Coordination Balances Mandates and Political Power

Organizations with the policy mandate for social safety nets are typically selected for their proximity to political power or for the alignment of social safety nets with their mandates. These choices point to strategies that are employed to generate legitimacy for social safety nets by lodging these programs within organizations with a mandate aligned with political interests or within organizations able to generate results—that is, organizations with the structures and the capacity to deliver the programs, including identifying eligible beneficiaries, making payments, monitoring activities, and so on. The relative importance of these factors may change. For instance, a program that emerges as a short-term response to an emergency may be located in a high-profile agency, such as the office of the president, where it may respond rapidly and with high visibility. However, as programs become more mature and become better integrated into longer-term social protection policy, a social ministry or agency with a policy mandate to serve the vulnerable may become a more appropriate home. There is a pattern between the chosen entity and the spending profile of programs. A large portion of the total social safety net financing overseen by social ministries is for cash transfer programs (44 percent), whereas when central institutions are in charge, spending is higher on public works (figure 4.3). When other arrangements (besides a ministry or central institution) are tapped, emergency programs or food aid are the largest share of government spending. There is a trade-off inherent in the choice of agency for coordination and oversight, as illustrated in the case of Nigeria's process for establishing a social safety net coordination function (box 4.3).

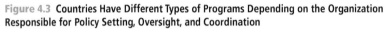

Figure 4.3 Countries Have Different Types of Programs Depending on the Organization Responsible for Policy Setting, Oversight, and Coordination

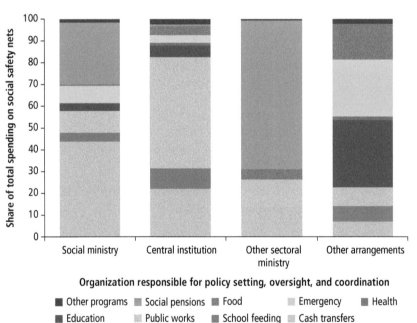

Sources: World Bank review of country documents; ASPIRE (Atlas of Social Protection Indicators of Resilience and Equity) (database), World Bank, Washington, DC, http://www.worldbank.org/aspire
Note: The category of social ministry includes organizations that are responsible for social assistance (including social affairs, social welfare, social protection, social cohesion, social action, human rights), employment (or labor), health, women (or gender), children and families, among others. The category of central institution includes organizations that play a central role in government, including offices of the president or prime minister, as well as ministries responsible for the economy, planning, and the budget or finance, depending on the country. The category of other sectoral ministry includes organizations that do not have a social mandate, including ministries responsible for local government, decentralization, local development, rural development, agriculture, forestry, transportation, and urban development, among others. Most often, these are ministries. The category called other arrangements includes situations when multiple ministries hold responsibility for policy setting, oversight, and coordination; or situations when responsibilities is given to an autonomous government agency or a nongovernmental organization. Typologies are described in appendix A, methodology in appendix B, and more details in appendix G, table G.6.

Responsibility for policy setting, oversight, and coordination is often housed in organizations with a mandate to support vulnerable populations. Across the sample, this responsibility is vested in a social organization in 22 of 38 countries reviewed; social ministries might include ministries of social action or affairs, labor; women, family and children; or social security (figure 4.4). The selection of a social ministry may reflect a desire to name a ministry that is already mandated to promote policies that support the poor and vulnerable. The decision might be to group together aspects of the social protection or social safety net system, such as social pensions or services for children, those affected by disability, or those affected by illness, an accident, or another emergency (whereas contributory pensions are usually managed by a separate agency). However, while social ministries may have the strongest mandate to support the poor, they often have limited financial resources and political influence, including limited authority to require other ministries to collaborate and to coordinate activities. These factors may undermine the ability of these ministries to achieve results and point to their limited legitimacy in some contexts.

BOX 4.3

Nigeria's Process to Establish a Coordination Function

In Nigeria, there were many questions about institutional and coordination functions and structures when the government embarked on the design of an ambitious new national social safety net program in 2015. The political economy of federalism implies a diverse landscape for potential reforms and a complex context for the implementation of national programs. While autonomy gives Nigerian states, particularly those with dynamic and progressive leadership, an opportunity to move ahead on their own, it also poses a challenge for building a national consensus across the various levels of government.

In developing a coordination function, the government of Nigeria reflected upon analyses of institutional arrangements that were focused on institutional forms and functions in countries with similar national social safety net programs, as well as the experience of countries that have established successful social safety nets. A number of functional capabilities emerged as common across programs, including convening ability, political visibility and influence, operational capabilities, ability to coordinate with other social programs, resilience, and transition capacity.

Using these capabilities as a guide, Nigerian agencies that could potentially house a national social safety net program were identified. Attention was paid to the implications of the Nigerian federal system, including the decentralization of roles and responsibilities among states. Several roundtable discussions were held with key government stakeholders and development partners. The government decided to house the main body for social safety net coordination and delivery in the Office of the President.

Source: Holmemo and Ort 2017.

Figure 4.4 Social Ministries Are the Typical—but Not the Only—Policy, Oversight, and Coordination Entities

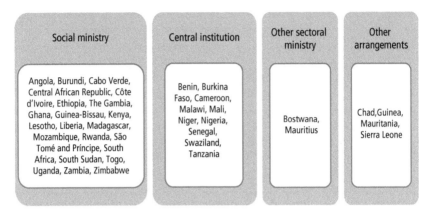

Social ministry	Central institution	Other sectoral ministry	Other arrangements
Angola, Burundi, Cabo Verde, Central African Republic, Côte d'Ivoire, Ethiopia, The Gambia, Ghana, Guinea-Bissau, Kenya, Lesotho, Liberia, Madagascar, Mozambique, Rwanda, São Tomé and Príncipe, South Africa, South Sudan, Togo, Uganda, Zambia, Zimbabwe	Benin, Burkina Faso, Cameroon, Malawi, Mali, Niger, Nigeria, Senegal, Swaziland, Tanzania	Bostwana, Mauritius	Chad,Guinea, Mauritania, Sierra Leone

Source: World Bank review of country documents for 38 countries.
Note: Central institutions include offices of the president or prime minister and ministries of the economy, planning, or finance. Other sectoral ministries include ministries of local government and rural development. See methodology in appendix A.2.2 and more details in appendix table D.1.

In many countries, central organizations are selected because they tend to have greater political influence through their proximity to powerful decision makers. Central organizations—the office of the prime minister, the office of the president, or ministries of finance and planning—are responsible for policy making and coordination in 10 of the 38 countries surveyed. While these organizations may enjoy considerable authority and often special procedures that allow them to act more swiftly than technical ministries, the organizational culture may be less sympathetic to the need of the vulnerable for social transfers. The focus in these organizations is generally on economic growth and expanding employment and productivity, while households that are in the most need of social safety net support tend to face the biggest challenges in gaining access to productive employment.

Locus of Program Management Reflects Organizational Mandates

The responsibility for the management and implementation of social safety net interventions is frequently housed in a different organization from that which oversees policy initiatives. Of the programs presented in table 4.3 (organized by type of organization responsible for policy, oversight, or coordination), about half are managed in the same agency that undertakes policy, coordination, and oversight. In Ethiopia, the Ministry of Labor and Social Affairs led the development of the national policy and is mandated to carry out coordination and oversight functions. But the largest program, the Productive Safety Net Program (PSNP), is managed by the Food Security Coordination Directorate in the

Ministry of Agriculture and Natural Resources. In countries where social safety net programs are nascent, as in Chad, some programs are typically managed by nongovernmental organizations (NGOs) and involve only limited government participation.

Generally, the management of social safety net programs is vested in ministries with a mandate that aligns with the aims of the program. Thus, social safety net programs with a protective focus, such as unconditional transfers to categorical groups considered vulnerable, tend to be housed in social ministries. This is the case of social safety net programs in Kenya (the Cash Transfer for Orphans and Vulnerable Children [OVC] Program, the cash transfer for the elderly, and the case transfer for people with severe disabilities), the Child Support Grant in South Africa, and social pensions in Uganda and Zanzibar. Programs that focus more on productive aspects may be more frequently housed in ministries of rural development, agriculture, roads, infrastructure, or water. One of Ghana's flagship social safety net programs, the Labor-Intensive Public Works Program, is managed by Ministry of Local Government and Rural Development. In Lesotho, the Public Works Program is managed by the Ministry of Forestry. In many countries, there are multiple social safety net programs and multiple ministries or agencies responsible for implementation.

In regions with a longer tradition of social safety net programs, the institutional arrangements often evolve. While programs are relatively new in Africa, and few have changed organizational home, experience in other regions shows that arrangements may alter. In Colombia, the conditional cash transfer program Familias en Acción was launched in the late 1990s as part of the Social Support Network created to offset the impact on poor households of a severe economic crisis. It was initially set to last three years and, in line with this short-term emergency mandate, was operated by Acción Social. As the crisis subsided, the original emergency role became obsolete, and programs were refocused more broadly on the promotion of human capital. The initial arrangements had allowed for rapid implementation because the operating rules were less constraining, but this had also resulted in isolating Familias en Acción from other, prevailing social organizations and coordination mechanisms. To establish links to other organizations and contribute to the broader human capital development strategy, the program began to be used as a liaison between service providers and the beneficiaries—the poorest households. This evolution, from emergency initiative to part of a broader social policy, required shifts in organizational arrangements. In 2011, the Departamento Administrativo de Prosperidad Social (Ministry for Social Prosperity) was created and took over the responsibility for management from the Office of the President. Today, Familias en Acción reaches over 2.5 million households, about a quarter of the population, and is strongly anchored in national legislation.

Table 4.3 Organizational Homes of Social Safety Nets Vary in Africa, Selected Programs

Organization responsible for policy setting, oversight, and coordination	Country	Program	Organization responsible for program management				Unit responsible for program implementation				
			Social ministry	Central institution	Other sectoral ministry	Other arrangements	Project implementation unit (PIU)	Special-purpose department	Preexisting department	Semiautonomous government agency (SAGA)	Nongovernmental institution
Social ministry	Angola	Proajuda Program (Cartão Kikuia)	✓						✓		
	Burundi	Cash transfer program (in preparation)	✓				✓				
	Côte d'Ivoire	Productive social safety net project	✓				✓				
	Côte d'Ivoire	Food-for-work and cash-for-work programs				✓					✓
	Ethiopia	Productive Safety Net Program (PSNP)			✓			✓			
	Ethiopia	Urban Productive Safety Net Project			✓		✓				
	Ghana	Livelihood Empowerment against Poverty (LEAP)	✓				✓				
	Ghana	Labor-intensive public works			✓			✓			
	Kenya	National safety net programs (transfers for orphans, vulnerable children, elderly, and disabled)	✓					✓			
	Kenya	Hunger Safety Net Program (HSNP)			✓		✓				
	Lesotho	Old-age pension		✓							
	Lesotho	Child Grant Program, Orphan Vulnerable Children Bursary Program, Public Assistance Program	✓					✓	✓		
	Lesotho	Public works program			✓				✓		

(Continued next page)

Table 4.3 Continued

Organization responsible for policy setting, oversight, and coordination	Country	Program	Organization responsible for program management				Unit responsible for program implementation				
			Social ministry	Central institution	Other sectoral ministry	Other arrangements	Project implementation unit (PIU)	Special-purpose department	Preexisting department	Semiautonomous government agency (SAGA)	Nongovernmental institution
	Liberia	Liberia Social Safety Nets Project	✓					✓			
	Madagascar	Productive Safety Nets Program, Human Development Cash Transfer Program		✓						✓	
	Mozambique	Basic Social Subsidy Program, Productive Social Action Program, Direct Social Action Program	✓							✓	
	Rwanda	Vision 2020 Umurenge Program (VUP)			✓					✓	
	South Sudan	Emergency food distribution programs				✓					✓
	South Sudan	Safety Net and Skills Development Project			✓				✓		
	Togo	Community Development Safety Nets	✓								✓
	Uganda	Social Assistance Grants for Empowerment	✓				✓				
	Uganda	Third Northern Uganda Social Action Fund		✓			✓				
	Zambia	Social Cash Transfer Scheme, Public Welfare Assistance Scheme, Food Security Pack, Women Empowerment Fund	✓						✓		
	Zimbabwe	Harmonized Social Cash Transfer Program	✓								
Central institution	Benin	Community-Driven Decentralized Services (public works and cash transfer programs)			✓			✓			
	Burkina Faso	Social Safety Net	✓				✓				
	Cameroon	Social safety net program		✓			✓				✓

(Continued next page)

201

Table 4.3 Continued

Organization responsible for policy setting, oversight, and coordination	Country	Program	Organization responsible for program management				Unit responsible for program implementation				
			Social ministry	Central institution	Other sectoral ministry	Other arrangements	Project implementation unit (PIU)	Special-purpose department	Preexisting department	Semiautonomous government agency (SAGA)	Nongovernmental institution
Social ministry	Malawi	MASAF PWP	✓							✓	
	Malawi	Social Cash Transfer Program (SCTP)	✓						✓		
	Mali	Jigisemejiri		✓			✓				
	Niger	Niger Safety Net Project		✓			✓				
	Senegal	Programme National de Bourses de Sécurité Familiale (national conditional cash transfer program, PNBSF)		✓						✓	
	Swaziland	Old-Age Grant and Orphans and Vulnerable Children Grant	✓						✓		
	Tanzania	Productive Social Safety Net (PSSN)		✓						✓	
Other sectoral ministry	Botswana	Orphan Care Program, Destitute Persons Program, Old-Age Pension, Public works (Ipelegeng) program			✓				✓		
	Mauritius	Pensions for retirement (old-age), invalid, widows, and orphans; Allowances for children, guardians (orphans), inmates, and carers (older people with disabilities)			✓			✓			
Other arrangements	Chad	Emergency safety nets (food security)		✓		✓					
	Mauritania	National Social Transfer Program Tekavoul				✓					✓
	Sierra Leone	National Social Safety Net Project				✓				✓	
	Sierra Leone	Labor-Intensive Public Works				✓				✓	

Source: World Bank review of program documents.

Note: Central institutions include offices of the president, offices of the prime minister, and ministries of planning or finance. More details are presented in appendix D, table D.3.

Early Choice of Organizational Home Can Shape the Evolution of Social Safety Nets

The choice of ministerial home shapes the evolution of the social safety net program, as different organizations—and the people who staff them—tend to focus on different outcomes. Programs tend to conform to the vision and mandate of the responsible organization. This occurs through the formal and informal rules that govern organizations. Social workers in a social ministry will focus on the specific needs of vulnerable groups—a reflection of their professional mandate and priorities, as well as their professional "customs" and views. This will affect how the program design evolves, with the possible inclusion of other vulnerable groups or extension of the program to other services required by these groups. Stakeholders and organizations involved in public works programs may have a different outlook, being more concerned about the contribution of programs to economic growth and graduation out of poverty than inclusion. The skills, interests, and incentives for the staff of these ministries—and the political will that backs these ministries—will prioritize those aspects of these programs that achieve the stated (or unstated) objectives. Experience from Kenya and Ethiopia, which is described below, shows how the choice of implementing ministry—and the different founding philosophy that leads to this choice—results in different implementation approaches and different results being achieved, which, in turn, lead to different trajectories.

In Kenya, the cash transfer for orphans and vulnerable children was launched in response to the growing number of children in households affected by HIV/AIDS. The government was keen to explore options that would provide support to orphans, while avoiding expansion in orphanages. The provision of cash transfers was expected to enable households to continue to care for orphans and vulnerable children. Responsibility was given to the unit responsible for the care of orphans, the Department of Children's Services, which is also supported by the United Nations Children's Fund (UNICEF), which played a key role in the pilot initiative. The early successes of the program influenced the Department of Social Development to pilot the cash transfer program for older persons, and for persons with severe disabilities. These pilots also gained political support, and overall coverage of these programs reached about 765,000 households in 2017. A similar trajectory is seen in Ghana.

In contrast, the PSNP in Ethiopia was initiated in response to chronic food insecurity. It was viewed as part of an overall food security strategy (associated with the launch of other resettlement and food security programs) and thus fell under the responsibility of the Ministry of Agriculture and Rural Development. Thus, the productive contribution of the program through the public works (such as investments in soil and water conservation) have been emphasized, with management of the works shifting to the Natural Resource Management Directorate of the Ministry, together with the ability of the social safety net transfers, when combined with livelihood support, to graduate people out of food insecurity. Yet, as the national social protection policy gained traction, the Ministry of Labor and Social Affairs was given the mandate to manage the aspect of the PSNP that supports those households that have no able-bodied adults and are thus unable to participate in public works.

Organizational Fragmentation Results from Multiple Views of Social Safety Nets

In some countries, there may be multiple views on the role of social safety nets, which reflect differing objectives, social norms, or political aims across countries (chapter 3). There may be a diversity of views within government, across development partners, and among other stakeholders on how social safety nets should be designed and operate. The existence of competing narratives enables different approaches to be tested, which can help identify the approach attracting the greatest political support and exerting the greatest impact, both of which are critical to expansion. But multiple approaches can also result in multiple fragmented institutions. In particular, best practice and the diverging preferences of development partners can lead to fragmentation. In Tanzania and Uganda, the coexistence of multiple narratives has led to the development of distinct programs, all providing transfers, but with different approaches and housed in different institutions (box 4.4).

Effective Coordination Requires Clear Mandates, Objectives, and Resources

A common feature of social protection policies is that the objectives span multiple sectors and therefore require interministerial collaboration. As such, social protection policies often include the creation of interministerial oversight bodies. These bodies are often chaired by ministers or cabinet secretaries in ministries with lower levels of decision-making and convening power or by ministers in central ministries with competing demands on time. Hence, forming such bodies or calling meetings once they are formed is rarely prioritized. For instance, in Burkina Faso, the intersectoral national council for social protection only meets once or twice a year, and mainly focuses on information sharing, whereby the main output is a list of programs and the resources spent. This lack of prioritization also arises because there are frequently no clear, time-bound outcomes that such committees are expected to produce. Instead, the stated roles include providing oversight, offering guidance, or ensuring integration. In contrast, successful coordination has involved leadership groups that are assigned specific output goals.

BOX 4.4

Contrasting Social Safety Net Narratives in Tanzania and Uganda

Uganda

Social safety nets have not yet gained a substantial foothold in Uganda. Two development partners—the UK Department for International Development and the World Bank—have joined with different government ministries on programs reflecting two approaches. Through the Expanding Social Protection Program, the former is providing support to the Ministry of Gender, Labour, and Social Development. Although this ministry is considered to have limited implementation capacity, it is identified in the social protection policy as the entity responsible for spearheading social protection. Investing in this entity is an appropriate long-term approach. The UK department's preference for unconditional cash transfers also informed the decision.

World Bank support for social safety nets is channeled through a third phase of the Northern Uganda Social Action Fund, which is managed by the Office of the Prime Minister. This phase will scale up public works. The World Bank's choice builds on an existing relationship and may help in promoting the government's commitment to social safety nets. Operational capacity has not been a significant consideration because district governments are responsible for most of the implementation.

Tanzania

In Tanzania in 2011, the World Bank was supporting pilot public works interventions and conditional cash transfers through the TASAF Tanzania Social Action Fund (under the Office of the President), while other actors were supporting unconditional categorical transfers, including the Kwa Wazee Pension Program, in which the main partner was the Ministry of Labour and Employment.

In 2012, the government reoriented the social action fund into the Productive Social Safety Net (PSSN), which provides a combination of unconditional cash transfers, conditional supplements linked to health care and education services, public works, and livelihood support. The PSSN has become a national program and operates in all districts. The fund's unrivaled capacity and the World Bank's relationship with the Office of the President have contributed to the decision to retain the institutional arrangements from earlier phases of the fund, despite the forthcoming social protection framework, which identifies the Ministry of Labour and Employment as the lead oversight agency in social protection.

Even after the launch of the PSSN, many stakeholders retained a strong interest in social pensions, including several NGOs and the United Nations Children's Fund. In 2016, the semiautonomous region of Zanzibar launched the Zanzibar Universal Pension Scheme, a social pension program to address poverty and vulnerability among the elderly who lacked formal pensions. The program is managed by the Zanzibar Ministry of Labour, Empowerment, Elderly, Youth, Women, and Children.

Source: Interviews with program experts.

However, social protection policies rarely establish the means by which joint oversight and interministerial collaboration can become functional. Many of the challenges described above may be attributed to the insufficient attention paid to identifying and reaching a consensus on the shared objectives of any coordination effort, the appropriate coordinating entity, and the targets of coordination. Typically, a general need for joint oversight is identified, along with initiatives to establish structures without clearly identifying the purpose and, therefore, the most appropriate mechanisms to achieve all goals. Often no specific staff members from ministries are assigned to the coordination efforts, nor are budgets allocated or objectives set out.

Ensuring That Organizations Can Effectively Implement Social Safety Net Programs

The Choice of Management Structure Matters for the Implementation of Programs

Across Africa, governments have put in place a variety of structures to manage and deliver social safety nets. Within the ministries selected for the management of social safety net programs, there are five main categories of management units (see table 4.3), that is, the structure within or outside the ministry that is effectively responsible for the daily management of programs, as follows:

- A *project implementation unit* (PIU): A team or unit that is created within a government organization to manage a project, the members of which are recruited or assigned for the sole purpose of managing the project and paid for by external agencies. This is the case for the social safety net programs in Cameroon and Uganda.

- A *special-purpose department*: A department that is established within a government organization with the specific mandate to manage one or several social safety net programs. An example is the Social Assistance Unit in Kenya that manages the OVC Program and cash transfers for the elderly and persons with severe disabilities.

- A *preexisting department*: A department within a government organization with a set mandate and range of responsibilities to which management of one or several social safety net programs is added. This is the case for the Lisungi cash transfer program launched in the Republic of Congo in 2013.

- A *semiautonomous government agency* (SAGA). A legal entity that has been created by a government to undertake specific functions that would have otherwise been carried out by the government. Such an entity is operationally autonomous from government. It may also be a fully autonomous agency. In Senegal, the National Agency for Social Protection and Solidarity (Délégation Nationale à la Protection Sociale et Solidarité Nationale), which reports to the Office of the President, is responsible for the management of the national cash transfer program and the social registry.

- *Nongovernmental institution.* This category includes nongovernmental organizations (NGOs) and agencies of the United Nations. These are more commonly used if capacity is limited, in fragile or humanitarian contexts, or for programs that are still small or at the pilot stage (such as in Somalia and South Sudan).

Management structures vary by context, although there is little evidence as to how these may evolve as social safety nets expand. Across a sample of programs examined, the most common form of management structure is the PIU (table 4.3). This is particularly the case among countries in which central ministries have vested responsibility for policy, oversight, and coordination. The use of PIUs also dominates if central ministries are responsible for program management. They are also a common form of management arrangement in social ministries. The rare exception to this trend seems to occur if management responsibilities are allocated to another sectoral ministry. The widespread use of PIUs may reflect the relatively recent establishment of government-managed social safety nets in many countries in Africa. The use of existing departments and SAGAs to manage social safety nets is the next most common type of management structure, followed by specialized departments and then NGOs.

The widespread use of PIUs may also reflect the fact that many government ministries lack the operational capacity and technical skills required to manage these programs. This may also be a product of the importance of development partner funding in social safety net programs given that PIUs are perceived to deliver results within the time frame of project financing. Lack of capacity and fiduciary concerns led to the decision to locate the Social Assistance Grants for the Empowerment Program in Uganda in PIUs. Specific arrangements were identified to manage the relevant funds, and the PIUs relied mostly on fixed-term contractors. In addition, PIUs offer other advantages, particularly in the short term. They may attract high-caliber staff through competitive employment terms and conditions (often involving consultancy contracts) and may operate outside regular government financial management and procurement systems. However, they are usually dependent on development partner financing and may not build long-term capacity within the public sector.[8] The experience in other sectors suggests that, while the creation of a PIU can quickly build the capacity that is needed to deliver results, there are risks to creating such islands of efficiency, which function well but do not respond to more systemic weaknesses within government systems.[9] Programs that are launched within separate PIUs may be migrated to regular departments within the responsible government organizations as they gain sustainability. For instance, in Indonesia, the management of the Program Keluarga Harapan was initially located within a PIU housed in the Ministry of Social Affairs and relied largely on consultants. To strengthen institutional sustainability, it was later moved to a directorate of the ministry, where civil servants carried out a greater range of tasks. Colombia has had a similar experience.

If programs are managed by existing government structures, departments are the most common form of management unit. It also appears that the use of existing departments is somewhat more common if social ministries are responsible for social safety net programs. If programs are small and new, they may be added as an extra responsibility to a preexisting government department. Selected staff within these departments may be assigned responsibility for the program, either in addition to their existing responsibilities or exclusively. As the programs become larger or more established, a special-purpose department might be established. Such departments tend to be formed only once programs have reached a certain size and governments have made political and financial commitments to ensure long-term implementation. This is the case in Kenya, where a social assistance unit was established to manage three programs that were initially run by existing departments within the Ministry of Gender, Children, and Social Development.[10] As the three programs were expanded and procedures were harmonized, the new unit was created to take over management.

SAGAs enjoy some degree of autonomy not experienced by core ministerial departments. They are usually answerable to a ministry or the office of the president and thus form a regular part of the government architecture, but operate under a different set of rules. The autonomy may extend to financing, personnel, or organization and may help ensure that the agency's structure and procedures reflect its needs and function. Such managerial and financial autonomy can enable the SAGA to make and enforce decisions more rapidly. SAGAs can often set up implementation structures that directly reach beneficiaries, thereby bypassing the multiple levels of government administration and various decision-making processes. For example, in Sierra Leone, the National Commission for Social Action has district offices that directly oversee the delivery of social safety net interventions.

Although existing SAGAs may be made responsible for social safety nets, the establishment of a new SAGA usually requires greater government commitment, especially in terms of the resources and the passage of specific legislation needed to establish a separate agency. Thus, the establishment of a dedicated SAGA may reflect strong political support for social safety nets. An example of a SAGA focused on a social safety net is the South African Social Security Agency, which is attached to the Ministry of Social Development. It was formed in response to perceived weak implementation by a ministerial department and decentralized government structures. The National Agency for Social Protection and Solidarity in Senegal is another example. Particularly in countries in which the social safety net program has evolved from a social fund, the responsibility for social safety nets has been allocated to existing SAGAs. In Rwanda, the Vision 2020 Umurenge Program (VUP) is run by the Local Administrative Entities Development Agency, a SAGA responsible for several rural development programs. In Sierra Leone, the social safety net is managed by the National Commission for Social Action (an autonomous government agency), which originally housed the country's social fund. This is also the case for Madagascar, Malawi, and Tanzania. There is no evidence on whether SAGAs evolve into other entities or if SAGAs may be a preferred type of delivery agency for social safety nets in Africa.

The choice of management structure influences the effectiveness of the organization because these structures may incentivize or constrain management and implementation in various ways. For instance, the functioning of government departments is typically hampered by the need to abide by ministerial procedures. In particular, fiduciary procedures or hiring standards and processes are typically more restrictive among departments within government ministries than those among SAGAs or PIUs. However, allocating responsibility for a social safety net to a government department offers the opportunity to embed the program in regular government systems, which creates management interest in and responsibility for the program. It is also a way of concretizing the views on the most appropriate types of programs without undertaking implementation. Reinforcing the mandate of a government department and strengthening its resources as needed can facilitate the grounding of social safety nets beyond the level of strategies.

Effective Implementation Often Requires Technical Coordination across Multiple Government Actors

The choice of management structure will also reflect the extent to which technical coordination is required to deliver the social safety net program. Universal or unconditional programs may be associated with simpler institutional arrangements run broadly by one sectoral entity and local and national representatives. Conditional programs often require the engagement of multiple sectors, such as ministries of health and education, and robust procedures for collecting information from health centers and schools on the compliance of individuals with conditions. Public works programs often require the involvement of diverse technical staff. Their implementation frequently depends heavily on local governments; some programs are effectively devolved to local agencies. They also often require coordination with departments involved in road, water, and natural resource management.

There are many examples in Africa of practical coordination across sectors in program implementation. The Rwanda VUP and the Tanzania PSSN have achieved significant interagency coordination, particularly at the local level. The effectiveness of the coordination structures established to implement the PSNP in Ethiopia benefited from the Safety Net Support Facility, which provided training and backup on leadership, understanding the terms of reference, preparing agendas, chairing meetings, dealing with nonattendance, and documenting action points. Table 4.4 drills down into details on three large social safety net programs, in Ghana, Rwanda, and Senegal.

Technical coordination can be supported through the development of centralized tools. As social safety nets expand, the need to establish centralized tools that can serve multiple programs becomes apparent. Registries, management information systems (MISs), and shared payment mechanisms are approaches that have been applied with some success (box 4.5). They help raise efficiency and foster coordination (chapter 5). However, while these tools and the formal rules that are associated with them can improve coordination, there has been little consideration for how they may interact with the informal rules and norms that shape their use. Most immediately, the technical skills required to design and operate these tools are scarce in many African countries, and hiring suitably skilled staff can thus be difficult. If such staff are identified, they often request higher salaries than those paid to civil servants, which can breed resentment.

Technical Coordination Often Extends Beyond Government

While policy oversight and coordination are increasingly being carried out by governments, nonstate actors are frequently involved in the delivery of social safety nets. The responsibility for certain aspects of social safety net programs is often outsourced to specialized agencies that are based in the private sector, such as payment providers or independent monitors. In many cases, NGOs and United Nations agencies provide social safety nets to hard-to-reach communities or in fragile or conflict-affected areas. The management of social safety nets thus may include coordination and management of the private sector or NGOs in the effort to achieve a common purpose. In the Democratic Republic of Congo, the United Nations Office for Project Services has become involved in carrying out labor-intensive public works for road rehabilitation. In Guinea, the World Food Programme has been conducting a school feeding initiative. In Burkina Faso, Cameroon, and Niger, social safety net benefit payments are provided through microfinance institutions or money transfer agencies under contract with the agency managing the program. The Urban Safety Net Program in Ethiopia is setting up a payment system through the Commercial Bank of Ethiopia. NGOs may support frontline service delivery, such registration in the case of Senegal

Table 4.4 The Type of Program Affects the Complexity of Implementation Arrangements

Level	Ghana unconditional transfer program, Livelihood Empowerment against Poverty Program (LEAP)	Senegal conditional transfer program, Programme National de Bourses de Sécurité Familiale (PNBSF)	Public works program, Rwanda VUP
National	LEAP is managed by the LEAP Secretariat within the Ministry of Gender, Children, and Social Protection. A national program steering committee provides oversight and enables coordination between the program and the Labor-Intensive Public Works Program.	PNBSF is managed by a team in the National Agency for Social Protection and National Solidarity, a SAGA in the Office of the President. A multisectoral safety net steering committee provides regular technical oversight, and key institutions (health care, education, nutrition) are expected to have more regular engagement.	The VUP is managed by the Social Protection Programs Division of the Local Administrative Entities Development Agency (in the Ministry of Local Government). The Social Protection Sector Working Group has been established to coordinate and share information. It is supported by a number of thematic subcommittees that meet more regularly.
Local	District social welfare officers, answerable to district assemblies (and thus under the Ministry of Local Government), are the main actors in the districts. Their main roles include supporting the targeting and enrollment processes and undertaking case management. Payments are managed by e-zwich, a national smart card payment system.	NGOs and their networks of social workers provide much of the frontline support for the program (registration, social promotion activities, case management, and so on). The delivery of social promotion activities by deconcentrated sectoral ministries is piloted in one region. Payments are managed by the postal service and a mobile telephone company.	Decentralized government line departments support planning, implementation, and quality control in public works and assist in the Ubedehe wealth-ranking process used to target the VUP and other programs. Support for planning and implementation includes ensuring that community plans fit with sectoral development plans, checking the adequate design of subprograms, and managing the provision of nonwage inputs into public works programs. Funds are transferred from local finance offices to savings and credit cooperatives, which make payments to beneficiaries.
Community	Community implementation committees consisting of community volunteers who identify potentially eligible households assist in household data collection for targeting and act as an information channel between the program and beneficiaries.	Local community committees identify potentially eligible households as part of the National Unique Registry, which is used to identify PNBSF beneficiaries.	Communities are expected to lead in the identification of public works subprograms through voluntary community meetings. Communities also play key roles in the Ubedehe wealth-ranking process and the subsequent identification of eligible households.

Source: World Bank compilation.

BOX 4.5

Tools for Coordination

In Kenya, the launch of the National Safety Net Program (NSNP) represented an attempt to coordinate four existing cash transfers: the Hunger Safety Net Program (HSNP) and cash transfer programs for old people, orphans and vulnerable children (the OVC Program), and people with severe disabilities. The consolidation strategy brought three of the four cash transfers under the management of a single unit, where all key functions at the national level are carried out by a single team. The staff of the fourth program participate in coordination meetings. At the local level, where the programs are implemented, the government has merged local community structures to support complaint processes and case management and is piloting a harmonized targeting approach. A shared registry of beneficiaries has been created from the MISs of the four programs, as well as data of the Cash for Works and Food for Asset Programs of the World Food Programme. There are plans to expand this registry to additional programs so it can act as a resource for multiple programs that may adopt the harmonized targeting approach.

The government of Senegal is building a registry to be used by programs that address chronic poverty and support vulnerable households. In 2012, it created a social protection agency housed in the Office of the President, to lead in the formulation of a social protection strategy, the design of social safety net interventions, and coordination. As a main pillar of this effort, the government has established the Registre National Unique (unified national registry), which, by 2017, included data on the 450,000 poorest households nationwide (around 30 percent of the population) (appendix D, table D.2). It already serves as an entry point for several targeted interventions, including the main conditional cash transfer program and the subsidized health insurance program, and its use is expected to expand, in particular to programs designed to respond to shocks. The registry is housed in a dedicated department, independent of the department in charge of the implementation of national cash transfer programs.

In the Republic of Congo and in Mali, the cash transfer programs have been steadily expanded since their launch in 2013, and the establishment of a unified national registry has been a key part of this process (appendix D, table D.2). The development of these two national registries was undertaken while the programs were being conceived. In Mali, the creation of the Registre Social Unifié (unified social registry) began with the establishment of the Jigisemejiri Cash Transfer Program. Its objectives are to reduce costs and program coverage overlap, and to facilitate the rapid expansion of programs to respond to shocks. In the Republic of Congo, a registry was developed through the conditional cash transfer program.

Source: Interviews with program experts.

(see table 4.4). Similarly, complementary services, such as behavioral change activities that target social safety net beneficiaries, are often managed by specialized United Nations agencies (such as the United Nations Children's Fund) or NGOs, as in Niger.

In fragile settings or in countries where humanitarian programs are prominent, NGOs and development partners frequently play a critical role. Indeed, the coordination and oversight of these large programs implemented outside of government are of large practical importance because of the size of the programs and the political nature of the response to shocks. In most Sahelian countries, humanitarian actors have initiated efforts to coordinate interventions, capitalize on good practices, and engage in advocacy (box 4.6). These initiatives have sometimes been formalized as alliances, such as in Mauritania, Niger, and Senegal. They can help support government efforts to coordinate the response to shocks.

Decentralization May Boost Flexibility and Adaptability, but Compromise Equity and Transparency

Across Africa, government decentralization is affecting the design, delivery, and, in some cases, the financing of social safety nets. Most countries have adopted some degree of decentralization, defined here to include deconcentration and devolution. Deconcentration occurs when decision making and management responsibilities are distributed to different entities of the central government and often involves shifting responsibilities from central government officials to central government actors working in regions, provinces, or districts. Devolution occurs when governments transfer authority for decision making, financing, and management to quasi-autonomous units of local governments, such as municipalities that elect their own mayors and councils, raise their own revenues, and exercise independent authority in investment decisions.[11] The argument in favor of the decentralization of services is that it distributes decision making closer to the people to increase the likelihood that the choices made by leaders reflect the preferences of the people and encourage greater responsiveness to local concerns across a wider range of issues. These is no strong evidence on the effects of devolution or deconcentration on the functioning of social safety nets. Two of the largest social safety net programs offer contrasting experiences.

Prospera, the conditional cash transfer program in Mexico, is centralized, while the operation of Brazil's Bolsa Família is deconcentrated to states. The case of South Africa offers some insights: prior to the launch of the South Africa Social Security Agency, nine provincial governments were responsible for the implementation of seven social grants offered by the government. This devolved implementation was characterized by delays in the processing of grant applications, delayed grant payments, concerns over fraud and corruption, and high

BOX 4.6

Sahel Humanitarian Coordination for Food Security

Humanitarian actors in West Africa are seeking to create links with government programs. In particular, technical collaboration has emerged in several countries in building unified national registries to identify and target households during responses to shocks.

In most Sahelian countries, humanitarian actors have initiated efforts to coordinate their interventions on food and nutrition security, capitalize on good practices, and engage in advocacy based on experiences. The nature of the efforts has depended on the country and has sometimes been formalized as an alliance, such as the Cadre Commun in Niger, Alliance Cash in Mauritania, and CORRIANS in Senegal, mainly with the financial support of the ECHO Project.

To harmonize their approaches in addressing food insecurity, humanitarian actors have developed or adopted common tools. For instance, the Cadre Harmonisé (regional framework), a methodology developed by the Permanent Interstate Committee for Drought Control in the Sahel (Comité permanent Inter-Etats de Lutte contre la Sécheresse dans le Sahel, CILSS) to analyze food security, is used for the early identification of areas that are at risk of food insecurity and the number of people projected to be affected. Humanitarian actors also support the collection of primary data, such as through the hunger biomass map of Action Against Hunger and improvements in national early warning systems. They have likewise harmonized a household targeting methodology through a community-based approach, Household Economy Analysis (HEA), which was developed by Save the Children UK in the mid-1990s. Program evaluation activities have been coordinated through a common postdistribution monitoring design (Niger) and a joint grievance mechanism (Senegal). Coordination has recently been strengthened through meetings of regional alliances (Niamey in 2015 and Dakar in 2016).

The coordinated effort of development partners is also promoting the creation of synergies with government programs. In particular, the inclusion of development partner interventions in government-led annual food insecurity response plans has improved coordination and has also highlighted the differences in intervention methods and principles among actors. Strengthening the dialogue between humanitarian actors and governments has helped to overcome misunderstandings linked to the constraints among humanitarian actors, who are limited in their collaboration by the short funding cycle.

A technical collaboration has emerged in several countries to build national unified registries (Burkina Faso, Chad, Niger) and use them in identifying and targeting households during responses to shocks (Mauritania, Senegal).

Source: Interviews with program experts.

administrative costs. The reform that led to the creation of the new central agency assigned the responsibility for the management and implementation of these grants to one administrative unit with a central office and service offices in each province.

In most African countries, most and perhaps all programs are funded centrally, and national organizations set out key parameters and guidelines; the notable exception is NGO-implemented programs that are not overseen or managed by national governments. The delivery of the various elements of social safety nets may remain with central ministries or be deconcentrated to local staff. Typically, if implementation is carried out through a PIU, as in Burkina Faso, the delivery is centralized, and staff are recruited by the ministry to coordinate local activities. SAGAs, such as in Sierra Leone and South Africa, establish offices or recruit local staff to deliver social safety net services. In other cases, the frontline delivery of social safety nets falls to staff who report directly to local governments (devolution). In these cases, the staff—who are likely the same professional cadre as the responsible ministry, such as social workers in the case of a social ministry—are required to follow centrally established guidelines and standards. But, in a devolved context, the national organization responsible for the program does not directly manage frontline workers. These staff are accountable to local authorities. In Botswana, social workers supporting the frontline implementation of the Social Cash Transfer Program are accountable to local authorities. In such situations, local authorities recruit staff based on locally defined criteria and pay them through locally managed budgets, which may be devolved from central authorities. Often, local authorities also establish the local priorities, which may or may not include the aims and objectives of the social safety net programs.

While national, standardized guidelines exist in most programs, these often contain provisions for some degree of local decision making. National guidelines typically describe the various procedures to be followed in implementing program targeting, registration, payments, case management, grievance mechanisms, and exits. These guidelines, however, sometimes allow local implementers in deconcentrated and devolved settings leeway in adapting programs to local conditions. Indeed, national standards enable consistent implementation, but some tasks can also benefit from devolved decision making so programs take local realities into account. This flexibility can result in more effective processes, such as in the context of some targeting processes, and can encourage local buy-in, thereby generating legitimacy for the program among communities and local leaders. However, it can also result in distortions or biases in the implementation of programs. In this case, local norms or practices may lead to favoritism, to the advantage of particular groups or objectives. Table 4.5 provides examples of the variation in the delegation of selected tasks and decision

Table 4.5 Decision Making and Implementation May Be Centralized, Delegated, or Devolved

Activity	Centralized	Delegated	Devolved (including to communities)
Budgeting			
Allocating resources for different regions or districts	In many countries, national poverty data are used to determine the number of beneficiaries in each district (and, hence, the budget allocation). In Cameroon, a quota is set nationally for the number of beneficiaries in each commune. In Burkina Faso's Burkin Nong Saya Program, regions are selected based on the national poverty map. At least one community in each commune in these regions participates in the program. This is important for equity across communes. However, the selection of participating communities within each commune is random because no poverty estimates exist below the regional level. [a]		In Ethiopia's PSNP, while the overall number of beneficiaries per district is determined nationally, the decisions on the number of beneficiaries in each subdistrict are left to district authorities
Targeting			
Choice of criteria and methodology	In almost all countries, the targeting methodology is determined at the central level.		The PSNP and Urban Productive Safety Net Project in Ethiopia and the Burkina Faso Burkin Nong Saya Program provide some flexibility to include locally appropriate targeting criteria.
Data collection	Senegal's PNBSF and Mauritania's Tekavoul Program depend on national registries to identify eligible households in each district. In Cameroon and Sierra Leone, data are collected by the central statistical office.	In Kenya, targeting is performed by enumerators managed by county and subcounty officers from the Department of Children's Services and the Department of Social Development, under the supervision of central authorities.	
Beneficiary selection	Many programs—Kenya's social assistance unit, Senegal's PNBSF, and Sierra Leone's Social Safety Net Program, Burkina Faso's Burkin Nong Saya Program, Niger's Projet Filets Sociaux—use a combination of community identification of potentially eligible households, a nationally applied poverty measure, and a community validation to select program beneficiaries. They do this either themselves or by relying on national registries that combine these elements. In Benin and Cameroon, communities first identify potentially eligible households, then finalize the selection using a national poverty measure.	In South Africa, branches of the South African Social Security Agency review applications to assess whether households meet national eligibility criteria.	In Ethiopia's PSNP, communities make key decisions on which households are targeted in the PSNP.

(continued next page)

Table 4.5 Continued

Activity	Centralized	Delegated	Devolved (including to communities)
Public works and conditions			
Rules regarding conditionality[b]	The conditions in most conditional programs are set nationally.		
Rules regarding public works parameters[c]	In national programs, norms are usually set at the national level; Ethiopia's PSNP provides for reduced work norms in hot lowland areas, but these are also set at the national level.		
Public works planning			All public works programs allow the district or community identification of public works to reflect local needs.
Assessing adherence to conditions and public works requirements	In a number of programs (Tanzania's PSSN conditional component), monitoring and reporting on conditions are a delegated responsibility, but the calculation of deductions takes place at the national level.	Where the responsibility for payment is delegated (Tanzania's PSSN public works component and Uganda's Northern Uganda Social Action Fund 3), decisions on which household should be penalized are delegated, but this decision is expected to adhere to national standards.	
Complaints and case management			
Documenting complaints and beneficiary information updates		Most programs with a national MIS or a unified registry have delegated responsibility to districts or communities for collecting reports on complaints or updates.	
Approving beneficiary updates and resolving complaints	Most programs with a national MIS or unified registry require central authorization to resolve major complaints or update beneficiary information.	Kenya's HSNP allows district and county staff to propose updates from within the MIS, but this still requires approval from the head office.	Ethiopia's PSNP has appeals committees established within local governments and is increasingly looking to local social accountability mechanisms as a means of identifying and resolving complaints.

Source: World Bank compilation.

a. In the expansion phase, the program is tending toward selecting communes based on the presence of social action offices and social workers instead of mandating that each commune be included.

b. This refers to the setting of conditionalities for households, which usually is related to cash transfer programs conditioned on health care visits or education outcomes (see chapter 1, box 5.1).

c. This refers to rules on working hours and other work conditions related to public works activities.

217

making to local structures. Local decision making may include community involvement in the identification of beneficiaries, community or district involvement in the choice of projects in public works schemes, district involvement in priority setting, and community or district decision making on the penalties for noncompletion of public works projects or failure to meet health care or education objectives.

Many of the challenges associated with coordination experienced at the national level are less apparent among local implementers. Indeed, proximity facilitates communication among the staff of national institutions at the local level in the context of deconcentration. In practice, staff offer mutual support in the implementation of their respective programs.

Beyond the staff and consultants who oversee targeting, make payments, or facilitate local planning, a range of local actors often influence and shape how various aspects of a social safety net are carried out. The involvement of communities—often through local leaders or committees comprising teachers, extension workers, and representatives of youth groups—is common in Africa (see table 4.5). Their involvement is most frequently seen in targeting, which enables communities to use their local knowledge to identify those people or households who meet the eligibility criteria or are considered by the community to deserve support. The involvement of local leaders can also lend legitimacy to these processes. In the Afar Regional State in Ethiopia, the regional government sought the participation of religious leaders in the targeting process in an effort to ensure that the poorest and most deserving of support were selected. Despite this, the extent to which local leaders (traditional chiefs, elders, tribal leaders) are assigned formal roles in social safety net programs varies. If such roles are not defined, this can create confusion as these leaders and their communities are left to play the roles appropriate to local dynamics of power.

Creating Incentives to Encourage Individual Actors to Deliver Results

Management structures and coordination mechanisms incentivize or constrain the people who oversee and deliver social safety nets. Programs may be delivered by government staff who are fully dedicated to the program or by government staff for whom social safety net activities are added to their other workloads. These may be civil servants or consultants. Key functions might also be subcontracted to private sector providers, such as administering payments (contracted to post offices and a mobile phone company in Senegal, for instance), organizing training activities (NGOs in Senegal's PNBSF), or even running the PIU (as is the case of Chad). Government staff may work full time on a program, but social safety net activities may represent only a small part of the labor burden of district staff, and core government staff may also work alongside contract staff. Many programs make use of voluntary community structures to realize elements of program implementation, particularly local planning and beneficiary selection. Most programs use a combination of these arrangements. Table 4.6 highlights selected strengths and weaknesses of various approaches.

A range of other factors that incentivize or constrain staff performance are becoming increasingly important for social safety nets in Africa. Incentives can come in many forms (de Neubourg 2002). Numerous studies have explored how low salaries, limited career advancement, and poor performance management lead to low motivation and general job dissatisfaction in the public sector. (These management structures are influenced to varying degrees by a country's civil service or public sector management reform; see Brinkerhoff and Brinkerhoff 2015). These factors can also lead to high rates of staff turnover, generating gaps in the capacity of social safety nets in countries such as Ethiopia, Malawi, Rwanda, and Uganda. In Sierra Leone, low remuneration rates have been identified as a key constraint in attracting qualified personal, as suggested by the widespread use of coping arrangements to offset the low public sector pay scale. Srivastava and Larizza (2013) identify the features of these coping arrangements as follows: (1) relatively well-paid technical assistance, often funded by development partners, in line positions; (2) PIUs; (3) externally funded line agencies; and, (4) other ad hoc salary increases. Interagency rivalry or competition for status or resources among government ministries can also lead to a lack of willingness to cooperate on programs, resulting in poor coordination. As social safety nets expand and are increasingly anchored in government systems, there will be a need to consider how the incentives and constrains inherent in the civil service affect the functioning of the program and to engage with and support broader civil service reform.

Development partner funding for social safety nets is often accompanied by rules and incentives with short- and long-term implications for staff motivation. Civil servants working on social safety net programs funded by development partners may have heavier workloads or be expected to perform to a higher standard than other civil servants. Yet, their remuneration often remains the same, guided by civil service scales and norms. This is frequently cited as the rationale for increases in the salaries of civil servants working on these programs, through fuel and telephone vouchers, for instance. In cases in which civil servants and hired externally funded consultants are working side, by side and interacting on a daily basis to deliver, for example, health extension services or agricultural extension services to beneficiaries (Burkina Faso, Cameroon, Ethiopia), competition and resentment may grow among the civil servants

Table 4.6 There Are Trade-Offs in the Various Approaches to Staffing

Approach	Strengths	Weaknesses	Most appropriate use
Staff dedicated exclusively to the program	Allows investment in the specific skills required for operationalizing social safety nets; ensures that tasks are not neglected by staff forced to prioritize other activities; performance incentive systems reflect social safety net tasks.	Can cause the implementation of social safety nets to occur in silos, that is, incapable of reciprocal operation through appropriate links with other, related services.	At headquarters, to ensure the adequate oversight and management of key tasks.
Staff for whom social safety nets are an additional activity	Limits the need to recruit new staff or set up new departments during the pilot phase of a program; can promote a better-integrated approach; may allow the engagement of staff in other activities that only require part-time efforts	Unless social safety net responsibilities are carefully written into job descriptions and performance contracts, they may be neglected; they may be viewed as additional responsibilities for which staff are not remunerated; they may also overburden staff and lead to unrealistic workloads.	If an integrated approach is needed that requires the participation of frontline staff; if core activities are shared in related programs, such as benefit schemes; if the engagement of other sectors is needed part time (responsibilities should be carefully written into job descriptions and performance contracts).
Consultants	Allows high-caliber consultants to be recruited through better pay and conditions; may facilitate a rapid surge in capacity.	May prevent capacity gaps from being structurally addressed; training and investments are provided to staff who will only work on the program for a limited duration; working relationships may be difficult with contract staff, who will lack authority and might be resented for their better pay and conditions.	To provide technical expertise not immediately available within the government; to work with government staff to develop skills and procedures; to provide surge capacity during periods of particularly substantial workloads.
Staff responsible for implementation coordinated among agencies	Allows different aspects of a social safety net to be delivered by the agency with the appropriate skills and procedures; facilitates links to complementary programs	The nonlead agency is likely to assign its own core activities a higher priority than social safety net implementation; may be difficult to establish coordination mechanisms that function as needed.	Necessary for public works programs and conditional transfer programs; however, it is important to find advocates within each agency; it is also important to consider social safety net tasks in staffing, job descriptions, and budget allocations.
Contracting key functions to the private sector (including NGOs)	May ensure that key functions, such as payments, are carried out by organizations with appropriate skills, operating procedures, and safeguards; may allow skills and procedures not readily available in the government to be accessed, such as MIS development; may promote independence in evaluations and audits; may limit capture.	There may be a lack of private sector organizations capable of undertaking tasks; difficulties in managing the contract as a result of poor contract management skills in the central agency; lines of accountability may be unclear, leading to confusion among beneficiaries on how to hold service providers to account.	For the technical design of key systems (targeting, MIS, and so on); for the provision of services in which the private sector has a comparative advantage (payment services, provision of training, family support, and so on).
Use of voluntary community structures	Builds community ownership of key program procedures, such as targeting; helps ensure program responsiveness to local needs, such as planning public works projects; facilitates outreach from district headquarters.	Risk of elite capture and may affect social relationships, particularly in targeting; difficult to ensure consistent quality in implementation; the opportunity costs of the time spent participating in community activities and performing tasks as volunteers (may result in demands for payment).	Most programs benefit from using volunteer community structures, but the risks need to be managed; in particular, wasting time in unnecessary meetings; needs to be avoided, and the community volunteers must not be overburdened, but must be adequately supervised.

Source: World Bank compilation.

because consultants are often paid higher salaries. More generally, studies in West Africa show that the position of focal point in a project funded by development partners is highly sought because it provides access to islands of functionality and resources; civil servants who are not working on these externally funded projects may become apathetic toward project objectives and activities because they do not receive the same benefits (Olivier de Sardan 2013).

Within devolved contexts, local administrative structures, priorities, and incentive systems often determine the motivation of locally recruited staff. In the case of devolution, if local governments manage the staff responsible for implementation, program activities must be adequately reflected in local government plans. The alignment of program objectives with the objectives of the local governments can help ensure the political and managerial support of local authorities. To be effective, however, this alignment of aims should be translated into the detailed terms of references, work plans, and performance reviews of local staff. Even in countries such as Botswana, where the social safety net program is mature and has been fostered mainly by national stakeholders, the widespread reliance on locally hired staff has not translated into the prioritization of the roles and functions of these staff members by the local authorities who hire and pay. In Rwanda, concerns have been raised about the availability of staff to undertake the tasks associated with the social safety net program in districts because of competing priorities and a lack of clarity on the accountability for monitoring and reporting. Within a devolved setting, the knowledge, priorities, and skills of local managers and elected leaders can thus significantly influence social safety net programs. If local managers understand the objectives of the program and are trained in leadership skills, they become more engaged. Experience with the Ethiopia PSNP shows that, for these reasons, local managers paid more attention to the technical experts who were carrying out tasks for the PSNP, such as facilitating local planning, organizing public works, and making payments. They were more confident in encouraging their teams to embrace shared objectives and responsibilities. Through a sense of engagement, leaders were able to build trust within their teams. Such changes in leadership have resulted in team members performing at a higher level. In contrast, low-performing districts are more often characterized by new or unengaged leaders than by the quality of the skills among the technical experts.[12]

In many countries, informal practices influence the ability and willingness of staff to carry out their functions. For example, it has become common for civil servants to use the per diems associated with training, workshops, and monitoring visits to supplement their salaries. The implications of this per diem culture are various. The desire to receive a per diem may bring people together to overcome a barrier in decision making or resolve technical issues. The desire to collect per diems may also undermine reforms. For instance, the introduction of e-payments and electronic reporting systems may be resisted by staff if these systems reduce the need for monitoring visits by staff, which enable them to draw per diems. In some countries, informal networks and personal or political connections influence hiring decisions within the civil service, thereby limiting the role played by technical expertise and merit and resulting in suboptimal program staffing.

Notes

1. This is echoed in the human rights approach to social protection. Thus, "social protection programmes must be enshrined and defined in national legal frameworks and supported by a national strategy and plan of action" (Sepúlveda and Nyst 2012, 26).
2. See "International Covenant on Economic, Social, and Cultural Rights," Office of the United Nations High Commissioner for Human Rights, Geneva, http://www.ohchr .org/EN/ProfessionalInterest/Pages/CESCR.aspx; "Universal Declaration of Human Rights," United Nations, New York, http://www.un.org/en/universal -declaration-human-rights/.
3. "African Charter on Human and Peoples' Rights," African Commission on Human and Peoples' Rights, Banjul, The Gambia, http://www.achpr.org/instruments/achpr/. See chapter 3, box 3.3.
4. See "R202, Social Protection Floors Recommendation, 2012 (No. 202): Recommendation Concerning National Floors of Social Protection," International Labour Organization, Geneva, http://www.ilo.org/dyn/normlex/en/f?p=NORMLE XPUB:12100:0::NO::P12100_ILO_CODE:R202.
5. See AU (2008); NANHRI (2006). For the Livingstone Call for Action, see "Zambia: Social Protection Conference Issues Call to Action," *Pambazuka News*, April 12, 2006, https://www.pambazuka.org/resources/zambia-social-protection-conference -issues-call-action. See also "Ouagadougou Declaration and Plan of Action on Accelerating Prisons and Penal Reforms in Africa," African Commission on Human and Peoples' Rights, Banjul, The Gambia, http://www.achpr.org/instruments /ouagadougou-planofaction/; "Yaoundé Declaration on the Implementation of the Sendai Framework in Africa," Declaration of the Fourth High Level Meeting on Disaster Risk Reduction Held in Yaoundé, Cameroon, on July 23, 2015, African Union, Addis Ababa, http://www.ifrc.org/Global/Publications/IDRL/regional /Yaounde%20Declaration%20DRR%20EN%2023072015.pdf.
6. Even countries without specific constitutional provisions—such as Chad, Republic of Congo, Mauritania, and Senegal—shave adapted relevant articles of the International Covenant on Economic, Social, and Cultural Rights and the Universal Declaration of Human Rights in their constitutions.
7. In the case of Uganda, this concern arose, in part, against a backdrop of significant national financing committed to antiretroviral drugs.
8. However, in Burkina Faso, even programs run by consultants financed by development partners must follow the rules set out in government decrees on hiring and staff compensation.

9. For example, Olivier de Sardan (2013) explains that, in West Africa, civil servants and local administrators are often focused on gaining formal or informal access to development aid.

10. The OVC Program was run by the Department of Children's Services, while the cash transfer programs for older persons and persons with severe disabilities were run by the Department of Social Development.

11. Deconcentration tends to involve only the delegation of certain tasks and decisions, though the upward accountability to supervising ministries tends to take precedence over any local accountability. Decentralization includes the relinquishment of power by the central government to actors at a lower level in a political-administrative hierarchy. At a minimum, it devolves substantial decision-making powers to locally representative bodies, but it may also include the decentralization of fiscal resources and revenue-generating powers. One type of decentralization is delegation, whereby responsibility for decision making and the administration of public functions are transferred to semiautonomous organizations not wholly controlled by the central government, but ultimately accountable to it, such as public enterprises or corporations, housing authorities, transportation authorities, and semiautonomous school districts. See Ribot (2002).

12. Personal communication, Paul Derksin, August 2017.

References

Andrews, Matt. 2013. *The Limits of Institutional Reform in Development: Changing Rules for Realistic Solutions.* Cambridge: Cambridge University Press.

AU (African Union). 2008. "Social Policy Framework for Africa." First Session of the AU Conference of Ministers in Charge of Social Development, Windhoek, Namibia, October 27–31, Document CAMSD/EXP/4(I), AU, Addis Ababa.

Barma, Naazneen H., Elisabeth Huybens, and Lorena Viñuela, eds. 2014. *Institutions Taking Root: Building State Capacity in Challenging Contexts.* New Frontiers in Social Policy Series. Washington, DC: World Bank.

Black Sash. 2010. *Social Assistance: A Reference Guide for Paralegals.* Cape Town: Black Sash.

Bridges, Kate. 2016. "Why the Iceberg Sinks: A Critical Look at Malawi's History of Institutional Reform." Background paper for, Malawi Country Economic Memorandum 2016, World Bank, Washington, DC.

Bridges, Kate, and Michael Woolcock. 2017. "How (Not) to Fix Problems That Matter: Assessing and Responding to Malawi's History of Institutional Reform." Policy Research Working Paper 8289, World Bank, Washington, DC.

Brinkerhoff, Derick W., and Jennifer M. Brinkerhoff. 2015. "Public Sector Management Reform in Developing Countries: Perspectives beyond NPM Orthodoxy." *Public Administration and Development* 35 (4): 222–37.

Carroll, Kate. 2011. "Addressing Inequality: Framing Social Protection in National Development Strategies." *IDS Bulletin* 42 (6): 89–95.

de Neubourg, Chris. 2002. "Incentives and the Role of Institutions in the Provision of Social Safety Nets." Social Protection Discussion Paper 226, Social Safety Net Primer Series, World Bank, Washington, DC.

d'Iribarne, Philippe, and Alain Henry. 2015. "The Cultural Roots of Effective Institutions." Background paper for, *World Development Report 2017: Governance and the Law*, World Bank, Washington, DC.

Devereux, Stephen. 2010. "Building Social Protection Systems in Southern Africa." Background paper for, European Report on Development, Centre for Social Protection, Institute of Development Studies, Brighton, UK.

Garcia, Marito H., and Charity M. T. Moore. 2012. *The Cash Dividend: The Rise of Cash Transfer Programs in Sub-Saharan Africa*. Directions in Development: Human Development Series. Washington, DC: World Bank.

Goyal, Radhika, Clare Leaver, Sally Murray, Pieter Serneels, and Andrew Zeitlin. 2014. "Strengthening Public Sector Performance Contracts in Rwanda." IGC Rapid Response Note, International Growth Centre, London School of Economics and Political Science, London.

Grindle, Merilee S. 1997. "Divergent Cultures? When Public Organizations Perform Well in Developing Countries." *World Development* 25 (4): 481–95.

Hickey, Samuel. 2012. "Turning Governance Thinking Upside-Down? Insights from the Politics of What Works." *Third World Quarterly* 33 (7): 1231–47.

Holmemo, Camillla, and Rachel Ort. 2017. "Institutional Design and Coordination of Social Safety Nets: Adapting Good Practice to Institutional and Political Realities in Nigeria." Working paper, World Bank, Washington, DC.

ILO (International Labour Organization), UNICEF (United Nations Children's Fund), and WFP (World Food Programme). 2015. "Capitalising on UN Experience: The Development of a Social Protection Floor in Mozambique." United Nations Joint Programme on Social Protection, Maputo, Mozambique.

Kaltenborn, Markus, Abdul-Gafaru Abdulai, Keetie Roelen, and Sarah Hague. 2017. "The Influence of Policy and Legal Frameworks on the Development of National Social Protection Systems." IDS Working Paper 501, Centre for Social Protection, Institute of Development Studies, Brighton, UK.

Krause, Philipp. 2013. "Of Institutions and Butterflies: Is Isomorphism in Developing Countries Necessarily a Bad Thing?" Background Note, Overseas Development Institute, London.

Leftwich, Adrian. 2006. "What Are Institutions." IPPG Briefing Paper 1, Research Programme Consortium on Improving Institutions for Pro-Poor Growth, University of Manchester, Manchester.

Leftwich, Adrian, and Kunal Sen. 2010. "Beyond Institutions: Institutions and Organizations in the Politics and Economics of Growth and Poverty Reduction, a Thematic Synthesis of Research Evidence." Research Programme Consortium on Improving Institutions for Pro-Poor Growth, University of Manchester, Manchester.

Mathauer, Inke. 2004. "Institutional Analysis for Safety Net Interventions." Social Protection Discussion Paper 418, World Bank, Washington, DC.

Mehta, Lyla, Melissa Leach, Peter Newell, Ian Scoones, K. Sivaramakrishnan, and Sally-Anne Way. 1999. "Exploring Understandings of Institutions and Uncertainty: New Directions in Natural Resource Management." IDS Discussion Paper 372, Institute of Development Studies, Brighton, UK.

MEPATI (Republic of Congo, Ministère de l'Economie, du Plan, de l'Administration du Territoire et de l'Intégration). 2012. *Document de Stratégie pour la Croissance, l'Emploi et la Réduction de la Pauvreté (DSCERP 2012–2016)*. Brazzaville: MEPATI.

Monchuk, Victoria. 2014. *Reducing Poverty and Investing in People: New Role of Safety Nets in Africa*. Directions in Development: Human Development Series. Washington, DC: World Bank.

North, Douglass C. 1989. "Institutions and Economic Growth: A Historical Perspective." *World Development* 17 (9): 1319–32.

North, Douglass C., John Joseph Wallis, Steven B. Webb, and Barry R. Weingast. 2007. "Limited Access Orders in the Developing World: A New Approach to the Problems of Development." Policy Research Working Paper 4359, World Bank, Washington, DC.

Olivier de Sardan, Jean-Pierre. 2013. "The Bureaucratic Mode of Governance and Practical Norms in West Africa and Beyond." In *Local Politics and Contemporary Transformations in the Arab World: Governance beyond the Center*, edited by Malika Bouziane, Cilja Harders, and Anja Hoffmann, 43–64. Governance and Limited Statehood Series. London: Palgrave Macmillan.

Ostrom, Elinor. 1990. *Governing the Commons: The Evolution of Institutions for Collective Action*. Cambridge, U.K.: Cambridge University Press.

Pritchett, Lant, Michael Woolcock, Matt Andrews. 2013. "Looking Like a State: Techniques of Persistent Failure of State Capability for Implementation." *Journal of Development Studies* 49 (1): 1–18.

Ribot, Jesse C. 2002. "African Decentralization: Local Actors, Powers, and Accountability." Democracy, Governance, and Human Rights Paper 8, United Nations Research Institute for Social Development, Geneva.

Ridde, Valéry. 2010. "Per Diems Undermine Health Interventions, Systems, and Research in Africa: Burying Our Heads in the Sand." *Tropical Medicine and International Health* 15 (7): E1–E4.

Robalino, David A., Laura Rawlings, and Ian Walker. 2012. "Building Social Protection and Labor Systems: Concepts and Operational Implications." Background paper for, Social Protection and Labor Strategy 2012–22, World Bank, Washington, DC.

Rodrik, Dani, and Arvind Subramanian. 2003. "The Primacy of Institutions (and What This Does and Does Not Mean)." *Finance and Development* 40 (2): 31–34.

Rubio, Gloria. 2011. "Measuring Governance and Service Delivery in Safety Net Programs." SP Discussion Paper 1119, World Bank, Washington, DC.

Scott, W. Richard. 2008. *Institutions and Organizations: Ideas and Interests*, 3rd ed. Thousand Oaks, CA: Sage Publications.

Scott, Zoë. 2011. "Evaluation of Public Sector Governance Reforms 2001–2011: Literature Review." May 31, Oxford Policy Management, Oxford.

Sepúlveda, Magdalena 2014. "The Rights-Based Approach to Social Protection in Latin America: From Rhetoric to Practice." Políticas Sociales 189, United Nations Economic Commission for Latin America and the Caribbean, Santiago.

Sepúlveda, Magdalena, and Carly Nyst. 2012. "The Human Rights Approach to Social Protection." Elements for Discussion Series, Unit for Development Communications, Ministry for Foreign Affairs, Helsinki.

Simons, Andrew M. 2016. "What Is the Optimal Locus of Control for Social Assistance Programs? Evidence from the Productive Safety Net Programme in Ethiopia." ESSP Working Paper 86 (April), Ethiopia Strategy Support Program, International Food Policy Research Institute, Washington, DC.

Srivastava, Vivek, and Marco Larizza. 2013. "Working with the Grain for Reforming the Public Service: A Live Example from Sierra Leone." International Review of Administrative Science 79 (3) 458–85.

UNDP (United Nations Development Programme). 2009. "Capacity Development: A UNDP Primer." Capacity Development Group, Bureau for Development Policy, UNDP, New York.

UNDP (United Nations Development Programme) and African Management Development Institute Network. 2017. "Report on the State of the Public Service in Africa: Experiences from the Water, Education, and Health Sectors in Selected Countries." UNDP, New York.

Vian, Taryn, Candace Miller, Zione Themba, and Paul Bukuluki. 2013. "Perceptions of Per Diems in the Health Sector: Evidence and Implications." Health Policy and Planning 28 (3): 237–46.

World Bank. 2012. "The World Bank's Approach to Public Sector Management 2011–2020: Better Results from Public Sector Institutions." February 3, World Bank, Washington, DC.

———. 2015. The State of Social Safety Nets 2015. Washington, DC: World Bank.

———. 2017. World Development Report 2017: Governance and the Law. Washington, DC: World Bank.

Chapter **5**

Harnessing Resources to Expand and Sustain Social Safety Nets

Lucilla Maria Bruni, Melis Guven, and Emma Monsalve

Expanding the coverage of programs represents a serious fiscal challenge. Currently, governments in Africa are spending about 1.2 percent of gross domestic product (GDP) on social safety nets. This is lower than the spending on other sectors, such as energy, health care, education, and, in some cases, the military. This level of spending and the predictability of expenditures are inadequate to face the high chronic poverty rates and vulnerability to shocks experienced in the region. Bringing these programs to scale will require a multipronged approach to fiscal systems.

First, countries need to make better use of existing resources. The operational efficiency of programs needs to be improved. The scale and quality of the operation of administrative tools are critical to greater efficiency. Governments across the region have recently put considerable emphasis on enhancing administrative processes and systems. Efficiency gains can also be harvested by raising allocative efficiency to expand the reach of programs among the poor and vulnerable.

The level and sustainability of financial resources must be upgraded. Development partners are crucial in the financing of social safety nets in Africa. Given the fiscal constraints facing many governments, development partner support will continue to be critical to bringing programs to scale in most countries. Governments must find the right mix of domestic, foreign, public, and nonpublic funding. Strengthening fiscal systems is the most sustainable option for financing social safety nets at scale because of the uncertainties in the global macroeconomic and political environment, the rising costs of borrowing, and the unpredictability of external financing. Reforming tax systems is a widely recognized imperative in Africa.

Finally, flexible financing strategies are needed to respond to shocks and crises efficiently and in a timely manner. Contingency or reserve funds could be established to finance relief, rehabilitation, reconstruction, and prevention activities to address emergencies. Risk transfer mechanisms, which are financial or insurance instruments, are another option to insure against shocks.

How to finance social safety nets at scale sustainably is a pressing issue for policy makers. This report argues that bringing social safety nets to scale is key to responding to the challenges of chronic poverty and vulnerability to shocks across the region. However, governments across the world, but especially in Africa, face competing fiscal demands and finite budgets.

Financing social safety net programs at scale in Africa is therefore a challenge. Rising to the challenge requires resolving both sides of the fiscal equation: expenditure and revenue. That means spending resources more effectively and boosting revenue. Considering social protection expenditure and revenue issues jointly boosts the likelihood of achieving revenue sufficiency for sustained programs.

Spending and Financing for Social Safety Nets: A Snapshot

Chapter 1 highlights the main traits of spending on social safety nets in the region. On average, the region devotes 1.2 percent of GDP on social safety nets (equivalent to 4.6 percent of total government spending), compared with the global average of 1.6 percent. This is lower than the spending on other sectors, such as energy subsidies, health care, education, and, in some cases, the military (figure 5.1; appendix G, table G.1). In particular, spending on energy subsidies—often cited as a means of supporting vulnerable households, but largely regressive in practice—is greater than spending on social safety nets in the region, with particularly high levels in Central and Eastern Africa and in low-income countries.

There is great variation across the Africa region in spending on social safety nets as a share of GDP. High-income and upper-middle-income countries spend an average of 2.5 and 2.2 percent of GDP (6.5 and 6.9 percent of total government expenditures, respectively), while low-income countries spend an average 1.4 percent of GDP (4.8 percent of total government expenditures; see figure 5.1 and appendix G, table G.3). Southern African countries spend an average 3.2 percent of GDP, three times more than countries in other subregions. Non-resource-rich countries devote more than twice as much to social safety nets (2.1 percent of GDP) as resource-rich countries (1 percent of GDP). Countries with lower exposure to droughts allocate fewer resources to these programs than countries facing high or medium exposure (appendix G, table G.3).

The composition of social safety net spending also varies. Overall, cash transfer programs account for 41 percent of all social safety net spending in Africa (chapter 1, figure 1.4, and appendix G, table G.6). Social pensions represent the second-highest share of spending (26 percent of total). In Southern Africa and upper-middle- or high-income countries, a larger share of social safety net spending goes to programs focused on the elderly. Spending on public

Figure 5.1 Spending Is Lower on Social Safety Nets Than on Other Sectors

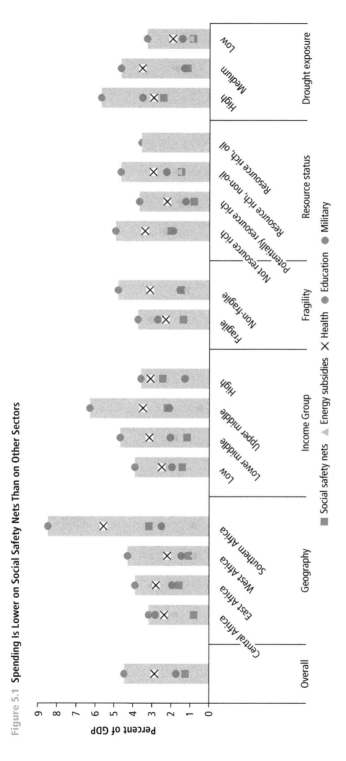

■ Social safety nets ▲ Energy subsidies ✕ Health ● Health ● Education ● Military

Sources: Spending data: ASPIRE (Atlas of Social Protection Indicators of Resilience and Equity) (database), Administrative data, World Bank, Washington, DC, http://www.worldbank.org/aspire. Energy subsidies: Coady et al. 2015. Other data: WDI (World Development Indicators) (database), World Bank, Washington, DC, http://databank.worldbank.org/data/reports aspx?source=world-development-indicators.

Note: Methodology presented in appendix B.4 and more details in appendix G, table G1. Data do not reflect reductions in subsidies which have taken place since 2015. Social safety net spending estimates are moderately different from those in World Bank (2018) due to data updates in this report and different treatment of outlier data points.

works programs represents 16 percent of all safety net spending in Africa; these programs exist in almost all low-income countries and fragile states. While overall poverty-targeted programs account for the majority of spending in the region, most of the social safety net spending in Central Africa and West Africa is categorically targeted (chapter 3, figure 3.4, and appendix G, table G.6).

Current spending is inadequate for confronting the high poverty rates and vulnerability to shocks in the region. Many of the poor do not have access to social safety net programs. Average coverage is 10 percent of the total population, while the average poverty rate is above 41 percent (appendix F, table F.2; chapter 1, figure 1.1). If one assumes that the targeting of social safety net interventions is perfect, this implies that around 24 percent of the poor are covered. Most countries in Africa spend much less on social safety nets than the aggregate poverty gap, which is, on average, 14 percent of GDP, while social safety net spending is 1.2 percent of GDP (see chapter 1).[1] Only upper-middle-income countries, some lower-middle-income countries, and countries in Southern Africa spend amounts on social safety nets that more or less match the poverty gap.

In terms of efficiency, the available data show that administrative costs represent an average 17 percent of program spending (appendix G, table G.9). This reflects the cost of the initial investments in systems and the small size of many programs. Though there are data limitations, the share of administrative costs appears to be lower in public works, school feeding, and social pension programs, possibly because of less costly targeting approaches. Administrative costs tend to fall, but not always, as programs increase in size. The administrative costs of the Social Safety Nets Project in Cameroon accounted for 65 percent of program spending at launch in 2015, but fell to 23 percent in 2016, while the number of beneficiaries quadrupled (figure 5.2). In Mali, the administrative costs of the Jigisemejiri (Tree of Hope) Safety Nets Project fell from 41.8 percent to 11.9 percent of program costs in 2014–16, while the number of beneficiaries grew from about 30,000 people to over 375,000 people. The administrative costs of the Mozambique Basic Social Subsidy Program decreased slightly when benefits were raised. However, expansion does not necessarily lead to immediate savings if new networks and systems need to be developed for geographic expansion, as occurred in the Tanzania Productive Social Safety Net (appendix G, table G.9).

On average, development partners finance 55 percent and governments the remaining 45 percent of social safety net spending in Africa (chapter 3, figure 3.3). Interventions supported by development partners often prioritize food-based programs, such as school feeding, food for work, and vouchers (appendix G, table G.8, presents detailed information for selected programs). Humanitarian aid represents the main source of funding in emergency situations, and development partners remain critical in many low-income and fragile contexts (chapter 1, figure 1.12). The average amount of humanitarian aid flowing to fragile and conflict-affected countries (3.9 percent of GDP) is larger

Figure 5.2 Administrative Costs Often Decline as Programs Grow, but Not Always

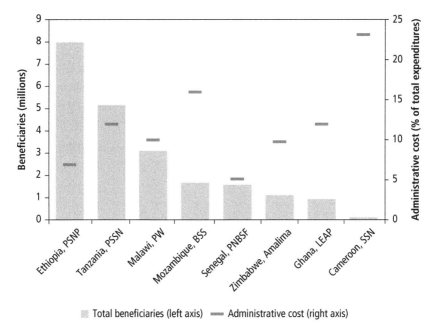

Total beneficiaries (left axis) ▬ Administrative cost (right axis)

Source: Spending data: ASPIRE (Atlas of Social Protection Indicators of Resilience and Equity) (database), Administrative data, World Bank, http://www.worldbank.org/aspire.
Note: See details in appendix G, table G.9; Amalima = Response to Humanitarian Situation; BSS = Basic Social Subsidy Programme; LEAP = Livelihood Empowerment against Poverty; MASAF PWP = Malawi Social Action Fund Public Works Program PNBSF = National Cash Transfer Program; PSNP = Productive Safety Net Program; PSSN = Productive Social Safety Net Program; SSN = Social Safety Net.

than the social safety net spending of the governments of these countries (1.4 percent of GDP). The Central African Republic and South Sudan are the largest recipients of humanitarian aid (21.6 and 11.3 percent of GDP, respectively), followed by Burundi, Chad, the Democratic Republic of Congo, Liberia, Mali, Niger, and Sierra Leone (appendix G, table G.1).

Making Better Use of Existing Resources

Maximizing the efficiency and effectiveness of social safety net programs is paramount given the tight fiscal environments and competing demands. For the purposes of this study, the general concept of efficiency reflects the achievement of desired outcomes at the lowest possible cost, while the concept of effectiveness encompasses the achievement of the highest possible impact for a given budget.

Desired outcomes and impacts depend on policy goals and preferences, country context, and specific programs. For example, the desired outcome of a particular cash transfer program could be limited to the immediate reduction of monetary poverty, while that of other programs might include enhancing the human capital of children, social cohesion, or resilience to natural disasters. (The discussion below mostly focuses on impact in terms of monetary poverty reduction because of the nature of the available data and the goal of facilitating cross-country comparisons.) Box 5.1 offers a more detailed discussion of the definition and measurement of efficiency and effectiveness in social safety nets used in this report.

BOX 5.1

How Are Efficiency and Effectiveness Defined and Measured?

The concepts of efficiency and effectiveness represent ways to gauge inputs, outputs, and outcomes (Farrell 1957). The definitions of the inputs, outputs, and outcomes of social safety net programs depend on the policy goals and parameters of each program. The outputs and outcomes of cash transfer programs might relate to child poverty, school attendance, earnings, and so on depending on the program objectives. Defining the relationship between these variables is challenging, given that most social outcomes are the result of many factors and not a single policy. Empirically, measurement is also often difficult because appropriate data are often not available or are of poor quality.

The social protection literature presents multiple approaches to measuring efficiency and effectiveness (Bui et al. 2015; Castro-Leal et al. 1999; Galang, Lavado, and Domingo 2013; Herrmann et al. 2008; Mandl, Dierx, and Ilzkovitz 2008; Nelson 2012; Sudaram, Strokova, and Vandeninden 2014). The two main ones are the analysis of performance indicators and frontier analysis. Performance indicators include metrics such as the coverage and targeting of the poor, benefit incidence analysis, poverty reduction decomposition, and cost-effectiveness analysis. However, these do not include information on the maximum possible achievements, the yardsticks at the core of efficiency analysis. In contrast, frontier analysis provides a benchmark to assess efficiency and effectiveness by building a production possibility frontier based on cross-country data. There are multiple techniques to estimate a production possibility frontier, either parametric (Free Disposal Hull, Data Envelopment Analysis) or nonparametric (econometric methods such as Stochastic Frontier Analysis).

Results of the parametric data envelopment analysis are presented below to illustrate the kind of analysis that may be performed, though this is by no means an exhaustive examination of social safety nets' efficiency and effectiveness. The methodology estimates the highest possible level of output that can be reached for a

(continued next page)

Box 5.1 (continued)

given level of spending (called effectiveness in this methodology), based on the performance of other countries (Farrell 1957). Figure B5.1.1 shows the frontier calculated using social safety net spending as a share of GDP as an input and coverage of the poor as an output (other inputs and outputs could be used). The vertical distance of a country to the frontier shows how much a country could increase its coverage of the poor, keeping constant its current spending level. Effectiveness scores measure how close a country is to the frontier (calculated as [d1/(d1+d2)] for Lesotho in the graph). Table B5.1.1 shows the effectiveness scores for different country groups (a higher score shows greater effectiveness).

Figure B5.1.1 Most Countries Can Improve Effectiveness

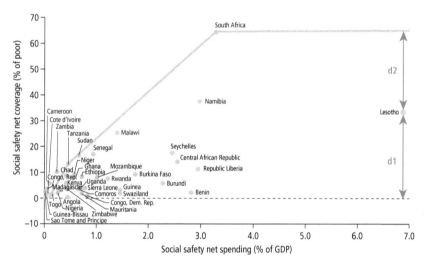

Sources: Spending and beneficiaries: ASPIRE (Atlas of Social Protection Indicators of Resilience and Equity) (database), Administrative data. World Bank, Washington, DC, http://www.worldbank.org/aspire. Other: WDI.
Note: Coverage is calculated as the number of beneficiaries (administrative data) divided by the number of poor (WDI), except for South Africa and Namibia, for which it is estimated using household surveys.

Table B5.1.1 Effectiveness Varies by Country Group

Country groups		Effectiveness score
Income group	Low income	32
	Lower middle income	47
	Upper middle income	81
	High income	61

(continued next page)

Table B5.1.1 Continued

Country groups		Effectiveness score
Fragility	Fragile	30
	Nonfragile	46
Overall development of social safety net system	No solid plans	17
	In progress	40
	In place	81
Social protection strategy or policy	Not present	57
	In progress	37
	Present	38
Organization responsible for policy setting, oversight, and coordination	Social ministry	35
	Central ministry	50
	Other	19
Social registry status	Not planned	56
	Planned	32
	Operating on small scale	34
	Operating on medium scale	40
	Operating on large scale	59
Development partner involvement	Yes	38
	No	57

Source: World Bank calculations.

The ability of programs to reduce poverty varies widely. Among others, programs' impact on poverty depends on their ability to reach the poor. For instance, while $0.72 of each dollar transferred to households by Rwanda's VUP Direct support program goes to the poor, this is only the case for $0.06 of each dollar transferred by the noncontributory pension in Mauritius (table 5.1). Programs' ability to reduce poverty also depends on the number of beneficiaries. In 2014, Rwanda's VUP Direct Support program only reached 1.1 percent of the population, while the noncontributory pension in Mauritius' coverage was 15.5 percent. Impact depends also on the value of transfers, and their ability to bring households above the poverty line (transfers represent about 22 percent of beneficiaries' consumption for the VUP Direct support program, and 27 percent for Mauritius's program). Therefore, Rwanda's VUP Direct support program performs well in terms of reaching the poor and providing them with relatively large transfers, but its impact on poverty is limited by its limited coverage. In Mauritius, the noncontributory pension has large impacts on poverty, but is a costly program, as transfers are large and many are not reaching the poor.

Overall, there is significant room to improve the effectiveness of social safety net spending in many countries. The frontier analysis described in box 5.1 shows that most countries can significantly improve their effectiveness by increasing

Table 5.1 **Performance Indicators for Selected Programs**

Country year	Program	Cost of program, (% of GDP)	Population covered (% of total population)	Benefit level (% of beneficiary welfare)	Transfers going to poor (% of total program expenditures)	Estimated impact of program (%)	
						Reduction in poverty rate	Reduction in poverty gap
Malawi 2013	Public works (MASAF PWP)	0.2	15.2	10.8	28	1.0	0.6
Mauritius 2012	Social aid program	0.04	3.4	16.7	11	34.0	52.0
	Noncontributory pension	3.2	15.5	27.0	6	87.0	94.6
Rwanda 2014	Vision 2020 Umurenge Program:						
	- Direct support	0.5	1.1	22.2	72	0.0	0.3
	- Classic public works	0.1	1.3	9.4	84	0.0	0.1
Senegal 2011	Community nutrition program	0.03	25.6	0.6	18	0.1	0.1
	Medical assistance for elderly	0.01	0.6	1.7	34	0.0	0.3
South Africa 2010	Grants for old-age, disability, veterans	1.2	5.6	22.2	19	49.0	73.9
	Grants for child support, care dependency, and foster care	1.1	21.3	14.6	23	46.0	67.0
Uganda 2012	Expanding social protection program, Direct income support	0.05	0.3	6.5	13	0.1	0.4

Sources: Cost of program and population covered: ASPIRE (Atlas of Social Protection Indicators of Resilience and Equity) (database), Administrative data, World Bank, Washington, DC, http://www.worldbank.org/aspire. Benefit level and estimated impacts: ASPIRE and household survey data. Other data: WDI.
Note: The reduction in the poverty rate [gap] is estimated as the difference between the pretransfer poverty [gap] (simulated using household survey) and the actual rate [gap], expressed in percentage of the pretransfer rate [gap].

their coverage of the poor while maintaining their current level of spending. Generally, countries with a strong social safety net system; with a central institution leading policy setting, oversight, and coordination; and with large social registries tend to be more effective (box 5.1, table B5.1.1). On the other hand, the presence of development partners and of a social protection strategy is negatively associated with effectiveness; this probably reflects lower effectiveness observed in poorer or fragile countries, where development partners and strategies are also more present. While these measures should only be taken as indicative, they suggest significant potential efficiency gains for many countries' programs.

Strong Delivery Mechanisms Are the Basis for an Efficient System

Well-functioning administrative tools are critical to ensuring the cost-effective delivery of social safety net transfers to the intended beneficiaries, and governments across the world have begun to emphasize improving administrative processes and systems. The essential elements of the effective administration of a social safety net system include processes for identification, targeting, enrollment, payments, service delivery, and case management. The government of South Africa achieved significant efficiency gains by overhauling administration, by introducing a specialized agency for centralized administration and payments (the South African Social Security Agency), by introducing biometric smart cards, by reregistering beneficiaries, and by undertaking regular biometric proof-of-life verifications (notwithstanding recent controversies surrounding the arrangements regarding the payment systems) (Alam, Mokate, and Plangemann 2016).

Upgrading administrative processes and introducing technology can be costly, but the benefits can be significant in the medium to long terms. During the first seven years of Mexico's Prospera Program, administrative costs fell from 51 percent of the program's overall budget to 6 percent. This was because of large up-front investments in systems—the purchase of equipment, the design of systems, the definition of procedures, and so on—that yielded benefits for multiple years, as well as a gradual increase in the number of beneficiaries served by the systems (Lindert, Skoufias, and Shapiro 2006). In Africa, the administrative costs associated with Cameroon's Social Safety Nets Project declined from an initial 60 percent of total spending to 23 percent after one year. During the first year of the program, most of the spending was allocated to establishing appropriate information infrastructure; but, after the first year, the program implementation unit (PIU) became more efficient, and benefit payments became the largest cost item.

The adoption of technology in all aspects of administration can lead in lowering the cost of administering social safety net programs. A shift from physical cash transfers to electronic payments generates substantial gains in efficiency by reducing leakage and allowing the integration of payments with information management. In Mexico, thanks to a campaign to integrate electronic payments and social assistance, 97 percent of 2.6 million pensioners are paid through a centralized electronic system, saving the equivalent of about $900 million annually in administrative costs.

The use of biometric smart cards is another example of how technology is able to boost efficiency by lowering administrative costs. In India, the introduction of biometric smart cards resulted in time savings to beneficiaries valued at $4.5 million and reduced annual leakage by approximately $38.5 million in the National Rural Employment Guarantee Scheme and $3.2 million in the social security pension program. The efficiency gains are particularly large relative to the total cost of the introduction of the smart cards, $2.3 million (Muralidharan, Niehaus, and Sukhtankar 2016).

Technology can also promote effectiveness. Thus, through a recent pilot program of the Fundación Capital in Colombia, recipients of the Más Familias en Acción conditional cash transfer program gained access to shared tablet computers and smartphones to use LISTA, an application designed as an alternative to in-person financial training through a peer-to-peer education methodology. Participants were able to access LISTA from home at their own pace and focus their learning on the choice of topics. Preliminary results indicate significant impacts on financial knowledge, attitudes toward formal financial services, the adoption of good financial practices, and financial outcomes.

Technology also holds promise for decreasing the cost and increasing the accuracy of targeting. The governments of Sierra Leone and Tanzania are using innovative spatial statistical modeling approaches to targeting. Georeferenced locational information (geotagged and satellite data) is combined with household survey data to generate poverty maps. In Tanzania, the maps are used to assess geographical targeting performance and will be used to select priority areas for retargeting and any eventual expansion of the social safety net program. In Sierra Leone, the maps are used to target multiple programs and are overlaid with other data, depending on the needs of each program; they are also used to help harmonize interventions across governmental and nongovernmental institutions (Gething and Rosas 2015; World Bank 2015).

Introducing technology does not guarantee cost savings, however. The quality of implementation and local conditions play a big role and there is often a learning period. In a cash-for-assets program in Kenya, electronic cash payments were 15 percent less costly to implement than the distribution of food of equivalent value (CGAP 2013). However, in the Malawi Cash and Food for Livelihoods Pilot Program, cash was more expensive to administer than food (though it assured greater food security) because the program was able to purchase food at much lower, more stable prices in the context of weak food market integration (Audsley, Halme, and Balzer 2010).

On the basis of international experiences, three crucial factors may be identified in determining whether technology can raise the efficiency and effectiveness of social safety nets. First, the quality of infrastructure and implementation is critical for the successful introduction of technology. In four cash transfer programs in low-income settings (Haiti, Kenya, the Philippines, and Uganda), efficiency gains from the introduction of electronic payments were not immediately realized because of the lack of adequate mobile infrastructure, a high-quality management information system (MIS), technical capacity among administrators, and recipient understanding (CGAP 2014). In Zambia, an innovative mobile technology enumeration and registration system for the Social Cash Transfer Program did not outperform the existing paper system in a small pilot initiative, because of challenges largely "related to an isolated design flaw in the application, logistical challenges with power and the network, and poor compatibility between the m-tech database and the existing management information system" (IDinsight 2015, 1).

Second, the start-up costs of technology are high, either because it requires infrastructure investments or because switching technologies implies transaction costs. A review of e-payments for emergency cash transfers in Kenya and Somalia found that the choice of payment modality is not a large determinant of overall costs and that e-payments are not necessarily cheaper than manual payments, often because of the higher start-up costs (O'Brien, Hove, and Smith 2013). Nonfinancial factors (such as timeliness, the burden on beneficiaries, safety, risk of fraud, and so on) may then be determining factors in the choice of payment modality. An e-voucher pilot initiative of the World Food Programme in Afghanistan found that, although the program was successful in many aspects, costs were not lower than the costs of traditional paper vouchers because of the high costs of monitoring the pilot initiative, costs that would disappear in follow-up phases.

Finally, the legal and procurement aspects of the introduction of technology need to be carefully managed. Contracting information technology service providers entails unique challenges because such services may be based on proprietary source codes or other asymmetric information that can create excessive negotiating or market power among the service providers. Governments are advised to manage this risk carefully through appropriate legal and procurement processes or by relying on open source systems to avoid vendor lock-in. While the South African social assistance identification and payment card is one of the most advanced in the world, the South African Constitutional Court declared, in 2014, that the tender process and, thus, the contract for provision were invalid. The contract with the service provider was continued to guarantee service, but the court ruled that the South African Social Security Agency must reopen the tender. Since then, the agency has encountered numerous challenges in attempting to comply with court's finding, and the same service provider is still administering payments, despite allegations of abuse of market power through the provision of complementary financial services using personal and biometric data collected through the grants payment system.

By Joining Programs and Tools, a System-Wide Approach May Promote Efficiency

All programs require basic administrative tools to identify and enroll beneficiaries, make payments, and manage information (box 5.2). Unifying these administrative tools and systems can lead to economies of scale and result in efficiency gains. Beyond more efficient delivery, a system-wide approach also encompasses program and policy integration, which can reduce costs and boost efficiency. Despite progress in achieving better coordination, social safety net programs in Africa are still largely fragmented, and responsibility for implementation is typically spread over several ministries (chapter 4). Governments can save resources by creating an integrated and coherent social protection system. The efficiency analysis presented above suggests that countries with a social protection strategy embodied in a ministry with a social protection mandate are able to establish a more efficient nationwide social safety net system. Systems enable governments to respond more efficiently and effectively to poverty and shocks and to promote well-being throughout the life cycle.

BOX 5.2

Key Instruments of Social Safety Net Programs and Systems

Social registries support outreach, intake, registration, and the assessment of needs and conditions. Beneficiary registries and benefit administration systems support decisions and notification along the delivery chain of a program. If several beneficiary registries are linked or integrated, they can support coordination across programs. Kenya is taking steps to enhance efficiency by consolidating some social safety net programs, including the Cash Transfer for Orphans and Vulnerable Children (OVC) Program, the cash transfer for older persons, the cash transfer for persons with severe disabilities, the Hunger Safety Net Program (HSNP), and the World Food Programme's Cash for Assets Program. An integrated beneficiary registry has been developed, and the new, unified registry has allowed more efficient program monitoring, reduced double registration, increased transparency and accountability, promoted the efficient transfer of data, and enhanced the quality of operations.

Unified national identification systems can support social protection systems. Unique identifiers are needed to integrate social safety net information systems and accomplish the following: (a) facilitate the verification and authentication of the identity of individuals, (b) link individuals to families and households, (c) eliminate duplication among registered individuals, and (d) access other information systems to share data or undertake cross-checks. India's Aadhaar unique identification number is a 12-digit random number issued to residents based on voluntary enrollment. Aadhar has been used in the rollout of several government social safety nets and other social programs. It is the largest biometric authentication system in the world.

(continued next page)

Box 5.2 (continued)

Payment systems support the administration and provision of payment services. Linking payment flows with other processes is especially critical to ensure the delivery of benefits to the intended individuals in a timely manner while minimizing costs. Case management systems support the management of individuals, families, and households participating in one or many programs through needs assessment, service planning and implementation, advocacy, establishing appropriate links with service providers and complementary programs, and monitoring the delivery and use of services, including monitoring conditionalities. Grievance redress mechanisms support eligibility appeals, complaint handling, the engagement of applicants, beneficiaries and potential beneficiaries of social programs, and feedback. Business intelligence and analytics support the generation, aggregation, analysis, and visualization of data to inform and facilitate evidence-based policy making and strategic decision support in social programs. Other applications include data mining, report preparation, time series analysis and predictive techniques, online analytical processing, and statistical analysis.

Interoperability protocols for data exchange—including application programming interfaces, web services, enterprise service bus implementation, and connections to a whole-of-government architecture—are also key components of an integrated social protection information system. Within the broader country context of digital governance, integrated social protection information systems interact with numerous other administrative systems—such as national identification systems, civil registries, and tax authorities—exchanging and cross-checking data across central and subnational governmental entities. The architecture of integrated social protection information systems includes feedback loops between the various information system components, for example, feeding back data on enrollment decisions in a beneficiary registry to a social registry.

Source: Selected information from World Bank 2017a.

Information systems are a key tool in the implementation of core processes. Thanks to recent improvements in technology, countries have developed methodologies to integrate aspects of program management into MISs. MISs are made up of components that automate various functions of the delivery chain in a complementary manner.

Experience across the world shows that the development of information systems can lead to significant savings. The National Database of Social Information of Brazil contains records on 34 types of social security benefits among 30 million beneficiaries, or 16 percent of the population. In 2009, the data were deemed legally sufficient as proof of eligibility for social security benefits, meaning that, if a beneficiary's records are complete, there is no need to provide additional documents attesting to the payment of contributions or the periods of employment. This led to a reduction of the time necessary to document a retirement to 30 minutes.

In addition, the unemployment insurance program processes 3.5 million requests per month and uses data from the national database to check in real time whether a person has another job or receives benefits. The database also provides information on an individual's wages during the last three months worked, which serves as the basis for calculating benefits. Benefits can be received for up to five months, and, every month, an automatic verification is performed to ensure that the eligibility criteria have been met before the benefit is paid. In 2013, approximately R$900 million ($385 million) in payments were blocked as result of cross-checking.

Various documented experiences in Eastern Europe show similar success (World Bank 2014). In Kazakhstan, people now receive 578 different services through the e-government portal. Since its launch, more than 77 million electronic services have been provided, including various certificates or statements. The e-government system has served more than 2.6 million users. In the Kyrgyz Republic, the transition to an automated system for the allocation and payment of social safety nets—the Corporate Information Systems of Social Assistance—has facilitated a significant decrease in the time needed to process cases, from several days to only around two minutes per report. The government of Romania is able to carry out cross-checks between social safety nets and external data by using a unique personal identification number in all major national databases (tax administration, social assistance, health care, pensions, and disability). In 2013, these checks led to the recovery of €1.5 million (approximately $1.65 million). Cross matchings are now a regular activity in various social safety net programs and social services. In the Russian Federation, the Moscow city targeted social safety net program switched from paper-based in-kind transfers to an automated system centered on the Moscow Residents Social Card. The elderly now receive payments directly on their social cards rather than a box of goods and are able to use the cards like cash in authorized retail stores in Moscow. The introduction of this automated system has reduced processing time from weeks to 72 hours.

A reliable public financial management system is a key element in the efficient allocation and effective use of social safety net resources. A program that is supported by a reliable, transparent, and accurate public financial management system is more likely to allocate social safety net resources appropriately so that the resources reach eligible beneficiaries in a timely manner with minimal or no leakage. Such a system also enables the preparation and publication of detailed, precise, and comprehensive reports. Such a system can typically be used to ensure policy-based and consultative budget preparation; effective budget execution processes, including the identification and registration of eligible beneficiaries and the timely transfer of funds to beneficiaries; accurate and timely reporting of transactions; and high-quality external audits to satisfy parliamentary scrutiny and follow-up. The system can support a ministry of finance in coding social protection expenditures to allow efficient and transparent social protection expenditure tracking and analysis.

Enhancing the administrative efficiency of existing programs can also improve political and public buy-in, thereby facilitating their increase in scale (chapter 3).

A Focus on the Identification of Beneficiaries

Social safety net programs vary in nature and have different objectives. While poverty reduction is often at the core of social safety nets, promoting equity, resilience, and opportunity encompasses a much wider variety of goals (see chapters 1 and 2). The specific scope and design of social safety net programs often depend on social norms and ideological factors and are therefore contingent on country-specific contexts and preferences (see chapter 3). Inevitably, intended beneficiary groups differ across countries and programs, and the methods applied by programs to identify intended beneficiaries vary accordingly.

Whatever the specific objective of programs, the programs should provide for carefully selecting and monitoring beneficiaries to maximize the effectiveness of spending. The availability of national personal identification systems, sound MISs, and common beneficiary registries across programs is crucial to the identification and management of beneficiaries and to reducing fraud and errors (box 5.3). In Lesotho, demographic projections suggest that up to 25 percent of the beneficiaries of old-age pensions might be ineligible (World Bank 2016a). The government is taking action to address this problem by performing periodic cross-checks with other databases (such as the national identification and civil registry database, and the Civil Service Pensions database), introducing regular proof-of-life verification, and implementing a new electronic payment system. Estimates suggest Lesotho could save up to 0.5 percent of GDP annually once these measures are in place.

If the main program objective is poverty reduction, targeting on the basis of poverty (using income, consumption, or welfare indicators) is often advocated as a cost-effective way to achieve poverty reduction and, more generally, as a way to prioritize among people in allocating scarce resources. Indeed, transfer programs targeted on the basis of poverty (sometimes combined with geographical or categorical targeting) account for the largest share of social safety net expenditures (chapter 1). A number of factors, however, determine whether poverty targeting will improve the cost-effectiveness of social safety nets in reducing monetary poverty.

Simulations based on data on Africa and Latin America suggest that income-targeted programs have greater poverty impacts than categorical programs, even if errors in targeting are taken into account (Acosta, Leite, and Rigolini 2011; Guven and Leite 2016). But, the higher the poverty rate, the lower the need for income targeting, because income targeting and universal approaches yield similar beneficiary groups. In 15 African countries with high poverty rates, perfect poverty targeting (with transfers only made to the poor) and

BOX 5.3

Ways to Combat Fraud and Errors in Social Safety Nets

The efficiency of social safety nets can be improved by systematically tackling fraud and errors. Fraud involves intentional behavior to defraud a program, while errors refer to unintentional mistakes on behalf of benefit claimants or program staff. Fraud and errors are inevitable in social safety net programs, and steps taken to reduce them should be cost-effective and strike a balance among prevention, deterrence, and detection.

Irrespective of their size and design, all social safety net programs are prone to fraud and errors, including in countries with more sophisticated systems, more transparent processes, and more robust governance structures. Reducing fraud and errors contributes to greater efficiency and effectiveness by ensuring that more resources reach the intended beneficiaries. Combating fraud and errors also helps build public confidence in and support for social safety net programs by demonstrating that taxpayer money is secure and is being used efficiently (see chapter 3).

Improving the clarity of business processes and introducing automation in the administration of social safety net programs can provide opportunities for program administrators to institute more advanced and effective strategies to reduce fraud and errors. The level of benefit fraud in the United Kingdom has fallen by over 60 percent since 2010 as a result of the actions taken by the Department for Work and Pensions, the institution responsible for social protection policy. A cost-benefit analysis has estimated that for every £1 invested in data matching, the automated system identifies £24 in irregularities (NAO 2008). These matching efforts have meant that fraud in the benefit system accounts for only 0.7 percent of total expenditures.

In Romania, the government decided to strengthen the institutions in charge of combating errors and fraud in 2010 by (a) implementing data matching across databases at the application stage to prevent ineligible households from registering for income or means-tested benefits that are intended for low-income households, (b) using risk profiles to target inspections by social inspectors on high-risk cases, and (c) introducing a sanctions policy to deter potential fraudulent claims and recover misspent resources. These efforts focused on large, high-risk programs and were accompanied by improved information technology and organizational structures. In particular, this included a review of the legislation supporting the legal power of social inspectors, a significant increase in the number of these inspectors, the allocation of inspectors proportionally across programs, the preparation of a manual, and the establishment of a risk analysis and profiling team. As a result of these efforts, spending decreased by $149 million from 2011 to 2012, and 84,000 beneficiary files were cancelled. In 2013, $58 million in resources misspent because of errors and fraud were recovered from beneficiaries.

universal transfers are simulated to have similar impacts on a poverty index (Kakwani, Veras Soares, and Son 2005). Programs that imperfectly target households on the basis of poverty and in which targeting costs 15 percent of administrative costs have been compared in simulations with a universal program in 13 countries in Latin America. The simulations indicate that, although poverty targeting tends to deliver higher poverty impacts, categorical targeting (combined with geographical targeting) yields better overall results in low-income countries with widespread pockets of poverty. In Nicaragua, for instance, a categorical program only achieves about the same poverty reduction as an imperfect income-targeted program that costs the same but does not leave out 30 percent of the poor. In contrast, in wealthier and more unequal countries, such as Colombia, the need to transfer larger amounts to a smaller pool of poor beneficiaries makes an imperfect poverty-targeted system more attractive than categorical targeting (Acosta, Leite, and Rigolini 2011).

The costs of implementing the chosen targeting methodology also influence the cost-effectiveness of the program. These include administrative costs associated with gathering the information necessary to determine eligibility, the costs of implementing targeting, and the indirect costs of targeting, such as any distortions in beneficiary behavior to qualify for benefits and the burden on beneficiaries (Samsen, van Niekerk, and Mac Quene 2011; Slater and Farrington 2009). These costs are not often calculated, so it is impossible to carry out an empirical analysis comparing the additional costs of targeting. Different targeting mechanisms imply various costs and levels of accuracy. Proxy-means-testing and hybrid mechanisms, such as the combination of community-based mechanisms and proxy-means-testing, are often costly to administer, but are relatively effective at excluding both the nonpoor and the poor, thereby increasing efficiency by decreasing leakage, but at the cost of substantial errors of exclusion (Brown, Ravallion, and van de Walle 2016; Karlan and Thuysbaert 2013).

Targeting affects the political acceptability of programs, which affects the willingness to allocate budgets to programs (chapter 3; Gelbach and Pritchett 2002). Treating budgets as fixed is therefore a simplistic approach. Depending on the country, there might be more or less support for poverty targeting versus universal or categorical targeting, and that choice might ultimately impact the total amount of resources. Choosing a politically unpalatable option (a narrow poverty-targeted program in a context of strong preferences for a broader or categorical program) might result in fewer resources available for the poor. The cost-effectiveness of targeting will therefore greatly depend on the country context, the methodology chosen, and the available technologies. Governments would therefore benefit from carefully choosing strategies on the ways to focus spending on the desired beneficiaries on the basis of effectiveness, but also equity within the wider political context.

A Focus on Programs That Have a Proven Impact on Stated Objectives

The effectiveness of social safety nets depends heavily on program choice and design. Indeed, even programs that have a poverty reduction mandate could have limited poverty reduction effects if their coverage of the poor is limited, they are poorly targeted, the amounts are too small, or there is a narrow causal link between the intervention and poverty reduction. Evidence on the effectiveness of alternative program choices, design, and implementation arrangements can help policy makers make effective choices (chapter 2).

Energy subsidies are an example of programs that have often been launched with a poverty mandate, but have weak poverty impacts because they tend to benefit the better off in society. Energy subsidies are typically regressive because large shares of benefits accrue to richer households that have the highest levels of consumption (Inchauste and Victor 2017). A number of countries have phased out or reduced energy subsidies in favor of social safety net programs that target the poor and vulnerable, thereby achieving stronger poverty impacts or fiscal savings. A key aspect of successful reforms has often been the parallel creation or expansion of social safety net programs as a compensation measure. For instance, in Iran in 2010, the government began a large energy subsidy reform, undertaking extensive public communication and using cash transfers as a means to compensate people for the loss of the subsidies. As a result, the reform had positive effects on poverty, inequality, and overall costs (Guillaume, Zytek, and Farzin 2011; Inchauste and Victor 2017). The government of the Dominican Republic adopted a similar approach, replacing an electricity subsidy with a targeted cash transfer to help poor households pay for the first 100 kilowatts of electricity each month. The effort was associated with an extensive community sensitization campaign, as well as the rehabilitation of electrical lines to guarantee access. The number of registered electricity users rose from 1.4 million to 2.3 million in three years, and the government achieved considerable savings, with annual costs of $150 million for the subsidy, versus $55 million for the cash transfer program (Inchauste and Victor 2017).

Overall, choosing programs with greater impact potential and selecting design features that maximize impacts are critical ways to improve the efficiency and effectiveness of social safety net spending. (Chapter 2 discussed some of the design features which are more likely to yield strong impacts on poverty and human development outcomes.) Instruments such as public expenditure reviews and distributional program analyses can greatly help assess how resources are being spent and their impact on poverty and other outcomes.

Securing Sustainable Resources to Expand and Sustain Coverage

While improving the efficiency and effectiveness of programs can bring gains, most countries in Africa will need to increase the amount of resources going to social safety nets to expand coverage to the poor and vulnerable, as well as create systems to make financing available to scale up coverage during crises. This section provides a broad overview of how governments can achieve this. The section focuses on ways to strengthen fiscal policy as a cornerstone to increasing government revenue, as well as options for alternative financing sources.

The literature on these themes abounds and extends well beyond social protection. For this reason, this section is not meant to be an exhaustive, in-depth discussion on these issues. Rather, it is meant to provide food for thought for policy makers on possible avenues to increase and strengthen financing.

Implement Measures to Boost Domestic Revenue

As with all government functions, strengthening fiscal policy is a cornerstone of the sustainable financing of social safety nets at scale. Given the uncertainties in the global macroeconomic and political context, the rising costs of borrowing, and the unpredictability of external financing, domestic revenue mobilization is the most durable way to create fiscal space (IMF 2015). An improved fiscal system also benefits the consolidation of the citizen-state compact and promotes the accountability of government to taxpaying citizens.

"Effective tax systems can be associated with a 'virtuous circle,'" writes Bastagli (2016, 22), "whereby the generation of government tax revenues leads to improved service provision, which in turn increases citizens' willingness to pay taxes." The reform of tax policy can also enhance overall governance. Expanding a country's domestic resource mobilization is likely to be politically feasible and sustainable only if it is associated with improved rule-of-law, accountability, and transparency standards (World Bank 2017b).

There is scope to increase the domestic fiscal envelope through increased taxation (IMF 2015; OECD 2017). At current GDP levels, the median country in Africa is estimated to have the potential to increase tax revenue by between 3.0 and 6.5 percentage points of GDP (IMF 2015). Given that average spending on social safety nets in the region is 1.2 [[12]] percent of GDP, such potential increases in tax revenue would allow at least a doubling of social safety net spending on average and still leave room for additional spending in other sectors. In Africa, total tax revenues stood at an average of about 21 percent of GDP between 2011 and 2014, compared with over 30 percent in high-income countries. While still comparatively low, this represents a remarkable improvement. The region has experienced the largest increase in tax revenue in the world since the turn of the millennium (IMF 2015). With the exception of Botswana,

Nigeria, Zambia, and a few fragile states, all African countries have managed to increase their tax-to-GDP ratio. This improvement partially reflects the lower starting point of Africa. Even so, progress in the median low-income country in the region was still greater despite a higher starting point than the median low-income country elsewhere in the world. The largest contribution to the average change in tax revenue was provided by taxes on income, profits, and capital gains, as well as taxes on goods and services (IMF 2015).

Finding the balance between direct and indirect taxes and determining the overall level of taxes are crucial to boosting domestic revenue effectively and equitably (IMF 2017). The share of direct taxes—such as income, property, and corporate taxes—in overall tax revenue has traditionally been lower in developing countries, reflecting low per capita incomes, administrative challenges, and the political hurdles of taxing the rich and local elites. However, given their progressive nature and relatively low starting base, direct taxes have the potential to be effective instruments for revenue mobilization (World Bank 2017b). Improvements in tax administration, compliance, and formalization can help boost the revenue from direct taxes. At the same time, while often dismissed as regressive, indirect taxation—such as value added taxes—presents an opportunity for more revenue than other tax instruments in many African countries in the short term (IMF 2015). This is because its overall effect on distribution can be progressive if it is used to finance strongly progressive spending (Bastagli 2015). Furthermore, a shift from labor to consumption taxes (value added taxes, excise taxes, and so on) could boost formal labor demand by lowering nonwage labor costs, which is paramount in light of the emerging potential negative employment impact of automation (Alesina, Battisti, and Zeira 2015; Kuddo and Weber 2017; Santos 2017). Indirect taxes can be implemented with a broad base, a fairly high threshold to avoid overburdening small businesses, and a single or limited number of rates to preserve simplicity and limit opportunities for rent seeking (IMF 2015). Concerns over the regressive burden of indirect taxes can also be mitigated by design options, including ensuring that taxes on the goods most often consumed by the poor are low (Bastagli 2016).

Improved tax administration and simplified tax systems are a fundamental pillar in increasing tax revenue and have contributed significantly to increasing fiscal revenue in a number of countries. In Rwanda, the government raised tax revenue by approximately 50 percent between 2001 and 2013 by establishing a revenue authority to cover nontax revenue and rationalize income taxation; introducing a value added tax; aligning the tax system with development priorities; introducing tax audits, appeals, and penalties for evasion; and harmonizing the domestic system with the system of the East African Community (IMF 2009). Through the expansion in tax revenues, the government was able to increase spending on infrastructure, education, health care, and social protection (AfDB 2010). In South Africa in 2009, the government simplified the tax revenue system by introducing a turnover tax on microbusinesses, the value added tax, the provisional tax, the capital gains tax, and the dividends tax. The additional revenue generated through the introduction of the turnover tax allowed the government to maintain the country's large social safety net system.

Innovative research points to the potential impact that behavioral nudging mechanisms can have on increasing tax compliance across the globe, including in Africa. Field experiments have been conducted around the world over the past few years to test mechanisms—such as reminders, messages, or well-designed default options—to incentivize taxpayers to pay their taxes, based on the concept that people evade taxes not only because of the expected net benefit of evading but also because of social and moral considerations (Kettle et al. 2016; Mascagni 2017). Social norms are more effective if tax evasion is perceived as an exception and if compliance is considered the norm. This is where the image of the tax administration plays an important role (World Bank 2017b). As a pioneer in Africa, the Rwanda Revenue Authority generated almost $9 million in additional revenue by sending messages to tax payers regarding their taxes. Messages highlighting the importance of tax payments for public services and reminders about deadlines were more effective than messages focused on deterrence and emphasizing sanctions and penalties for noncompliance, and routine mailings outperformed more expensive letters in promoting increases in declared taxes (ICTD 2016; Mascagni, Nell, and Monkam 2017). While the validity of these type of interventions in other African countries has yet to be explored, this is a promising avenue for governments to follow, hand in hand with other policies.

Formalization can boost overall tax revenue, but evidence on the progress and future potential of this phenomenon for fiscal policy is mixed. Informality entails a loss in budget revenues by reducing the payment of taxes and social security contributions and, accordingly, the provision of public goods and services (Kuddo and Weber 2017). Formalization can be promoted by cutting the cost of compliance and regulation by simplifying administrative processes, enhancing the perceived benefits of formalization, and supplying a comprehensive package of support to firms, such as through training, support in opening business bank accounts, and help in dealing with tax authorities and tax mediation services.[2] However, overall progress in the formalization of employment across the world has been slow, and emerging trends point to the need to rethink traditional fiscal mechanisms such as payroll-based systems (Kuddo and Weber 2017; Palacios 2017). The share of people of working age contributing to formal social security systems in developing countries has not increased significantly over the past 20 years. At the same time, there has been a shift in many countries toward shorter-term employment, more fragmented careers, and a progressive deindustrialization process, suggesting that emerging economies might not follow the same path of industrialization and experience a premature deindustrialization (Palacios 2017; Rodrik 2016). These developments point to the need for government leaders of developing countries to think innovatively about fiscal strategy.

Technological progress can offer new opportunities for the collection of tax revenue in this context because governments will be able to track and tax earnings and incomes without the need for payroll-based systems. The impressive innovations in digital payments and e-commerce across the world, but especially in Africa and Asia, over the last 15 years, combined with inclusion, are effectively formalizing large parts of economies by opening these transactions as a new source of contribution collection with minimal transaction costs (Palacios 2017). Digital, unique identification systems and linked administrative datasets could allow governments to more effectively target fiscal policies, such as negative income taxes or subsidies, and to tailor contributions to income levels (Palacios 2017). Given the challenges developed countries might face in reforming or eliminating well-established but obsolete tax systems and their legacies, governments across Africa can potentially leapfrog developed countries in adopting innovative fiscal instruments.

Governments can also explicitly link a specific tax revenue source to social safety net financing to help establish a predictable and accountable domestic funding source for social safety nets. In Ghana, a share of value added tax and payroll tax revenues is earmarked to finance the country's National Health Insurance System, improving the consistency of health financing and increasing spending on health care. There is debate about whether earmarking tax revenue for specific sectors is desirable (World Bank 2017b). In general, the literature agrees that appropriate levels of taxation of some temptation goods, such as alcohol or tobacco, can be used to finance social sector spending directly. In low- and middle-income countries, tax rates on such undesirable goods are relatively modest, and there is large scope for heavier taxation (World Bank 2017b). Raising taxes on tobacco products is a cost-effective measure that reduces consumption of products that lead to premature mortality, while generating substantial revenue for health care and other social programs (Savedoff and Alwang 2015; World Bank 2017b). Through tobacco tax reform, Moldova raised the value of tobacco taxes from 1 percent to 6 percent of total taxes from 2009 to 2016. Armenia has rapidly increased tobacco taxes, reaching 1 percent of GDP. The Philippines boosted tobacco tax revenues by a factor of 1.5 in three years, and this was used to increase the health care budget and the number of people receiving health subsidies (World Bank 2017c).

In resource-rich countries, one option is the use of natural resource revenue to finance human capital investment, including direct dividend payments, that is, cash transfers (de la Brière et al. 2017; Devarajan and Giugale 2013). Historically, reliance on natural resource revenues has been associated with volatility, instability, and financing sustainability concerns, as well as possible lower government accountability before citizens because the revenues are unearned (Bastagli 2016). Some countries have avoided the resource curse and effectively promoted long-run development by pursuing a balanced approach that includes investment in human capital (de la Brière et al. 2017). In Mongolia, for instance, the government has levied royalty rates of 5 percent on the extraction of natural resources, applied a 10 percent corporate income tax on profits, and established royalties and licensing fees for exploration and production. A fund was created using such revenues to finance expenditures on health insurance and pensions, housing payments, cash transfers, and medical and education service payments (ILO 2016). Direct dividend payments could present an opportunity to avoid the resource curse by "using cash transfers to hand the money directly to citizens and thereby protect the social contract between the government and its people" (Devarajan and Giugale 2013, ii). The authors' estimates suggest that a country with a large natural resource base relative to population size would be able to provide citizens with considerable cash transfers financed directly through resource revenues. Angola, Gabon, and Equatorial Guinea could close the poverty gap by distributing 10 percent of resource revenues in cash transfers. Less resource-rich or more highly populated countries would be able to cover less, but still a considerable share of the poverty gap, such as Nigeria (39 percent) and Tanzania (26 percent).

Curtailing illicit financial flows—that is, capital associated with illegal activities or money that crosses borders that has been illegally earned, transferred, or used—can also help governments raise additional resources for social safety nets (World Bank 2016b). Illicit financial flows include traded goods that are mispriced to avoid tariffs, wealth transferred to offshore accounts to evade income taxes, and unreported movements of cash. In 2012, almost $1 trillion in illicit financial flows were estimated to have been drained from developing countries, and these flows amounted to almost 10 times the total aid received by developing countries (Kar, Cartwright-Smith, and Hollingshead 2010; Ortiz, Cummins, and Karunanethy 2015).

Attracting Alternative Resources

While it is a fundamental instrument, fiscal policy alone may not supply the financing needed to take social safety nets to scale in Africa. Governments can therefore also seek alternative funding sources. An assessment of Ethiopia's taxation and social protection system finds that it does not have the capacity to achieve the desired level of redistribution by applying higher marginal rates on relatively high incomes, nor to close the poverty gap or fully fund the main social safety net program using domestic income sources alone (Hirvonen, Mascagni, and Roelen 2016).

Development partner financing is an obvious option that already plays an important role in financing social protection spending. It is particularly strategic in financing initial investments in the sector, for instance, in establishing the building blocks for delivery. It can also be a catalyst for gathering domestic resources for social protection. In Mozambique, development partners were key in advocating for an increase in budget allocations for the social protection strategy and plan (Bastagli 2015). Responsibility for financing can gradually shift to governments once initial investments have been made and country systems are in place. The financing and implementation of social safety nets have gradually been taken over by the governments of Ethiopia, Lesotho, and Senegal (box 5.4). Ethiopia's Productive Safety Net Program (PSNP) is an example of the successful integration of government and development partner funding, as well as of development partner harmonization. Eleven development partners coalesced and created effective implementation arrangements that span multiple ministries and now provide a unified stream of technical advice in support of the government-led program (Monchuk 2014).

Other options include development impact bonds, which are innovative tools that governments can use to mobilize private sector financing for development objectives, including those of social safety nets. Development impact bonds "provide funding for development programs by private investors, who are remunerated by development partners or host-country governments—and earn a return—if evidence shows that programs achieve pre-agreed outcomes" (CGD and Social Finance 2013). The returns to investment are contingent on the achievement of the envisaged development objectives (Coleman 2016). The principle of this approach is that socially motivated private investors provide upfront funding for a development program. Development impact bonds are the developing-country adaptation of social impact bonds, which are used in higher-income countries to promote socially desirable results, mostly in the areas of criminal justice, homelessness, and the workforce. Most development bonds are still at the design stage, but early lessons are emerging (Gustafsson-Wright and Gardiner 2016; Gustafsson-Wright, Gardiner, and Putcha 2015).

Diaspora bonds could also be used to direct remittances toward development goals. They are debt instruments issued by a government to raise financing from its diaspora (Ketkar and Ratha 2007). The bonds are long-dated securities that may be redeemed only upon maturity. Typically, investors who purchase diaspora bonds are motivated by a desire to contribute to the development of their country of origin. Diaspora bonds have been successfully introduced in India, Israel, and Nigeria. Through such bonds, the State Bank of India had raised over $11 billion by 2007, while Nigeria issued $100 million in diaspora bonds in 2013, and, given the success of the first issue, decided to raise €300 million from a second diaspora bond issue under the 2016–18 borrowing plan (Ketkar and Ratha 2007; Ozaki 2016).

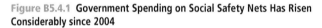

BOX 5.4

How Senegal Finances Most of Its Main Social Safety Net Programs

In the mid-2000s, social safety net spending in Senegal was low, around 0.4 percent of GDP in 2004. Social safety net funding was largely dependent on development partner financing. Of the nine programs on which there is funding information, development partners financed 62 percent of costs (World Bank 2013). Since then, however, government spending on social safety nets has increased significantly (figure B5.4.1). This follows the adoption by the government of its flagship conditional cash transfer program as a key element of the 2012 national development strategy. Government leadership has helped mobilize substantial national resources, and development partners now mostly focus on supporting the development of tools, instruments, and systems.

Figure B5.4.1 **Government Spending on Social Safety Nets Has Risen Considerably since 2004**

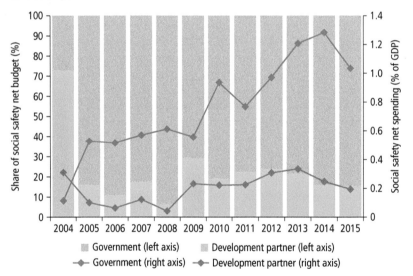

Sources: Spending data: ASPIRE (Atlas of Social Protection Indicators of Resilience and Equity) (database), Administrative data, World Bank, Washington, DC, http://www.worldbank.org/aspire. Other data: WDI (World Development Indicators) (database), World Bank, Washington, DC, http://data.worldbank.org/products/wdi.

Corporate social responsibility (CSR), relative to other social sectors and regions, might be an underutilized source for financing social safety nets in Africa. A few governments have developed strategies and tools to access these resources to fund economic and development strategies. In El Salvador, multinational companies have supported the creation of two major foundations in education and in broader socioeconomic development. In Mauritius, the Ministry of Finance requested that all firms spend 2 percent of their profits on CSR activities approved by the government or transfer the funds to the government to be used for social and environmental projects. Some elements required for CSR to bring additional funding for social safety net programs in Africa include (1) placing social protection on the global business development agenda as a sector of CSR activity, (2) building government leadership in the development of CSR within countries, (3) developing a national CSR strategy among public sector companies, (4) ensuring that CSR activities are aligned with the development objectives of social safety nets to maximize synergy, and (5) defining the needs in social safety nets that can be effectively addressed by CSR activities and resources (Forstater et al. 2010; GIZ 2012; Visser and Tolhurst 2010).

Developing a Financing Strategy for a Reliable, Effective Emergency Response

Current financing strategies to manage crises, including humanitarian support and commercial insurance, cover only a fraction of disaster losses, creating a protection gap that leaves many of the vulnerable exposed. Only around 30 percent of catastrophe losses have been covered by insurance over the past 10 years, which means that close to 70 percent of catastrophe losses have been borne directly by individuals, firms, and governments (Swiss Re 2016). Furthermore, humanitarian assistance is struggling to keep up with growing needs. Almost half the humanitarian appeals of the United Nations were left unmet in 2016 (UNHCR 2017). Finances are strained, and the status quo in financing for disaster response may suffer because of delays in mobilization, during which livelihoods suffer, particularly those of the poor.

To manage the risk of shocks effectively, ensure predictable and timely access to resources, and ultimately mitigate long-term fiscal impacts, many governments are adopting a strategic approach to disaster risk financing that relies on a range of preplanned, prenegotiated financial instruments. In a number of countries in Africa, these disaster risk financing strategies and shock-responsive social safety nets are being developed or considered. This builds on several global initiatives that seek to improve the financial resilience of low- and middle-income countries. There is growing interest in the international community to build the financial resilience of such countries, which is evidenced by the multiple global initiatives. The most relevant for Africa is the G7's German-presidency-sponsoreds InsuResilience Initiative, which looks to expand climate risk insurance to an additional 400 million poor and vulnerable people in these nations by 2020.

Disaster risk financing involves planning ahead and mobilizing resources to finance shock-responsive activities before the impacts of the shock affect households. Emerging evidence on this approach is promising, demonstrating significant cost savings over the status quo. In Ethiopia, every $1.00 secured beforehand for early drought response can save up to $5.00 in future costs, and well-targeted early interventions in slow-onset disasters, such as droughts, cost a fraction of emergency aid after a famine develops (Clarke and Hill 2013; Hess, Wiseman, and Robertson 2007).

Contingency or reserve funds have been established in many countries to finance relief, rehabilitation, reconstruction, and prevention activities associated with national emergencies. Funds specifically dedicated to disaster response exist in Colombia, Costa Rica, India, Indonesia, the Lao People's Democratic Republic, the Marshall Islands, Mexico, the Philippines, and Vietnam. In the Philippines, the National Disaster Risk Reduction and Management Fund finances a range of disaster-related expenditures, but is not able to disburse rapidly in response to a crisis. For that reason, the government created the Quick Response Fund, which focuses on emergency response. In Mexico, FONDEN was created as a budgetary tool to allocate federal funds rapidly for emergency response and the rehabilitation of public infrastructure affected by disasters. A number of African countries are working on the establishment of similar funds. In Kenya, the government is in the final stages of operationalizing a national contingency fund dedicated to drought emergencies. Efforts are also under way to create such funds in Madagascar and Mozambique.

Contingent financing consists of financial instruments designed to offer countries access to liquidity prior to or immediately following an exogenous shock, such as a terms-of-trade shock, financial shock, or natural disaster. Contingent loans have been used by multilateral development banks to strengthen national capacities in risk management and supply countries with access to liquidity immediately following an exogenous shock. These instruments promote early responses, which can help mitigate the risks of exacerbating crisis situations and reduce overall costs.

Risk transfer financial instruments enable governments to transfer the risk of specific meteorological or geological events (droughts, hurricanes, earthquakes, and floods) or commodity price shocks to actors in the market (insurance companies, reinsurance companies, banks, and investors) that are willing to accept them. These market-based risk transfer products use scientific information and actuarial modeling to estimate losses that would be sustained because of a specific event and price the risk. Payments are triggered by the performance of a prespecified, underlying parametric index, such as levels of rainfall, length and intensity of drought, or commodity price movements. Risk transfer products can be implemented in various forms, including direct access to insurance, reinsurance, and capital markets (derivative contracts or catastrophe bonds or indirect access through a dedicated vehicle such as a catastrophe risk pool) (World Bank 2017d). Catastrophe risk pools create a platform that allows governments to take a collective and standard approach to quantitative analysis and modeling, improve information sharing, coordinate response, lower the costs of coverage (through the pooling of diverse exposures, the retention of some risk, and the transfer of excess risks to capital and reinsurance markets), and strengthen subregional and regional cooperation and policy dialogue. Examples include the Caribbean Catastrophe Risk Insurance Facility, the Pacific Catastrophe Risk Assessment and Financing Initiative facility, and African Risk Capacity. Governments can also purchase indemnity insurance for public assets, such as buildings and other key infrastructure. This, however, is not typically an approach used to deal with risk and secure reliable financing for social safety nets.

Each instrument serves different purposes and the frequency and severity of the risks to be managed vary by country. Hence, governments should to take a strategic approach—possibly combining or layering instruments. Such an approach prioritizes cheaper sources of funding, ensuring that the most expensive instruments are only used in exceptional circumstances. Insurance may be cost-effective to cover extreme events (though it could be prohibitively expensive in countries frequently affected by extreme events), but it may be inefficient and costly in the case of low-intensity, recurring events. For such disasters, a dedicated contingency fund may be a more appropriate solution. Figure 5.3 provides a graphic representation of this risk-layering approach. Combining instruments also enables governments to take into account the evolving needs for funds, from emergency response to long-term reconstruction. For instance, a government could decide to purchase (ex ante) quick-disbursing risk transfer instruments to ensure immediate liquidity just before or in the aftermath of extreme events, but raise the larger sums required to finance reconstruction efforts through (ex post) budget reallocations or by issuing bonds.

Figure 5.3 Governments Can Layer Financing Instruments That Address Different Needs

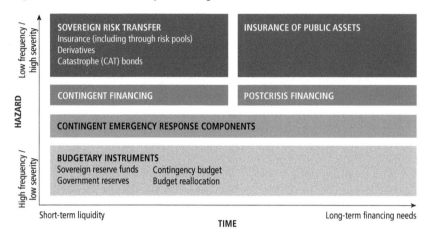

Source: World Bank 2017d.

In addition to natural disasters, social safety nets can play a central role during economic contractions. In the face of macroeconomic shocks, the demand for social safety nets typically rises, while governments must operate on tighter budgets. During these times, social safety net spending needs to be protected and even increased to prevent the long-lasting negative impacts of the lack of protection for the poor. Several countries have made efforts in this direction. Thus, the government of Ghana set targets for social safety net spending to mitigate the impact of fiscal consolidation under its arrangements with the International Monetary Fund in 2015–18.

Governments in Africa must find the appropriate financing mix to ensure that social safety nets are funded sustainably and that resources are available if and when needed both for permanent programs and for emergency responses. Each option explored in this chapter has advantages and disadvantages (table 5.2), which largely depend on country contexts. Governments can fund a larger share of the social safety net over the medium term through a range of efficiency improvements, strengthened domestic revenue, leveraging alternative financial sources, and using risk financing mechanisms.

Table 5.2 Options for Increasing Social Safety Net Resources Are Available

Financing methods	Advantages	Challenges
Increased efficiency in administration of social safety nets	Creates fiscal space without raising taxes; increases acceptability of social safety nets	Implementation of administrative reforms can be difficult; the amount saved is often insufficient to finance the effort of brining programs to scale
Reallocation of expenditures toward desired beneficiaries and goals	Creates fiscal space without raising taxes; can increase the productivity of government outlays and efficiency by reducing unproductive expenditures; can increase the acceptability of public spending, depending on the social contract and expectations; feasible in the short term on a small scale, particularly if low-hanging fruit can be identified	Requires significant commitment by the government to implement changes and face trade-offs; requires detailed analysis of public expenditure programs and medium-term commitments by the government; may imply winners and losers among previous and new beneficiaries, leading to potential political discontent
Boosting domestic revenue	Most sustainable option in the medium to long expenditures; may have a positive redistributive effect depending on balance in the tax mix; increases the overall productivity of the government if it is achieved through improvements in tax administration, compliance, or design; potentially improves the transparency of resource revenues	Tax reforms can be difficult to implement administratively and politically; higher taxation may have direct and indirect effects on economic growth and the poor; needs to be designed well; tax increase may produce limited returns, given the narrow fiscal base, and may be politically unpopular
Leveraging alternative resources	Development partners can provide financing in the short and medium terms; usually associated with technical assistance for the design of reforms; innovative instruments (for example, development impact bonds) can be sustainable mechanisms for long-term financing	Cyclicality of funding and downward trend can imply unreliable development partner or private sector financing; bureaucratic or policy requirements may hinder government ownership; development partner coordination may be a challenge; long-term performance of innovative instruments has yet to be tested
Tools for crisis financing	Different risk-financing instruments are available to cover risks that vary in frequency and severity	Choice among instruments requires careful risk assessment and financial planning during normal times (risk-layering strategy)

257

Notes

1. The poverty gap is the mean shortfall of the total population from the poverty line. It is expressed as a percent share of the poverty line. It counts the shortfall of the nonpoor at 0.0 percent. The gap reflects the incidence and the depth of poverty.
2. Rwanda and South Africa offer examples. See on tax administration reform above in the text. See also Bastagli (2015); Benhassine et al. (2016).

References

Acosta, Pablo, Phillippe G. Leite, and Jamele Rigolini. 2011. "Should Cash Transfers Be Confined to the Poor? Implications for Poverty and Inequality in Latin America." Policy Research Working Paper 5875, World Bank, Washington, DC.

AfDB (African Development Bank). 2010. "Domestic Resource Mobilization for Poverty Reduction in East Africa: Rwanda Case Study." November, Regional Department East A, AfDB.

Alam, Asad, Renosi Mokate, and Kathrin A. Plangemann, eds. 2016. *Making It Happen: Selected Case Studies of Institutional Reforms in South Africa*. Directions in Development: Public Sector Governance Series. Washington, DC: World Bank.

Alesina, Alberto, Michele Battisti, and Joseph Zeira. 2015. "Technology and Labor Regulations: Theory and Evidence." NBER Working Paper 20841, National Bureau of Economic Research, Cambridge, MA.

Audsley, Blake, Riikka Halme, and Niels Balzer. 2010. "Comparing Cash and Food Transfers: A Cost-Benefit Analysis from Rural Malawi." In *Revolution: From Food Aid to Food Assistance, Innovations in Overcoming Hunger*, edited by Steven Were Omamo, Ugo Gentilini, and Susanna Sandström, 89–102. Rome: World Food Programme.

Bastagli, Francesca. 2015. "Bringing Taxation into Social Protection Analysis and Planning." ODI Working Paper 421, Overseas Development Institute, London.

———. 2016. "Bringing Taxation into Social Protection Analysis and Planning." Guidance Note, Overseas Development Institute, London.

Benhassine, Najy, David McKenzie, Victor Pouliquen, and Massimiliano Santini. 2016. "Can Enhancing the Benefits of Formalization Induce Informal Firms to Become Formal? Experimental Evidence from Benin." Policy Research Working Paper 7900, World Bank, Washington, DC.

Brown, Caitlin, Martin Ravallion, and Dominique van de Walle. 2016. "A Poor Means Test? Econometric Targeting in Africa." Policy Research Working Paper 7915, World Bank, Washington, DC.

Bui, Anthony L., Rouselle F. Lavado, Elizabeth K. Johnson, Benjamin P. Brooks, Michael K. Freeman, Casey M. Graves, Annie Haakenstad, Benjamin Shoemaker, Michael Hanlon, and Joseph L. Dieleman. 2015. "National Health Accounts Data from 1996 to 2010: A Systematic Review." *Bulletin of the World Health Organization* 93 (8): 566–76.

Castro-Leal, Florencia, Julia Dayton, Lionel Demery, and Kalpana Mehra. 1999. "Public Social Spending in Africa: Do the Poor Benefit?" *World Bank Research Observer* 14 (1): 49–72.

CGAP (Consultative Group to Assist the Poor). 2013. "Cash for Assets: World Food Programme's Exploration of the In-Kind to E-Payments Shift for Food Assistance in Kenya." September, CGAP, World Bank, Washington, DC.

———. 2014. "Electronic G2P Payments: Evidence from Four Lower-Income Countries." CGAP, World Bank, Washington, DC.

CGD (Center for Global Development) and Social Finance. 2013. *Investing in Social Outcomes: Development Impact Bonds—The Report of the Development Impact Bond Working Group.* London: Social Finance Ltd; Washington, DC: CGD.

Clarke, Daniel J., and Stefan Dercon. 2016. *Dull Disasters? How Planning Ahead Will Make a Difference.* Washington, DC: World Bank; Oxford, U.K.: Oxford University Press.

Clarke, Daniel J., and Ruth Vargas Hill. 2013. "Cost-Benefit Analysis of the African Risk Capacity Facility." IFPRI Discussion Paper 1292, International Food Policy Research Institute, Washington, DC.

Coleman, David. 2016. "Variations on the Impact Bond Concept: Remittances as a Funding Source for Impact Bonds in Low- and Middle-Income Countries." September Brookings Institution, Washington, DC.

de la Brière, Bénédicte, Deon Filmer, Dena Ringold, Dominic Rohner, Karelle Samuda, and Anastasiya Denisova. 2017. *From Mines and Wells to Well-Built Minds: Turning Sub-Saharan Africa's Natural Resource Wealth into Human Capital.* Directions in Development: Human Development Series. Washington, DC: World Bank.

Devarajan, Shantayanan, and Marcelo Giugale. 2013. "The Case for Direct Transfers of Resource Revenues in Africa." With Hélène Ehrhart, Tuan Minh Le, and Huong Mai Nguyen. CGD Working Paper 333, Center for Global Development, Washington, DC.

Farrell, Michael James. 1957. "The Measurement of Productive Efficiency." *Journal of the Royal Statistical Society, Series A (General)* 120 (3): 253–90.

Forstater, Maya, Simon Zadek, Yang Guang, Kelly Yu, Chen Xiao Hong, and Mark George. 2010. "Corporate Responsibility in African Development: Insights from an Emerging Dialogue." Corporate Social Responsibility Initiative Working Paper 60 (October), Harvard University, Cambridge, MA.

Galang, Roberto Martin N., Rouselle F. Lavado, and Gabriel Angelo B. Domingo. 2013. "Why Do Asian Firms Say That Their Governments Are Corrupt: Assessing the Impact of Firm-Level Characteristics on Corruption Perceptions." AIM Working Paper 14–004, Asian Institute of Management, Makati, Manila.

Gelbach, Jonah B., and Lant H. Pritchett. 2002. "Is More for the Poor Less for the Poor: The Politics of Means-Tested Targeting." *B. E. Journal of Economic Analysis and Policy* 2 (1): 1–28.

Gething, Peter, and Nina Rosas. 2015 "Developing a Poverty Map for Targeting of Social Safety Net Programs in Sierra Leone." Social Protection and Labor Global Practice, World Bank, Washington, DC.

GIZ (Deutsche Gesellschaft für Internationale Zusammenarbeit). 2012. *Shaping CSR in Sub-Saharan Africa: Guidance Notes from a Mapping Survey.* Bonn GIZ.

Guillaume, Dominique M., Roman Zytek, and Mohammad Reza Farzin. 2011. "Iran: The Chronicles of the Subsidy Reform." IMF Working Paper 11/167, International Monetary Fund, Washington, DC.

Gustafsson-Wright, Emily, and Sophie Gardiner. 2016. "Education Plus Development: Educate Girls Development Impact Bond Could Be a Win-Win for Investors and Students." #GirlsEdu (blog), July 18. https://www.brookings.edu/blog/education-plus-development/2016/07/18/educate-girls-development-impact-bond-could-be-win-win-for-investors-and-students/.

Gustafsson-Wright, Emily, Sophie Gardiner, and Vidya Putcha. 2015. "The Potential and Limitations of Impact Bonds: Lessons from the First Five Years of Experience Worldwide." Global Economy and Development Series, Brookings Institution, Washington, DC.

Guven, Melis U., and Phillippe G. Leite. 2016. "Benefits and Costs of Social Pensions in Sub-Saharan Africa." Social Protection and Labor Discussion Paper 1607, World Bank, Washington, DC.

Herrmann, Peter, Arno Tausch, Almas Heshmati, and Chemen S. J. Bajalan. 2008. "Efficiency and Effectiveness of Social Spending." IZA Discussion Paper 3482, Institute for the Study of Labor, Bonn.

Hess, Ulrich, William Wiseman, and Tim Robertson. 2007. "Ethiopia: Integrated Risk Financing to Protect Livelihoods and Foster Development." Discussion Paper (November), World Food Programme, Rome.

Hirvonen, Kalle, Giulia Mascagni, and Keetie Roelen. 2016. "Linking Taxation and Social Protection: Evidence on Redistribution and Poverty Reduction in Ethiopia." ICTD Working Paper 61 (December), International Centre for Tax and Development, Institute of Development Studies, Brighton, UK.

ICTD (International Centre for Tax and Development). 2016. "Africa's First Large-Scale Tax Experiment: Researching Compliance in Rwanda." Summary Brief, ICTD, Institute of Development Studies, Brighton, UK.

IDinsight. 2015. "Evaluation of M-Tech and Paper Enumeration of Social Cash Transfer Beneficiaries in Zambia: Implementation Guide." November 25, IDinsight, New Delhi.

ILO (International Labour Organization). 2016. "Delivering Social Protection for All." Issue Brief, Inter-Agency Task Force on Financing for Development, International Labour Office, Geneva.

IMF (International Monetary Fund). 2009. "Some Observations on Domestic Revenue Mobilization." IMF staff presentation during mission to Rwanda, October–November, Kigali, Rwanda.

———. 2015. Sub-Saharan Africa: Dealing with the Gathering Clouds. Regional Economic Outlook, October. World Economic and Financial Surveys. Washington, DC: IMF.

———. 2017. Sub-Saharan Africa: Fiscal Adjustment and Economic Diversification. Regional Economic Outlook, October. World Economic and Financial Surveys. Washington, DC: IMF.

Inchauste, Gabriela, Nora Lustig, Mashekwa Maboshe, Catronia Purfield, and Ingrid Woolard. 2015. "The Distributional Impact of Fiscal Policy in South Africa." CEQ Working Paper 29, Commitment to Equity, Inter-American Dialogue, Washington, DC; Center for Inter-American Policy and Research and Department of Economics, Tulane University, New Orleans.

Inchauste, Gabriela, and David G. Victor, eds. 2017. The Political Economy of Energy Subsidy Reform. Directions in Development: Public Sector Governance Series. Washington, DC: World Bank.

Kakwani, Nanak, Fábio Veras Soares, and Hyun H. Son. 2005. "Conditional Cash Transfers in African Countries." Working Paper 9, International Poverty Centre, United Nations Development Programme, Brasília.

Kar, Dev, Devon Cartwright-Smith, and Ann Hollingshead. 2010. "The Absorption of Illicit Financial Flows from Developing Countries: 2002–2006." Global Financial Integrity, Center for International Policy, Washington, DC.

Karlan, Dean, and Bram Thuysbaert. 2013. "Targeting Ultra-Poor Households in Honduras and Peru." NBER Working Paper 19646, National Bureau of Economic Research, Cambridge, MA.

Ketkar, Suhas L., and Dilip Ratha. 2007. "Development Finance via Diaspora Bonds: Track Record and Potential." Policy Research Working Paper 4311, World Bank, Washington, DC.

Kettle, Stewart, Marco Hernandez, Simon Ruda, and Michael Sanders. 2016. "Behavioral Interventions in Tax Compliance: Evidence from Guatemala." Policy Research Working Paper 7690, World Bank, Washington, DC.

Kuddo, Arvo, and Michael Weber. 2017. "Policies on Taxation of Labor." Working note, World Bank, Washington, DC.

Lindert, Kathy, Emmanuel Skoufias, and Joseph Shapiro. 2006. "Redistributing Income to the Poor and the Rich: Public Transfers in Latin America and the Caribbean. Social Protection Discussion Paper 0605 (August), Social Safety Nets Primer Series, World Bank, Washington, DC.

Mandl, Ulrike, Adriaan Dierx, and Fabienne Ilzkovitz. 2008. "The Effectiveness and Efficiency of Public Spending." Economic Paper 301, Directorate-General for Economic and Financial Affairs, European Commission, Brussels.

Mansour, Mario. 2014. "A Tax Revenue Dataset for Sub-Saharan Africa: 1980–2010." FERDI Working Paper I19, Fondation pour les études et recherches sur le développement international, Clermont-Ferrand, France.

Mascagni, Giulia. 2017. "From the Lab to the Field: A Review of Tax Experiments." *Journal of Economic Surveys.* http://onlinelibrary.wiley.com/doi/10.1111/joes.12201 /abstract.

Mascagni, Giulia, Christopher Nell, and Nara Monkam. 2017. "One Size Does Not Fit All: A Field Experiment on the Drivers of Tax Compliance and Delivery Methods in Rwanda." ICTD Working Paper 58, International Centre for Tax and Development, Institute of Development Studies, Brighton, UK.

Monchuk, Victoria. 2014. *Reducing Poverty and Investing in People: New Role of Safety Nets in Africa.* Directions in Development: Human Development Series. Washington, DC: World Bank.

Muralidharan, Karthik, Paul Niehaus, and Sandip Sukhtankar. 2016. "Building State Capacity: Evidence from Biometric Smartcards in India." *American Economic Review* 106 (10): 2895–2929.

NAO (National Audit Office). 2008. "Tackling External Fraud." Good Practice Guide, NAO, London.

Nelson, Kenneth. 2012. "Improving the Efficiency of Social Protection: Synthesis Report." Peer Review in Social Protection and Social Inclusion Series 2011, European Commission, Brussels.

O'Brien, Clare, Fidelis Hove, and Gabrielle Smith. 2013. "Factors Affecting the Cost-Efficiency of Electronic Transfers in Humanitarian Programmes." Oxford Policy Management.

OECD (Organisation for Economic Co-operation and Development). 2017. "Social Protection in East Africa: Harnessing the Future." OECD, Paris.

Ortiz, Isabel, Matthew Cummins, and Kalaivani Karunanethy. 2015. "Fiscal Space for Social Protection: Options to Expand Social Investments in 187 Countries." ESS Working Paper 48, Extension of Social Security, International Labour Office, Geneva.

Ozaki, Mayumi. 2016. "Asia Could Use Diaspora Bonds to Finance Development." Asian Development Blog, May 27. https://blogs.adb.org/blog/asia-could-use-diaspora-bonds-finance-development.

Palacios, Robert. 2017. "Death of the Payroll Tax." Draft policy note, World Bank, Washington, DC.

Rodrik, Dani. 2016. "Premature Deindustrialization." *Journal of Economic Growth* 21 (1): 1–3.

Samsen, Michael, Ingrid van Niekerk, and Kenneth Mac Quene. 2011. *Designing and Implementing Social Transfer Programmes*, 2nd ed. Cape Town: Economic Policy Research Institute.

Santos, Indhira. 2017. "Implications of the Digital Revolution for Social Protection, Taxation, and Labor Market Institutions." Working paper, World Bank, Washington, DC.

Savedoff, William, and Albert Alwang. 2015. "The Single Best Health Policy in the World: Tobacco Taxes." CGD Policy Paper 062, Center for Global Development, Washington, DC.

Slater, Rachel, and John Farrington. 2009. "Targeting of Social Transfers: A Review for DFID." With inputs from Marcella Vigneri, Mike Samson, and Shaheen Akter. Overseas Development Institute, London.

Sudaram, Ramia, Victoria Strokova, and Frieda Vandeninden. 2014. "Effectiveness and Efficiency of Social Protection in Europe and Central Asia: A Post-Crisis Assessment." Paper presented at the European Association of Development Research and Training Institute's 14th General Conference, "Responsible Development in a Polycentric World: Inequality, Citizenship, and the Middle Classes," June 23–26, Bonn.

Swiss Re (Swiss Reinsurance Company Ltd.). 2016. "Global Insurance Review 2016 and Outlook 2017/18." Swiss Reinsurance Company Ltd., Zürich.

UNHCR (United Nations High Commissioner for Refugees). 2017. "Biennial Program Budget Data." Global Focus, UNHCR, Geneva. http://reporting.unhcr.org/financial#tabs-financial-budget.

Visser, Wayne, and Nick Tolhurst, eds. 2010. *The World Guide to CSR: A Country-by-Country Analysis of Corporate Sustainability and Responsibility*. Sheffield, UK: Greenleaf.

World Bank. 2013. "Republic of Senegal: Social Safety Net Assessment." Report ACS7005, World Bank, Washington, DC.

———. 2014. "Impact of Strengthening the Information Systems in Social Assistance Programs." Working paper, World Bank, Washington, DC.

———. 2015. "Developing a High Resolution Poverty Map for Tanzania: Final Report." Social Protection and Labor Global Practice, World Bank, Washington, DC.

———. 2016a. "Project Appraisal Document on a Proposed Credit to the Kingdom of Lesotho for a Social Assistance Project." Report PAD1377, World Bank, Washington, DC.

———. 2016b. "The World Bank Group's Response to Illicit Financial Flows: A Stocktaking." World Bank, Washington, DC.

———. 2017a. "Social Protection and Labor Delivery Systems: Taxonomy of Core Terminology." World Bank, Washington, DC.

———. 2017b. "Strengthening Domestic Resource Mobilization." World Bank, Washington, DC.

———. 2017c. "Tobacco Taxation Conference: Summary of Proceedings." World Bank, Washington, DC.

———. 2017d. "Sovereign Climate and Disaster Risk Pooling: World Bank Technical Contribution to the G20." World Bank, Washington, DC.

———. 2018. *The State of Social Safety Nets 2018*. World Bank, Washington, DC.

Appendix A

Definitions and Data Sources

A.1 Definition of Social Safety Nets

Social safety nets are defined in this report as noncontributory programs targeting the poor or vulnerable. They may be designed, implemented, and supported by governments, international organizations, or nongovernmental organizations (NGOs). Their distinctive feature is their noncontributory nature, that is, beneficiaries do not have to contribute financially to receive the benefits. This differentiates them from contributory forms of social protection, whereby prior contributions or participation in the labor market determine benefit eligibility.

The definition of social safety nets used in this report includes social assistance programs, social care services, and programs that support productive activities. The range of programs included is detailed in the next section. In this report, general health care and education interventions or general consumer price subsidies (including energy, electricity, and food subsidies) are not considered part of social safety nets.

A.2 Typologies Used in This Report

A.2.1 Typologies of Social Safety Net Programs

Building on the ASPIRE database classification, this report relies on four typologies to classify social safety net programs. For each typology, the categories have been systematically built to be mutually exclusive. Where relevant, the ASPIRE categories covered under each category are specified to allow readers to compile similar aggregates from the ASPIRE database.

Program Typology 1: Program Type
This classification groups programs into nine categories, building on Grosh et al. (2008). It reflects differences in program benefits, program objectives, and the intended beneficiaries. See Grosh, Margaret E., Carlo del Ninno, Emil Tesliuc, and Azedine Ouerghi, 2008, *For Protection and Promotion: The Design and Implementation of Effective Safety Nets*, Washington, DC: World Bank.

- *Cash transfer programs*: Cash transfer programs offer periodic monetary transfers to beneficiaries with a view to providing regular, predictable income support. This category includes poverty reduction programs; family and child allowance (including orphan and vulnerable children benefits); public-private charity; disability pensions, allowance, or benefits; war veterans' pensions, allowances, or benefits; noncontributory funeral grants; burial allowances; entrepreneurship support and startup incentives (grants, loans, training); and other cash programs. Both conditional and unconditional cash transfer programs are included in this category. In this report, this category excludes public works, emergency, scholarships, and social pension programs, which are covered in other categories. This corresponds to the following categories in ASPIRE: 1.1.1, 1.1.2, 1.1.3, 1.1.8, 1.1.9, 1.1.10, 1.1.12, 1.2.8, and 3.2.5.

- *School feeding programs*: This category includes school feeding programs, which supply meals or snacks for children at school to encourage their enrollment and attendance and improve their nutritional status and ability to learn. It also includes take-home food rations for children's families. This corresponds to the following category in ASPIRE: 1.2.3.

- *Public works programs*: This category includes public works, workfare, and direct job creation programs providing support in cash or food (including food-for-training or food-for-assets programs). Public works programs offer short-term employment at low wages on labor-intensive projects, such as road construction and maintenance, irrigation infrastructure, reforestation, soil conservation, and social services. Support is typically in the form of either cash or food transfers. This corresponds to the following categories in ASPIRE: 1.1.11 and 1.2.10.

- *Education interventions*: In the report typology, this category includes scholarships and targeted subsidies in education (for example, orphans and vulnerable children [OVC] bursaries). It excludes general education interventions (such as free basic education). Educational fee waivers and scholarships assist households in meeting the cost of educational services by covering part of the fees or other selected expenditures. This corresponds to the following categories in ASPIRE: 1.1.6. and 1.2.7.

- *Health interventions*: In the report typology, this category includes targeted subsidies and fee waivers in health (such as reduced medical fees for the vulnerable population). It excludes general health interventions (for instance, free health care/treatments and campaigns). These programs assist selected households in meeting the costs of health services. This corresponds to the following category in ASPIRE: 1.2.6.

- *Emergency programs*: This category includes programs providing emergency support in cash and in kind (including support for refugees and returning migrants). Emergency support programs supply cash or in-kind transfers to individuals or households in case of emergency or in response to shocks. The shocks may encompass weather shocks (droughts, floods), pandemics, food insecurity, human-made crises, and economic downturns. The transfers are usually temporary, typically over a period of a few months. This corresponds to the following categories in ASPIRE: 1.1.5 and 1.2.5.

- *Food-based programs*: In the report typology, food-based programs include programs providing food stamps and vouchers, food distribution programs, and nutritional programs that involve therapeutic feeding distribution and promote good feeding practices. This category excludes food-for-work programs, emergency in-kind transfer programs, and meals provided at schools, which are classified in other groups. This corresponds to the following categories in ASPIRE: 1.2.1, 1.2.2, and 1.2.4.

- *Social pensions*: This category includes old-age social pensions, allowances, or benefits. Social pensions are regular cash transfers provided exclusively to the elderly. Unlike contributory pensions or social insurance programs, social pensions do not require prior contributions. Old-age social pensions may be universal or targeted to the poor. This corresponds to the following category in ASPIRE: 1.1.7.

- *Other programs*: This category includes other noncontributory programs targeting the poor or vulnerable, such as programs distributing school supplies, tax exemptions, social care services, and other programs not included in the other eight categories. This corresponds to the following categories in ASPIRE: 1.2.9, 1.2.11, 1.2.12, and 1.3, 4.

Program Typology 2: Life Cycle

This classification categorizes programs in terms of their targeted population, organized along the life cycle. There are five categories, which are mutually exclusive:

- *Children*: This category includes family and child allowances (including programs for orphans and vulnerable children), scholarships, school feeding programs, education interventions, school supplies, nutritional programs, and care services for children and youth. This corresponds to the following categories in ASPIRE: 1.1.2, 1.1.6, 1.2.3, 1.2.7, 1.2.9, 1.2.4, and 4.1.

- *Working-age population*: This category includes programs that are directed at adults. It includes public works programs, workfare programs, direct job creation programs, entrepreneurship support, start-up incentives, and care services for vulnerable working-age individuals. This corresponds to the following categories in ASPIRE: 1.1.11, 1.2.10, and 4.3.
- *The elderly*: This category includes old-age social pensions, allowances, or benefits as well as war veterans pensions, allowances, or benefits. This corresponds to the following categories in ASPIRE: 1.1.17 and 1.1.9.
- *Households and families*: This category includes programs that target entire households or families, rather than specific individuals. It includes poverty reduction programs, public-private charity, allowances for housing and utilities, food stamps and vouchers, food distribution programs, targeted subsidies in health care and housing or utilities, tax exemptions, noncontributory funeral grants, burial allowances, care services for families, and other social assistance This corresponds to the following categories in ASPIRE: 1.1.1, 1.1.3, 1.1.4, 1.2.1, 1.2.2, 1.2.6, 1.2.8, 1.2.11, 1.3, 1.1.10, 1.1.12, and 4.2.
- *Special groups*: This category includes programs that target other groups, outside the four categories described above. In the report typology, it includes disability social pensions, allowances, and benefits and emergency support in cash and in kind (including support for refugees and returning migrants). This corresponds to the following categories in ASPIRE: 1.18, 1.1.5, and 1.2.5.

Program Typology 3: Targeting Method

This classification categorizes programs according to the method they use to identify beneficiaries. Programs have been organized into five mutually exclusive categories.

- *Categorical*: This category includes programs that target individuals or households that belong to an easily identifiable and specific social or demographic group. It typically involves defining eligibility in terms of characteristics that are fairly easy to observe and difficult to manipulate, such as age, sex, ethnicity, disability status, or land ownership. Age is a commonly used category in cash child allowances, school feeding programs, and social pensions.
- *Geographical*: This category includes programs that only use geographical criteria to identify beneficiaries (focusing on specific regions, villages, neighborhoods, and so on).
- *Geographical and categorical*: This category includes programs that combine both geographical and categorical targeting.
- *Poverty*: This category includes programs that only use targeting methods that approximate a potential beneficiary's poverty, welfare, or vulnerability status.

These include various methods that are often combined, such as methods based on community targeting (whereby the communities identify their poorest or most vulnerable members); a measure of potential beneficiary consumption or income; indicators that proxy consumption or income (proxy-means-test); receipt or level of pensions received by potential beneficiaries; or some form of self-targeting (such as transfers in public works programs designed to attract the poor).

- *Poverty and geographical/categorical*: This category includes programs that combine poverty-based targeting methods with either geographical or categorical targeting or with both.
- *N/A:* This category includes programs for which information on the targeting method is not available.

Program Typology 4: Nature of Benefits

This classification organizes programs according to the type of benefits or services they provide to the beneficiaries. Four categories are defined, which are mutually exclusive:

- *Cash*: This category includes cash transfer programs that provide only cash benefits. It corresponds to the following category in ASPIRE: 1.1, which is also coded as Benefit type 1.
- *Food*: This category includes food programs that provide only food benefits such as food stamps and vouchers, food distribution programs, school feeding programs, nutritional programs, and food-for-work programs. This corresponds to the following categories in ASPIRE: 1.2.1, 1.2.2, 1.2.3, 1.2.4, and 1.2.10, which are also coded as Benefit type 3.
- *Other in kind*: This category includes programs that provide in-kind benefits other than food. These include targeted interventions in health care, education, housing, and utilities; school supplies; tax exemptions; social care services, and other programs. This corresponds to the following categories in ASPIRE: 1.2.5, 1.2.6, 1.2.7, 1.2.8, 1.2.9, 1.2.11, 1.2.12, and 1.3, 4 that are also coded as Benefit type 2, 3, or 4.
- *Mix*: Any program with a combination of cash, food, or other in-kind benefits. This corresponds to all programs coded in ASPIRE as Benefit type 5.

A.2.2 Typologies of Social Safety Net Institutions and Systems

Building on system and program documents, this report uses typologies to compare across countries and regions according to the development of social safety net institutions and systems. The categories are mutually exclusive for each typology.

Institution/System Typology 1: Overall Development of Social Safety Net System
This classification categorizes countries according to the extent of development of their social safety net system. The classification of countries is presented in appendix D, table D.3.

- *No social safety net program*: This category includes countries that have no or extremely limited social safety net programs.
- *No solid plans*: This category includes countries that have individual social safety net programs or elements of programs, but have not laid the foundations of a coordinated social safety net system.
- *In progress*: This category includes countries that have one or more programs in place, are starting to harmonize development partner involvement, and are working toward a consolidated system.
- *In place*: This category includes countries that have adequate social safety net policies and delivery capacity.

Institution/System Typology 2: Social Protection Strategy or Policy
This classification categorizes countries according to the development of their national social safety net or social protection policy or strategy. The classification of countries is presented in appendix D, table D.1.

- *Not present*: If no social safety net or social protection strategy or policy has been drafted or is in preparation.
- *In progress*: If the country is in the process of developing or validating a national social safety net or social protection strategy or policy.
- *Present*: If the country has adopted a national social safety net or social protection strategy or policy.

Institution/System Typology 3: Organizations
This classification is used to categorize organizations. It is used in this analysis to classify organizations responsible for policy setting, oversight, and coordination, as well as the organizations responsible for program management. The classification of countries is presented in appendix D, tables D.1 and D.3.

- *Social ministry*: This category includes organizations that are responsible for social assistance (including social affairs, social welfare, social protection, social cohesion, social action, human rights), employment (or labor), health, women (or gender), and children and families, among others.
- *Central institution*: This category includes organizations that play a central role in government, including offices of the president or prime minister, as well as ministries responsible for the economy, planning, budget, or finance, depending on the country.

- *Other sectoral ministry*: This category includes organizations that do not have a social mandate, including organizations responsible for local government, decentralization, local development, rural development, agriculture, forestry, transportation, and urban development, among others.
- *Other arrangement*: This category includes situations in which multiple ministries hold joint responsibility for policy setting, oversight, and coordination; or situations in which responsibilities are given to an autonomous government agency or an NGO.
- *N/A*: This category includes countries for which data on the organization responsible for policy setting, oversight, and coordination is not available, namely: Cabo Verde, Central African Republic, Comoros, Democratic Republic of Congo, the Republic of Congo., Gabon, Guinea, Namibia, São Tomé and Príncipe, Seychelles, Somalia, and Sudan.

Institution/System Typology 4: Unit Responsible for Program Implementation
This classification categorizes countries and programs according to the unit responsible for program implementation. There are five categories, which are mutually exclusive. The classification of selected programs is presented in appendix D, table D.2.

- *Project implementation unit* (PIU): A team or unit that is created within a government organization to manage a project and the members of which are recruited or assigned for the sole purpose of managing the project and paid for by a development partner.
- *Special-purpose department*: A department that is established within a government organization with the specific mandate to manage one or several social safety net programs.
- *Preexisting department*: A department within a government organization with a set mandate and range of responsibilities to which the management of one or several social safety net programs is added.
- *Semiautonomous government agency* (SAGA): A legal entity that has been created by a government to undertake specific functions that would have otherwise be carried out by the government. It may be fully or semiautonomous, but is typically operationally autonomous from the government.
- *Nongovernmental institution*. This category includes NGOs and agencies of the United Nations.

Institution/System Typology 5: Social Registry Status
This classification categorizes countries according to the extent of development of their social registry. Social registries can help improve the identification and targeting of beneficiaries. These systems support outreach, the collection and processing of needs assessment data, and registration and eligibility information

for social safety net programs. They also represent a platform so individuals or households may be considered across various programs (Karippacheril, Leite, and Lindert 2017). The classification of countries is presented in appendix D, table D.2.

- *Not planned*: This category includes countries that do not have a social registry and have no plans to develop one.
- *Planned*: This category includes countries that have plans to implement a social registry, but have not yet started implementation.
- *Operating on small scale*: This category includes countries that have a social registry in place that is operating on a small scale, usually covering less than 5 percent of the population.
- *Operating on medium scale*: This category includes countries that have a social registry in place that is operating on a medium scale, usually covering between 5 percent and 15 percent of the population.
- *Operating on large scale*: This category includes countries that have a social registry in place that is operating on a significant scale, usually covering more than 15 percent of the population.
- *N/A:* This category includes countries for which data on social registries are not available, namely, Namibia.

Institution/System Typology 6: Measures to Deal with Crises

This classification categorizes countries according to the extent to which they have taken measures to promote the use of social safety nets in responses to crises. The definition is based on Monchuk (2014, see Data Sources). The classification of countries is presented in appendix D, table D.1.

- *Limited or no measures*: This category includes countries that have not put in place any significant measure to use social safety net programs to respond to shocks or crises.
- *Moderate*: This category includes countries that have started to put in place some measures to use social safety net programs during a crisis—for instance, through the use of targeting or payment systems to reach households affected by shocks—but have not done so in a systemic manner.
- *Strong*: This category includes countries that have taken systemic measures to use social safety nets or some elements of the social safety net system to respond to shocks and crises.

Institution/System Typology 7: Development Partner Involvement

This classification categorizes countries according to the level of development partner involvement in social safety nets. The classification of countries is presented in appendix D, table D.2.

- *Yes*: This category includes countries in which development partners are involved in social safety nets.
- *No*: This category includes countries in which there is no or limited involvement of development partners in social safety nets.

A.2.3 Typologies of Countries

This report uses five country typologies. Country classifications for these five typologies are presented in table A.1.

Country Typology 1: Geography

This classification categorizes countries into four subregions according to the classification of the United Nations Department of Economic and Social Affairs database (see below), except for Sudan, which is classified in that

Table A.1 **List of Countries and Country Groups**

Country name	Geography	Income group	Fragility	Resource status	Drought exposure
Angola	Central Africa	Lower middle income	Nonfragile	Resource-rich, Oil	Medium
Benin	West Africa	Low income	Nonfragile	Not resource-rich	Medium
Botswana	Southern Africa	Upper middle income	Nonfragile	Resource-rich, Non-oil	High
Burkina Faso	West Africa	Low income	Nonfragile	Not resource-rich	High
Burundi	East Africa	Low income	Fragile	Not resource-rich	Low
Cabo Verde	West Africa	Lower middle income	Nonfragile	Not resource-rich	N/A
Cameroon	Central Africa	Lower middle income	Nonfragile	Resource-rich, Oil	Low
Central African Republic	Central Africa	Low income	Fragile	Potentially resource-rich	Low
Chad	Central Africa	Low income	Fragile	Resource-rich, Oil	High
Comoros	East Africa	Low income	Fragile	Not resource-rich	N/A
Congo, Dem. Rep.	Central Africa	Low income	Fragile	Resource-rich, Non-oil	Low
Congo, Rep.	Central Africa	Lower middle income	Fragile	Resource-rich, Oil	N/A
Côte d'Ivoire	West Africa	Lower middle income	Fragile	Resource-rich, Oil	Low
Equatorial Guinea	Central Africa	Upper middle income	Nonfragile	Resource-rich, Oil	N/A
Eritrea	East Africa	Low income	Fragile	Not resource-rich	High
Ethiopia	East Africa	Low income	Nonfragile	Not resource-rich	Medium
Gabon	Central Africa	Upper middle income	Nonfragile	Resource-rich, Oil	N/A
Gambia, The	West Africa	Low income	Fragile	Not resource-rich	High
Ghana	West Africa	Lower middle income	Nonfragile	Potentially resource-rich	Low
Guinea	West Africa	Low income	Nonfragile	Resource-rich, Non-oil	Low

(continued next page)

Table A.1 (Continued)

Country name	Geography	Income group	Fragility	Resource status	Drought exposure
Guinea-Bissau	West Africa	Low income	Fragile	Not resource-rich	Low
Kenya	East Africa	Lower middle income	Nonfragile	Not resource-rich	Medium
Lesotho	Southern Africa	Lower middle income	Nonfragile	Not resource-rich	High
Liberia	West Africa	Low income	Fragile	Resource-rich, Non-oil	N/A
Madagascar	East Africa	Low income	Nonfragile	Potentially resource-rich	Low
Malawi	East Africa	Low income	Nonfragile	Not resource-rich	Medium
Mali	West Africa	Low income	Fragile	Resource-rich, Non-oil	High
Mauritania	West Africa	Lower middle income	Nonfragile	Resource-rich, Non-oil	High
Mauritius	East Africa	Upper middle income	Nonfragile	Not resource-rich	N/A
Mozambique	East Africa	Low income	Fragile	Potentially resource-rich	Medium
Namibia	Southern Africa	Upper middle income	Nonfragile	Resource-rich, Non-oil	High
Niger	West Africa	Low income	Nonfragile	Resource-rich, Non-oil	Medium
Nigeria	West Africa	Lower middle income	Nonfragile	Resource-rich, Oil	Low
Rwanda	East Africa	Low income	Nonfragile	Not resource-rich	Low
São Tomé and Príncipe	Central Africa	Lower middle income	Nonfragile	Not resource-rich	N/A
Senegal	West Africa	Low income	Nonfragile	Not resource-rich	High
Seychelles	East Africa	High income	Nonfragile	Not resource-rich	N/A
Sierra Leone	West Africa	Low income	Fragile	Potentially resource-rich	N/A
Somalia	East Africa	Low income	Fragile	Not resource-rich	Medium
South Africa	Southern Africa	Upper middle income	Nonfragile	Resource-rich, Non-oil	Medium
South Sudan	East Africa	Low income	Fragile	Not resource-rich	High
Sudan	East Africa	Lower middle income	Fragile	Resource-rich, Oil	High
Swaziland	Southern Africa	Lower middle income	Nonfragile	Not resource-rich	Medium
Tanzania	East Africa	Low income	Nonfragile	Potentially resource-rich	Medium
Togo	West Africa	Low income	Fragile	Potentially resource-rich	Medium
Uganda	East Africa	Low income	Nonfragile	Potentially resource-rich	Low
Zambia	East Africa	Lower middle income	Nonfragile	Resource-rich, Non-oil	Medium
Zimbabwe	East Africa	Low income	Fragile	Not resource-rich	High

system as part of North Africa and which we consider here as part of East Africa.

- *Central Africa*: This category includes Angola, Cameroon, the Central African Republic, Chad, the Democratic Republic of Congo, the Republic of Congo, Equatorial Guinea, Gabon, and São Tomé and Príncipe.
- *East Africa*: This category includes Burundi, the Comoros, Eritrea, Ethiopia, Kenya, Madagascar, Malawi, Mauritius, Mozambique, Rwanda, Seychelles, Somalia, South Sudan, Sudan, Tanzania, Uganda, Zambia, and Zimbabwe.
- *West Africa*: This category includes Benin, Burkina Faso, Cabo Verde, Côte d'Ivoire, The Gambia, Ghana, Guinea, Guinea-Bissau, Liberia, Mali, Mauritania, Niger, Nigeria, Senegal, Sierra Leone, and Togo.
- *Southern Africa*: This category includes Botswana, Lesotho, Namibia, South Africa, and Swaziland.

Country Typology 2: Income Group

This classification categorizes countries according to income level based on the World Development Indicators database for 2017 (see Data Sources).

- *Low income*: This category includes countries with a per capita income of $1,025 or less. It includes Benin, Burkina Faso, Burundi, the Central African Republic, Chad, the Comoros, the Democratic Republic of Congo, Eritrea, Ethiopia, The Gambia, Guinea, Guinea-Bissau, Liberia, Madagascar, Malawi, Mali, Mozambique, Niger, Rwanda, Senegal, Sierra Leone, Somalia, South Sudan, Tanzania, Togo, Uganda, and Zimbabwe.
- *Lower middle income*: This category includes countries with a per capita income between $1,026 and $4,035. It includes Angola, Cabo Verde, Cameroon, the Republic of Congo, Côte d'Ivoire, Ghana, Kenya, Lesotho, Mauritania, Nigeria, São Tomé and Príncipe, Sudan, Swaziland, and Zambia.
- *Upper middle income*: This category includes countries with a per capita income between $4,035 and $12,475. It includes Botswana, Gabon, Equatorial Guinea, Mauritius, Namibia, and South Africa.
- *High income*: This category includes countries with a per capita income of $12,476 or more. It includes Seychelles.

Country Typology 3: Fragility

This classification categorizes countries into two categories and is based on the World Bank Harmonized List of Fragile Situations Fiscal Year 18 (see Data Sources).

- *Fragile*: This category includes Burundi, the Central African Republic, Chad, the Comoros, the Democratic Republic of Congo, the Republic of Congo,

Côte d'Ivoire, Eritrea, The Gambia, Guinea-Bissau, Liberia, Mali, Mozambique, Sierra Leone, Somalia, South Sudan, Sudan, Togo, and Zimbabwe.

- *Nonfragile:* This category includes Angola, Benin, Botswana, Burkina Faso, Cabo Verde, Cameroon, Equatorial Guinea, Ethiopia, Gabon, Ghana, Guinea, Kenya, Lesotho, Madagascar, Malawi, Mauritania, Mauritius, Namibia, Niger, Nigeria, Rwanda, São Tomé and Príncipe, Senegal, Seychelles, South Africa, Swaziland, Tanzania, Uganda, and Zambia.

Country Typology 4: Resource Status
This typology classifies countries according to the importance of natural resources in the economy, measured in terms of natural resource revenues or exports. It is based on de la Brière et al. (2017, see Data Sources), itself partly based on work of the International Monetary Fund (IMF 2012), which defines countries as resource rich if they had either natural resource revenue of at least 20 percent of total revenue or natural resource exports of at least 20 percent of total exports in 2006–10. It also includes additional countries not covered by IMF (2012), such as Côte d'Ivoire, Liberia, Niger, Namibia, and South Africa. Countries are classified in four categories.

- *Not resource-rich:* This category includes Benin, Burkina Faso, Burundi, Cabo Verde, the Comoros, Eritrea, Ethiopia, The Gambia, Guinea-Bissau, Kenya, Lesotho, Malawi, Mauritius, Rwanda, São Tomé and Príncipe, Senegal, Seychelles, Somalia, South Sudan, Swaziland, and Zimbabwe.

- *Potentially resource-rich:* This category includes countries with identified reserves where production has not begun or reached significant levels, namely, the Central African Republic, Ghana, Madagascar, Mozambique, Sierra Leone, Tanzania, Togo, and Uganda.

- *Resource-rich, non-oil:* This category includes countries with resources mostly other than oil, namely, Botswana, the Democratic Republic of Congo, Guinea, Liberia, Mali, Mauritania, Namibia, Niger, South Africa, and Zambia.

- *Resource-rich, oil:* This category includes countries with resources mostly oil, namely, Angola, Cameroon, Chad, the Republic of Congo, Côte d'Ivoire, Equatorial Guinea, Gabon, Nigeria, and Sudan.

Country Typology 5: Drought Exposure
This classification is based on estimations by Cervigni and Morris (2016, see Data Sources) of the share of a country's population exposed to droughts and other shocks (population living in dryland areas, classified according to the aridity index as hyperarid, arid, semiarid, or dry subhumid).

- *High:* This category includes countries where more than 75 percent of the population lives in dryland areas. It includes Botswana, Burkina Faso, Chad,

Eritrea, The Gambia, Lesotho, Mali, Mauritania, Namibia, Senegal, South Sudan, Sudan, and Zimbabwe.

- *Medium*: This category includes countries where 35 to 74 percent of the population lives in dryland areas. It includes Angola, Benin, Ethiopia, Kenya, Malawi, Mozambique, Niger, Somalia, South Africa, Swaziland, Tanzania, Togo, and Zambia.

- *Low*: This category includes countries where less than 35 percent of the population lives in dryland areas. It includes Burundi, Cameroon, Central African Republic, Democratic Republic of Congo, Côte d'Ivoire, Ghana, Guinea, Guinea-Bissau, Madagascar, Nigeria, Rwanda, and Uganda.

- *N/A:* This category includes countries for which data on dryland areas are not available. It includes Cabo Verde, Comoros, Republic of Congo, Equatorial Guinea, Gabon, Liberia, Mauritius, São Tomé and Príncipe, Seychelles, and Sierra Leone.

A.3 Data Sources

A.3.1 ASPIRE Administrative Data

The main source of information for this report is the program-level administrative data collected in the ASPIRE database for Africa. The database contains information on 46 of the 48 countries in the region (Equatorial Guinea and Eritrea are not included for lack of data) and on 695 active social safety net programs. See ASPIRE (Atlas of Social Protection Indicators of Resilience and Equity) (database), World Bank, Washington, DC, http://datatopics.worldbank .org/aspire/.

Sources used to develop the ASPIRE database include primary sources (from official reports and information systems) and secondary sources (from reports analyzing social safety nets, often prepared in the context of the elaboration of social safety net strategies and often with the support of the ILO, the United Nations Children's Fund (UNICEF), the World Bank, and other key partners.

The database was substantially updated for African countries during 2016–17, building on data collection efforts by implementing agencies and World Bank teams. Extensive efforts were made during the preparation of this report to cross-check and verify these data, and significant updates to the ASPIRE database were made during this process. Nonetheless, data limitations, errors, or omissions might remain.

A.3.2 Household Survey Data

Nationally representative household survey data (income, expenditure, or consumption surveys) are sometimes used in the report to complement the

Table A.2 **Household Surveys Used**

Country	Survey year	Survey
Ghana	2012	Ghana Living Standards Survey VI
Lesotho	2014	CMS Quarter III 2013/2014
Malawi	2013	Third Integrated Household Survey
Mauritania	2014	Enquête Permanente sur les Conditions de Vie des Ménages
Mauritius	2012	Household Budget Survey
Nigeria	2012	General Household Survey, Panel Wave 2
Rwanda	2014	Integrated Household Living Conditions Surveys
Senegal	2011	Enquête de Suivi de la Pauvreté au Sénégal
Sierra Leone	2011	Integrated Household Survey
South Africa	2010	Income and Expenditure Survey
Uganda	2012	Uganda National Panel Survey

analysis based on administrative data, especially to assess the performance of specific programs.

In particular, in chapters 1 and 5, 11 household surveys collected after 2010 with instruments that allow for the capture of (some) social safety net programs are used to assess the coverage, targeting accuracy, and distributional impact of these programs (table A.2). Otherwise, because of the data limitations described in appendix B, box B.1, household survey data are generally not used to estimate the number of beneficiaries of social safety nets or coverage rates. Whenever household survey data are used, they are identified in the text to ensure clarity.

A.3.3 Databases

World Development Indicators Database (WDI)
The World Development Indicators database (WDI) is used for some of the indicators reported in this study. The WDI is one of the World Bank's primary collections of development indicators, compiled from officially recognized international sources to report national, regional, and global estimates. In this study, the WDI is used for information on the income groups of countries, gross domestic product (GDP), purchasing power parity (PPP), poverty rates, education indicators, and health indicators. The data available as of July 2017 are used. See WDI (World Development Indicators) (database), World Bank, Washington, DC, http://data.worldbank.org/products/wdi.

United Nations Department of Economic and Social Affairs Database (DESA)
The United Nations Department of Economic and Social Affairs database is used as a source to classify countries into four subregions and to estimate

population data. The databases can be accessed at https://unstats.un.org/unsd /methodology/m49/ (geographical classification) and https://esa.un.org/unpd /wpp/Download/Standard/Population/ (population).

Harmonized List of Fragile Situations
In this report, countries in fragile situations are identified on the basis of the list established in http://pubdocs.worldbank.org/en/189701503418416651 /FY18FCSLIST-Final-July-2017.pdf.

Population Statistics Database of the United Nations High Commissioner for Refugees (UNHCR)
We use the Office of the United Nations High Commissioner for Refugees database, available at http://popstats.unhcr.org/, as a source for data on internally displaced persons (IDPs). The data only include people who have been forced to leave their homes or places of habitual residence as a result of conflict and to whom the Office of the United Nations High Commissioner for Refugees extends protection or assistance. Data available as of January 2017 are used.

World Economic Outlook (IMF WEO) Database
This report uses the World Economic Outlook database of the IMF for macro-economic data, including government finance indicators, such as total spending, tax revenues, and government overall balance (chapter 5). Data available as of April 2017 are used. See WEO (World Economic Outlook Database), International Monetary Fund, Washington, DC, https://www.imf.org/external /pubs/ft/weo/2016/01/weodata/index.aspx.

IMF Country-Level Subsidy Estimates
We use the information available at www.imf.org/external/np/fad/subsidies /data/codata.xlsx for estimates of energy subsidies. These estimates were prepared in the context of the preparation of Coady, David P., Ian W. H. Parry, Louis Sears, and Baoping Shang, 2015, "How Large Are Global Energy Subsidies?" IMF Working Paper 15/105 (May 18), International Monetary Fund, Washington, DC, http://www.imf.org/external/pubs/ft/wp/2015/wp15105.pdf.

Development Initiatives
We use the information for 2014 available at http://devinit.org/methodology and http://data.devinit.org for estimates of humanitarian assistance received by countries, defined as the financial resources for humanitarian action, delivered during and in the aftermath of disasters caused by natural hazards and crises caused by human action. The data include the bilateral and multilateral humanitarian assistance of members of the Development Assistance Committee of the Organisation for Economic Co-operation and Development, as well as assistance from development partners (see definitions in http://devinit.org/wp -content/uploads/2017/06/GHA-Report-2017-Chapter-6.pdf).

A.3.4 Reports and Studies

de la Brière et al. (2017)
de la Brière, Bénédicte, Deon Filmer, Dena Ringold, Dominic Rohner, Karelle Samuda, and Anastasiya Denisova, 2017, *From Mines and Wells to Well-Built Minds: Turning Sub-Saharan Africa's Natural Resource Wealth into Human Capital*, Directions in Development: Human Development Series, Washington, DC: World Bank is used to classify countries according to their resource status.

Cervigni and Morris (2016)
Cervigni, Raffaello, and Michael Morris, eds., 2016, *Confronting Drought in Africa's Drylands: Opportunities for Enhancing Resilience*, Africa Development Forum Series, Washington, DC: Agence Française de Développement and World Bank is used to classify countries in terms of their level of drought exposure.

Monchuk (2014)
Monchuk, Victoria, 2014, *Reducing Poverty and Investing in People: New Role of Safety Nets in Africa*, Directions in Development: Human Development Series, Washington, DC: World Bank is used to classify countries according to the measures they have in place to use social safety nets to deal with crises and shocks.

Appendix B

Estimating the Number of Programs, the Number of Beneficiaries, Coverage, and Spending

For each country, the analysis considers programs that were operating as of March 2017. However, because data on beneficiaries or spending are not systematically available for all programs for 2016 and because there is year-on-year variation, the report's estimates are based on data over a few years. The following rule is applied. The reference year for each country is defined as the most recent year for which there are data on any programs; for example, the most recent data for Mauritania are for 2016, for one program. Then, the most recent data are considered for each program going back a maximum of three years before a country's reference year; thus, in the case of Mauritania, data are included for 2013, 2014, 2015, and 2016. So, if a program was operating in March 2017, but only produced information older than this (the reference year, plus three previous years), then this program was not included. Also, any data that predate 2010 are systematically excluded to avoid using severely outdated information.

Throughout the report, each country is given equal weight, irrespective of its size, when estimating averages for groups of countries, except where explicitly specified (appendix G, table G.6). The results are therefore not population-weighted.

The main source of information for estimating the number of beneficiaries and spending is the ASPIRE administrative database (see Data Sources).

B.1 Methodology to Estimate the Number of Programs

The number of social safety net programs for each country is estimated as the number of programs or their components if separated (data presented in appendix E, table E.1). For instance, the Tanzania Productive Social Safety Net (PSSN) is counted as three programs, since it has three distinct components: conditional cash transfer, public works, and livelihood enhancement.

When estimating the average number of social safety net programs for country groups, each country is given an equal weight (data presented in appendix E, table E.2). When a country has no data for a particular category of program, it is assumed that the country has no programs in that category.

When estimating the share of different types of social safety net programs for country groups, the share for a group is the average of the shares of all countries belonging to each country group, giving equal weight to each country (presented in appendix E, table E.3).

B.2 Methodology to Estimate the Number of Beneficiaries

The number of beneficiaries from social safety net programs is derived from the ASPIRE administrative database and is based on program administrative data (box B.1).

In the ASPIRE database, the number of beneficiaries is reported either as the number of households or the number of individuals, depending on the nature of each program. One important aspect that has bearing on measuring the number of beneficiaries is the distinction between direct and indirect beneficiaries. Depending on a program's target group, its direct beneficiary may be an individual or a household. For some of the programs that provide benefits to individuals, however, the report considers other household members as indirect beneficiaries if the benefit is expected to be shared within the household. In other programs, the benefit is not expected to be shared more broadly, and no indirect beneficiaries are assumed.

In presenting information on the number of beneficiaries, this report considers both direct and indirect beneficiaries for cash transfers, public works, food distribution, emergency programs, and other programs, but only direct beneficiaries for old-age pensions, school feeding, education fee waivers and scholarships, and health fee waivers.

Within the first group of programs, administrative data typically report both the direct and the indirect beneficiaries for food distribution programs, emergency interventions, and other programs (that is, the number reported is the total number of people in beneficiary households), and typically report only the number of direct beneficiaries for cash transfer programs and public works programs. So, in the case of estimates of the total number of beneficiaries, or coverage, the number of direct beneficiaries of cash transfer and public works programs is multiplied by the average household size in the country to obtain estimates of the number of direct and indirect beneficiaries. If multiple individuals are beneficiaries within a single household, this will result in an overestimation of the number of total beneficiaries because the method will count household members multiple times.

BOX B.1

The Challenges in Measuring Social Safety Net Coverage in Africa

To measure program coverage in terms of the number of beneficiaries, there are two potential data sources that can be used: administrative data from programs and household survey data (such as national budget surveys or other surveys that collect socioeconomic data and identify program participation). There are advantages and disadvantages to these sources.

Typically, administrative data are regularly collected, whereas household surveys do not exist annually, may not be available for recent years, and may not collect data on specific program participation, in the survey questionnaires.

Administrative data are usually program-specific within a country because most countries do not maintain a single database on beneficiaries of all programs. Double counting will therefore occur if beneficiaries benefit from multiple programs. This will result in overestimation of the total number of beneficiaries. By contrast, household surveys provide information for each household on the set of programs considered in the survey questionnaire, which allows one to avoid double counting in estimating coverage.

Household surveys include information on socioeconomic characteristics, thereby allowing one to profile beneficiaries, whereas administrative data offer only basic details on beneficiaries. Surveys also provide information on nonbeneficiaries, which can supply information on errors of exclusion.

Household surveys in the region are typically too small in terms of sample size, and too clustered in sample design, to be accurate at representing small programs. Thus, these surveys can, at best, provide accurate information only about larger programs that have broad geographic coverage.

Because of these differences, these two sources often do not produce similar estimates of the number of beneficiaries in a given country. The shortcomings in the household surveys, together with the low frequency of survey data collection in many countries in Africa, limit the ability of household survey data to report on the number of beneficiaries or assess the precision of targeting, except in a few countries, such as Ethiopia and South Africa.

As a result, in this report, administrative data are preferred as the main source for the estimates of the number of beneficiaries. Household surveys are only sometimes used in selected countries, and their use is noted explicitly in such cases.

Because of the data limitations discussed above, country-level estimates of the number of beneficiaries for a given program type will be overestimated if beneficiaries receive benefits through more than one program of the same type.

In the presentation of information on the overall number of beneficiaries of social safety net programs, the number of beneficiaries of cash transfers, food-based transfers, and public works programs only are summed. Beneficiaries of the other six program types—old-age social pension, school feeding, emergency, health fee waivers, education fee waivers, and other programs—are not included because they are more likely to overlap with the beneficiaries of the three selected types of programs and would likely result in large overestimates of coverage.

B.3 Methodology to Estimate Coverage Rates

In presenting coverage rates by program type, the report relies on different population groups as denominators.

For overall coverage and cash transfers, public works, food distribution, health fee waivers, and other programs, the total population is used as a denominator. For old-age social pensions, school feeding, and educational fee waivers and scholarships, the following age groups are used as denominators: (1) the program's age-eligibility criteria for old-age social pension programs (Botswana 65, Cabo Verde 60, Kenya 65, Lesotho 70, Mauritius 60, Namibia 60, Nigeria 65, São Tomé and Príncipe 60, Seychelles 63, South Africa 60, Swaziland 60, and Uganda 65), (2) the population of 5- to 14-year-olds for school feeding programs, and (3) the population of 15- to 24-year-olds for educational fee waivers and scholarships. However, specific country programs included in each category may not precisely follow these target groups. For instance, individuals below the required age may benefit from social pensions on other grounds, or a 16-year-old might benefit from school feeding. As a result, coverage will be overestimated.

In the estimates of coverage rates using the categorization by life cycle, the following population groups are used as denominators: (1) 0- to 14-year-olds for programs for children, (2) 15- to 64-year-olds for programs for the working-age population, (3) 65-year-olds or older people for programs for the elderly; and (4) the entire population for programs for families, households, or special groups. For the estimates of coverage rates using the categorizations by the nature of benefits or by the targeting method, the total population is used as the denominator.

Coverage rates for different program types are calculated by summing the number of beneficiaries for all programs within the category of interest. This method could overestimate coverage if there are beneficiaries who receive benefits from more than one program in the same category.

The overall coverage rate for social safety nets (presented in overview: figure O.5, chapter 1: figure 1.9; and appendix F, table F.1) is approximated by summing up the number of direct and indirect beneficiaries of cash transfers, food-based transfers, and public works programs only. The beneficiaries of the other six program types (old-age social pensions, school feeding, emergency, health and education fee waivers, and other programs) are not included because the beneficiaries of these programs are more likely to overlap with the beneficiaries of the other programs, which would result in overestimated coverage rates.

In the estimates of coverage rates, 2016 population data are used in the presentations of data for multiple countries, and population data are used for each year in presenting trends for a specific country.

When estimating the coverage rate of different types of social safety nets for country groups, the coverage for a group is the average of the coverage rates for all countries belonging to each country group, giving equal weight to each country (presented in chapter 1: figure 1.5, 1.6; and appendix F, table F.2). When no data are available for a category of program for a country, we assume that country has zero coverage in that category.

B.4 Methodology to Estimate Spending on Social Safety Nets

The amount spent on social safety nets is derived from program-level administrative data in the ASPIRE database. This typically includes spending on benefits, as well as on administrative costs. There is no differentiation by the source of the funding (whether development partner funds or government revenues). Data on spending are converted to U.S. PPP dollars (at constant 2011 prices) to allow for cross-program and cross-country comparisons. Overall social safety net spending for a country is measured by summing up the program-level amounts for all active programs. When spending is presented as a share of GDP, the information is expressed in terms of the GDP in 2015 (presented in chapter 1: figure 1.11; and appendix G, tables G.1 and G.2).

When estimating social safety net spending (as percentage of GDP) for country groups, spending (as percentage of GDP) for a group is the average of the spending (as percentage of GDP) for all countries in each country group, giving equal weight to each country (presented in the overview: figure O.12; in chapter 1: figure 1.12; in chapter 5: figure 5.1; and appendix G, table G.3). When no data are available for a category of program for a country, we assume that country has zero spending in that category.

When estimating the distribution of spending on social safety net programs across categories for country groups, the share of each category for a group is the average of the share of that category for all countries in each country group, giving equal weight to each country (presented in appendix G, table G.5). When no data are available for a category of program for a country, we assume that country has zero spending in that category.

In the section on spending, we also present an additional table which brings together all the resources deployed by all countries belonging to a particular country group (for instance, for the group "fragile," all the spending in dollars incurred in the 18 fragile countries is summed). Table G.6 presents the distribution of all these aggregated resources across program categories—showing, for instance, that 27 percent of all the safety net spending incurred in all countries of Central Africa is devoted to cash transfer programs. In this report, these numbers are used in overview: figure O.4 and O.10; in chapter 1: figure 1.4; in chapter 3: figures 3.4 and 3.5; and in chapter 4: figure 4.3.

Appendix **C**

The Country Context

Table C.1 Main Indicators, by Country

Country	Population, 1,000s	GDP per capita, constant 2011 PPP $	Average GDP growth, 2010–15	Poverty headcount, national	Poverty headcount ratio at $1.90 a day (2011 PPP $), % of population	Poverty headcount ratio at $3.10 a day (2011 PPP $), % of population	Prevalence of stunting, height-for-age, % of children under 5	Gross enrollment ratio, secondary, %	Gini index, World Bank estimate	Population ages 0–14, % of total	Population ages 15–59, % of total	Population ages 60 and above, % of total	Number of IDPs, 1,000s
Angola	27,860	6,025	3.9	37	30	55	29	29	43	47	49	4	–
Benin	10,576	2,010	4.2	36	53	76	34	57	43	43	52	5	–
Botswana	2,209	15,513	5.1	19	18	36	31	77	60	32	62	6	–
Burkina Faso	18,111	1,595	5.5	40	44	75	35	34	35	46	51	4	–
Burundi	10,200	721	2.4	65	78	92	58	42	33	45	51	4	79
Cabo Verde	534	6,075	1.8	27	8	25	21	93	47	31	62	7	–
Cameroon	22,834	3,046	4.8	38	24	44	32	58	47	43	52	5	82
Central African Republic	4,546	648	–2.3	62	66	82	41	17	56	44	51	5	369
Chad	14,010	1,846	4.3	47	38	65	40	22	43	48	48	4	–
Comoros	777	1,411	2.4	45	13	32	32	60	56	40	55	5	–
Congo, Dem. Rep.	76,196	742	6.9	64	77	91	43	44	42	46	49	5	1,492
Congo, Rep.	4,994	5,301	3.9	47	37	60	21	55	49	42	52	5	–
Côte d'Ivoire	23,112	3,448	6.3	46	29	55	30	44	43	43	53	5	24
Ethiopia	99,874	1,608	10.2	30	34	71	40	35	33	42	53	5	–
Gabon	1,933	16,786	5.1	33	8	24	18	53	42	36	58	6	–
Gambia, The	1,978	1,566	2.9	48	45	68	25	57	47	46	51	4	–
Ghana	27,583	3,980	7.1	24	25	49	19	62	43	39	56	5	–
Guinea	12,089	1,215	2.5	55	35	69	36	39	34	43	52	5	–
Guinea-Bissau	1,769	1,466	3.7	69	67	84	28	33	51	42	53	5	–

(continued next page)

Table C.1 (Continued)

Country	Population, 1,000s	GDP per capita, constant 2011 PPP $	Average GDP growth, 2010–15	Poverty headcount, national	Poverty headcount ratio at $1.90 a day (2011 PPP $), % of population	Poverty headcount ratio at $3.10 a day (2011 PPP $), % of population	Prevalence of stunting, height-for-age, % of children under 5	Gross enrollment ratio, secondary, %	Gini index, World Bank estimate	Population ages 0–14, % of total	Population ages 15–59, % of total	Population ages 60 and above, % of total	Number of IDPs, 1,000s
Kenya	47,237	2,926	6.0	46	34	59	26	60	49	41	55	4	—
Lesotho	2,174	2,808	4.5	57	60	77	33	54	54	36	58	7	—
Liberia	4,501	754	4.3	64	69	90	32	37	36	42	53	5	—
Madagascar	24,234	1,396	2.5	75	78	90	49	38	43	42	54	5	—
Malawi	17,574	1,084	4.3	51	71	88	42	43	46	45	51	4	—
Mali	17,466	1,963	4.1	44	49	78	39	41	33	48	48	4	90
Mauritania	4,182	3,572	4.3	42	6	22	22	31	32	40	55	5	—
Mauritius	1,258	19,549	3.7	—	1	3	14	96	36	19	65	15	—
Mozambique	28,009	1,128	6.6	55	69	88	43	32	46	45	50	5	—
Namibia	2,427	9,812	5.0	29	23	46	23	65	61	37	58	5	—
Niger	19,898	907	6.2	49	46	75	43	21	34	50	46	4	50
Nigeria	181,181	5,439	4.3	46	53	76	33	56	43	44	51	4	1,385
Rwanda	11,629	1,774	7.3	45	60	81	44	37	50	41	55	5	—
São Tomé and Príncipe	195	2,993	4.7	62	32	68	17	86	31	44	52	4	—
Senegal	14,978	2,380	4.5	47	38	66	19	50	40	43	52	5	—
Seychelles	95	26,319	5.4	39	1	2	8	82	47	22	66	12	—
Sierra Leone	7,237	1,366	5.2	53	52	80	38	43	34	43	53	4	—
Somalia	13,907	—	0.0	—	—	—	25	7	—	47	49	4	1,133

(continued next page)

Table C.1 (Continued)

Country	Population, 1,000s	GDP per capita, constant 2011 PPP $	Average GDP growth, 2010–15	Poverty headcount, national	Poverty headcount ratio at $1.90 a day (2011 PPP $), % of population	Poverty headcount ratio at $3.10 a day (2011 PPP $), % of population	Prevalence of stunting, height-for-age, % of children under 5	Gross enrollment ratio, secondary, %	Gini index, World Bank estimate	Population ages 0–14, % of total	Population ages 15–59, % of total	Population ages 60 and above, % of total	Number of IDPs, 1,000s
South Africa	55,291	12,260	2.0	54	17	35	24	99	63	29	63	8	–
South Sudan	11,882	1,808	–5.9	51	43	63	31	10	46	42	53	5	1,643
Sudan	38,647	4,385	2.7	47	15	39	38	43	35	41	53	5	2,343
Swaziland	1,320	7,734	3.0	63	42	63	26	66	51	38	58	5	–
Tanzania	53,880	2,583	6.8	28	47	76	35	32	38	45	50	5	–
Togo	7,419	1,382	4.8	55	54	75	28	55	46	42	53	5	–
Uganda	40,146	1,714	5.3	20	35	65	34	23	41	48	48	3	–
Zambia	16,100	3,636	5.6	61	64	79	40	20	56	45	51	4	–
Zimbabwe	15,778	1,860	7.9	72	21	46	28	48	43	41	54	4	–

Sources: WDI; United Nations High Commissioner for Refugees population statistics database.
Note: IDPs = internally displaced persons.

Social Safety Net Institutions and Systems

Table D.1 Social Protection Policies and Strategies, by Country

Country	Overall development of social safety net system	Social protection strategy or policy		Organizations responsible for policy setting, oversight, and coordination		Measures to deal with crises	Development partner involvement
		Status	Year	Nature	Name		
Angola	No solid plans	In progress		Social ministry	Ministério da Acção Social, Família e Promoção da Mulher	Strong	Yes
Benin	In progress	Present	2014	Central institution	Ministry of Planning and Development and Ministry of Social Affairs and Microfinance	Strong	Yes
Botswana	In place	Not present		Other sectoral ministry	Ministry of Local Government and Rural Development	Moderate	No
Burkina Faso	In progress	Present	2012	Central institution	Prime Minister's Office, chair of the National Social Protection Council	Strong	Yes
Burundi	In progress	Present	2011	Social ministry	Minister of Gender, Social Affairs and Human Rights	Moderate	Yes
Cabo Verde	In place	Present	2012	Social ministry	Direção Nacional de Inclusao Social, which is under the Ministerio da Familia e Inclusão Social	Limited or no measures	No
Cameroon	In progress	Not present		Central institution	Ministry of Economy, Planning, and Regional Development	Moderate	Yes
Central African Republic	In progress	In progress	2019	Social ministry	Ministry of Social Action and National Reconciliation and Ministry in charge of the promotion of women and family and the protection of children	Limited or no measures	Yes
Chad	In progress	Present	2015	Other arrangements	Ministry of Economics, Planning, and International Cooperation, and Ministry of Social Affairs	Limited or no measures	Yes
Comoros	No solid plans	Present	2016			Moderate	Yes

(continued next page)

Table D.1 (Continued)

Country	Overall development of social safety net system	Social protection strategy or policy		Organizations responsible for policy setting, oversight, and coordination		Measures to deal with crises	Development partner involvement
		Status	Year	Nature	Name		
Congo, Dem. Rep.	No solid plans	In progress	2017			Limited or no measures	Yes
Congo, Rep.	In progress	Present	2013			Limited or no measures	Yes
Côte d'Ivoire	In progress	Present	2014	Social ministry	Ministry of Employment and Social Protection	Limited or no measures	Yes
Ethiopia	In progress	Present	2014	Social ministry	Ministry of Labor and Social Affairs	Strong	Yes
Gabon	In progress	Not present				Limited or no measures	No
Gambia, The	No social safety net program	Present	2015	Social ministry	Ministry of Health and Social Welfare	Limited or no measures	Yes
Ghana	In progress	Present	2015	Social ministry	Ministry of Gender, Children, and Social Protection	Moderate	Yes
Guinea	In progress	Present	2017	Other arrangements	Ministry of Planning and of International Cooperation and Ministry of Social Action and Promotion of Women and Children	Limited or no measures	Yes
Guinea-Bissau	No solid plans	In progress		Social ministry	Ministry of Women, Family and Social Cohesion	Limited or no measures	Yes
Kenya	In progress	Present	2011	Social ministry	Ministry of East African Community, Labour, and Social Protection	Strong	Yes
Lesotho	In progress	Present	2015	Social ministry	Ministry of Social Development	Moderate	Yes

(continued next page)

Table D.1 (Continued)

Country	Overall development of social safety net system	Social protection strategy or policy		Organizations responsible for policy setting, oversight, and coordination		Measures to deal with crises	Development partner involvement
		Status	Year	Nature	Name		
Liberia	In progress	Present	2013	Social ministry	Ministry for Gender, Children, and Social Protection	Moderate	Yes
Madagascar	In progress	Present	2015	Social ministry	Ministry of Population, Social Protection, and the Promotion of Women	Strong	Yes
Malawi	In progress	Present	2012	Central institution	Ministry of Finance, Economic Planning, and Development (Directorate of Poverty Reduction and Social Protection)	Moderate	Yes
Mali	In progress	Present	2016	Central institution	Ministry of Economy, Finance, and Budget	Moderate	Yes
Mauritania	In progress	Present	2013	Other arrangements	Ministry of Economy and Finance; Ministry of Social Action, Children, and the Family	Limited or no measures	No
Mauritius	In place	Not present		Other sectoral ministry	Ministry of Social Security, National Solidarity, and Reform Institutions	Moderate	No
Mozambique	In progress	Present	2010 (updated in 2016)	Social ministry	Ministry of Women and Social Action	Moderate	Yes
Namibia	In place	Not present				No information	No
Niger	In progress	Present	2011	Central institution	Prime Minister's Office (National Institution for the Prevention and Management of Food Crisis)	Strong	Yes
Nigeria	In progress	Present	2017	Central institution	Ministry of Budget and National Planning, with coordination shifting to the National Social Safety Net Coordination Office under the Office of the Vice President	Moderate	Yes

(continued next page)

Country	Overall development of social safety net system	Social protection strategy or policy		Organizations responsible for policy setting, oversight, and coordination		Measures to deal with crises	Development partner involvement
		Status	Year	Nature	Name		
Rwanda	In progress	Present	2013	Social ministry	Ministry of Local Government	Moderate	Yes
São Tomé and Príncipe	In progress	Present	2014	Social ministry	Ministerio de Emprego e Assuntos Sociais e Direcao da Protecao Social e Solidaridade	Limited or no measures	No
Senegal	In progress	Present	2005 (updated in 2017)	Central institution	Délégation Générale à la Protection Sociale et la Solidarité, attached to the Presidency	Limited or no measures	Yes
Seychelles	In place	Not present				Moderate	No
Sierra Leone	In progress	Present	2011	Other arrangements	National Social Protection Program Inter-Agency Forum, chaired by the Chief of Staff (Office of the President) and the Minister of Finance	Moderate	Yes
Somalia	In place	In progress				Moderate	Yes
South Africa	In place	Present	1997	Social ministry	Department of Social Development	Moderate	No
South Sudan	In progress	Present	2014	Social ministry	Ministry of Gender, Child, and Social Welfare	Limited or no measures	Yes
Sudan	No solid plans	In progress				Limited or no measures	Yes
Swaziland	No solid plans	Not present		Central institution	Department of Social Welfare within the Deputy Prime Minister's Office	Limited or no measures	Yes

(continued next page)

Table D.1 (Continued)

Country	Overall development of social safety net system	Social protection strategy or policy		Organizations responsible for policy setting, oversight, and coordination		Measures to deal with crises	Development partner involvement
		Status	Year	Nature	Name		
Tanzania	In place	In progress		Central institution	Prime Minister's Office	Strong	Yes
Togo	In progress	Present	2012	Social ministry	Ministry of Health and Social Protection	Moderate	Yes
Uganda	In progress	Present	2015	Social ministry	Ministry of Gender, Labour and Social Development	Moderate	Yes
Zambia	In progress	Present	2014	Social ministry	Ministry of Community Development and Social Services	Limited or no measures	Yes
Zimbabwe	No solid plans	Present	2016	Social ministry	Ministry of Public Service, Labour, and Social Welfare	Moderate	Yes

Source: World Bank review of program documents.

Table D.2 **Social Registries, by Country**

Country	Social registry status	Programs served, number	Total households, 1,000s	Percent of population covered
Angola	Planned			
Benin	Operating on medium scale	2	248	11.7
Botswana	Planned			
Burkina Faso	Operating on small scale	1	24	0.8
Burundi	Planned			
Cabo Verde	Operating on large scale	2	17	13.7
Cameroon	Not planned			
Central African Republic	Planned			
Chad	Operating on small scale	1	25	0.9
Comoros	Operating on small scale	1	4.5	3.4
Congo, Dem. Rep.	Not planned			
Congo, Rep.	Operating on small scale	2	41	3.4
Côte d'Ivoire	Operating on small scale	1	80	2.8
Ethiopia	Planned			
Gabon	Operating on large scale	19	518 (individuals)	26.8
Gambia, The	Planned			
Ghana	Operating on small scale	2	132	2.1
Guinea	Planned			
Guinea-Bissau	Planned			
Kenya	Operating on large scale	6	763	7.1
Lesotho	Operating on large scale	3	235	51.9
Liberia	Planned			
Madagascar	Operating on medium scale	1	100	2.0
Malawi	Planned			
Mali	Operating on small scale	2	60	2.1
Mauritania	Operating on small scale	3	53	7.7
Mauritius	Operating on medium scale	5	41	11.4
Mozambique	Operating on small scale	1	22	0.3
Namibia	N/A			
Niger	Planned			
Nigeria	Operating on small scale	3	200	0.5
Rwanda	Operating on large scale	4	2,400	88.7
São Tomé and Príncipe	Operating on medium scale	2	1	2.1
Senegal	Operating on large scale	3	450	24.0

(continued next page)

Table D.2 (Continued)

Country	Social registry status	Programs served, number	Total households, 1,000s	Percent of population covered
Seychelles	Not planned			
Sierra Leone	Operating on small scale	4	48	3.9
Somalia	Planned			
South Africa	Operating on medium scale	8	2,200	14.3
South Sudan	Planned			
Sudan	Planned			
Swaziland	Operating on small scale	1	11	4.0
Tanzania	Operating on large scale	1	1,100	9.6
Togo	Planned			
Uganda	Planned			
Zambia	Operating on small scale	5	3	0.1
Zimbabwe	Operating on small scale	1	42	1.1

Source: World Bank review of program documents.
Note: The registry in Kenya is a single registry of beneficiaries, which covers six programs. Tanzania has a unified registry of beneficiary for the PSNP program and established by TASAF. In Mauritania, the plan for the registry is to cover 150,000 households by 2020.

Table D.3 Organizational Homes of Selected Social Safety Net Programs

Organization responsible for policy setting, oversight, and coordination	Country	Program	Organizations responsible for program management		Unit responsible for program implementation	
			Nature	Name	Nature	Name
Social ministry	Angola	Proajuda Assistance for Work Program (Cartão Kikuia)	Social ministry	Ministry of Family and Social Assistance	Pre-existing department	
	Burundi	Cash transfer program (under preparation)	Social ministry	Ministry of Human Rights, Social Affairs and Gender	PIU	Project Implementation Unit
	Burundi	Public work programs	Other sectoral ministry	Ministry of Agriculture (MAE), the Ministry of Transport, Burundi Agency for Public Programs, and Ministry of the Interior		
	Côte d'Ivoire	Productive social safety net project	Social ministry	Ministry of Employment, Social Affairs, and Professional Training	PIU	Unité de Gestion du Projet
	Côte d'Ivoire	Food-for-work and cash-for-work programs	Other arrangements	Ministry of Employment and Social Protection, Ministry of Agriculture, and Ministry of Women and Women's Affairs	Nongovernmental institutions	
	Ethiopia	Productive Safety Net Program	Other sectoral ministry	Ministry of Agriculture and Rural Development	Special-purpose department	Food Security Coordination Directorate
	Ethiopia	Urban Productive Safety Net Program	Other sectoral ministry	Ministry of Urban Development and Housing	PIU	Project Coordination Unit
	Ghana	Livelihoods Empowerment Against Poverty (LEAP)	Social ministry	Ministry of Gender, Children and Social Protection	PIU	Unit within the Social Welfare Department
	Ghana	Labour Intensive Public Works (LIPW)	Other sectoral ministry	Ministry of Local Government and Rural Development	PIU	

(continued next page)

Table D.3 (Continued)

Organization responsible for policy setting, oversight, and coordination	Country	Program	Organizations responsible for program management		Unit responsible for program implementation	
			Nature	Name	Nature	Name
Social ministry	Kenya	National safety net program (NSNP) (Transfers for orphans, vulnerable children, elderly, and disabled)	Social ministry	Ministry of East African Community, Labour and Social Protection	Special-purpose department	Social Protection Secretariat
	Kenya	Hunger Safety Net Program	Other sectoral ministry	National Drought Management Authority	PIU	Program Learning and Implementation Unit
	Lesotho	Old-age pension (OAP, universal social pension)	Central institution	Ministry of Finance	Pre-existing department	Pension Directorate
	Lesotho	Child Grant Programme (CGP)	Social ministry	Ministry of Social Development	Pre-existing department	Social Assistance Department
	Lesotho	Orphan Vulnerable Children Bursary Program (OVC), Public Assistance program (PA)	Social ministry	Ministry of Social Development	Pre-existing department	Social Assistance Department
	Lesotho	Public works program (IWM)	Other sectoral ministry	Ministry of Forestry	Pre-existing department	
	Lesotho	Post Primary Bursary (PPB)	Social ministry	Ministry of Social Development		
	Liberia	Liberia Social Safety Nets Project (LSSN-P)	Social ministry	Ministry for Gender, Children and Social Protection	Special-purpose department	National Social Safety Net Secretariat
	Madagascar	Productive Safety Nets Program (PSN), Human Development Cash Transfer Program (HDCT)	Social Ministry	Ministry of Social Protection	SAGA	Intervention Fund for Development (FID)
	Mozambique	Basic Social Subsidy Program (PSSB), Productive Social Action Program (PASP), Direct Social Action Program (PASD)	Social ministry	Ministry of Gender, Children and Social Action	SAGA	National Institute for Social Action (INAS)

(continued next page)

Organization responsible for policy setting, oversight, and coordination	Country	Program	Organizations responsible for program management		Unit responsible for program implementation	
			Nature	Name	Nature	Name
Social ministry	Rwanda	Vision 2020 Umurenge Program	Social ministry	Ministry of Local Government	SAGA	Local Administrative Entities Development Agency (LODA)
	South Sudan	Emergency food distribution programs	Other arrangements	Most interventions are funded by development partners and NGO implemented	Nongovernmental institutions	
	South Sudan	Safety Net and Skills Development Project	Other sectoral ministry	Ministry of Agriculture, Forestry, Cooperatives, and Rural Development	Pre-existing department	
	Togo	Community Development and Safety Nets Project (CDSNP)	Social ministry	Ministry of Community Development, Handicraft, Youth and Youth Employment	Nongovernmental institutions	AGAIB (Agences d'Appui aux Initiatives de Base), private non-profit entities (Board includes NGOs, Government and civil society)
	Uganda	Expanding Social Protection Program	Social ministry	Ministry of Gender, Labour and Social Development	PIU	
	Uganda	Labor-intensive public works	Central institution	Office of the Prime Minister	PIU	Northern Uganda Social Action Fund
	Zambia	Social Cash Transfer Scheme (SCTS), Public Welfare Assistance Scheme (PWAS), Food Security Pack (FSP) and Women Empowerment Fund (WEF)	Social ministry	Ministry of Community Development and Social Services	Pre-existing department	
	Zimbabwe	Harmonized Social Cash Transfer (HSCT)	Social ministry	Ministry of Public Service, Labour and Social Welfare	Nongovernmental institutions	UNICEF operates as fund manager

(continued next page)

301

Table D.3 (Continued)

Organization responsible for policy setting, oversight, and coordination	Country	Program	Organizations responsible for program management		Unit responsible for program implementation	
			Nature	Name	Nature	Name
Central institution	Benin	Community-Driven Decentralized Services (public works and cash transfer programs)	Other sectoral ministry	Ministry of Decentralization, Local Government, and Administration and Development of the Territory	Special-purpose department	Secretariat for Decentralized Community Driven Services, in coordination with Ministry of Social Affairs and Microfinance
	Burkina Faso	Social Safety Net Program (Burkin Naong Saya)	Social ministry	Ministry of Social Action and National Solidarity	PIU	Management Unit (Unité de Gestion)
	Cameroon	Social safety net program	Central institution	Ministry of Economy, Planning, and Regional Development	PIU	Project Management Unit
	Malawi	MASAF Public works program	Other sectoral ministry	Ministry of Local Government	SAGA	Malawi Social Action Fund (MASAF) Local Development Fund technical support team
	Malawi	Social Cash Transfer Program	Social ministry	Ministry of Gender, Children and Social Welfare	Pre-existing department	
	Mali	Jigisemejiri	Central institution	Ministry of Economy, Finance and Budget	PIU	Safety Nets Technical Management Unit
	Niger	Safety Net Program	Central institution	DNPGCCA in the Office of the Prime Minister	PIU	Safety Nets Unit (cellule de filets sociaux, CFS)

(continued next page)

Table D.3 (Continued)

Organization responsible for policy setting, oversight, and coordination	Country	Program	Organizations responsible for program management		Unit responsible for program implementation	
			Nature	Name	Nature	Name
Central institution	Senegal	National Conditional Cash Transfer Program (PNBSF)	Central institution	General Delegation for Social Protection and Solidarity (Délégation Générale à la Protection Sociale et la Solidarité) under the President's Office	SAGA	
	Swaziland	Old Age Grant, Orphans and Vulnerable Children Grant	Social ministry	Department of Social Welfare	Pre-existing department	
	Tanzania	Productive Social Safety Net	Central institution	Office of the President	SAGA	Tanzania Social Action Fund (TASAF)
Other sectoral ministry	Botswana	Orphan Care Program (OCP), Destitute Persons Program (DPP), Old Age Pension (OAP), Public works (Ipelegeng) program	Other sectoral ministry	Ministry of Local Government & Rural Development	Pre-existing department	
	Mauritius	Pensions for retirement (old-age), invalid, widows and orphans; Allowances for children, guardians (orphans), inmates, and carers (older people with disabilities)	Other sectoral ministry	Ministry of Social Security, National Solidarity and Reform Institutions		
Other arrangements	Chad	Emergency safety nets (food security)	Other arrangements	Most interventions funded by development partners and implemented by NGOs	Nongovernmental institutions	
	Mauritania	National Social Transfer Program Tekavoul	Central institution	Presidency	SAGA	Tadamoun Agency against the consequences of slavery, for insertion and against poverty
	Sierra Leone	National Safety Net Program	Other arrangements	National Commission for Social Action	SAGA	
	Sierra Leone	Labor Intensive Public Works (LIPW)	Other arrangements	National Commission for Social Action (NaCSA)	SAGA	

Source: World Bank review of program documents.

Appendix **E**

Typologies of Social Safety Net Programs

Table E.1 Number of Social Safety Net Programs, by Program Typology and Country

Total

Country	Total	Cash transfer	School feeding	Public works	Education interventions	Health interventions	Emergency	Food-based	Social	Other	Children	Working age	Elderly	Households/families	Special groups	Categorical	Geographical	Geographical and categorical	Poverty	Poverty and geographical/categorical	N/A	Cash	Food	Other in kind	Mix
					Program type								Life cycle					Targeting method					Nature of benefits		
Angola	8	2					2	2		2	3		1	4		7			1			1	3	2	2
Benin	16	13		1	1	1					2	1		8		5	1		6	2	2	9	1	4	2
Botswana	8	3						2	1	2		7	1	1		2	1		2			2	1	1	4
Burkina Faso	56	8	3	8	8	3	6	8		12	19	11	3	16	1	8		6	9		33	21	11	21	3
Burundi	21	4	1	6	1	2	1	2		4	4	6		9	2	14		1		4	2	6	3	7	5
Cabo Verde	39	5	2	1	5	2		5	3	16	16	3	4	15	1	17		1		2	19	9	7	21	2
Cameroon	22	11	1	5	3	1		1			5	13	1	4		8	1	6	1	4	2	11	2	1	8
Central African Republic	35	1		6			20	2		6	6	6	5	5	20	18	3	5	3	5	1	9	2	23	1
Chad	54	3	3	4			34	10			8	4		8	34	2		4		5	43	10	11	26	7
Comoros	3	1		2							2	2		1						3		3			
Congo, Dem. Rep.	6	2		1	1		2				2	1		1	2					6		3		3	
Congo, Rep.	2	2										2		2		1				1			2		
Côte d'Ivoire	5	3	1						3		2	2		2		1		4				1	1	1	2
Ethiopia	5	2	1	2						1	2	2		2		1			2		2		1	1	3
Gabon	2	1				1				1	1			1		2						1		1	1

(continued next page)

Table E.1 (Continued)

Country	Total	Program type									Life cycle					Targeting method						Nature of benefits			
		Cash transfer	School feeding	Public works	Education interventions	Health interventions	Emergency	Food-based	Social	Other	Children	Working age	Elderly	Households/families	Special groups	Categorical	Geographical	Geographical and categorical	Poverty	Poverty and geographical/categorical	N/A	Cash	Food	Other in kind	Mix
Gambia, The	11	3	1	1	1			3		2	7	1		3	2	6		3		5	1	5	4	2	2
Ghana	16	4	2			1			1	2	9	3		4	1	8			2	4	3	4	4	3	4
Guinea	7	2		1	5	1					9	2		4	2	8		3		3	4	4	3	3	2
Guinea-Bissau	3	1			1	1		1			1	1		1	1	1						1	1	1	
Kenya	11	3	2	2	3	1	1	3	1	2	4	2	1	2	2	6	1	3	2	5	1	5	4	2	1
Lesotho	8	2	1	1	3						5	1		2	2	2	1	1		5		4	2	1	1
Liberia	15	2	2	4			2	4		1	5	4		4	2	5	1	3	1	4	1	4	6	3	1
Madagascar	22	7	2	1			6	4		2	9	1		6	6			6	1	14	1	8	5	8	1
Malawi	7	2	2	2			1	1			2	3		1	1	2			3	1	1	2	2	2	1
Mali	13	2	2	1		1	4	1		3	3	2		4	4	1	2	3	3	3		3	4	5	1
Mauritania	3	1	2			1	2				1	1		1	2	1	1			3		1	1	2	
Mauritius	10	7	1						1	2	5	4		3	1	8			2			7	2	2	1
Mozambique	17	5	1		2	1		4	1	4	7	4	1	6	1	9		2	2	4		5	5	4	3
Namibia	11	9	1						1	1	2	1	6	1	1	11						8	1	1	1

(continued next page)

Table E.1 (Continued)

Country	Total	Cash transfer	School feeding	Public works	Education interventions	Health interventions	Emergency	Food-based	Social	Other	Children	Working age	Elderly	Households/families	Special groups	Categorical	Geographical	Geographical and categorical	Poverty	Poverty and geographical/categorical	N/A	Cash	Food	Other in kind	Mix
		Program type									Life cycle					Targeting method						Nature of benefits			
Niger	10	3	1	3			1	2		2	3	3		3	1	1		2	1		2	6	3		1
Nigeria	14	4	1	6	1		1		2	1	3	6	2	4	2	7		1	2	1	2	6		1	7
Rwanda	10	5		1	1		2			1	1		1	5	2	5		1	3	2		7		2	1
São Tomé and Príncipe	3	1						2		2	1		2	1	1	3						3	1		1
Senegal	24	10	2		1	3	6		3	2	7	6	4	5	6	13		2	1	8		8	1	9	6
Seychelles	12	5			1		2		2	4	2		4	4	2	9			1	2		4			
Sierra Leone	21	4	2		2		2	2		9	8	1	1	8	3	16			1	1	3	5	4	11	1
Somalia	8	4		2			2	2			2	2	3	4	2		1			8		6	1	1	
South Africa	17	7	1	3				1	1	4	5	5	3	2	2	5			2	9	1	10	1	4	2
South Sudan	10	1	1	1	1	1	2	2	1	4	4	1	2	3	2	8		1	2	1	1	2	2	6	
Sudan	11	2	1	1	1	1	1	3		1	6	1	2	1	1	5	1	1	1	3	1	1	4	3	3
Swaziland	16	5	1	2	1	2	2	2	1	2	3	2	2	5	6	8		1	1	6		9	2	5	
Tanzania	14	4	3	2			1	2		2	7	5		1	1		1	4	2	2		2	6	6	

(continued next page)

Table E.1 (Continued)

Country	Program type										Life cycle					Targeting method						Nature of benefits			
	Total	Cash transfer	School feeding	Public works	Education interventions	Health interventions	Emergency	Food-based	Social	Other	Children	Working age	Elderly	Households/families	Special groups	Categorical	Geographical	Geographical and categorical	Poverty	Poverty and geographical/categorical	N/A	Cash	Food	Other in kind	Mix
Togo	12	3	1	1		2					6	1		5		8		2	2			4	6	2	
Uganda	39	7	1	7	1			5	1	21	15	8	1	11	4		1	6	2	29	1	11	2	21	5
Zambia	20	6	1	2	3		1	2		9	7	3		5	5	9	4		1		6	3	1	13	3
Zimbabwe	29	12		2	2	2	3			9	7	11	2	5	4	11	4	1	5	7	1	10	1	17	1

Note: See methodology in Appendix B.1. Benin has several school feeding, public works, education, and health programs, which were not included due to data limitations.

Table E.2 **Number of Social Safety Net Programs, by Program Typology and Country Group**
Average number of programs

Country groups		Total	Cash transfer	School feeding	Public works	Education interventions	Health interventions	Emergency	Food-based	Social	Other	Children	Working age	Eslderly	Households/families	Special groups	Categorical	Geographical	Geographical and categorical	Poverty	Poverty and geographical/categorical	N/A	Cash	Food	Other in-kind	Mix
			Program type									Life cycle					Targeting method						Nature of benefits			
Overall		15	4	2	2	1	1	2	1	0	3	5	3	1	4	3	5	0	1	1	4	3	5	2	6	2
Geography	Central Africa	16	3	1	1	1	0	7	2	0	1	3	3	0	3	7	5	1	2	1	3	6	5	2	7	2
	East Africa	15	5	1	2	1	1	0	1	0	4	3	3	1	4	2	5	1	1	2	5	1	6	2	6	2
	West Africa	16	4	1	2	2	1	1	2	0	3	5	3	1	5	2	6	0	1	1	3	6	6	3	6	2
	Southern Africa	12	5	1	1	1	0	2	1	1	1	3	2	3	2	2	6	0	0	1	5	0	7	1	3	2
Income group	Low income	18	4	1	1	1	1	4	2	0	3	4	4	0	5	4	5	0	2	2	4	4	6	3	7	2
	Lower middle income	13	4	1	2	2	0	2	1	2	2	4	3	1	4	1	5	0	1	1	3	2	5	2	4	2
	Upper middle income	10	5	0	1	0	0	0	1	1	2	3	1	2	2	1	6	0	0	1	3	0	6	2	2	2
	High income	12	5	0	0	1	0	0	0	2	4	2	0	4	4	2	9	0	0	1	2	2	8	0	4	0
Fragility	Fragile	15	3	1	2	1	0	4	2	0	2	4	3	0	4	4	6	1	1	1	4	3	6	3	6	2
	Nonfragile	15	5	1	2	1	1	1	1	1	3	5	3	1	4	2	5	0	1	1	4	3	6	2	5	2
Resource status	Not resource-rich	15	5	1	2	1	1	1	1	1	3	4	3	1	5	2	6	0	1	1	4	3	6	2	5	1
	Potentially resource-rich	22	4	1	2	1	0	4	3	0	6	8	4	0	6	4	7	0	3	3	7	1	6	4	10	2
	Resource-rich, non-oil	11	4	1	2	2	0	1	1	0	2	2	2	1	3	2	4	0	1	1	4	1	4	2	4	1
	Resource-rich, oil	14	3	1	2	1	0	4	2	0	0	3	3	3	3	4	4	0	1	1	3	6	4	4	4	4

(continued next page)

Table E.2 (Continued)

Country groups		Total	Program type									Life cycle					Targeting method						Nature of benefits			
			Cash transfer	School feeding	Public works	Education interventions	Health interventions	Emergency	Food-based	Social	Other	Children	Working age	Elderly	Households/families	Special groups	Categorical	Geographical	Geographical and categorical	Poverty	Poverty and geographical/categorical	N/A	Cash	Food	Other in-kind	Mix
Drought exposure	High	20	5	1	2	2	1	5	2	0	3	6	3	1	4	5	5	1	2	1	4	7	6	3	8	2
	Medium	12	5	1	2	0	0	1	1	0	2	4	4	0	4	3	4	0	1	2	3	1	5	3	3	1
	Low	17	4	1	3	1	0	3	1	0	3	5	4	1	5	1	6	0	2	2	6	1	6	2	6	3
	N/A	12	3	1	1	2	1	5	2	1	3	6	3	1	4	5	5	1	2	1	4	3	6	2	5	1
Overall development of social safety net system	No social safety net program	21	1	1	3	2	0	10	1	0	3	4	3	0	4	10	10	2	4	2	5	0	6	2	13	1
	No solid plans	11	3	1	2	1	1	1	1	1	2	3	3	1	3	2	5	1	0	1	3	0	4	2	4	1
	In progress	16	4	1	1	1	1	3	2	0	3	5	3	0	5	3	5	0	2	2	4	4	6	3	6	2
	In place	15	6	1	1	1	1	0	1	1	4	5	2	2	4	1	7	0	1	2	3	3	7	2	5	1
Social protection strategy or policy	Not present	14	5	0	2	1	1	3	1	1	2	3	3	2	3	4	8	1	2	1	3	0	7	1	5	1
	In progress	8	3	0	1	0	0	1	1	0	1	3	2	0	2	1	3	1	1	1	3	0	2	2	2	1
	Present	17	4	1	2	1	1	2	2	0	3	5	3	1	5	3	5	0	2	1	5	4	6	2	6	2

(continued next page)

Table E.2 (Continued)

Country groups		Total	Program type									Life cycle					Targeting method						Nature of benefits			
			Cash transfer	School feeding	Public works	Education interventions	Health interventions	Emergency	Food-based	Social	Other	Children	Working age	Elderly	Households/families	Special groups	Categorical	Geographical	Geographical and categorical	Poverty	Poverty and geographical/categorical	N/A	Cash	Food	Other in-kind	Mix
Organizations responsible for policy setting, oversight, and coordination	Social ministry	15	4	1	2	1	1	2	2	0	3	2	3	1	4	2	5	1	2	1	5	0	2	3	5	1
	Central institution	19	6	2	0	0	1	2	3	0	2	5	6	1	4	2	6	1	1	2	4	4	8	3	5	2
	Other sectoral ministry	9	5	1	2	1	0	1	1	0	2	5	3	1	4	2	5	0	3	2	2	4	5	3	2	2
	Other arrangements	26	3	0	1	1	1	13	1	1	3	3	1	1	6	13	6	1	1	0	3	15	6	1	13	3
	N/A	12	3	2	1	0	0	2	4	0	2	3	2	0	3	2	6	0	0	0	3	2	5	5	5	1
Social registry status	Not planned	11	5	0	2	2	0	1	2	0	3	3	3	0	4	2	4	0	2	2	4	0	6	3	2	2
	Planned	13	3	1	2	0	1	1	2	0	3	3	3	1	3	2	5	1	1	1	4	1	3	5	5	2
	Operating on small scale	17	4	1	2	1	0	4	2	0	3	3	3	1	5	4	5	0	1	1	4	6	6	3	7	1
	Operating on medium scale	14	7	1	1	1	1	1	1	1	2	5	3	1	4	2	4	0	1	2	6	1	7	1	4	2
	Operating on large scale	18	5	2	1	1	1	2	2	1	4	7	3	1	5	2	7	0	2	2	3	4	5	1	8	2
	N/A	17	4	0	3	0	0	7	1	0	2	7	3	2	3	7	11	1	2	1	3	0	7	1	9	1
Measures to deal with crises	Limited or no measures	14	3	1	0	0	0	4	1	0	2	4	2	0	4	5	6	0	1	2	3	4	4	2	7	1
	Moderate	15	5	2	2	1	1	1	3	0	2	6	4	1	5	2	6	1	1	2	5	1	4	2	7	2
	Strong	18	5	2	2	1	0	1	1	0	3	6	4	1	4	2	6	1	0	2	5	1	7	4	5	1
	N/A	11	9	1	0	0	0	0	0	1	0	2	1	6	1	1	11	0	0	0	0	0	8	1	1	1

(continued next page)

Table E.2 (Continued)

Country groups		Total	Cash transfer	School feeding	Public works	Education interventions	Health interventions	Emergency	Food-based	Social	Other	Children	Working age	Elderly	Households/families	Special groups	Categorical	Geographical	Geographical and categorical	Poverty	Poverty and geographical/ categorical	N/A	Cash	Food	Other in-kind	Mix
			Program type									**Life cycle**					**Targeting method**						**Nature of benefits**			
Development partner involvement	Yes	16	4	0	1	1	1	0	1	1	3	4	1	2	2	3	6	0	0	1	2	3	5	3	6	2
	No	12	4	1	2	1	0	3	2	0	3	5	3	0	4	1	5	1	2	1	4	2	5	1	4	1

Source: ASPIRE (Atlas of Social Protection Indicators of Resilience and Equity) (database), Administrative data, World Bank, Washington, DC, http://datatopics.worldbank.org/aspire/. The data only presents information on active programs.

Note: See methodology in appendix B.1. Rounding might result in small discrepancies. Benin has several school feeding, public works, education, and health programs, which were not included in the averages due to data limitations.

Table E.3 **Distribution of Social Safety Net Programs, by Program Typology and Country Group**
% of total number of programs

Country groups		Program type									Life cycle					Targeting method						Nature of benefits			
		Cash transfer	School feeding	Public works	Education interventions	Health interventions	Emergency	Food-based	Social	Other	Children	Working age	Elderly	Households/families	Special groups	Categorical	Geographical	Geographical and categorical	Poverty	Poverty and geographical/categorical	N/A	Cash	Food	Other in-kind	Mix
Geography	Central Africa	38	3	8	5	7	19	7	8	5	25	13	10	33	19	54	2	6	2	26	11	51	9	30	10
	East Africa	33	7	17	3	2	9	7	2	19	30	23	4	30	13	35	3	8	15	34	4	43	16	31	11
	West Africa	31	9	11	6	6	10	10	1	14	30	20	2	34	13	41	2	8	9	27	13	36	20	32	11
	Southern Africa	43	7	11	9	3	3	6	9	10	31	15	22	20	12	46	0	4	9	41	1	53	10	20	17
Income group	Low income	29	8	17	4	4	15	10	0	14	28	23	1	31	17	34	3	10	12	32	9	40	18	33	9
	Lower middle income	36	8	9	10	3	7	6	8	12	31	17	10	32	10	44	2	6	5	35	9	43	15	26	16
	Upper middle income	56	3	6	0	10	0	6	7	11	35	10	19	28	9	67	0	0	11	21	1	55	5	23	16
	High income	42	0	0	8	0	0	0	17	33	17	0	33	33	17	75	0	0	8	17	0	67	0	33	0
Fragility	Fragile	30	7	14	4	4	15	12	0	14	28	19	1	34	18	41	3	7	6	34	8	38	20	33	9
	Nonfragile	37	7	12	6	4	7	6	6	14	30	19	10	29	12	41	2	8	13	29	8	46	13	28	13

(continued next page)

Table E.3 (Continued)

Country groups		Program type									Life cycle					Targeting method						Nature of benefits			
		Cash transfer	School feeding	Public works	Education interventions	Health interventions	Emergency	Food-based	Social	Other	Children	Working age	Elderly	Households/families	Special groups	Categorical	Geographical	Geographical and categorical	Poverty	Poverty and geographical/categorical	N/A	Cash	Food	Other in-kind	Mix
Resource status	Not resource-rich	36	8	15	5	5	8	5	6	14	28	20	9	30	12	46	2	6	12	27	8	51	13	27	9
	Potentially resource-rich	22	8	9	7	3	13	16	0	22	41	17	1	27	15	37	2	14	14	27	5	29	24	40	7
	Resource-rich, non-oil	34	6	14	5	1	16	9	3	13	24	18	8	28	21	29	2	7	8	46	7	42	13	34	11
	Resource-rich, oil	42	6	10	5	8	9	9	2	8	27	20	3	41	9	49	2	5	3	27	13	38	15	23	24
Drought exposure	High	29	6	7	7	3	20	12	3	14	32	14	8	24	22	37	3	8	7	30	15	33	17	37	13
	Medium	36	11	16	4	3	6	11	2	12	29	25	4	31	10	33	3	10	19	29	5	42	23	24	11
	Low	32	7	16	8	6	12	4	1	14	26	24	2	32	16	39	1	8	7	41	5	40	11	33	16
	N/A	42	3	11	3	6	3	5	11	16	29	12	14	39	6	62	1	3	4	23	8	62	9	26	4
Overall development of social safety net system	No social safety net program	27	9	9	9	0	0	27	0	18	64	9	0	27	0	55	0	27	9	0	9	36	9	27	0
	No solid plans	31	9	16	7	8	9	7	1	11	29	20	5	30	16	46	3	1	5	43	2	42	18	27	8
	In progress	32	7	13	6	4	13	8	4	13	28	20	4	32	15	39	2	9	10	30	10	42	15	31	12
	In place	45	5	9	3	1	4	7	8	18	29	15	17	27	12	44	1	4	14	30	7	51	11	26	12

(continued next page)

Table E.3 (Continued)

Country groups		Program type									Life cycle					Targeting method						Nature of benefits			
		Cash transfer	School feeding	Public works	Education interventions	Health interventions	Emergency	Food-based	Social	Other	Children	Working age	Elderly	Households/families	Special groups	Categorical	Geographical	Geographical and categorical	Poverty	Poverty and geographical/categorical	N/A	Cash	Food	Other in-kind	Mix
Social protection strategy or policy	Not present	52	3	7	4	10	2	4	8	11	29	13	18	30	10	67	1	5	9	17	1	56	6	23	15
	In progress	27	11	12	5	6	19	10	0	9	31	15	2	28	24	41	4	6	10	38	2	31	22	37	10
	Present	32	7	14	6	3	11	9	4	15	29	21	5	32	13	36	2	8	10	32	11	43	16	30	11
Organizations responsible for policy setting, oversight, and coordination	Social ministry	28	9	11	7	4	8	11	5	18	35	17	7	29	12	47	2	9	9	26	7	38	20	32	10
	Central institution	35	10	18	5	4	11	6	2	9	26	33	3	26	12	28	5	13	19	23	12	40	18	25	17
	Other sectoral ministry	54	0	0	0	0	11	13	0	16	38	6	11	34	11	53	0	0	23	25	0	48	6	16	30
	Other arrangements	22	4	6	6	4	35	7	0	14	17	10	1	36	36	31	0	2	1	43	23	33	10	53	4
	N/A	51	2	15	4	7	8	3	1	5	22	16	11	40	12	46	1	0	0	49	1	65	6	23	6
Social registry status	Not planned	42	2	13	13	2	11	2	6	11	24	25	11	23	17	37	2	9	4	45	3	56	3	29	12
	Planned	25	9	18	13	5	2	3	1	13	31	19	2	34	13	45	3	9	11	29	4	35	23	28	14
	Operating on small scale	33	6	12	3	6	15	6	1	17	23	22	3	34	18	33	2	6	7	37	16	41	13	34	12
	Operating on medium scale	52	3	6	7	1	2	5	17	17	32	16	19	24	10	48	1	5	15	26	5	64	6	21	9
	Operating on large scale	34	9	8	8	11	9	5	4	12	40	16	6	28	15	40	2	10	15	7	7	41	16	35	8
	N/A	82	9	0	0	0	0	0	9	0	18	9	55	9	9	100	0	0	0	0	0	73	9	9	9

(continued next page)

Table E.3 (Continued)

Country groups		Program type									Life cycle					Targeting method						Nature of benefits			
		Cash transfer	School feeding	Public works	Education interventions	Health interventions	Emergency	Food-based	Social	Other	Children	Working age	Elderly	Households/families	Special groups	Categorical	Geographical	Geographical and categorical	Poverty	Poverty and geographical/categorical	N/A	Cash	Food	Other in-kind	Mix
Measures to deal with crises	Limited or no measures	32	6	7	5	8	17	7	5	13	29	12	5	33	21	49	1	4	2	31	11	40	12	40	8
	Moderate	33	6	17	7	2	6	8	4	16	29	24	6	30	10	40	3	7	13	34	4	45	14	25	16
	Strong	35	12	16	3	3	8	13	1	10	32	24	3	31	9	22	3	16	20	28	12	40	26	24	9
	N/A	82	9	0	0	0	0	0	9	0	18	9	55	9	9	100	0	0	0	0	0	73	9	9	9
Development partner involvement	Yes	32	8	15	6	4	11	9	1	14	29	22	2	32	14	37	3	9	11	33	9	40	18	30	12
	No	45	2	4	2	6	7	5	9	14	29	7	23	27	14	61	0	0	7	25	6	56	5	30	10

Source: ASPIRE (Atlas of Social Protection Indicators of Resilience and Equity) (database), Administrative data, World Bank, Washington, DC, http://datatopics.worldbank.org/aspire/. The data only present information on active programs. The table presents the share of programs for each category within each program typology.

Note: See methodology in appendix B.1. Benin has several school feeding, public works, education, and health programs, which were not included in the averages due to data limitations.

Coverage of Social Safety Net Programs

Table F.1 Coverage of Social Safety Nets, by Program Typology and Country
% of population

Column groups: *Program type* = Overall → Other; *Life cycle* = Children → Special groups; *Targeting method* = Categorical → N/A; *Nature of benefits* = Cash → Mix.

Country	Overall	Cash transfer	School feeding	Public works	Education interventions	Health interventions	Emergency	Food-based	Social pensions	Other	Children	Working age	Elderly	Households/families	Special groups	Categorical	Geographical	Geographical and categorical	Poverty	Poverty and geographical/categorical	N/A	Cash	Food	Other in-kind	Mix
Angola	0.4				0.1			0.4		0.0	0.0	0.3		0.4		0.0	0.4				0.4	0.0	0.4		
Benin	2.1	1.6	0.6	10.9						0.0	0.0	1.3	1.3			0.0		0.9	1.2	0.0	1.9	1.9	0.2	0.0	0.2
Botswana	38.9	9.3	10.9				18.7	129.0		0.1	58.8	4.7	8.5	0.9		6.2		29.2	8.4	15.7		15.7	17.4	0.1	10.7
Burkina Faso	9.2	1.6	59.3	4.4	1.9	3.9	0.7	3.3		0.3	44.2	1.5	0.1	5.9	0.7	4.4		16.7		4.8	5.2	6.2	20.0	4.9	0.1
Burundi	5.7	0.1	11.7	4.6	0.8	0.1		1.1		0.4	8.2	1.9		1.3		4.9		4.2		0.4		0.3	4.2	0.5	4.6
Cabo Verde			2.9	14.4						0.7	11.9	0.7		0.7		2.3		0.6		1.5		1.6	0.6	2.2	
Cameroon	5.7	4.6	0.9	0.2	0.0	0.2		0.9			2.8	0.7		3.2		0.2	0.0	1.9	0.0	3.1	1.0	0.6	1.2	0.2	4.2
Central African Republic	14.1	1.7	10.5				21.8	1.8		1.4	0.8	3.9		4.6	21.8	14.8	7.3	3.1	0.2	10.2	1.7	12.4	1.8	22.1	1.0
Chad	8.7	0.4	7.6	0.6			15.6	7.7			11.7	0.2		5.2	15.6	1.8		2.5		1.4	20.8	1.4	8.5	12.1	4.7
Comoros	3.5	0.3	3.2									1.0		0.3					3.5	3.5		3.5			
Congo, Dem. Rep.	1.9	0.1		1.8	0.3			4.3			0.1	1.6		0.1	4.3				6.2			1.9		4.4	
Congo, Rep.	3.7	3.7												3.7		3.4				0.3		3.7		3.7	
Côte d'Ivoire	1.9	1.9	17.8							0.8	11.0	0.2		2.0		4.7				2.7		1.2	4.7	0.8	0.7

(continued next page)

Table F.1 (Continued)

Country	Overall	Program type									Life cycle					Targeting method						Nature of benefits			
		Cash transfer	School feeding	Public works	Education interventions	Health interventions	Emergency	Food-based	Social pensions	Other	Children	Working age	Elderly	Households/families	Special groups	Categorical	Geographical	Geographical and categorical	Poverty	Poverty and geographical/categorical	N/A	Cash	Food	Other in-kind	Mix
Ethiopia	8.2	0.0	2.6	8.2							1.6	15.4				0.0	0.7			8.0		0.2	0.7		8.0
Gabon	0.0	2.6				25.0							25.0			25.0						25.0			
Gambia, The	23.1	6.7	21.8	8.3	0.4		8.1		0.3		33.0	2.0		0.3		21.7		7.5	0.2		0.1	15.0	14.2		0.3
Ghana	8.1	3.7	25.9	2.6	7.0	24.3		1.7			24.2	1.2		27.7		3.2			24.5	12.2		6.5	8.0	25.2	0.3
Guinea	3.2	0.6		2.5						0.0	0.6	0.8		0.6		3.2						0.0			
Guinea-Bissau	0.3	0.3	32.0								19.6	0.8		0.3	0.3	8.5				3.2		0.3	8.2		
Kenya	5.7	4.7	13.5	1.1		0.4	0.7		25.4		10.5	0.4	15.9	1.3	1.1	1.7	0.7	1.9	3.7	3.1		5.9	4.1		
Lesotho	33.4	8.0	78.6	25.4	3.8			146.7			55.7	9.2	57.9	2.6		18.1				37.9		37.3	17.9	0.8	
Liberia	11.3	0.9	53.9	6.9			3.4			0.7	42.1	2.6		0.9	0.7	4.1	0.7	14.4	0.9	6.6		7.8	17.8		0.7
Madagascar	3.2	3.0		0.4				0.2		10.4	25.6	2.1		0.4				2.0	0.0	12.0	0.0	3.0	0.2	10.8	0.0
Malawi	25.4	5.5	61.3	19.9			0.7				38.7	8.9		4.5	0.7	17.3	0.7		7.7	17.7		22.1	17.3	0.7	
Mali	n/a																								
Mauritania	1.0	1.0		2.6										1.0	2.6					3.7		1.0		2.6	
Mauritius	15.9	15.9							101.3	0.2	12.3			101.3	0.4	31.4					0.2	24.1		2.6	7.3

(continued next page)

Table F.1 (Continued)

Country	Program type										Life cycle					Targeting method						Nature of benefits			
	Overall	Cash transfer	School feeding	Public works	Education interventions	Health interventions	Emergency	Food-based	Social pensions	Other	Children	Working age	Elderly	Households/families	Special groups	Categorical	Geographical	Geographical and categorical	Poverty	Poverty and geographical/categorical	N/A	Cash	Food	Other in-kind	Mix
Mozambique	8.0	7.1	5.5	0.2	0.0			0.6		0.6	4.8	0.2	7.5	5.3		1.2		1.1	0.2			7.1	2.2	0.6	0.3
Namibia	37.5	47.6	53.3						111.8		35.4		111.8	31.8	5.3	66.0					0.1	21.8	12.4		31.8
Niger	9.1	1.6	5.1	1.6			2.5	5.9		0.6	14.9	0.6	1.4	2.5		1.2		4.0		7.8	0.1	3.2	7.4		2.5
Nigeria	2.0	2.0		0.1	0.0		0.4			0.0	0.0	0.0	0.3	1.9	0.0	0.0		0.0	0.1		0.0	2.0	0.0		0.1
Rwanda	7.5	3.6		3.9			0.2			1.7		1.7	0.5	5.3	0.2	0.1			5.3	4.1		7.5	1.7		0.2
São Tomé and Príncipe	2.6	2.6							38.1		1.4		38.1			4.1						4.1			
Senegal	17.0	17.0	16.4		3.6	5.9	6.8			1.0	0.1		22.0	6.8		7.9		4.3		23.5		16.9	2.3	13.7	2.9
Seychelles	17.5	17.5			14.5				99.0	3.1	10.0		115.0	12.3	5.2	18.6			11.6	2.8		29.9		3.1	
Sierra Leone	3.8	2.3	6.6		0.3			1.6		3.5	8.0		5.7		0.1	6.9			0.4	1.9		2.3	3.3	3.5	
Somalia	0.8	0.7		0.1							0.0	0.0	0.7	0.8	0.7	0.9				0.8	0.8	0.2	0.2	0.0	0.6
South Africa	64.4	62.8	87.1	2.8					69.4	0.9	76.0	1.3	70.2	0.8	8.0				0.8	86.8	0.2	71.1	16.6	0.9	0.1
South Sudan	4.6	2.5		0.3			33.8	1.9		4.3	19.1	0.1	4.1	33.8	4.1	40.0			0.0	0.3	2.5	2.8	1.9	38.1	0.1

(continued next page)

Table F.1 (Continued)

Country	Program type										Life cycle					Targeting method						Nature of benefits			
	Overall	Cash transfer	School feeding	Public works	Education interventions	Health interventions	Emergency	Food-based	Social pensions	Other	Children	Working age	Elderly	Households/families	Special groups	Categorical	Geographical	Geographical and categorical	Poverty	Poverty and geographical/categorical	N/A	Cash	Food	Other in-kind	Mix
Sudan	16.6	14.1	9.6	1.6	2.6	40.7	5.4	0.9		0.0	12.2	0.5		48.1	5.4	10.0	0.0		6.7	8.3	40.7	7.4	3.4	46.1	8.8
Swaziland	1.8	1.8	103.1					100.8			66.1	100.8	1.8			29.7				1.8		6.7	24.8		
Tanzania	13.3	10.2	1.5	3.1		1.7		0.1		2.9	7.4	1.5		9.6	1.7	0.0		0.5	17.1	0.7	1.8	12.2	0.9		5.1
Togo	1.4	0.7	2.0	0.3				0.4			2.2	0.6		0.7		0.4		0.9	0.7			1.0	0.9		
Uganda	3.9	2.2		1.4	1.2				10.5	1.2	3.5	0.8		1.9	0.0		0.9	0.2	0.7	4.5		3.4	0.2	1.2	0.7
Zambia	10.2	10.2	23.1		1.1		0.2	0.2		0.4	15.0	0.9		8.1	0.2	0.3		0.9	0.2	0.3	2.5	7.8	6.5	0.8	2.4
Zimbabwe	3.6	0.6		3.0	6.0	0.2	1.7			0.1	3.9	3.5	0.2	0.3	1.7	0.1	4.7		0.4	1.6	0.0	0.6	0.0	3.2	3.0

Source: ASPIRE (Atlas of Social Protection Indicators of Resilience and Equity) (database), Administrative data, World Bank, Washington, DC, http://datatopics.worldbank.org/aspire/.

Note: See methodology in appendixes B.2 and B.3. The overall coverage rates for Namibia and South Africa are based on household survey data. Due to data limitations, information is not available for Mali. Benin has several school feeding, public works, education, and health programs, which were not included due to data limitations.

Table F.2. Coverage of Social Safety Nets, by Program Typology and Country Group
% of population

Country groups		Overall	Program type									Life cycle					Targeting method						Nature of benefits			
			Cash transfer	School feeding	Public works	Education interventions	Health interventions	Emergency	Food-based	Social pensions	Other	Children	Working age	Elderly	Households/families	Special groups	Categorical	Geographical	Geographical and categorical	Poverty	Poverty and geographical/categorical	N/A	Cash	Food	Other in-kind	Mix
Overall	Overall	10	16	3	3	1	2	2	1	18	1	16	2	16	6	3	8	0	2	2	7	2	9	5	5	2
Geography	Central Africa	5	2	1	2	0	3	5	1	5	0	2	1	5	5	5	6	1	1	0	3	3	3	8	5	1
	East Africa	9	6	8	3	2	2	3	0	14	2	10	2	14	6	3	7	0	2	3	4	3	8	2	7	2
	West Africa	6	3	16	2	2	2	1	0	0	0	15	1	0	5	1	4	0	3	2	5	3	6	6	4	0
	Southern Africa	35	26	64	8	1	0	0	4	112	0	58	3	84	9	3	24	0	0	2	31	0	31	18	0	9
Income group	Low income	8	3	11	3	1	0	4	1	0	1	12	2	0	3	4	5	1	3	1	5	3	5	4	5	1
	Lower middle income	7	4	20	2	2	5	0	0	22	0	15	1	15	7	3	6	0	1	3	6	1	6	5	6	1
	Upper middle income	31	27	28	3	0	5	1	4	82	0	36	1	72	13	4	26	0	0	3	23	0	27	9	5	10
	High income	17	17	0	0	15	0	0	0	99	3	10	0	115	12	5	19	0	0	12	3	0	30	0	3	0
Fragility	Fragile	7	3	10	2	1	2	5	2	0	1	10	1	5	5	5	7	1	2	1	3	4	4	4	8	0
	Nonfragile	12	9	19	3	2	2	1	1	30	1	19	2	25	7	2	9	0	2	3	10	0	11	6	4	3
Resource status	Not resource-rich	9	5	20	4	2	1	2	1	26	1	18	2	21	3	3	11	0	1	2	6	0	9	6	4	2
	Potentially resource-rich	7	4	5	2	1	3	3	1	1	2	10	1	7	3	3	3	1	1	2	6	0	6	2	9	0
	Resource-rich, non-oil	20	15	25	3	0	0	1	3	34	0	27	1	29	6	3	9	0	4	5	16	0	15	9	1	5
	Resource-rich, oil	5	3	4	0	0	8	3	1	0	0	5	0	0	11	3	6	0	1	1	2	8	1	2	11	2

(continued next page)

Table F.2 (Continued)

Country groups		Overall	Cash transfer	School feeding	Public works	Education interventions	Health interventions	Emergency	Food-based	Social pensions	Other	Children	Working age	Elderly	Households/families	Special groups	Categorical	Geographical	Geographical and categorical	Poverty	Poverty and geographical/categorical	N/A	Cash	Food	Other in-kind	Mix
Drought exposure	High	18	10	22	5	0	3	6	4	35	1	26	2	23	12	7	16	0	3	1	10	6	11	9	11	6
	Medium	12	8	23	3	1	2	5	0	15	1	18	1	14	3	5	4	0	2	3	10	1	11	6	1	1
	Low	5	2	7	1	3	0	0	1	1	0	8	2	1	4	1	3	0	1	3	5	0	4	2	6	1
	N/A	6	5	7	2	3	3	6	4	26	1	10	8	28	5	1	11	0	2	3	2	2	9	2	4	1
Overall development of social safety net system	No social safety net	23	7	22	1	0	0	0	8	0	0	33	2	0	0	0	22	0	8	0	0	0	15	14	0	0
	No solid plans	4	2	21	1	1	6	6	2	15	1	15	1	14	7	3	7	0	0	1	3	0	3	5	8	2
	In progress	8	3	14	2	2	2	2	3	8	0	12	2	4	5	3	6	0	2	3	6	0	6	5	6	1
	In place	24	20	18	2	4	4	0	2	64	1	26	1	60	8	4	16	0	3	2	6	6	22	6	1	6
Social protection strategy or policy	Not present	17	14	22	2	2	4	4	4	77	0	26	1	73	12	3	25	0	0	3	5	0	14	8	4	8
	In progress	7	4	6	2	0	6	6	0	0	1	6	0	0	9	5	5	1	1	3	4	6	8	4	11	1
	Present	10	5	16	3	2	8	5	0	9	1	16	2	6	4	4	5	0	1	1	8	1	9	5	4	5
Organizations responsible for policy setting, oversight, and coordination	Social ministry	10	6	17	4	2	1	3	3	13	1	17	2	9	3	3	6	1	2	2	9	0	9	5	5	1
	Central institution	10	5	28	3	1	1	2	2	11	0	21	2	11	6	3	7	0	3	3	7	1	8	8	3	1
	Other sectoral ministry	27	13	0	5	1	0	0	9	115	0	36	2	90	4	4	19	0	0	4	15	0	20	9	0	9
	Other arrangements	4	1	4	1	0	0	5	5	0	1	5	0	0	3	5	2	0	1	0	3	1	2	3	5	1
	N/A	10	10	8	1	2	8	1	0	26	0	7	0	28	15	3	15	0	0	2	3	5	9	2	10	5

(continued next page)

Table F.2 (Continued)

Country groups		Overall	Program type – Cash transfer	School feeding	Public works	Education interventions	Health interventions	Emergency	Food-based	Social pensions	Other	Life cycle – Children	Working age	Elderly	Households/families	Special groups	Targeting method – Categorical	Geographical	Geographical and categorical	Poverty	Poverty and geographical/categorical	N/A	Nature of benefits – Cash	Food	Other in-kind	Mix
Social registry status	Not planned	8	7	7	0	5	0	1	0	33	1	4	1	38	5	3	6	0	1	4	4	0	11	0	3	1
	Planned	10	3	12	5	0	3	4	3	9	0	16	3	5	5	4	8	1	2	2	6	3	0	7	2	2
	Operating on small scale	5	3	19	1	1	2	2	3	8	0	15	1	8	5	2	4	0	3	2	3	2	4	6	4	1
	Operating on medium scale	18	17	17	1	2	0	0	1	42	2	23	0	42	1	3	7	0	0	0	20	0	21	3	2	2
	Operating on large scale	11	6	16	5	3	4	1	0	25	1	14	2	11	9	1	8	0	1	4	10	1	12	4	7	0
	N/A	38	48	53	0	0	0	0	0	112	0	35	0	112	32	5	66	0	0	0	0	0	22	12	0	32
Measures to deal with crises	Limited or no measures	7	14	14	2	1	4	5	1	8	0	13	1	8	7	5	10	0	2	0	4	4	5	6	10	1
	Moderate	14	8	18	4	2	1	0	2	29	1	18	2	23	5	1	6	0	1	3	12	0	13	6	2	2
	Strong	38	48	53	0	0	0	0	0	112	0	35	0	112	32	5	66	0	0	0	0	0	22	12	0	32
	N/A	6	3	10	2	0	1	1	1	3	2	13	2	2	3	1	1	0	3	3	5	1	4	4	3	1
Development partner involvement	Yes	8	4	16	3	1	2	3	1	8	1	14	2	5	5	3	6	0	2	2	6	2	6	5	6	2
	No	20	17	16	2	3	3	3	2	61	1	23	1	57	9	3	17	0	0	2	14	0	19	5	4	6

Source: ASPIRE (Atlas of Social Protection Indicators of Resilience and Equity) (database), Administrative data, World Bank, Washington, DC, http://datatopics.worldbank.org/aspire/.
Note: See methodology in appendixes B.2 and B.3. Due to data limitations, estimates do not include information on Mali. Benin has several school feeding, public works, education, and health programs, which were not included in the averages due to data limitations.

Spending on Social Safety Net Programs

Table G.1 Spending on Social Safety Nets and Other Sectors, Tax Revenue, and Humanitarian Assistance, by Country
% of GDP

Country name	Social safety net spending	Labor market spending	Contributory public pension spending		Energy subsidies	Health Spending	Education spending	Military expenditures	Humanitarian assistance	Government total Spending	Government total tax revenue	Government balance
			Pensions	Other social insurance								
Angola	0.4		1.7		0.7	2.1	3.5	2.9	0.0	29.7	24.8	−2.9
Benin	2.8		1.5		0.0	2.3	4.4	1.1	0.1	24.4	16.9	−6.7
Botswana	1.2				0.6	3.2	9.6	3.4	0.0	37.5	33.4	−9.6
Burkina Faso	1.8	0.1	0.8	0.0	0.9	2.6	4.1	1.2	0.5	21.9	19.6	−1.6
Burundi	2.3				.	4.0	5.4	2.2	1.3	28.5	22.9	−4.7
Cabo Verde	2.4	0.0	0.8	0.2	2.2	3.6	5.0	0.6	0.2	30.0	26.2	−2.3
Cameroon	0.1	0.0			2.2	0.9	3.0	1.6	0.2	20.5	17.9	−2.3
Central African Republic	2.6				.	2.1	1.2	2.6	21.6	14.9	14.3	−0.1
Chad	0.4				.	2.0	2.8	2.8	1.5	17.1	12.2	−4.6
Comoros	0.7		0.8		.	2.2	4.3		0.2	27.3	31.6	4.4
Congo, Dem. Rep.	0.7				1.9	1.6	2.2	1.3	1.6	14.7	14.6	0.2
Congo, Rep.	0.0				4.5	4.2	6.2	7.2	0.1	46.2	27.8	−18.1
Côte d'Ivoire	0.1	0.2	0.7		2.6	1.7	5.0	1.2	0.2	24.1	21.1	−1.4
Ethiopia	0.7				1.2	2.9	4.5	0.7	1.0	18.6	16.1	−2.1
Gabon	0.2		0.0	0.0	0.0	2.4	2.7	1.4	0.0	22.6	21.3	0.8
Gambia, The	n/a		0.0									

(continued next page)

Table G.1 (Continued)

Country name	Social safety net spending	Labor market spending	Contributory public pension spending		Energy subsidies	Health Spending	Education spending	Military expenditures	Humanitarian assistance	Government total Spending	Government total tax revenue	Government balance
			Pensions	Other social insurance								
Ghana	0.6	0.0	0.9		0.0	2.1	6.2	0.4	0.0	23.9	19.2	1.8
Guinea	1.5				.	2.7	3.2	2.5	1.1	27.8	19.0	−7.8
Guinea-Bissau	0.0		0.6		.	1.1	2.2	1.6	0.6	26.8	19.8	−6.3
Kenya	0.4				0.2	3.5	5.3	1.3	0.6	27.8	19.5	−5.6
Lesotho	6.9		1.0		1.4	8.1	11.4	1.8	0.2	59.0	59.2	1.1
Liberia	3.0	0.0	0.2		0.0	3.2	2.8	0.6	8.3	43.7	32.3	−9.7
Madagascar	0.3		1.4		1.0	1.5	2.1	0.6	0.2	15.1	11.8	−2.5
Malawi	1.4				2.4	6.0	5.6	0.6	0.9	28.9	23.8	−1.8
Mali	0.6	0.0	1.9	0.7	1.0	1.6	3.7	2.6	1.7	20.9	19.1	−1.2
Mauritania	0.8				1.0	1.9	2.9	3.0	1.0	32.6	29.2	−2.3
Mauritius	3.3		1.8	0.0	.	2.4	4.9	0.2	0.0	26.1	22.7	−1.0
Mozambique	1.0	0.0	1.4		5.6	3.9	6.5	1.0	0.2	35.4	28.0	−6.1
Namibia	3.0		1.5	0.2	0.9	5.4	8.3	4.4	0.0	42.3	34.2	−6.5
Niger	0.6			0.0	.	3.2	6.7	2.2	2.7	32.7	23.6	−8.5
Nigeria	0.3	0.0			0.1	0.9	3.1	0.4	0.0	11.0	7.2	−2.7
Rwanda	1.2				0.3	2.9	3.6	1.2	0.3	28.1	25.0	−2.3
São Tomé and Príncipe	0.0				.	3.6	3.8		0.5	34.2	28.0	−5.5
Senegal	0.9	0.0	1.8	0.2	1.6	2.4	7.4	1.7	0.2	29.9	25.1	−2.8
Seychelles	2.5	0.0	0.9	0.0	.	3.1	3.6	1.3		32.8	34.7	5.0

(continued next page)

| Country name | Social safety net spending | Labor market spending | Contributory public pension spending | | Energy subsidies | Health Spending | Education spending | Military expenditures | Humanitarian assistance | Government total Spending | Government total tax revenue | Government balance |
			Pensions	Other social insurance								
Sierra Leone	0.7	0.0	0.0		.	1.9	2.7	0.8	8.1	20.1	15.7	−3.6
Somalia	0.0				0.0		1.3	0.0	8.9			
South Africa	3.3	0.0		0.0	0.7	4.2	6.0	1.1	0.0	33.5	29.6	−0.6
South Sudan	10.1				.	1.1	1.8	12.8	11.3	50.2	25.0	−24.2
Sudan	0.7		0.5			1.8	2.2	2.8	0.6	12.9	11.0	−1.1
Swaziland	1.5	0.1	1.8		.	7.0	7.0	1.8	0.3	33.3	27.7	−4.4
Tanzania	0.5		1.6		1.9	2.6	3.5	1.1	0.1	18.0	14.8	−1.6
Togo	0.2		0.0	0.0	.	2.0	5.2	1.9	0.1	28.5	21.8	−4.9
Uganda	0.8	0.1	0.6	0.0	1.2	1.8	2.2	1.6	0.4	18.1	15.4	−1.0
Zambia	0.2	0.0	0.4		7.1	2.8	1.1	1.5	0.0	27.2	18.2	−6.3
Zimbabwe	0.4	0.0	3.8		18.8	2.5	8.4	2.2	0.5	28.6	27.5	0.0

Source: Social protection spending: ASPIRE (Atlas of Social Protection Indicators of Resilience and Equity) (database), Administrative data, World Bank, Washington, DC, http://datatopics.worldbank.org/aspire/. WDI for spending on education, health, and the military. IMF WEO for government energy subsidies, total spending, and tax revenue. Humanitarian assistance from Development Initiatives.

Note: See methodology in appendix B.4. Data are not available for The Gambia. Benin has several school feeding, public works, education, and health programs, which were not included due to data limitations.

Table G.2 Spending on Social Safety Nets, by Program Typology and Country

% of GDP, unless otherwise specified

Country name	Total	Total (share of total government spending)	Program type									Life cycle					Targeting method						Nature of benefits			
			Cash transfer programs	School feeding programs	Public works programs	Education interventions	Health interventions	Emergency programs	Food-based programs	Social pensions	Other programs	Children	Working age population	The elderly	Households/families	Special groups	Categorical	Geographical	Geographical and categorical	Poverty	Poverty and geographical/categorical	N/A	Cash	Food	Other in-kind	Mix
Angola	0.4	1.9	0.2	0.0		0.2			0.0			0.2	0.1	0.2	0.1	0.4	0.4		0.0	0.1		0.0	0.2	0.0	0.1	0.2
Benin	2.8	13.3	2.8				0.0				0.0	0.0	0.0	2.7			2.3	0.0			0.4		2.7	0.0	0.0	0.1
Botswana	1.2	3.6	0.3		0.5				0.2			0.2	0.5	0.3	0.3	0.0	0.4		0.3	0.3	0.5		0.7	0.0	0.0	0.5
Burkina Faso	1.8	7.6	0.1	0.3	0.3	0.2			0.4	0.3	0.0	0.9	0.3	0.6	0.0	0.0	0.2			0.1	0.8		0.6	0.8	0.4	0.0
Burundi	2.3	10.3	0.1	0.1	1.0	0.3	0.2	0.1	0.0		0.6	1.0	0.3	0.0	0.3	0.1	2.2		0.3		0.0	1.3	1.3	0.6	0.4	0.3
Cabo Verde	2.4	8.0	0.2	0.2	0.0	0.1	0.6	0.2	0.0		0.4	0.3	0.2	1.1	0.9	0.0	0.5				0.9	1.1	1.1	0.2	1.0	0.2
Cameroon	0.1	0.4	0.1		0.0	0.0	0.0				0.0	0.0	0.1		0.0		0.0	0.0	0.1	0.0	0.0	1.1	1.1	0.0	0.0	0.1
Central African Republic	2.6	20.3			1.0	0.0	0.0		0.0		0.5	0.4	1.0		0.1	1.1	0.9	0.3	0.4	0.1	0.9	0.0	1.1	0.0	1.4	0.1
Chad	0.4	2.7	0.0	0.0	0.0			1.1	0.0	1.0		0.1	0.0		0.2	0.0	0.1		0.4		0.2		0.0	0.0	0.0	0.1
Comoros	0.7	2.2	0.0	0.0	0.7			0.0	0.3			0.0	0.7		0.7				0.0		0.7	0.7	0.1	0.1	0.0	0.0
Congo, Dem. Rep.	0.7	5.1	0.0	0.0	0.0			0.7				0.0	0.0			0.7					0.7		0.0	0.7	0.0	0.2

(continued next page)

Table G.2 (Continued)

Country name	Total	Total (share of total government spending)	Program type									Life cycle					Targeting method						Nature of benefits			
			Cash transfer programs	School feeding programs	Public works programs	Education interventions	Health interventions	Emergency programs	Food-based programs	Social pensions	Other programs	Children	Working age population	The elderly	Households/families	Special groups	Categorical	Geographical	Geographical and categorical	Poverty	Poverty and geographical/categorical	N/A	Cash	Food	Other in-kind	Mix
Congo, Rep.	0.0	0.1	0.0								0.0	0.0			0.0		0.0	0.0				0.0	0.0	0.0		
Côte d'Ivoire	0.1	0.3	0.1	0.0								0.1			0.0		0.1						0.1	0.0		
Ethiopia	0.7	3.9			0.7						0.0		0.7							0.1	0.6			0.1		0.6
Gabon	0.2	0.9	0.1				0.1					0.1			0.1		0.2						0.1			0.1
The Gambia	n/a	n/a																								
Ghana	0.6	2.2	0.1	0.1	0.0	0.3	0.0				0.0	0.4			0.1	0.1	0.3	0.1		0.1	0.2	0.0	0.3	0.1	0.1	0.1
Guinea	1.5	6.8	0.1		0.3	1.1	0.1					1.1	0.3		0.1		1.1				0.3		0.3			1.1
Guinea-Bissau	0.0	0.1		0.0				0.0	0.0			0.0			0.0			0.0	0.0					0.0	0.0	
Kenya	0.4	1.5	0.2	0.0				0.0	0.0	0.1		0.1		0.1	0.1	0.1	0.0	0.0	0.0	0.1	0.2		0.3	0.0	0.0	0.1
Lesotho	6.9	13.8	1.9	0.7		2.5				1.8		5.1		1.8						2.3	3.8		3.7	0.7	0.2	2.3
Liberia	3.0	8.2	0.1	0.8	1.0				0.5		0.5	1.1	1.0		0.8	0.1	0.4	0.1		0.1	0.9	1.4	0.9	1.3	0.6	0.2

(continued next page)

Table G.2 (Continued)

Country name	Total	Total (share of total government spending)	Program type									Life cycle					Targeting method						Nature of benefits			
			Cash transfer programs	School feeding programs	Public works programs	Education interventions	Health interventions	Emergency programs	Food-based programs	Social pensions	Other programs	Children	Working age population	The elderly	Households/families	Special groups	Categorical	Geographical	Geographical and categorical	Poverty	Poverty and geographical/categorical	N/A	Cash	Food	Other in-kind	Mix
Madagascar	0.3	1.8	0.2	0.0	0.0			0.0	0.0		0.0	0.2	0.0		0.1	0.0		0.1		0.0	0.0	0.2	0.2	0.0		0.0
Malawi	1.4	5.0		1.0	0.4							1.0	0.4				1.0			0.4	0.2		0.4	1.0		
Mali	0.6	2.7	0.1	0.1	0.1			0.2	0.1		0.1	0.2	0.1			0.2	0.2	0.1	0.2	0.0	0.1		0.1	0.2	0.3	0.0
Mauritania	0.8	2.8	0.0					0.8							0.0	0.8		0.2	0.0	0.1		0.8		0.8		
Mauritius	3.3	13.2	0.2							3.1	0.0	0.2		3.1			3.3						3.3			0.0
Mozambique	1.0	3.2	0.4	0.1	0.1	0.1			0.1		0.2	0.3	0.1		0.6		0.3		0.2	0.0	0.5		0.6	0.2	0.2	0.0
Namibia	3.0	7.1	2.0	0.1						0.9		0.3	0.0	1.6	0.0	1.0	3.0						2.9	0.1	0.0	0.0
Niger	0.6	2.2	0.1	0.0	0.0			0.1	0.3			0.2	0.0		0.3	0.1			0.2	0.0	0.2	0.2	0.1	0.4		
Nigeria	0.3	2.6	0.0		0.3								0.3		0.0		0.3						0.0		0.2	0.2
Rwanda	1.2	4.7	0.8		0.1			0.3			0.0	0.0	0.1	0.1	0.7	0.3	0.3			0.5	0.4		0.9	0.0	0.0	0.3
São Tomé and Príncipe	0.0	0.1	0.0							0.0		0.0		0.0									0.0	0.0	0.2	0.0
Senegal	0.9	3.1	0.2	0.0				0.2			0.0	0.5	0.0		0.3	0.2	0.6			0.0	0.3		0.7	0.0	0.2	0.0

Table G.2 (Continued)

Country name	Total	Total (share of total government spending)	Cash transfer programs	School feeding programs	Public works programs	Education interventions	Health interventions	Emergency programs	Food-based programs	Social pensions	Other programs	Children	Working age population	The elderly	Households/families	Special groups	Categorical	Geographical	Geographical and categorical	Poverty	Poverty and geographical/categorical	N/A	Cash	Food	Other in-kind	Mix
																							Nature of benefits			
Seychelles	2.5	6.5	0.6			0.1				1.7	0.1	0.1	0.1	1.8	0.3	0.3	2.1			0.3	0.0		2.4		0.1	
Sierra Leone	0.7	3.0	0.2	0.3		0.0					0.1	0.4	0.0	0.0	0.2	0.0	0.5			0.0	0.1	0.1	0.2	0.4	0.1	0.0
Somalia	0.0	0.0	0.0					0.0							0.0					0.0	0.0		0.0			0.0
South Africa	3.3	10.0	1.7	0.1	0.2				0.0	1.2	0.0	1.4	0.2	1.2	0.0	0.5	0.0			0.0	3.3	0.0	3.2	0.1	0.0	0.0
South Sudan	10.1	4.7			0.0			10.0					0.0			10.0	10.0				0.0				10.0	0.0
Sudan	0.7	5.8	0.2	0.0	0.0	0.0	0.3	0.1	0.0		0.0	0.1	0.0		0.5	0.1	0.1	0.0		0.0	0.2	0.3	0.1	0.0	0.4	0.1
Swaziland	1.5	4.0		0.1	0.1	0.6	0.2	0.0		0.4	0.0	0.7	0.1	0.4	0.2	0.0	1.1		0.1	0.2	0.1		1.1	0.1	0.3	
Tanzania	0.5	2.5	0.2	0.1	0.1			0.0			0.0	0.1	0.1		0.2	0.0		0.0	0.1	0.3	0.0		0.3	0.1	0.0	
Togo	0.2	0.5		0.0			0.1	0.0				0.0			0.1		0.1		0.0	0.0			0.0	0.0	0.1	
Uganda	0.8	4.2	0.1		0.2	0.1			0.0	0.1	0.2	0.4	0.3	0.1	0.0	0.0	0.2	0.0	0.0	0.0	0.8	0.0	0.3	0.0	0.2	0.2
Zambia	0.2	1.0	0.0	0.0		0.2					0.0	0.2	0.0		0.0	0.0	0.2	0.0	0.0	0.0	0.0	0.0	0.0	0.0	0.2	0.0
Zimbabwe	0.4	1.5	0.0	0.0	0.1	0.0	0.0	0.2			0.0	0.1	0.0	0.0	0.0	0.2	0.0	0.2	0.0	0.0	0.0	0.0	0.1	0.0	0.3	0.1

Source: ASPIRE (Atlas of Social Protection Indicators of Resilience and Equity) (database), Administrative data, World Bank, Washington, DC, http://datatopics.worldbank.org/aspire/.
Note: See methodology in appendix B.4. Data are not available for The Gambia. Benin has several school feeding, public works, education, and health programs, which were not included due to data limitations.

Table G.3 Spending on Social Safety Nets, by Program Typology and Country Group

% of GDP, unless otherwise specified

Country groups		Total	Total (share of total government spending)	Program type									Life cycle					Targeting method						Nature of benefits			
				Cash transfer programs	School feeding programs	Public works programs	Education interventions	Health interventions	Emergency programs	Food-based programs	Social pensions	Other programs	Children	Working age population	The elderly	Households/families	Special groups	Categorical	Geographical	Geographical and categorical	Poverty	Poverty and geographical/categorical	N/A	Cash	Food	Other in-kind	Mix
Overall		1.2	4.6	0.3	0.1	0.2	0.0	0.1	0.0	0.1	0.2	0.1	0.4	0.2	0.3	0.2	0.1	0.5	0.0	0.1	0.1	0.4	0.1	0.7	0.2	0.2	0.1
Geography	Central Africa	0.6	3.9	0.1	0.0	0.1	0.2	0.0	0.2	0.0	0.0	0.0	0.1	0.1	0.0	0.1	0.1	0.2	0.0	0.1	0.0	0.2	0.1	0.2	0.0	0.3	0.1
	East Africa	1.6	4.2	0.2	0.1	0.2	0.1	0.0	0.6	0.0	0.0	0.2	0.2	0.2	0.3	0.1	0.2	1.2	0.0	0.0	0.0	0.2	0.0	0.7	0.1	0.7	0.1
	West Africa	1.1	4.2	0.3	0.0	0.1	0.1	0.1	0.1	0.1	0.0	0.1	0.3	0.1	0.1	0.4	0.1	0.4	0.1	0.0	0.3	0.2	0.0	0.5	0.2	0.3	0.0
	Southern Africa	3.2	7.7	1.2	0.2	0.1	0.6	0.1	0.0	0.0	0.9	0.0	1.5	0.1	1.1	0.1	0.3	1.1	0.0	0.5	0.0	1.5	0.0	2.3	0.2	0.1	0.6
Income group	Low income	1.4	4.8	0.2	0.1	0.2	0.1	0.0	0.5	0.0	0.0	0.1	0.3	0.2	0.0	0.0	0.5	0.8	0.0	0.1	0.1	0.3	0.1	0.5	0.1	0.6	0.1
	Lower middle income	1.0	3.2	0.2	0.1	0.0	0.3	0.1	0.0	0.1	0.2	0.0	0.5	0.2	0.3	0.1	0.1	0.3	0.0	0.2	0.0	0.5	0.0	0.5	0.1	0.2	0.2
	Upper middle income	2.2	6.9	0.9	0.0	0.1	0.0	0.0	0.0	0.0	1.1	0.0	0.4	0.0	1.2	0.1	0.3	1.4	0.0	0.0	0.1	0.7	0.0	2.0	0.0	0.0	0.0
	High income	2.5	6.5	0.6	0.0	0.0	0.1	0.0	0.0	0.0	1.7	0.1	0.1	0.0	1.8	0.3	0.3	2.1	0.0	0.0	0.0	0.0	0.3	2.4	0.0	0.1	0.0
Fragility	Fragile	1.4	4.2	0.1	0.1	0.2	0.0	0.0	0.7	0.0	0.0	0.0	0.2	0.2	0.0	0.2	0.7	0.9	0.0	0.1	0.0	0.3	0.0	0.3	0.2	0.8	0.2
	Nonfragile	1.4	4.8	0.1	0.1	0.1	0.2	0.0	0.1	0.1	0.4	0.1	0.5	0.1	0.4	0.2	0.1	0.6	0.0	0.1	0.0	0.5	0.1	0.9	0.1	0.2	0.2

(continued next page)

Table G.3 (Continued)

Country groups		Total	Total (share of total government spending)	Program type									Life cycle					Targeting method						Nature of benefits			
				Cash transfer programs	School feeding programs	Public works programs	Education interventions	Health interventions	Emergency programs	Food-based programs	Social pensions	Other programs	Children	Working age population	The elderly	Households/families	Special groups	Categorical	Geographical	Geographical and categorical	Poverty	Poverty and geographical/categorical	N/A	Cash	Food	Other in-kind	Mix
Resource status	Not resource-rich	2.1	5.4	0.4	0.1	0.2	0.2	0.1	0.6	0.1	0.4	0.1	0.5	0.2	0.4	0.3	0.6	1.3	0.0	0.1	0.1	0.1	0.4	1.0	0.2	0.7	0.2
	Potentially resource-rich	0.8	4.7	0.2	0.2	0.2	0.2	0.0	0.1	0.0	0.0	0.1	0.3	0.2	0.0	0.2	0.1	0.3	0.0	0.1	0.1	0.3	0.0	0.4	0.1	0.3	0.0
	Resource-rich, non-oil	1.5	5.0	0.4	0.1	0.2	0.1	0.0	0.2	0.1	0.2	0.1	0.5	0.2	0.3	0.2	0.4	0.5	0.0	0.1	0.0	0.7	0.0	0.8	0.2	0.4	0.1
	Resource-rich, oil	0.3	1.8	0.0	0.0	0.0	0.1	0.0	0.1	0.0	0.1	0.0	0.1	0.1	0.0	0.1	0.0	0.1	0.0	0.0	0.1	0.1	0.1	0.1	0.0	0.1	0.1
Drought exposure	High	2.4	5.0	0.5	0.1	0.1	0.3	0.0	1.1	0.0	0.3	0.0	0.7	0.1	0.3	0.2	1.1	1.4	0.0	0.3	0.0	0.6	0.1	0.8	0.2	1.2	0.3
	Medium	1.0	3.8	0.4	0.1	0.1	0.1	0.1	0.0	0.0	0.1	0.0	0.1	0.1	0.1	0.3	0.1	0.4	0.0	0.0	0.1	0.4	0.1	0.7	0.2	0.2	0.3
	Low	0.9	4.9	0.4	0.1	0.2	0.1	0.0	0.0	0.0	0.0	0.0	0.3	0.3	0.0	0.1	0.2	0.4	0.0	0.0	0.1	0.3	0.1	0.4	0.1	0.3	0.1
	N/A	1.4	4.7	0.2	0.1	0.2	0.0	0.1	0.0	0.0	0.0	0.1	0.2	0.2	0.0	0.3	0.0	0.1	0.0	0.1	0.0	0.3	0.1	1.0	0.2	0.2	0.0
Overall development of social safety net system	No social safety net program	n/a																									
	No solid plans	0.6	2.9	0.1	0.0	0.1	0.1	0.1	0.0	0.1	0.0	0.1	0.2	0.1	0.1	0.1	0.1	0.2	0.0	0.2	0.0	0.3	0.1	0.3	0.0	0.2	0.0
	In progress	1.4	4.5	0.3	0.1	0.2	0.2	0.2	0.4	0.0	0.1	0.1	0.4	0.2	0.1	0.3	0.3	0.7	0.0	0.0	0.0	0.4	0.1	0.5	0.2	0.6	0.1
	In place	2.0	6.4	0.7	0.1	0.1	0.1	0.0	0.0	0.0	1.0	0.1	0.3	0.1	1.1	0.2	0.2	1.2	0.0	0.0	0.0	0.6	0.1	1.7	0.1	0.1	0.1

(continued next page)

Table G.3 (Continued)

Country groups		Total	Total (share of total government spending)	Cash transfer programs	School feeding programs	Public works programs	Education interventions	Health interventions	Emergency programs	Food-based programs	Social pensions	Other programs	Children	Working age population	The elderly	Households/families	Special groups	Categorical	Geographical	Geographical and categorical	Poverty	Poverty and geographical/categorical	N/A	Cash	Food	Other in-kind	Mix
				Program type →									Life cycle →					Targeting method →						Nature of benefits →			
Social protection strategy or policy	Not present	1.7	5.1	0.5	0.0	0.1	0.2	0.0	0.0	0.0	0.0	0.0	0.2	1.0	0.2	0.1	0.2	1.5	0.0	0.1	0.1	0.0	0.0	1.5	0.0	0.1	0.1
	In progress	0.7	5.1	0.1	0.1	0.2	0.1	0.1	0.1	0.1	0.0	0.1	0.1	0.2	0.1	0.1	0.3	0.2	0.0	0.1	0.0	0.3	0.1	0.2	0.0	0.0	0.5
	Present	1.5	4.3	0.1	0.1	0.2	0.2	0.0	0.0	0.0	0.0	0.1	0.2	0.1	0.2	0.3	0.4	0.7	0.0	0.1	0.0	0.5	0.1	0.6	0.2	0.5	0.1
Organizations responsible for policy setting, oversight, and coordination	Social ministry	1.8	4.9	0.3	0.1	0.2	0.2	0.0	0.6	0.1	0.2	0.1	0.5	0.2	0.2	0.5	0.6	0.8	0.0	0.2	0.1	0.6	0.1	0.7	0.2	0.7	0.2
	Central institution	1.0	4.3	0.4	0.2	0.1	0.1	0.0	0.0	0.1	0.0	0.1	0.2	0.2	0.0	0.1	0.3	0.0	0.2	0.1	0.1	0.2	0.0	0.2	0.3	0.1	0.2
	Other sectoral ministry	2.3	8.4	0.0	0.0	0.0	0.1	0.1	0.1	0.0	1.7	0.1	0.2	0.2	1.7	0.2	0.1	1.9	0.0	0.0	0.0	0.1	0.2	2.0	0.0	0.0	0.0
	Other arrangements	0.9	3.9	0.1	0.1	0.1	0.1	0.0	0.0	0.2	0.0	0.1	0.1	0.1	0.0	0.2	0.4	0.4	0.0	0.2	0.2	0.2	0.0	0.1	0.1	0.0	0.1
	N/A	1.0	3.5	0.0	0.1	0.0	0.3	0.0	0.1	0.0	0.3	0.0	0.1	0.1	0.2	0.2	0.3	0.7	0.0	0.0	0.2	0.4	0.0	0.8	0.0	0.0	0.2
Social registry status	Not planned	1.1	4.0	0.2	0.0	0.0	0.0	0.0	0.0	0.0	0.0	0.0	0.0	0.6	0.0	0.6	0.3	0.7	0.0	0.1	0.0	0.3	0.1	0.8	0.0	0.2	0.0
	Planned	1.7	5.2	0.1	0.1	0.3	0.1	0.0	0.8	0.0	0.6	0.1	0.4	0.3	0.6	0.2	0.4	1.1	0.0	0.1	0.0	0.4	0.0	0.8	0.2	0.2	0.1
	Operating on small scale	0.6	2.6	0.1	0.1	0.1	0.1	0.0	0.1	0.0	0.0	0.1	0.2	0.0	0.0	0.2	0.8	0.2	0.0	0.1	0.0	0.7	0.0	0.3	0.1	0.2	0.0
	Operating on medium scale	1.9	7.7	0.0	0.0	0.1	0.0	0.1	0.0	0.1	0.9	0.0	0.4	0.1	0.9	0.6	0.1	1.1	0.0	0.0	0.1	0.7	0.1	1.9	0.0	0.0	0.0
	Operating on large scale	1.8	4.9	0.1	0.0	0.0	0.4	0.1	0.1	0.1	0.4	0.1	0.9	0.0	0.4	0.3	0.1	0.3	0.0	0.4	0.0	0.8	0.2	0.1	0.1	0.2	0.4
	N/A	3.0	7.1	2.0	0.1	0.1	0.0	0.0	0.0	0.0	0.9	0.0	0.3	0.0	1.6	0.0	1.0	3.0	0.0	0.0	0.0	0.0	0.0	2.9	0.1	0.0	0.0

(continued next page)

Table G.3 (Continued)

Country groups		Program type											Life cycle					Targeting method						Nature of benefits			
		Total	Total (share of total government spending)	Cash transfer programs	School feeding programs	Public works programs	Education interventions	Health interventions	Emergency programs	Food-based programs	Social pensions	Other programs	Children	Working age population	The elderly	Households/families	Special groups	Categorical	Geographical	Geographical and categorical	Poverty	Poverty and geographical/categorical	N/A	Cash	Food	Other in-kind	Mix
Measures to deal with crises	Limited or no measures	1.4	4.1	0.1	0.0	0.1	0.1	0.8	0.0	0.0	0.1	0.1	0.2	0.1	0.1	0.2	0.8	0.9	0.0	0.0	0.0	0.3	0.1	0.3	0.0	1.0	0.0
	Moderate	1.5	4.9	0.3	0.2	0.2	0.1	0.0	0.0	0.1	0.4	0.1	0.6	0.2	0.4	0.2	0.1	0.6	0.0	0.2	0.1	0.6	0.0	1.0	0.2	0.2	0.2
	Strong	0.9	4.3	0.5	0.1	0.1	0.0	0.0	0.0	0.1	0.0	0.0	0.2	0.0	0.2	0.5	0.0	0.4	0.0	0.1	0.1	0.2	0.0	0.6	0.2	0.1	0.1
	N/A	3.0	7.1	2.0	0.1	0.0	0.0	0.0	0.0	0.0	0.0	0.0	0.3	0.0	1.6	0.0	1.0	3.0	0.0	0.0	0.0	0.0	0.0	2.9	0.1	0.0	0.0
Development partner involvement	Yes	1.3	5.8	0.2	0.1	0.2	0.0	0.0	0.4	0.1	0.0	0.1	0.4	0.2	0.1	0.2	0.4	0.7	0.0	0.1	0.1	0.2	0.4	0.5	0.2	0.5	0.1
	No	1.9	4.3	0.6	0.0	0.1	0.0	0.0	0.0	0.0	0.9	0.1	0.3	0.1	1.0	0.2	0.3	1.1	0.0	0.0	0.1	0.6	0.1	1.5	0.0	0.2	0.1

Source: ASPIRE (Atlas of Social Protection Indicators of Resilience and Equity) (database), Administrative data, World Bank, Washington, DC, http://datatopics.worldbank.org/aspire/.

Note: See methodology in appendix B.4. Due to data limitations, averages do not include The Gambia. Benin has several school feeding, public works, education, and health programs, which were not included in the averages due to data limitations.

Table G.4 Distribution of Spending on Social Safety Nets, by Program Typology and Country

% of social safety net spending

Country name	Program type									Life cycle					Targeting method						Nature of benefits			
	Cash transfer programs	School feeding programs	Public works programs	Education interventions	Health interventions	Emergency programs	Food-based programs	Social pensions	Other programs	Children	Working age population	The elderly	Households/families	Special groups	Categorical	Geographical	Geographical and categorical	Poverty	Poverty and geographical/categorical	N/A	Cash	Food	Other in-kind	Mix
Angola	41	6		36			1		16	42	3	41	18	1	99				1		36	7	16	41
Benin	100			0					0	0	3	97			82	0		3		15	97	0	1	2
Botswana	26		37				14	22		0	14	37	26	1	36			25	39		59	1		40
Burkina Faso	5	19	16	13	3	1	25		19	49	18	0	33	1	14		16		26	44	32	44	23	2
Burundi	4	3	42	11	9	3	25		2	39	42	14		5	98				1	1	58	28	15	
Cabo Verde	7	6	0	2	23		1	43	18	11	6	44	39	0	19	1	44		36		45	7	41	6
Cameroon	89		4	4	3					4	61		35		9	1	53		33	3	36	3		61
Central African Republic		39				41	2		18	17	39		3	41	35	11	15	2	37		42	2	54	2
Chad	9	3	5			11	71			30	5		54	11	26		4		50	19	13	28	11	48
Comoros	1	99									99		1						100		100			
Congo, Dem. Rep.			5			95					5			95					100			5	95	
Congo, Rep.	100												100						100		100			
Cote d'Ivoire	91	9								9	91				9				91		0	0	0	91

(continued next page)

Table G.4 (Continued)

Country name	Program type									Life cycle					Targeting method						Nature of benefits			
	Cash transfer programs	School feeding programs	Public works programs	Education interventions	Health interventions	Emergency programs	Food-based programs	Social pensions	Other programs	Children	Working age population	The elderly	Households/families	Special groups	Categorical	Geographical	Geographical and categorical	Poverty	Poverty and geographical/categorical	N/A	Cash	Food	Other in-kind	Mix
Ethiopia			100							100					100						10			90
Gabon	28	72								28			72					10		90	28	72		
Gambia, The																								
Ghana	21	24	1	43	7					68	12		20		45			17	34	4	48	24	18	11
Guinea	5	18		73	4					73	18		9		77				23		23	77		
Guinea-Bissau	47				53					47			53		100						47	53		
Kenya	47	5	7	4	11	2	24			33	7	24	21	15	2	11	4	30	52		75	10	15	
Lesotho	27	10		36				27		73		27				11	34		56		54	10	2	34
Liberia	5	26	33				17		15	37	33		27	3	13	4	31	4	48		32	44	19	5
Madagascar	84	13	0				1		1	75	0		24	1			38	0	62		84	13	2	
Malawi		71	29							71			29		71				29		29	71		
Mali	12	9	12			40	17		10	26	12		22	40	29	9	34	6	13	8	18	38	44	0
Mauritania	1						99					99	1			100					1		99	
Mauritius	7							92	1	7		92	1		99			1			99	1		

(continued next page)

Table G.4 (Continued)

Country name	Program type									Life cycle					Targeting method						Nature of benefits			
	Cash transfer programs	School feeding programs	Public works programs	Education interventions	Health interventions	Emergency programs	Food-based programs	Social pensions	Other programs	Children	Working age population	The elderly	Households/families	Special groups	Categorical	Geographical	Geographical and categorical	Poverty	Poverty and geographical/categorical	N/A	Cash	Food	Other in-kind	Mix
Mozambique	41	6	13	9			11		20	27	14		59		31		17	1	51		61	17	20	1
Namibia	68	2						29		10	0	53	1	35	100			1			96	2	0	1
Niger	10	4	2			25	60			30	2		44	25			28	1	37	34	12	63	25	
Nigeria	2		98							1	98		2		97				3		6			94
Rwanda	66		10			24				1	10	7	58	24	25			42	33		77			23
São Tomé and Príncipe	37							63		37		63			100						100			
Senegal	24	3		44	10	16			2	50	3		31	16	63		3	0	34		69	1	26	4
Seychelles	24			4		2	70		2	4		71	14	10	87			12	1		98		2	
Sierra Leone	21	47		5			10		16	62	1	0	34	3	73			1	19	8	23	57	19	1
Somalia	100												100						100		1			99
South Africa	53	4	6				0	37	0	42	6	37	0	14	0			0	99		96	4	0	0
South Sudan	0		0		100						0	0	100		100				0		0		100	
Sudan	29	2	1	3	53	10	2		1	13	1		76	10	14		4	7	25	53	22	4	64	11
Swaziland	2	5	4	43	13	3		27	3	49	4	28	16	3	76		4	11	9		76	5	19	

(continued next page)

Table G.4 (Continued)

Country name	Program type									Life cycle					Targeting method						Nature of benefits			
	Cash transfer programs	School feeding programs	Public works programs	Education interventions	Health interventions	Emergency programs	Food-based programs	Social pensions	Other programs	Children	Working age population	The elderly	Households/families	Special groups	Categorical	Geographical	Geographical and categorical	Poverty	Poverty and geographical/categorical	N/A	Cash	Food	Other in-kind	Mix
Tanzania	54	29	13			4	1		0	30	13		54	4	0		30	70	1		66	30		4
Togo	3	21			67		9			30			70		50		23	28			3	30		67
Uganda	16		23	17			4	9	31	51	34	9	5	1		0	3	0	96	0	38	4	31	27
Zambia	13	6		73		0			8	79	1	0	13	7	82		13	4	4	1	12	6	81	1
Zimbabwe	28		14	9	1	46			2	33	17	0	3	46	2	55	4	4	35	0	28	4	58	9

Source: ASPIRE (Atlas of Social Protection Indicators of Resilience and Equity) (database), Administrative data, World Bank, Washington, DC, http://datatopics.worldbank.org/aspire/.

Note: Data on The Gambia are not available. Benin has several school feeding, public works, education, and health programs, which were not included due to data limitations.

Table G.5 Distribution of Spending on Social Safety Nets, by Program Typology and Country Group

% of social safety net spending

Country groups		Program type									Life cycle					Targeting method						Nature of benefits			
		Cash transfer programs	School feeding programs	Public works programs	Education interventions	Health interventions	Emergency programs	Food-based programs	Social pensions	Other programs	Children	Working age population	The elderly	Households/families	Special groups	Categorical	Geographical	Geographical and categorical	Poverty	Poverty and geographical/categorical	N/A	Cash	Food	Other in-kind	Mix
Overall		30	9	14	10	7	10	6	10	4	30	19	12	28	12	43	2	8	6	36	5	46	14	24	16
Geography	Central Africa	38	1	7	5	9	18	9	8	4	20	14	13	35	18	59	2	9	0	28	3	45	5	31	19
	East Africa	30	8	21	7	4	12	3	11	4	27	22	12	26	13	36	4	6	10	40	3	51	11	23	15
	West Africa	20	14	12	7	11	12	9	3	6	33	20	3	32	12	45	1	9	4	31	11	27	24	34	14
	Southern Africa	35	4	10	16	3	1	3	28	1	38	10	33	9	11	45	0	8	7	41	0	76	4	4	15
Income group	Low income	24	12	19	7	6	16	10	0	5	31	20	1	32	17	35	3	10	7	39	5	37	21	30	13
	Lower middle income	36	5	8	7	6	9	0	13	4	30	20	16	24	10	47	1	8	5	32	8	44	6	26	25
	Upper middle income	36	1	9	0	14	0	3	36	0	20	9	41	20	10	67	0	0	5	28	0	76	1	15	8
	High income	24	0	0	4	0	0	0	0	2	4	0	71	14	10	87	0	0	12	1	1	98	0	2	0

(continued next page)

Table G.5 (Continued)

Country groups		Program type									Life cycle					Targeting method						Nature of benefits			
		Cash transfer programs	School feeding programs	Public works programs	Education interventions	Health interventions	Emergency programs	Food-based programs	Social pensions	Other programs	Children	Working age population	The elderly	Households/families	Special groups	Categorical	Geographical	Geographical and categorical	Poverty	Poverty and geographical/categorical	N/A	Cash	Food	Other in-kind	Mix
Fragility	Fragile	26	10	15	2	11	21	10	0	5	22	21	0	36	21	40	5	8	3	39	5	30	18	36	16
	Nonfragile	31	7	13	14	5	7	4	16	4	33	17	18	23	9	46	0	8	8	32	5	54	11	20	16
Resource status	Not resource-rich	25	9	17	9	6	11	3	18	3	27	18	19	25	12	50	4	3	6	32	5	55	12	19	14
	Potentially resource-rich	30	18	11	9	9	6	5	1	11	45	14	1	34	6	29	1	16	15	37	1	46	22	27	5
	Resource-rich, non-oil	19	5	11	15	0	26	11	9	3	31	11	11	14	32	34	1	11	4	46	4	35	16	44	5
	Resource-rich, oil	49	2	13	5	16	3	9	0	2	16	32	5	45	3	57	0	7	1	25	9	30	6	21	43
Drought risk	High	21	4	8	10	6	29	12	7	3	27	8	9	22	33	36	6	9	4	34	11	36	12	39	14
	Medium	36	12	13	12	6	3	6	7	4	33	14	10	38	5	38	1	9	12	36	4	44	19	19	18
	Low	32	8	20	12	6	14	3	1	5	32	34	1	19	14	41	1	9	5	43	1	35	11	29	26
	N/A	26	9	15	1	11	1	3	30	6	21	16	30	32	2	66	0	3	2	23	6	69	12	17	1

(continued next page)

Table G.5 (Continued)

Country groups		Cash transfer programs	School feeding programs	Public works programs	Education interventions	Health interventions	Emergency programs	Food-based programs	Social pensions	Other programs	Children	Working age population	The elderly	Households/families	Special groups	Categorical	Geographical	Geographical and categorical	Poverty	Poverty and geographical/categorical	N/A	Cash	Food	Other in-kind	Mix
Overall development of social safety net system	No social safety net program	n/a																							
	No solid plans	14	8	17	13	17	22	0	4	3	26	18	10	24	22	42	8	1	3	39	8	38	10	44	9
	In progress	29	9	15	11	6	13	8	4	5	33	21	4	28	13	45	1	11	5	34	5	39	17	27	17
	In place	42	5	7	1	3	0	2	37	3	15	8	40	29	8	43	0	4	13	35	6	70	5	6	18
Social protection strategy or policy	Not present	35	1	6	7	12	0	2	34	1	17	15	38	24	7	72	0	8	7	12	0	71	1	14	15
	In progress	32	12	8	6	15	21	1	0	5	21	8	6	43	21	35	2	6	11	38	8	25	13	41	22
	Present	27	9	17	11	4	12	8	7	5	33	21	7	25	13	39	3	8	5	39	6	43	17	26	15
Organizations responsible for policy setting, oversight, and coordination	Social ministry	28	9	14	11	8	11	3	10	6	36	20	12	20	12	39	4	9	7	39	2	43	13	28	16
	Central institution	30	14	18	10	3	9	10	3	3	31	24	3	33	9	44	1	17	9	18	10	44	25	14	16
	Other sectoral ministry	17	0	19	0	0	0	7	57	1	11	19	57	13	0	68	0	0	13	20	0	79	0	1	20
	Other arrangements	9	13	6	19	1	28	20	0	4	41	6	0	24	28	44	0	1	0	48	7	15	21	52	12
	N/A	44	1	13	1	16	13	0	12	0	7	13	16	45	19	50	0	0	2	41	6	56	29	14	14

(continued next page)

345

Table G.5 (Continued)

Country groups		Program type — Cash transfer programs	School feeding programs	Public works programs	Education interventions	Health interventions	Emergency programs	Food-based programs	Social pensions	Other programs	Life cycle — Children	Working age population	The elderly	Households/families	Special groups	Targeting method — Categorical	Geographical	Geographical and categorical	Poverty	Poverty and geographical/categorical	N/A	Nature of benefits — Cash	Food	Other in-kind	Mix
Social registry status	Not planned	38	0	3	3	1	32	0	23	1	3	22	24	16	35	32	0	18	5	44	1	46	0	33	20
	Planned	16	12	22	9	12	12	2	6	6	31	21	5	30	12	46	1	7	5	35	6	24	20	35	21
	Operating on small scale	25	9	19	14	1	14	9	2	1	31	27	2	26	15	42	5	7	3	38	6	37	17	28	18
	Operating on medium scale	56	3	1	0	0	0	10	38	0	32	2	38	24	3	56	0	8	1	32	3	95	3	1	1
	Operating on large scale	36	8	4	12	16	8	0	13	3	32	6	14	39	8	31	2	10	20	30	6	59	8	23	10
	N/A	68	2	0	0	0	0	0	29	0	10	0	0	0	53	100	0	0	0	0	0	96	2	0	1
Measures to deal with crises	Limited or no measures	22	5	5	15	14	23	5	8	3	28	11	8	29	24	56	1	2	1	32	7	34	7	49	10
	Moderate	27	11	21	7	4	6	5	13	5	11	25	13	25	7	39	3	10	7	39	1	48	17	15	20
	Strong	43	9	17	6	1	1	5	3	11	32	18	8	36	6	25	1	15	14	33	12	52	21	11	17
	N/A	68	2	0	0	0	0	0	29	0	10	0	53	1	35	100	0	0	0	0	0	96	2	0	1
Development partner involvement	Yes	29	10	16	12	6	12	7	2	5	32	21	4	30	13	40	3	10	7	36	5	39	17	27	18
	No	28	1	5	1	11	11	0	40	2	17	6	42	17	18	60	0	0	0	31	5	69	1	24	5

Source: ASPIRE (Atlas of Social Protection Indicators of Resilience and Equity) (database), Administrative data, World Bank, Washington, DC, http://datatopics.worldbank.org/aspire/.
Note: See methodology in appendix B.4. This table presents the share of each category for a group, calculated as the average of the share of that category for all countries in each country group, giving equal weight to each country. Averages do not include data from The Gambia. Benin has several school feeding, public works, education, and health programs, which were not included in the averages due to data limitations.

Table G.6 Distribution of Social Safety Net Spending Aggregated within Country Groups

% of social safety net spending

Country groups		Program type									Life cycle					Targeting method						Nature of benefits			
		Cash transfer programs	School feeding programs	Public works programs	Education interventions	Health interventions	Emergency programs	Food-based programs	Social pensions	Other programs	Children	Working age population	The elderly	Households/families	Special groups	Categorical	Geographical	Geographical and categorical	Poverty	Poverty and geographical/categorical	N/A	Cash	Food	Other in-kind	Mix
Overall		41	5	16	4	2	3	2	26	2	35	27	9	12	12	20	0	2	3	71	3	74	6	7	13
Geography	Central Africa	27	3	4	18	3	29	6	0	9	25	7	20	19	29	59	1	4	0	35	1	26	6	41	27
	East Africa	18	6	20	4	8	29	2	12	3	17	21	12	21	30	45	2	4	11	31	7	36	7	40	16
	West Africa	18	6	48	12	2	5	4	1	3	21	51	1	21	5	69	0	4	3	16	8	29	11	14	46
	Southern Africa	52	4	7	1	0	0	1	36	0	41	7	37	22	14	5	0	1	1	94	0	94	4	0	2
Income group	Low income	19	7	22	6	1	34	5	1	5	20	23	1	22	34	45	1	6	8	35	5	31	12	41	16
	Lower middle income	20	5	39	13	10	5	1	5	3	20	41	9	21	5	60	1	3	6	20	10	27	6	20	47
	Upper middle income	51	4	7	0	0	0	1	38	0	40	7	39	1	14	7	0	0	1	92	0	95	4	0	1
	High income	24	0	0	4	0	0	0	70	2	4	0	71	14	10	87	0	0	12	1	0	98	0	2	0
Fragility	Fragile	12	3	5	2	13	57	5	0	3	11	6	0	25	57	20	2	4	2	23	13	15	7	73	5
	Nonfragile	43	5	17	4	1	1	1	28	1	36	17	29	7	11	20	0	2	3	73	1	78	6	4	13

(continued next page)

Table G.6 (Continued)

Country groups		Program type									Life cycle					Targeting method						Nature of benefits			
		Cash transfer programs	School feeding programs	Public works programs	Education interventions	Health interventions	Emergency programs	Food-based programs	Social pensions	Other programs	Children	Working age population	The elderly	Households/families	Special groups	Categorical	Geographical	Geographical and categorical	Poverty	Poverty and geographical/categorical	N/A	Cash	Food	Other in-kind	Mix
Resource status	Not resource-rich	18	5	20	6	2	31	2	15	2	18	20	15	16	31	57	2	4	6	27	5	42	8	34	17
	Potentially resource-rich	33	17	12	17	2	2	3	2	12	47	18	2	31	3	20	0	13	23	42	1	52	20	18	9
	Resource-rich, non-oil	50	4	7	1	0	3	1	34	0	40	7	35	1	17	5	0	1	1	93	0	91	4	4	1
	Resource-rich, oil	18	1	53	7	13	3	2	0	3	11	55	6	25	3	74	0	1	1	10	13	16	3	19	63
Drought exposure	High	19	3	5	7	10	41	5	7	2	18	5	9	22	45	57	2	5	3	19	14	31	7	54	8
	Medium	50	5	11	2	0	0	1	31	1	39	11	32	6	12	7	0	1	3	88	0	87	6	2	5
	Low	13	3	56	11	1	10	1	1	4	20	60	1	9	10	63	0	2	4	30	1	23	5	18	55
	N/A	11	5	3	1	5	0	2	68	4	14	4	69	13	1	84	0	3	1	8	3	82	8	9	1
Overall development of social safety net system	No social safety net program	n/a																							
	No solid plans	26	3	2	15	24	22	1	2	5	23	3	14	39	22	40	3	0	4	30	23	27	4	52	17
	In progress	17	6	36	9	2	22	4	4	5	21	38	3	16	22	57	1	5	5	29	4	28	9	29	34
	In place	51	4	7	0	0	0	1	37	0	39	7	38	2	14	7	0	1	3	89	0	94	4	0	1

(continued next page)

Table G.6 (Continued)

Country groups		Program type: Cash transfer programs	School feeding programs	Public works programs	Education interventions	Health interventions	Emergency programs	Food-based programs	Social pensions	Other programs	Life cycle: Children	Working age population	The elderly	Households/families	Special groups	Targeting method: Categorical	Geographical	Geographical and categorical	Poverty	Poverty and geographical/categorical	N/A	Nature of benefits: Cash	Food	Other in-kind	Mix
Social protection strategy or policy	Not present	33	1	3	3	3	0	3	50	1	12	9	57	10	12	83	0	2	6	0	9	86	1	4	10
	In progress	32	8	5	10	20	19	1	0	5	22	5	10	19	19	31	1	7	17	25	20	33	10	43	14
	Present	40	4	17	3	1	0	8	25	1	35	17	25	44	17	20	0	2	2	75	1	72	6	10	12
Organizations responsible for policy setting, oversight, and coordination	Social ministry	44	4	10	3	0	0	8	28	1	38	11	29	26	19	13	1	1	2	83	0	79	5	10	6
	Central institution	22	9	51	5	1	0	4	1	2	17	53	1	26	4	67	0	8	9	9	7	33	14	7	46
	Other sectoral ministry	14	0	13	0	0	5	4	68	1	10	13	68	9	0	78	0	0	9	13	0	86	0	1	14
	Other arrangements	7	7	9	31	2	26	16	0	2	45	9	0	20	26	47	0	1	0	47	5	16	14	60	10
	N/A	36	1	2	2	27	21	1	11	0	10	2	18	39	32	42	0	0	3	30	25	44	2	48	5
Social registry status	Not planned	15	0	4	1	0	72	0	8	0	1	12	8	6	73	11	0	7	2	80	0	19	0	73	8
	Planned	12	4	24	8	9	32	3	2	5	12	25	18	33	12	53	1	4	1	32	9	20	7	48	25
	Operating on small scale	10	7	54	11	2	6	6	1	5	22	56	1	15	6	66	2	5	3	18	6	21	12	15	52
	Operating on medium scale	52	4	6	0	0	0	0	37	0	40	6	37	3	13	0	0	0	0	93	7	96	4	0	0
	Operating on large scale	42	11	6	13	5	9	1	12	1	38	7	13	33	10	18	6	0	9	32	25	66	13	12	9
	N/A	68	2	0	0	0	0	0	29	0	10	0	53	1	35	0	0	0	0	0	100	96	2	0	1

(continued next page)

Table G.6 (Continued)

Country groups		Program type									Life cycle					Targeting method						Nature of benefits			
		Cash transfer programs	School feeding programs	Public works programs	Education interventions	Health interventions	Emergency programs	Food-based programs	Social pensions	Other programs	Children	Working age population	The elderly	Households/families	Special groups	Categorical	Geographical	Geographical and categorical	Poverty	Poverty and geographical/categorical	N/A	Cash	Food	Other in-kind	Mix
Measures to deal with crises	Limited or no measures	11	1	2	10	14	57	2	1	1	15	3	1	23	57	61	0	2	2	23	13	16	2	77	5
	Moderate	43	5	16	2	0	1	1	31	1	38	16	31	3	12	16	0	1	2	81	0	82	5	2	11
	Strong	37	8	31	8	1	3	5	3	5	24	31	10	32	3	30	2	8	17	36	8	47	14	9	31
	N/A	68	2	0	0	0	0	0	29	0	10	0	53	1	35	100	0	0	0	0	0	96	2	0	1
Development partner involvement	Yes	20	6	30	10	5	20	3	2	4	22	31	4	21	21	52	1	5	7	28	7	30	9	31	30
	No	51	4	6	0	0	1	1	38	0	39	7	39	1	15	15	0	0	1	91	0	95	4	1	1

Source: ASPIRE (Atlas of Social Protection Indicators of Resilience and Equity) (database), Administrative data, World Bank, Washington, DC, http://datatopics.worldbank.org/aspire/.

Note: This table brings together all the resources deployed by all countries belonging to a particular country group (for instance, for the group "fragile," all the spending in dollars incurred in the 18 fragile countries is summed). The table presents the distribution of all these aggregated resources across program categories, showing, for instance, that 27 percent of all the safety net spending incurred in Central Africa is devoted to cash transfer programs. Averages do not include data from The Gambia. Benin has several school feeding, public works, education, and health programs, which were not included in the averages due to data limitations.

Table G.7 Distribution of Spending on Social Safety Nets, by Population Quintile

Country name	Total social safety net spending (% of GDP)	Share of total social safety net beneficiaries in each quintile (%)					Social safety net spending received by each quintile (% of GDP)				
		Quintile					Quintile				
		1	2	3	4	5	1	2	3	4	5
Ethiopia	1.30	24	25	19	20	12	0.3	0.3	0.2	0.3	0.2
Ghana	0.61	20	18	23	24	15	0.1	0.1	0.1	0.1	0.1
Lesotho	5.42	25	23	22	20	11	1.3	1.3	1.2	1.1	0.6
Malawi	1.18	18	22	22	21	18	0.2	0.3	0.3	0.2	0.2
Mauritius	3.46	23	21	19	19	18	0.8	0.7	0.7	0.7	0.6
Nigeria	0.26	18	36	17	19	10	0.0	0.1	0.0	0.0	0.0
Rwanda	1.32	22	20	20	21	18	0.3	0.3	0.3	0.3	0.2
South Africa	3.33	28	26	22	16	7	0.9	0.9	0.7	0.5	0.2
Tanzania	0.73	20	18	22	21	19	0.1	0.1	0.2	0.2	0.1

Source: ASPIRE (Atlas of Social Protection Indicators of Resilience and Equity) (database), Administrative data, World Bank, Washington, DC, http://datatopics.worldbank.org/aspire/. Incidence is estimated on the basis of household surveys.
Note: The share of beneficiaries in each quintile is calculated as the number of individuals in the quintile who are direct or indirect beneficiaries as a share of the total number of direct and indirect beneficiaries. The social safety net spending received by quintile is calculated by allocating total social safety net spending to each quintile in proportion to its share of beneficiaries.

Table G.8 Share of Development Partner Financing, Selected Programs

% of total program expenditures

Country	Program	Main source of financing	Share of development partner spending		Period
			Period 1	Period 2	
Benin	Decentralized Partnership for Employment project	Government and others	10	4	2008–11
Benin	Health Fund for the Poor	Government and others		9	2013
Benin	Support for the Promotion of Youth Employment	Government, UNDP	78	96	2009–11
Burundi	Aid to persons affected by HIV/AIDS	Government and development partners (World Bank, WFP, UNDP, IFAD, Enabel)	83	98	2010–13
Burundi	Aid to persons with disabilities	Government and development partners (World Bank, WFP, UNDP, IFAD, Enabel)	96	22	2011–13
Burundi	Aid to vulnerable children	Government and development partners (World Bank, WFP, UNDP, IFAD, Enabel)	93	96	2010–13
Burundi	Food supplements for malnutrition	Government and development partners (World Bank, WFP, UNDP, IFAD, Enabel)	100	100	2010–12
Burundi	Humanitarian assistance, including aid for repatriation	Government and development partners (World Bank, WFP, UNDP, IFAD, Enabel)	89	87	2010–13
Burundi	Labor-intensive PWPs	Government and development partners (World Bank, WFP, UNDP, IFAD, Enabel)	100	99	2010–13
Burundi	Promotion of women and gender equality	Government and development partners (World Bank, WFP, UNDP, IFAD, Enabel)	71	58	2010–13
Burundi	School feeding	Government and development partners (World Bank, WFP, UNDP, IFAD, Enabel)	100	67	2010–13
Cameroon	Employment-Intensive Investment Approaches (HIMO)	AFD		100	2016
Chad	Food Assistance for Assets (Volunteer cooks)	WFP		100	2017
Chad	Girls' take-home rations	WFP		100	2017

(continued next page)

Table G.8 (Continued)

Country	Program	Main source of financing	Share of development partner spending		
			Period 1	Period 2	Period
Chad	School meals	WFP		100	2017
Comoros	Productive safety net	World Bank	100	100	2015–16
Côte d'Ivoire	Productive SSN Program	World Bank (IDA) and Government		90	2017
Côte d'Ivoire	National program for Orphans and Children affected by HIV/AIDS (PNOEV)	Government and external partners		100	2015
Ethiopia	Agricultural Growth Program	Communities, government, and development partners	99	99	2010–13
Ethiopia	Emergency Food Aid	Development partners	100	100	2012–13
Ethiopia	Food for Education	WFP	100	100	2009–13
Ethiopia	Household Asset Building Program	Government and development partners	13	31	2011–13
Ethiopia	Pilot social cash transfer—Tigray	UNICEF	100	100	2012–13
Ethiopia	Productive Safety Net (PSNP)	Government and development partners	98	99	2009–16
Ethiopia	Urban Productive Safety Net (UPSNP)	Government and World Bank		66	2016
Ethiopia	Targeted Supplementary Feeding	Development partners	100	100	2010–13
Ethiopia	Urban HIV/AIDS Program	WFP	100	100	2009–13
Ghana	Labor-intensive public works program (LIPW)	World Bank-financed Ghana social opportunities project	100	100	2011–16
Kenya	Blanket supplementary feeding program	WFP		100	2017
Kenya	Cash transfer for OVC	Government of Kenya and development partners, including UNICEF, World Bank, and DFID	57	16	2008–16
Kenya	Health Insurance Subsidy Program (HISP)	World Bank	100	100	2014–16
Kenya	Hunger Safety net program (HSNP)	Government of Kenya and DFID	100	79	2008–16

(continued next page)

Table G.8 (Continued)

Country	Program	Main source of financing	Share of development partner spending			Period
			Period 1	Period 2		
Kenya	Regular school meals program	Government, WFP, and other development partners	100	100		2008–16
Kenya	WFP Kenya Rural Resilience	WFP		100		2017
Kenya	WFP cash for assets	CGAP, DFID	100	100		2011–16
Kenya	WFP food for assets	CGAP, DFID	100	100		2008–16
Lesotho	Child Grants Program (CGP)	Government (European Union–UNICEF-financed transfer until 2012, administrative costs until 2014)		100		2012
Lesotho	School feeding program	Government and development partner (WFP)	75	100		2010–12
Liberia	Lean season safety nets	WFP	100	100		2009–10
Liberia	Liberian Agricultural Upgrading, Nutrition and Child Health (LAUNCH)	USAID	100	100		2009–10
Liberia	Livelihood Asset Rehabilitation (LAR)	WFP	100	100		2009–10
Liberia	OVS	Save the Children		100		2011
Liberia	Take-home ration WFP	WFP	100	100		2009–10
Liberia	Program for Refugees	UNICEF		100		2011
Liberia	Food for Peace Strategic Plan	USAID		100		2011
Liberia	School feeding	WFP	100	100		2009–10
Madagascar	Conditional Cash Transfer	World Bank	100	100		2014–18
Madagascar	Human Development Cash Transfer	World Bank	100	100		2016–19
Madagascar	Let Us Learn (LUL)	UNICEF		100		2000
Madagascar	Growth Monitoring and Promotion	World Bank		100		2017
Madagascar	Productive Safety Net	World Bank	100	100		2016–19

(continued next page)

Table G.8 (Continued)

Country	Program	Main source of financing	Share of development partner spending		
			Period 1	Period 2	Period
Malawi	MASAF Public works program	World Bank, European Union, government	9	9	2011–16
Mali	Appareillage Orthopédique et rééducation fonctionnelle	Budget du government, handicap international, ICRC, and others		25	2016
Mali	Assistance Alimentaire aux Déplacés et Urgence saisonière	Development partners	100	100	2015–16
Mali	Assistance Alimentaire pour la Création d'Actifs (3A)	Development partners	100	100	2015–16
Mali	Fonds de Solidarité Nationale (FSN)	Government and development partners		30	2016
Mali	Fonds pour l'autonomisation de la Femme (FAFE)	Government and development partners		2	2016
Mali	Jigisemejiri	Government and World Bank	94	95	2015–16
Mali	Programme de repas scolaire	WFP	100	100	2015–16
Mozambique	Basic Social Subsidy Program	National Social Action Institute, United Kingdom, DFID, government of the Netherlands, International Labour Organization, UNICEF, European Union, Irish Aid, SIDA	13	9	2012–15
Mozambique	Productive Social Action Program	Government of Mozambique, World Bank	100	94	2012–15
Mozambique	School Feeding	WFP		100	2010
Mozambique	Support for Orphans and Vulnerable Children Program (Apoio aos Órfãos e Crianças)	WFP		100	2010
Namibia	National School Feeding Program for Orphans and Vulnerable Children	WFP and government	53	100	2008–13
Nigeria	Youth Employment and Social Support Operation (YESSO)	World Bank		100	2016
Senegal	Food insecurity riposte (Food Security Agency, CSA)	Government and development partners	36	76	2012–15
Senegal	National conditional cash transfer program (PNBSF)	Government, World Bank		3	2015
Senegal	Security Response Program (WFP)	WFP	100	100	2010–15

(continued next page)

Table G.8 (Continued)

Country	Program	Main source of financing	Share of development partner spending		Period
			Period 1	Period 2	
Senegal	School Lunch Program (WFP)	WFP	100	100	2010–15
Senegal	Cash transfer nutritional program	World Bank	72	94	2009–15
Senegal	National funds for women's entrepreneurship	Government and development partners		27	2014
Senegal	Universal health coverage	Government and development partners		16	2015
Sierra Leone	Caregiver and Supplementary Feeding	Development partners		100	2012
Sierra Leone	Decentralized Service Delivery Program	World Bank		100	2012
Sierra Leone	Feeding assistance PLHIV/ TB	WFP and BRAC/PLAN International		100	2012
Sierra Leone	Refugees	United Nations High Commissioner for Refugees		100	2012
Sierra Leone	School feeding	WFP, DFID, and other development partners		100	2012
Sierra Leone	Victims of Sexual Violence	United Nations Peacebuilding Fund, UNTF		100	2012
South Sudan	Emergency Operation for IDPs and returnees	WFP	100	100	2012–16
South Sudan	Protracted Relief and Recovery Operation	WFP	100	100	2013–16
Sudan	Food for assets	WFP and World Vision	100	100	2014–15
Sudan	General Food distribution program	WFP and World Vision	100	100	2014–15
Sudan	Integrated Blanket Supplementary Feeding Program	WFP and World Vision	100	100	2014–15
Sudan	School Feeding Program	WFP, Zakat, NGOs, and community	100	100	2013–15
Sudan	Targeted Supplementary Feeding Program	WFP	100	100	2014–15
Sudan	UNICEF's Nutrition Program	ECHO, OFDA, Japan, USAID, DFID, CERF, SHF, KOICA, government		86	2013
Tanzania	Food for Assets (FFA)	Canada, Russian Federation, United Nations, United States, Republic of Korea	100	100	2011–16

(continued next page)

Table G.8 (Continued)

Country	Program	Main source of financing	Share of development partner spending		
			Period 1	Period 2	Period
Tanzania	Moderate Acute Malnutrition treatment (Supplementary Feeding Program)	WFP, Canada, Russian Federation, United Nations, United States, Republic of Korea	100	100	2011–16
Tanzania	Productive Social Safety Net (PSSN)—Livelihood Enhancement	World Bank	100	100	2014–16
Tanzania	Productive Social Safety Net (PSSN)—Conditional Cash Transfer	World Bank, DFID, SIDA, United Nations agencies, Bill & Melinda Gates Foundation, government	100	100	2014–16
Tanzania	Productive Social Safety Net (PSSN)—Public Works	World Bank	100	100	2015–16
Tanzania	Stunting prevention (Mother and Child Health and Nutrition program)	WFP, Canada, Russian Federation, United Nations, United States, Republic of Korea	100	100	2012–16
Togo	Nutrition program	UNICEF		100	2009
Uganda	Community Agricultural Infrastructure Improvement Program (CAIIP)	African Development Bank, IFAD, government	95	93	2009–16
Uganda	Northern Uganda Social Action Fund (II)—Household Income Support Program	World Bank	100	100	2014–16
Uganda	Sustainable Comprehensive Responses for vulnerable children and their families (SCORE)—Food and Nutrition Component	AVSI Foundation, USAID	100	100	2011–15
Zambia	Expanded Food Security Pack (EFSP)	Norway		100	2016
Zambia	School Feeding Program	Government and WFP		16	2016
Zimbabwe	Amalima—Response to Humanitarian Situation	USAID	100	100	2014–15
Zimbabwe	Basic Education Assistance Module (BEAM)	Government and development partners	100	100	2010–14
Zimbabwe	ENSURE—Humanitarian assistance	USAID	100	100	2013–15
Zimbabwe	Harmonized Social Cash Transfer	Child Protection Fund, government	100	100	2012–15
Zimbabwe	Small Enterprise Development Cooperation (SEDCO)	Government and development partners	65	10	2010–14

(continued next page)

Table G.8 (Continued)

Country	Program	Main source of financing	Share of development partner spending		
			Period 1	Period 2	Period
Zimbabwe	WFP—Lean Season Assistance	WFP, Brazil, Canada, European Commission, Finland, Japan, Luxembourg, Spain, Switzerland, UNICEF Common Funds and Agencies, United Kingdom, United States, Zimbabwe	100	100	2010–15
Zimbabwe	WFP—Productive Asset Creation Program	WFP, Brazil, Canada, European Commission, Finland, Japan, Luxembourg, Spain, Switzerland, UNICEF Common Funds and Agencies, United Kingdom, United States, Zimbabwe	100	100	2010–15

Source: ASPIRE (Atlas of Social Protection Indicators of Resilience and Equity) (database), Administrative data, World Bank, Washington, DC, http://datatopics.worldbank.org/aspire/.

Note: AFD = Agence Française de Développement; CERF = Central Emergency Response Fund; CGAP = Consultative Group to Assist the Poor; DFID = UK Department for International Development; ECHO = European Community Humanitarian Aid Office; Enabel = Belgian development agency; ICRC = International Committee of the Red Cross; IFAD = International Fund for Agricultural Development; KOICA = Korea International Cooperation Agency; OFDA = Office of US Foreign Disaster Assistance; SHF = Somalia Humanitarian Fund; SIDA = Swedish International Development Cooperation Authority; UNDP = United Nations Development Programme; UNTF = UN Trust Fund to End Violence against Women; USAID = US Agency for International Development; WFP = World Food Programme.

Overview: figure O.9 and Chapter 3: figure 13.3 present aggregated data by country. Data are from the ASPIRE database for Angola, Burkina Faso, Cameroon, the Republic of Congo, the Democratic Republic of Congo, Gabon, Kenya, Liberia, Malawi, Mauritius, Mozambique, Namibia, Senegal, Seychelles, Sierra Leone, Somalia, South Sudan, Sudan, Tanzania, Uganda, and Zimbabwe. Data are from Monchuk, Victoria. 2014. *Reducing Poverty and Investing in People: New Role of Safety Nets in Africa*, Directions in Development: Human Development Series, Washington, DC. for Benin, Botswana, and Mauritania. Data are from World Bank. 2016. *République centrafricaine Jeter de nouvelles bases pour la stabilité et la croissance.* Washington, DC for the Central African Republic; from World Bank. 2016. *Republic of Chad: Shaping Adaptive Safety Nets to Address Vulnerability.* Washington, DC for Chad; from Kiringai, Jane Wangui; Geiger, Michael Tobias; Bezawagaw, Mesfin Girma; and Jensen, Leif. 2016. *Ethiopia public expenditure review.* Washington, DC: World Bank for Ethiopia; from UNICEF. 2013. *Moving towards an Integrated and Equitable Social Protection in The Gambia.* Banjul: The Government of The Gambia for The Gambia; from Marques, Jose Silverio, and Honorati, Maddalena. 2016. *Ghana—Social protection assessment and public expenditure review.* World Bank. Washington, DC for Ghana; from World Bank (forthcoming). *Guinea-Bissau: Social Safety Net Assessment.* Washington, DC for Guinea Bissau; and from World Bank (forthcoming). *Social Protection Financing Diagnostics for Mali.* Washington, DC for Mali.

Table G.9 **Administrative Costs for Selected Programs**

Country	Program	Administrative cost (% of total program expenditures)			Number of beneficiaries		
		Year 1	Year 2	Period	Year 1	Year 2	Period
Benin	Support Fund for National Solidarity and Social Action	8.9	22.5	2000–13	1,570	8,670	2000–13
Burkina Faso	Child Development program through sponsorship	15.3	12.0	2008–15	16,795	60,651	2008–15
Burkina Faso	Special Program of job creation for young people and women (PSCE/JF)		1.0	2014		46,610	2014
Cameroon	Social Safety Net Project (Projet Filets Sociaux)	65.6	23.2	2015–16	24,000	103,200	2015–16
Cameroon	Program 559: National Solidarity and Social Justice	9.2	0.8	2013–16	52,800	569,808	2013–16
Cameroon	Root, Tuber, and Plantain Development and Valorization Program (PDVRTP)	20.0	18.9	2013–16	240	720	2014–16
Ethiopia	Agricultural Growth Program (AGP)	7.2	8.4	2010–13			
Ethiopia	Household Asset Building Program (HABP)	13.0	30.7	2011–13	148,356	187,344	2011–13
Ethiopia	Urban HIV/AIDS Program	0.1	3.3	2009–13	116,161	91,630	2009–13
Ethiopia	Productive Safety Net (PSNP)	7.3	6.9	2009–16	7,574,480	7,997,218	2009–16
Ghana	Livelihood Empowerment Against Poverty (LEAP)	12.0	12.0	2009–12	75,086	172,242	2009–10
Ghana	Local Enterprises and Skills Development Programme (LESDEP)	7.1	8.7	2011–12	196,834		2011
Ghana	School Feeding Programme		1.1	2012	1642,271		2011
Ghana	National Health Insurance Scheme indigent exemptions (NHIS)	4.5		2011	326,182		2011
Lesotho	Old age pension	7.0	6.3	2012–13	83,000		2012
Madagascar	Conditional Cash Transfer	46.0	23.4	2015–16	27,989	27,989	2015–16
Madagascar	Human Development Cash Transfer	35.9	48.8	2015–16	127,272	127,272	2015–16
Malawi	School Meals Programme (SMP)	48.8	17.6	2008–13	642,109		2008
Malawi	MASAF PWP	10.0	10.0	2011–16	1,151,224	3,105,000	2011–16
Mali	Jigisemejiri	41.8	11.9	2014–16	30,758	376,433	2014–16

(continued next page)

359

Table G.9 (Continued)

Country	Program	Administrative cost (% of total program expenditures)		Period	Number of beneficiaries		Period
		Year 1	Year 2		Year 1	Year 2	
Mali	Pilot Monetary Transfer program (Mopti region)		21.5	2014		1,200	2014
Mali	Food distribution	29.1	31.2	2014–16	1,425,758	430,958	2014–16
Mozambique	Direct Social Support program	12.6	24.6	2011–12		149,547	2012
Mozambique	Basic Social Subsidy Programme	27.3	16.0	2012–15	1,205,710	1,671,340	2012–15
Namibia	Provision of Social Assistance	3.2	4.6	2005–12	80,753	122,316	2005–12
Namibia	Old Age Grant	4.7	3.5	2001–12	97,373	143,562	2001–12
Senegal	National conditional cash transfer programme (PNBSF)	14.3	5.0	2013–15	392,704	1,582,008	2013–15
Senegal	Community-Based Re-Adaptation Program	39.5	18.7	2006–15	15,200	25,000	2010–15
Senegal	Old Age Support Program	23.7	26.8	2008–15	1,040	6,464	2008–15
Senegal	National Solidarity Fund		24.8	2013			
Senegal	Government School Lunch Program	1.6	1.9	2004–14	100,000	301,999	2006–14
Senegal	Kindergarten	44.4	28.0	2009–15	84,780	144,760	2009–15
Senegal	Food insecurity response (Food Security Agency, CSA)	9.6	4.2	2005–15	141,000	927,416	2012–15
Sierra Leone	Social Safety Nets Program	7.4	13.6	2015–16	81,485	136,768	2015–16
Tanzania	Disaster relief food response	15.0	6.6	2006–16	1,166,639	910,653	2006–16
Tanzania	Productive Social Safety Net (PSSN)—Conditional Cash Transfer	12.0	12.0	2014–16	1,219,410	5,164,623	2014–16
Tanzania	Most Vulnerable Children (MVC)—Child welfare care services	44.5	40.8	2010–11	206,398	400,803	2010–11
Tanzania	Most Vulnerable Children (MVC)—Child protection services	44.5	40.8	2010–11	96,281	206,392	2010–11
Uganda	Compassion International Child Development Programme	21.1	20.8	2013–16	76,880	94,457	2013–16
Zimbabwe	Harmonized cash transfer	12.5	9.6	2012–15	20,000	52,000	2012–15

(continued next page)

Table G.9 (Continued)

Country	Program	Administrative cost (% of total program expenditures)			Number of beneficiaries		
		Year 1	Year 2	Period	Year 1	Year 2	Period
Zimbabwe	Small Enterprise Development Cooperation (SEDCO)	15.8	2.9	2010–14	5,863	134	2010–14
Zimbabwe	Youth Development Loan Facility for income generating projects through CABS Bank	4.8	4.8	2012–15	7,535	2,554	2012–15
Zimbabwe	Youth Development Loan Facility for income generating projects through CBZ Bank	5.0	5.0	2010–14	1,709	437	2010–14
Zimbabwe	Basic education Assistance Module (BEAM) primary	8.0	10.0	2010–15	537,594	118,408	2010–15
Zimbabwe	Basic education Assistance Module (BEAM) secondary	10.0	10.0	2010–13	198,229	92,917	2010–13
Zimbabwe	Amalima—Response to Humanitarian Situation	10.9	9.8	2014–15	135,888	266,277	2014–15
Zimbabwe	ENSURE—Humanitarian assistance	20.0	8.2	2013–15	30,000	80,900	2013–15
Zimbabwe	WFP Lean Season Assistance	10.4	16.9	2010–15	1,278,293	263,237	2010–15
Zimbabwe	Community Recovery and Rehabilitation Programme	19.3	23.8	2010–15	621	281	2010–15
Zimbabwe	Food mitigation program	9.3	8.9	2010–15	389,365	756,000	2010–15
Zimbabwe	WFP Productive Asset Creation Program	10.4	16.9	2010–15	2,300,928	473,827	2010–15

Source: ASPIRE (Atlas of Social Protection Indicators of Resilience and Equity) (database), Administrative data, World Bank, Washington, DC, http://datatopics.worldbank.org/aspire/.

Main Social Safety Net Programs, by Program Type

Table H.1 The Five Largest Programs of Each Type, Ranked by Number of Beneficiaries

Type	Country	Program	Year started	Targeting method	Number of beneficiaries	Coverage % relevant population group	Coverage Year	Spending % GDP	Spending Year
Cash transfer programs	South Africa	Child Support Grant	2004	Categorical and means/income	27,949,636	50.6	2015	1.1	2015
	Tanzania	Productive Social Safety Net (PSSN)—Conditional Cash Transfer	2012	Community-based and proxy means	5,164,623	9.6	2016	0.2	2016
	South Africa	Disability grant	2004	Categorical and means/income	4,005,587	7.2	2015	0.5	2015
	Sudan	Social Initiatives Program (SIP)	2011	Proxy means and community-based	2,850,000	7.4	2016	0.1	2016
	Sudan	Solidarity fund		Self-targeting	2,599,673	6.7	2016	0.0	2016
School feeding programs	South Africa	National School Nutrition Programme	1994	Categorical and means/income	9,200,000	87.1	2013		2014
	Burkina Faso	Government School feeding program (primary education)		Geographical and categorical	2,906,000	57.1	2016	0.3	2016
	Malawi	WFP—Government School Meals Programme	1999	Categorical	2,230,000	45.0	2016		
	Ghana	Ghana School Feeding Programme	2005	Geographical, categorical, community-based and self-targeting	1,700,000	25.5	2014	0.1	2014
	Côte d'Ivoire	Integrated Program for Sustainability of School Canteens (PIPCS)	1989	Categorical	1,086,721	17.8	2016	0.0	2016
Public works programs	Ethiopia	Productive Safety Net (PSNP)	2005	Geographical and community-based	7,997,218	8.0	2016	0.6	2016
	Malawi	MASAF PWP		Categorical, community-based, and proxy means	3,105,000	17.7	2016	0.4	2016
	Tanzania	Productive Social Safety Net (PSSN)—Public Works	2014	Community-based and proxy means	1,405,159	2.6	2016	0.1	2016
	Congo, Dem. Rep.	Eastern Recovery Project	2014	Geographical, categorical, and community-based	1,353,226	1.8	2016	0.0	2016
	South Africa	Extended Public Works Programme (EPWP)	2004	Geographical, categorical, community-based, and self-targeting	1,260,245	6.2	2013		

(continued next page)

Table H.1 (Continued)

Type	Country	Program	Year started	Targeting method	Coverage Number of beneficiaries	Coverage % relevant population group	Coverage Year	Spending % GDP	Spending Year
Education interventions	Ghana	Metro Mass Transport		Categorical	242,850	4.5	2010		
	Sudan	National Student Welfare Fund	1996	Geographical, categorical, community-based, and means/income	200,000	2.6	2016	0.0	2016
	Ghana	Scholarships		Categorical	136,769	2.5	2014	0.1	2014
	Zimbabwe	Basic education Assistance Module (BEAM) primary	2002	Categorical and community-based	118,408	3.6	2015	0.0	2015
	Senegal	University scholarship		Categorical	107,632	3.6	2015	0.4	2015
Health interveantionsa	Sudan	Heath insurance	1995		15,725,537	40.7	2016	0.3	2016
	Ghana	National Health Insurance Scheme indigent exemptions (NHIS)	2003	Means/income	6,700,000	24.3	2014	0.0	2014
	Senegal	Universal Health Coverage	2015	Proxy means	792,985	5.3	2015	0.1	2015
	Burkina Faso	Subsidy for emergency obstetric and neonatal care for indigent women	2006	Categorical	702,083	3.9	2014		2015
	Gabon	Health insurance plan for economically weak Gabonese	2007	Categorical	483,000	25.0	2014	0.1	2014
Emergency programs	Congo, Dem. Rep.	WFP food distribution	2013	Geographical, categorical, community-based, and other	3,233,000	4.2	2016	0.7	2016
	Ethiopia	Emergency Food Aid		Categorical	2,550,579	2.6	2013	0.3	2013
	South Sudan	Emergency Operation for IDPs and returnees	2012	Categorical	2,208,005	18.6	2016	4.6	2016
	Sudan	General food distribution program		Categorical	2,095,568	5.4	2015	0.1	2015
	South Sudan	Proacted Relief and Recovery Operation	2012	Categorical	1,808,869	15.2	2016	5.5	2016

(continued next page)

Table H.1 (Continued)

Type	Country	Program	Year started	Targeting method	Number of beneficiaries	Coverage		Spending	
						% relevant population group	Year	% GDP	Year
Food-based programs	Niger	WFP Récupération Nutritionnelle	2017	Geographical, categorical, and other	1,178,830	5.9	2015	0.2	2015
	Ghana	Targeted supplementary feeding for malnourished children		Categorical	480,000	1.7	2011		
	Chad	Food aid to vulnerable / food-insecure households	2016		422,457	3.0	2016		
	South Sudan	Nutrition	2012	Categorical	412,332	3.5	2015		
	Botswana	Vulnerable Group Feeding Program	1988	Categorical and means/income	383,392	17.4	2013		
Social pensions	South Africa	Old-age grant	2004	Categorical and means/income	3,086,851	69.4	2015	1.2	2015
	Kenya	Older Persons Cash Transfer	2007	Categorical, community-based, and proxy means	310,000	25.4	2017	0.1	2017
	Mauritius	Basic Retirement Pension (zero pillar)	1950	Categorical	195,591	101.3	2016		
	Namibia	Old Age Grant	1990	Categorical	146,482	111.8	2013		2014
	Botswana	Old-Age Pension	1996	Categorical	105,754	129.0	2016	0.3	2016
Other programs	Madagascar	Growth monitoring and promotion	2014	Geographical, categorical, and self-targeting	2,508,000	10.3	2016		2017
	Tanzania	Most Vulnerable Children (MVC)—Child welfare care services	2010	Community-based and means/income	1,062,939	2.0	2016	0.0	2016
	Tanzania	Most Vulnerable Children (MVC)—Child protection services	2010	Community-based and means/income	489,166	0.9	2016	0.0	2016
	South Africa	HIV and AIDS Life Skills Education Programme	2000	Means/income	459,815	0.8	2013	0.0	2013
	South Sudan	Children reached with critical child protection services		Categorical	318,834	2.7	2015		

Source: ASPIRE (Atlas of Social Protection Indicators of Resilience and Equity) (database), Administrative data, World Bank, Washington, DC, http://datatopics.worldbank.org/aspire/.

Table H.2 **The Five Largest Programs of Each Type, Ranked by Coverage as a Share of the Population**

Type	Country	Program	Year started	Targeting method	Number of beneficiaries	Couverture % relevant population group	Couverture Year	Spending % GDP	Spending Year
Cash transfer programs	South Africa	Child Support Grant	2004	Categorical, means/income	27,949,636	50.6	2015	1.1	2015
	Namibia	Provision of Social Assistance		Categorical	772,900	31.8	2013	0.0	2013
	Senegal	National conditional cash transfer programme (PNBSF)	2013	Geographical, community-based, proxy means	2,400,000	16.0	2016		
	Seychelles	Social Welfare Assistance		Means/income	11,019	11.6	2015	0.3	2015
	Tanzania	Productive Social Safety Net (PSSN)—Conditional Cash Transfer	2012	Community-based, proxy means	5,164,623	9.6	2016	0.2	2016
School feeding programs	Swaziland	National School Meal Program	1982	Categorical	328,000	103.1	2011		
	South Africa	National School Nutrition Programme	1994	Categorical and means/income	9,200,000	87.1	2013		2014
	Lesotho	School feeding program	2005	Categorical	389,000	78.6	2014		
	Burkina Faso	Government School feeding program (primary education)		Geographical and categorical	2,906,000	57.1	2016	0.3	2016
	Liberia	WFP school feeding		Geographical and categorical	648,000	53.9	2011		

(continued next page)

Table H.2 (Continued)

Type	Country	Program	Year started	Targeting method	Number of beneficiaries	Couverture % relevant population group	Year	Spending % GDP	Year
Public works programs	Lesotho	Integrated Watershed Management Public Works Program		Categorical and self-targeting	552,000	25.4	2012		
	Malawi	MASAF PWP		Categorical community-based, proxy means	3,105,000	17.7	2016	0.4	2016
	Botswana	Ipelegeng (self-reliance)	2008	Categorical community-based self-targeting	240,500	10.9	2014		2015
	Ethiopia	Productive Safety Net (PSNP)	2005	Geographical and community-based	7,997,218	8.0	2016	0.6	2016
	Central African Republic	Support to the stabilization and early recovery of communities at risk in CAR (SIRIRI) Phase 2	2015	Categorical and proxy-means	318,000	7.0	2015	0.6	2015
Education interventions	Seychelles	Post-Secondary Bursary		Categorical	1,890	14.5	2015	0.1	2015
	Gambia, The	President's Empowerment of Girls' Education Program		Geographical, categorical	36,000	9.2	2012		
	Cabo Verde	School tuition		Categorical, means/income	8,000	7.0	2014		
	Cabo Verde	Cape Verdean Foundation for Social and Educational Action (FICASE)		Categorical	7,420	6.5	2014		
	Ghana	Metro Mass Transport		Categorical	242,850	4.5	2010		

(continued next page)

Table H.2 (Continued)

Type	Country	Program	Year started	Targeting method	Number of beneficiaries	Couverture % relevant population group	Year	Spending % GDP	Year
Health interventions	Sudan	Heath insurance	1995		15,725,537	40.7	2016	0.3	2016
	Gabon	Health insurance plan for economically weak Gabonese	2007	Categorical	483,000	25.0	2014	0.1	2014
	Ghana	National Health Insurance Scheme with indigent exemptions (NHIS)	2003	Means/income	6,700,000	24.3	2014	0.0	2014
	Senegal	Universal health coverage	2015	Proxy means	792,985	5.3	2015	0.1	2015
	Burkina Faso	Additional subsidy of emergency obstetric and neonatal care for indigent women	2006	Categorical	702,083	3.9	2014		2015
Emergency programs	South Sudan	Emergency Operation for IDPs and returnees	2012	Categorical	2,208,005	18.6	2016	4.6	2016
	South Sudan	Proacted Relief and Recovery Operation	2012	Categorical	1,808,869	15.2	2016	5.5	2016
	Central African Republic	Resuming agriculture and income opportunities for communities affected by the crisis in selected areas	2015	Geographical	319,500	7.0	2015	0.3	2015
	Senegal	Food insecurity response (Food security agency, CSA)	1974	Geographical, categorical, community-based	927,416	6.2	2015	0.1	2015
	Sudan	General Food distribution program		Categorical	2,095,568	5.4	2015	0.1	2015

(continued next page)

Table H.2 (Continued)

Type	Country	Program	Year started	Targeting method	Number of beneficiaries	Couverture		Spending	
						% relevant population group	Year	% GDP	Year
Food-based programs	Botswana	Vulnerable Group Feeding Program	1988	Categorical, means/income	383,392	17.4	2013		
	Niger	WFP Récupération Nutritionnelle	2017	Geographical, categorical, and other	1,178,830	5.9	2015	0.2	2015
	South Sudan	Nutrition	2012	Categorical	412,332	3.5	2015		
	Liberia	Supplementary feeding		Categorical	152,000	3.4	2010		
	Chad	Food aid to vulnerable / Food insecure Households	2016		422,457	3.0	2016		
Social pensions	Lesotho	Old age pension	2004	Geographical, categorical, and pensions-tested	85,087	146.7	2015		
	Botswana	The Old-Age Pension (OAP)	1996	Categorical	105,754	129.0	2016	0.3	2016
	Namibia	Provision of Social Assistance—Old Age Grant	1990	Categorical	146,482	111.8	2013		2014
	Mauritius	Basic Retirement Pension (BRP) zero pillar retirement only	1950	Categorical	195,591	101.3	2016		
	Swaziland	Old Age Grant (OAG)	2005	Categorical	63,500	100.8	2014		

(continued next page)

Type	Country	Program	Year started	Targeting method	Number of beneficiaries	Couverture		Spending	
						% relevant population group	Year	% GDP	Year
Other programs	Madagascar	Growth Monitoring and Promotion	2014	Geographical, categorical, self-targeting	2,508,000	10.3	2016		2017
	Sierra Leone	Decentralized Service Delivery Program (Education)		Categorical	250,000	3.5	2012	0.0	2012
	Seychelles	Home Care Program		Categorical and means/income	2,641	2.8	2015	0.0	2015
	South Sudan	Children reached with critical child protection services		Categorical	318,834	2.7	2015		
	Tanzania	Most Vulnerable Children (MVC)—Child welfare care services	2010	Community-based and means/income	1,062,939	2.0	2016	0.0	2016

Source: ASPIRE (Atlas of Social Protection Indicators of Resilience and Equity) (database), Administrative data, World Bank, Washington, DC, http://datatopics.worldbank.org/aspire/.

Generosity of Social Safety Net Programs

Table I.1 Generosity of Selected Cash Transfer Programs

Country	Program	Benefit	Year	Benefit monthly, $ PPP 2011	Benefit as a share of GDP per capita (2015)	National poverty line		$1.90 international poverty line	
						% Poverty line	% poverty gap	% poverty line	% poverty gap
Burkina Faso	Social Safety net project Burkin-Nong-Saya	CFA 30,000/trimester for mothers with less than 5 children under the age of 15 CFA 40,000 for a mother with 5 children or younger than 15.	2015	49	6	17	1	14	1
Cameroon	Social Safety Nets Cash transfers	CFA 360,000 monetary transfers and 180,000 emergency transfers	2016	75	6	14	1	27	4
Chad	Pilot Social Safety Nets Program (Cash transfers)	Cash transfers: 15,000 FCFA/month for poor households with children under 12 and/or pregnant women	2017	70	9	17	1	23	2
Ethiopia	Urban Productive Safety Net (UPSNP)—Direct Support	ETB 170 per person/month	2017	18	3	6	1	7	1
Ghana	Livelihood Empowerment Against Poverty (LEAP)	Benefit varies depending on the number of eligible members per beneficiary household (GH¢ 24 per month for one member, GH¢ 30 for two members, GH¢ 36 for three members, GH¢ 45 for four or more members)	2015	28	2	0	0	11	1
Kenya	Cash transfer for OVC (CT-OVC)	KES 2,000 per month per household on a bimonthly basis	2016	40	4	9	1	16	1
Kenya	Cash Transfer for Persons with Severe Disabilities (PwSD-CT)	KES 2,000 per month per household on a bimonthly basis	2016	40	4	9	1	16	1
Kenya	Hunger Safety net program (HSNP)	KES 5,400 every two months	2016	53	5	12	1	21	2
Lesotho	Child Grants Program (CGP)	Lesotho Loti 360–750	2015	25	2	13	0	9	0
Madagascar	Let Us Learn (LUL)	Ar 10,000 per child per month	2016	11	2	9	0	4	0

(continued next page)

Table I.1 (Continued)

Country	Program	Benefit	Year	Benefit monthly, $ PPP 2011	Benefit as a share of GDP per capita (2015)	National poverty line		$1.90 international poverty line	
						% Poverty line	% poverty gap	% poverty line	% poverty gap
Madagascar	Human Development Cash Transfer	Ar 10,000 as basic amount plus Ar 5,000 per child aged 6-12	2016	11	2	9	0	4	0
Madagascar	Filets Sociaux de Sécurité (FSS) TMC	Ar 10,000 as basic amount plus Ar 5,000 school incentive per child per month	2014	9	2	8	0	3	0
Madagascar	Emergency National Cash Program Fiavota	Basic household needs and average consumption	2016	33	6	27	1	12	0
Malawi	Social Cash Transfer Scheme (SCTS)	Transfer varies based on household size and number of children enrolled in primary and secondary school	2016	18	4	9	0	7	0
Mauritania	Tekavoul—National Social Transfer Programme	MRO 1,500 per household per trimester (expressed in new currency, introduced in 2018)	2016	50	3	7	1	14	10
Mauritius	Guardian's Allowance	MUR1,000, independent of number of orphans under a person's care	2016	57	1	8		28	256
Mauritius	Inmate's Allowance		2015	41	1	5		20	183
Mauritius	Child's Allowance	MUR 1,400 per child under 10 and MUR 1,500 per child aged 10 and over	2016	82	1	11		41	371
Mauritius	Basic Invalidity Pension	MUR 3,000 as basic retirement pension for severely handicapped individuals	2016	171	3	23		84	767
Mauritius	Basic Orphan's Pension	MUR 2,750 for children under 15 years or age and not enrolled in full-time education and MUR 4,250 for children aged 3 to 20 enrolled in full-time education	2016	199	3	27		98	895
Mauritius	Basic Widow's Pension	MUR 5,250 for basic widow pension	2016	299	5	40		148	1342

(continued next page)

Table I.1 (Continued)

Country	Program	Benefit	Year	Benefit monthly, $ PPP 2011	Benefit as a share of GDP per capita (2015)	National poverty line		$1.90 international poverty line	
						% Poverty line	% poverty gap	% poverty line	% poverty gap
Mozambique	Basic Social Subsidy Programme	From MZN310 per household, up to a maximum of MZN 610 per month for a household with four dependents	2015	18	4	4	0	7	0
Namibia	Foster Care Grant		2014	41	1	12	1	16	2
Namibia	Provision of Social Assistance		2014	98	3	28	3	39	6
Namibia	Veterans Welfare Development—Veterans monthly subvention		2014	360	10	104	12	142	21
Niger	Cash transfer of the Social Safety Net Project	CFA 10,000 per month (about 15% of poverty line for a rural household) over a period of 24 months	2011	45	10	11	1	13	1
Senegal	Support to orphans' children	CFA 30,000 per month	2015	128	8	13	1	28	2
Senegal	Conditional cash transfer for Orphans and Vulnerable Children (UNICEF)	CFA 7,500 per month for a child, up to CFA 15,000 per month for multiple children	2015	32	2	3	0	7	1
Senegal	National Conditional Cash Transfer Program (PNBSF)	CFA 25,000 per household per trimester	2015	36	2	4	0	8	1
Seychelles	Invalidity Benefits		2015	628	8			294	683
Seychelles	Social Welfare Assistance	Benefits differ depending on family size, income, and expenses	2015	211	3			99	230
Sierra Leone	Social Safety Nets Program	15.2 percent of average monthly household consumption among extremely poor households	2011	42	6	9	1	12	1
South Africa	Care Dependency Grant	R 1,350 per month	2008	362	10			174	36

(continued next page)

Table I.1 (Continued)

Country	Program	Benefit	Year	Benefit monthly, $ PPP 2011	Benefit as a share of GDP per capita (2015)	National poverty line		$1.90 international poverty line	
						% Poverty line	% poverty gap	% poverty line	% poverty gap
South Africa	War Veteran's Grant	R 1,370 per month	2008	365	10			175	36
South Africa	Foster Child Grant	R 830 per month per child	2008	219	6			105	22
South Africa	Child Support Grant	R 310 per month per child	2008	84	2			40	8
South Africa	Disability grant	R 1,350 per month	2008	362	10			174	36
Sudan	SIP (Social Initiatives Program)		2013	67	3	11	1	20	5
Swaziland	Public assistance		2011	21	1	3	0	7	0
Tanzania	Productive Social Safety Net (PSSN)—Conditional Cash Transfer	Ranges from TZS 10,000 to TZS 38,000 per month	2012	21	2	8	1	8	1
Togo	CCT with conditions on nutrition	XOF 5,000 per month	2015	21	4	5	0	9	0
Uganda	Direct Income Support under the Expanding Social Protection Program (ESP)	UGX 25,000 per month	2010	32	5	24	5	12	1
Uganda	Social Assistance Grants for Empowerment—Vulnerable Families Grant	UGX 25,000 per month	2016	20	3	15	3	7	1

(continued next page)

Table I.1 (Continued)

Country	Program	Benefit	Year	Benefit monthly, $ PPP 2011	Benefit as a share of GDP per capita (2015)	National poverty line		$1.90 international poverty line	
						% Poverty line	% poverty gap	% poverty line	% poverty gap
Zambia	Social Cash Transfer Scheme	ZMW70 per month per household, paid on a bimonthly basis ZMW 140 per month for households with persons with severe disabilities, paid on a bimonthly basis	2016	21	1	0	0	7	0
Zimbabwe	Public assistance /relief of distress		2013	38	6			15	3
Zimbabwe	Harmonized cash transfer	HH$ 10 for one person, HH$ 15 for two persons, HH$30 for three persons and HH$25 for four or more persons	2013	16	3			7	1

Source: ASPIRE (Atlas of Social Protection Indicators of Resilience and Equity) (database), Administrative data, World Bank, Washington, DC, http://datatopics.worldbank.org/aspire/.
Note: To estimate the share of benefit levels in GDP per capita, poverty lines, and poverty gaps, the benefit per capita is estimated by dividing the total benefit level by the average household size.

Table I.2 Generosity of Selected Public Works Programs

Country	Program	Benefit	Year	Benefit monthly, $ PPP 2011	Benefit as a share of GDP per capita (2015)	National poverty line		$1.90 International poverty line		Minimum wages	
						% Poverty line	% Poverty gap	% Poverty line	% Poverty gap	% Wage	Monthly $ PPP 2011
Botswana	Ipelegeng (self-reliance)	BWP 510 per month for six-hour work for 20 or 22 working days (BWP 590 per month for supervisors). Since 2012/13, daily meal also supplied (BWP 140 per month) for overall pay of BWP 650 per month	2015	151	3	62	5	71	12	142	107
Burkina Faso	Special Program of job creation for young people and women (PSCE / JF)	CFA 37,000 per month	2014	163	21	55	4	48	4	104	156
Burkina Faso	Repairing roads by using labor-intensive public works	CFA 1,500 per day (CFA 45,000 per month)	2014	198	25	67	4	58	5	127	156
Burkina Faso	Cash for work		2015	307	39	104	7	90	8	196	156
Burkina Faso	Youth Employment and skills development Project	CFA 1,480 per day (CFA 36,000 per month)	2015	153	20	52	3	45	4	98	156
Cameroon	HIMO Technical Unit		2016	597	49	113	9	215	28	395	151
Cameroon	Social Safety Nets—Labor intensive public works	CFA 78,000	2016	155	13	29	2	56	7	103	151
Chad	Pilot Social Safety Net Programs	1,200 CFS per day (5 hours per day), 80 days	2017	135	17	32	2	44	3		
Comoros	Productive safety net	KMF 1,000 per day (three periods of 20 days of work per year)	2016	41	6	5	0	12	3	16	256
Ethiopia	Productive Safety Net (PSNP)—public works	ETB 70 per person for five days in a month and for six months in a year.	2011	342	54	110	14	126	14		

(continued next page)

Table I.2 (Continued)

Country	Program	Benefit	Year	Benefit monthly, $ PPP 2011	Benefit as a share of GDP per capita (2015)	National poverty line % Poverty line	National poverty line % Poverty gap	$1.90 International poverty line % Poverty line	$1.90 International poverty line % Poverty gap	Minimum wages % Wage	Minimum wages Monthly $ PPP 2011
Ethiopia	Urban Productive Safety Net (UPSNP)—Public Works	60 ETB per day. Up to 4 household members can participate. Each beneficiary household will receive support for 3 years (1st year up to 60 days/person; 2nd year up to 40 days/person; 3rd year up 20 days/person).	2017	155	25	50	6	57	6	93	141
Ghana	Labor-intensive public works program (LIPW)	Average of US$5 (2011PPP) for a six-hour working day	2015	131	9	0	0	52	6	93	141
Kenya	WFP cash for assets CFA	KES 2,000 per month per household paid on a bimonthly basis	2016	23	2	5	0	9	1	19	123
Liberia	Youth, Employment, Skills (YES)	$3 per day for unskilled workers ($5 for skilled workers) for a total of $120 per participant	2014	126	39	27	1	43	2	184	69
Madagascar	Productive safety net	MGA 4,000 per day (four periods of 20 days of work per year)	2016	105	19	88	3	38	1	75	140
Malawi	MASAF Public works program	MWK 600 per day (program runs in 24-day cycles, total payment of MWK 14,400)	2016	73	17	38	2	27	1	70	104
Mozambique	Productive Social Action Program		2015	34	8	8	0	14	0	19	179
Niger	DNPGCA—Argent CT		2017	131	28	32	2	37	3	98	135
Rwanda	Vision 2020 Umurenge (VUP)		2012	130	21	139	9	52	2		

(continued next page)

Table I.2 (Continued)

Country	Program	Benefit	Year	Benefit, monthly, $ PPP 2011	Benefit as a share of GDP per capita (2015)	National poverty line		$1.90 International poverty line		Minimum wages	
						% Poverty line	% Poverty gap	% Poverty line	% Poverty gap	% Wage	Monthly $ PPP 2011
South Africa	Extended Public Works Programme (EPWP)	ZAR75.10 per day or task in 2014	2014	319	9			154	31		
Tanzania	Productive Social Safety Net (PSSN)—Public Works	TZS 2,300 per household per day (15 days per month, and maximum of 4 months per year)	2012	60	6	23	3	22	2	116	51
Uganda	Northern Uganda Social Action Fund (II)—Public Works Programme	Payment commensurate with the lowest-paid civil servant	2016	78	12	59	11	29	3	1528	5

Source: ASPIRE (Atlas of Social Protection Indicators of Resilience and Equity) (database), Administrative data, World Bank, Washington, DC, http://datatopics.worldbank.org/aspire/.
Notes: Monthly amounts are systematically computed assuming 24 days of work when payments are reported per day. This assumption will overestimate benefits for some programs (for example, the Ethiopia PSNP offers five days in a month). To estimate the benefit as a share of GDP per capita, poverty lines, and poverty gaps, the benefit per capita is estimated by dividing the benefit by the average household size.

Table I.3 **Generosity of Selected Social Pensions**

Country	Program	Benefit level	Year	Benefit monthly, $ PPP 2011	Benefit as a share of GDP per capita (2015)	National poverty line		$1.90 International poverty line	
						% Poverty line	% Poverty gap	% Poverty line	% Poverty gap
Botswana	The Old-Age Pension (OAP)	BWP250 per eligible citizen over 65	2016	53	1	22	2	25	4
Kenya	Older Persons Cash Transfer OPCT	KES 2,000 per month per household paid on a bimonthly basis	2016	40	4	9	1	16	1
Lesotho	Old age pension	LSL700 per month	2015	101	13	73	2	51	2
Mauritius	Basic Retirement Pension (BRP) zero pillar retirement only	MUR 5,250 for 60–90 years old, MUR 15,250 for 90–100 years old, and MUR 20,250 for those 100 years and older	2016	299	5	40		148	1342
Namibia	Provision of Social Assistance—Old Age Grant		2014	98	3	28	3	39	6
Nigeria	Ekiti State Social Security Scheme	NGN 5,000	2015	54	3	19	1	21	1
São Tomé and Príncipe	Social pension—continuous subsidy		2014	6	1	2		4	0
São Tomé and Príncipe	Social pension—subsidy to the unknown		2014	9	1	1		3	0
Seychelles	Retirement Pension		2015	628	8			294	683
South Africa	Old-age grant	R 1,350 per month (R 1,370 if individuals 75 years or older)	2008	84	2			40	8
Swaziland	Old-age grant		2011	17	1	3	0	6	0

Source: ASPIRE (Atlas of Social Protection Indicators of Resilience and Equity) (database), Administrative data, World Bank, Washington, DC, http://datatopics.worldbank.org/aspire/.
Note: To estimate the share of benefit levels in GDP per capita, poverty lines, and poverty gaps, the benefit per capita is estimated by dividing the total benefit level by the average household size.

Appendix J

Tax Revenue

Table J.1 Tax Revenue, by Type of Revenue and Country
% of GDP

Country	Total tax revenue	Of which, taxes on:		
		International trade	Goods and services	Income
Angola	24.9	1.5	2.0	20.1
Benin	16.7	8.6	3.4	1.9
Botswana	24.3	9.5	4.4	8.2
Burkina Faso	15.7			
Burundi	11.3	1.0	7.5	2.8
Cabo Verde	18.8	3.6	8.9	5.6
Cameroon	14.0	2.3	6.9	4.6
Central African Republic	6.2	1.6	3.4	1.2
Chad	8.9	1.6	0.8	5.7
Comoros	12.7	2.1	7.2	3.2
Congo, Dem. Rep.	10.4	2.0	4.5	3.9
Congo, Rep.	18.3	3.7	7.7	6.4
Côte d'Ivoire	15.1	5.3	2.6	4.9
Ethiopia	12.7	4.4	3.8	4.4
Gabon	14.3	4.9	2.9	
Gambia, The	17.7	5.5	7.6	4.5
Ghana	16.3	2.7	6.6	7.0
Guinea	19.5	4.0	9.7	2.8
Guinea-Bissau	9.2	2.8	3.9	2.5
Kenya	17.5	1.3	7.0	9.2
Lesotho	50.9	1.1	10.6	12.8

(continued next page)

Table J.1 (Continued)

Country	Total tax revenue	Of which, taxes on:		
		International trade	Goods and services	Income
Liberia	19.2	8.9	2.4	7.6
Madagascar	9.9	5.2	2.6	2.1
Malawi	16.8	1.7	6.8	8.1
Mali	16.6	2.2	9.3	5.1
Mauritania	18.2	2.3	8.9	6.0
Mauritius	19.2	0.3	11.4	5.7
Mozambique	21.7	2.1	9.4	9.1
Namibia	32.1	10.7	7.8	13.3
Niger	17.6	4.9	6.8	4.6
Nigeria	5.9	0.5	1.7	3.0
Rwanda	13.5	1.0	7.0	5.6
São Tomé and Príncipe	15.0	7.2	1.3	4.6
Senegal	18.7	2.1	10.1	
Seychelles	28.4	1.5	14.2	9.8
Sierra Leone	8.6	1.4	3.6	3.0
South Africa	24.7	-0.3	9.0	14.7
South Sudan	2.8			
Sudan	5.5	1.6	3.1	0.7
Swaziland	26.2	13.4	6.1	6.7
Tanzania	12.4	0.9	5.4	4.5
Togo	16.2	8.3	3.3	2.2
Uganda	13.0	1.2	7.2	4.5
Zambia	13.3	1.1	5.4	6.8
Zimbabwe	26.9	2.8	12.0	8.9

Source: IMF.

Table J.2 **Tax Revenue, by Type and Country Group**
% of GDP

Categories		Total tax revenue	Of which, taxes on:		
			International trade	Goods and services	Income
Geography	Central Africa	13.9	2.8	3.8	6.6
	East Africa	15.7	1.9	7.3	5.7
	Southern Africa	31.6	6.9	7.6	11.1
	West Africa	15.6	4.2	5.9	4.3
Income group	Low income	14.6	3.3	6.0	4.5
	Lower-middle income	18.6	3.4	5.6	7.0
	Upper-middle income	25.1	5.1	8.1	10.5
	High income	28.4	1.5	14.2	9.8
Fragility	Fragile	14.0	3.3	5.5	4.5
	Nonfragile	19.2	3.6	6.7	7.1
Resource status	Not resource-rich	19.5	3.6	7.6	6.0
	Potentially resource-rich	13.1	2.9	5.2	4.2
	Resource-rich, non-oil	19.6	4.5	6.8	7.3
	Resource-rich, oil	13.2	2.4	3.6	6.5
Drought exposure	High	22.0	3.9	7.5	7.2
	Medium	18.4	4.0	5.7	7.7
	Low	12.0	2.5	5.3	3.7
	N/A	17.5	3.6	7.1	5.7

Source: IMF.
Note: For each country group, the tax revenue (as % of GDP) is calculated as the average tax revenue (as % of GDP) for all countries in the group, giving equal weight to each country. Burkina Faso, Gabon, and South Sudan are not included for lack of data.